Fundamentals of Technology Project Management

Colleen Garton
with Erika McCulloch

MC PRESS

First Edition
First Printing—December 2004

ISBN: 1-58347-053-0

Corporate Offices
125 N. Woodland Trail
Lewisville, TX 75077 USA

Sales and Customer Service
P.O. Box 4300
Big Sandy, TX 75755-4300 USA
www.mcpressonline.com

Fundamentals
of Technology
Project Management

About The Authors

Colleen Garton

Colleen Garton has over 21 years of experience in technology and technology management. She has an educational background in Electronic/Electrical Engineering and Business Management and possesses extensive experience in technical management, project management, Internet development, business analysis, technical writing, and engineering. This experience includes 11 years in the entertainment and professional audio industries in the United Kingdom and Europe and 10 years in management consulting and technology project management in the United States. In addition to working in project management positions for successful technology companies such as Intuit Inc., she has owned and operated two management and technical consulting companies. Ms. Garton possesses strong project management and team-building skills and has a proven record of accomplishment for successfully managing and deploying large, complex, multimillion dollar projects as well as smaller projects in very diverse market spaces. She has in-depth knowledge and experience of project management tools and methodologies in addition to extensive knowledge of leadership and management styles and philosophies. Ms. Garton has formal training and project experience in quality management processes such as Six Sigma and SEI CMMi. She has participated in numerous management, leadership, communication, mentoring, and conflict management training over the last ten years.

Colleen Garton is the coauthor of the book *The AS/400 & Microsoft Office Integration Handbook*, published by MC Press in 1998.

Erika McCulloch

Erika McCulloch has worked on projects and project teams for more than 12 years. She has worked directly with multiple customers at all levels and has successfully managed projects of all types, sizes, and budgets in a variety of industries. She has in-depth experience with project management tools and methods as well as with business analysis and Internet development. Mrs. McCulloch possesses strong project management skills for large, complex projects spanning diverse platforms and has experience as a hands-on IT architect, which gives her an edge in the project management field. This experience has given her firsthand experience with the technical aspects and methodologies of design and development. She has completed many leadership skills, e-business technologies, and architecture courses. In addition to working in project management positions for successful technology services and distribution companies such as International Business Machines (IBM) and Ingram Micro, she has taught technology and e-business topics and has assisted in the development of educational programs for technology architects. She holds teaching certificates in both California and Texas. She is currently working as a consultant and is teaching industry-specific business practices and project management courses at California high schools. Mrs. McCulloch holds a Bachelors Degree in Business Management, and she is currently working on her MBA.

For Mark Perry
For your inspiration and your ready smile.
For your love of life, and family, and golf.
You will be loved and remembered forever.

—Colleen Garton

To my beautiful daughter, Piper Alexandria
Thank you for your patience and love.
For your radiant smile to get me through the day.
For just being you!!!
Mommy loves you!

—Erika McCulloch

Contents

Introduction

The term "project management" refers to the carefully planned and organized effort to complete a specific task in a specific timeline. Project management has been around since the beginning of time. It may not have been called "project management," and the leaders of the projects may not have considered themselves project managers. Nonetheless, they started with a plan and a goal, and they followed a process to accomplish a desired outcome. In other words, they managed the project.

Stonehenge, the megalithic ruin located on Salisbury Plain in Southern England, began construction around 2950 BC. It is believed that there were three main phases of construction that occurred at different times over a number of years. The last phase of development concluded around 1650 BC. This would definitely be considered a long-term project by today's standards! The building of Stonehenge, both the *why* and the *how,* remain a mystery and the subject of much speculation to this day. How were the stones moved from their original sites to the site of Stonehenge that was many, many miles away? What was the purpose of Stonehenge? Was it a giant observatory or a place of worship? There are many theories and legends on the subject, but what interests us most is how they approached this huge undertaking. It is hardly likely that a group of people got together and said, "Let's bring a lot of big stones from as far away as we can and put them in holes in the ground here," and then all went off independently and started moving rocks around. There must have been a *vision* for what Stonehenge was going to be, a plan for how it would be accomplished, and someone must have coordinated the execution of the plan. A significant amount of manpower would have been needed to move the stones, together with some ingenious method, or methods, for moving them such a great distance. There must have been a reason that those particular stones were the ones that had to be used. We must also assume that there was a design for the arrangement of the stones and a specific purpose for the stone circle after construction was complete. Someone must have managed each phase of the project to accomplish such an amazing feat.

Let us bring ourselves forward a few thousand years and explore how project management has evolved into the structured discipline that it is today. In the early 1900s, Frederick Taylor (1856–1915) began his work on scientific management. Up until then it had been assumed that the only way to increase productivity was to make people work longer and harder. Applying his scientific reasoning to the work being performed in steel mills, Taylor showed that output could be increased by improving the processes used to achieve that output. During this same time period, Henry Gantt (1861–1919), studied the order of operations in Navy ship construction before and during WWI. His *Gantt charts*, task bars, and milestone markers, outline the sequence and duration of all tasks in a process. Gantt charts are used to this day as a standard analytical tool for project managers. Gantt is also credited for bringing a human element to management by his emphasis that a favorable work environment has a positive psychological effect on workers. During the few decades up to and including WWII, a growing emphasis on marketing approaches, industrial psychology, and human relations began to further change the face of business management.

In the 1940s, a postwar shortage of labor, combined with the ever-increasing complexity of projects, required changes in organizational structures to support the changing environment. PERT charts and the *critical path method* (CPM) were introduced. These new methods enabled managers to effectively control intricately engineered and extremely large and complex projects such as military weapon systems. The new management methodologies being utilized for military projects were soon incorporated into other industries as business leaders looked for new ways to manage growth and development in a fast-changing and competitive business environment.

In the early 1960's, general system theories of science began to emerge as the drivers of business processes. At the same time, project management, as a career in its own right, came into being. Since the 1960s, numerous theories, methodologies, and standards have been introduced into the management of systems, knowledge, workflow, projects, and data. There has been a growing emphasis on business strategy, organizational change, and human relations skills. Every decade brings with it a need to develop projects with even greater complexity and speed. At the same time, projects must be implemented with fewer resources, lower costs, and higher quality. The ever-increasing diversity and complexity required for managing people, systems, and data has led to the substantial growth in the project management field.

As recently as 10 years ago, project management was not seen as an important or necessary role in many companies. Those companies spent millions of unnecessary dollars, and thousands of unnecessary hours, implementing projects without the use of the advanced tools, techniques, and methodologies required to create the timelines, cost controls, and risk management necessary for cost-effective development. In the last decade, the project management landscape has changed dramatically. It is no longer seen as a superfluous "middle management" position but as a critical role in meeting business demands for high quality, quick-to-market products and services.

Project management has gained enormous popularity over the last several decades due to significant changes in the way companies do business. These changes have been driven by the demands of global competition, rapid technological growth, down sizing (requiring more cost-effective and efficient development), higher quality goods and services, and faster time to market.

Project management is one of the fastest-growing career fields today, and this growth is predicted to continue for the foreseeable future. Project management skills are becoming a required core competency for many management positions in growth- and quality-oriented organizations. Today, project managers are in high demand worldwide to implement projects worth billions of dollars in both the public and the private sector for corporations, governments, healthcare, and nonprofit organizations.

About This Book

This book is a practical guide to project management in the technology sector. The book assumes no previous knowledge of project management. It has been written with the needs of the beginner- to intermediate-level project manager in mind. However, this is also an excellent book for seasoned project managers who are ready to take project management to a new level by adding more structure and methodology to the project management process. The book is an informational and easy-to-follow guide that not only explains what is required to successfully complete each phase of the project life cycle; it also explains in understandable terms how to do it. The book includes 60 project document templates designed to lead you methodologically through each of the six phases of the project life cycle: planning, design, development, integration, deployment, and post-deployment. The book includes techniques for consistently and accurately monitoring the health of the project and simple methods for analyzing the results to quickly and easily recognize when trouble is brewing. You will be taken step by step through processes to help you minimize the effect of problems as they arise and to get the project back on track swiftly and efficiently. This book clearly defines the process, the documentation, and the skill sets required to implement projects successfully—on time, within budget, and with high quality. It includes proven methods for building motivated and energized teams and suggestions on actions to take to deal with difficult or negative team members. You will learn how to maintain the right balance between people management, task management, schedule management, and personal career management. Armed with the knowledge and tools in this book, you will be well prepared to effectively and confidently manage any technology project and will be well positioned for maximum success in today's competitive marketplace.

The case study in Appendix A has been used as a guide for the examples that appear throughout this book. The CD-ROM includes the 60 templates for the documents that you will need to create during the project Life Cycle.

Special Thanks

We would like to thank the following people for their contributions during the creation of this book:

A special thank you to Charlie Swanson and Mark McCulloch for their unwavering support, enthusiasm, and encouragement during the creation of this book. Thanks also to Merrikay Lee at MC Press for her confidence and support for this project and to Mark Garner, Stuart Bishop, and Michael Scott for taking the time to give valuable input.

CHAPTER 1

Concepts of Project Management

A project without a project manager is like an orchestra without a conductor. You can have the best musicians (or engineers) in the world, but without the leadership of a talented conductor (or manager) who understands how everyone's piece must fit precisely together, in the right order, to produce the final product, the orchestra (or the team) is not going to perform well, and the results will be poor. To realize their full potential for a great symphony or a great technology product, a team needs direction and guidance from a leader who can see the "big picture," but who understands enough about the details to be able to lead the team to success. In technology, this person is the project manager. The project manager's value to the organization is the same value that the conductor brings to the orchestra. Successful orchestras would not dream of performing a concert without one. Successful companies should not dream of launching a project without a project manager. It happens, but not as often these days as in the past. Companies have learned from their project nightmare lessons! The project manager is the glue that holds the project team together. It is a vital role and carries with it a lot of responsibility. The success of a project is determined primarily by the quality of the project manager. Never underestimate the value that the project manager brings to the team or to the project results.

The Role of a Project Manager

A *project manager* (*PM*) has various functions or roles. A project manager will find himself or herself wearing many different hats during the various phases of his or her projects (and very likely at different times during the duration of each day). The specific roles a project manager will need to fulfill will differ to some extent depending on the company for whom the project is being managed. It will also differ depending on the particular needs and requirements of the department or client for whom the project is being developed and the nature of the actual project itself.

There are different types of project managers. You will find that most project managers fit into one of these broad categories: There are technical project managers who have a background in technology. They have a technical or engineering degree and have some, if not a lot, of experience in the engineering field. There are also career project managers. They have some level of technical skill and knowledge but have opted for the project management career path rather than the engineer and developer one. These individuals usually possess excellent organizational and leadership skills, which led them into a career in technology project management. Some companies specifically require one or the other of these types of project manager for their open positions. Others will be open to either. By choosing a career in technology project management, it is beneficial to have both strong project management skills and strong technical skills. However, companies are more likely to hire a very strong project manager with little to no technical experience than to hire a technical manager with little or no project management experience.

A project manager wears many different hats and is known by many different names. These are not the names that your project team may call you behind your back when you ask them to work the weekend, but the different names used to describe this role in an organization. One of the names you may find used is "program manager." This title is generally used to describe the different role of managing the actual products, rather than the process to build and deploy the product. Some companies interchange these titles, and some companies use them to describe different roles. To make matters even more confusing, the project manager role can also be referred to as a "technical manager" or a "project coordinator." In some companies, a project coordinator is an assistant to the project manager and is responsible for managing the schedule updates and status reports only. The more commonly used title is "project manager." When searching for a project manager position, check under all of these titles and always read the job descriptions thoroughly.

Management

The most important role of a project manager is to manage the project through all six stages of the project Life Cycle. This will include ensuring that the project stays within budget and is delivered on time and with high quality. This book is designed to guide you through each stage of the project by giving you the tools, skills, and knowledge you will need to consistently deliver successful projects.

Communication

A vital key to successful project management is communication; not just any old kind of communication, but two-way, open communication. Quantity is never a good substitute for quality. Communication must be tailored for your specific audience. A one-size-fits-all approach is not going to work. You will be communicating with different groups of stakeholders that could include sales people, marketing, product management, engineering, clients, quality assurance, senior management, accounting, and outside vendors. These different groups of stakeholders will be looking for different information from you with differing levels of detail. Personality types will also determine how much and how detailed the data you share and present needs to be.

So how do you figure out what information each group or person needs from you? One sure way of finding out is to ask them. You may talk to one stakeholder who tells you "I only want to know whether there is a problem. I will assume things are going well unless you tell me otherwise." Another may tell you, "Don't come to me with a problem unless you have a solution. If I cannot do anything about it, then I would rather not know. Let me know once the problem is solved and just tell me what the schedule impact is and what plans you have in place to counteract the impact." Then there are the people who want to know every little detail of what is going on, "Send me an e-mail every day/week to update me on where we are with every aspect of the project. Let me know when each and every milestone is completed, and inform me immediately of any potential issues that you anticipate in the following week." The list of responses to this question can go on and on. Never assume that you know what someone needs from you, and never assume it is the same as what someone else needs. People always appreciate being asked for their opinions and preferences. It not only makes them feel that their opinions are important; it also makes you look like you are a good manager who is setting a solid foundation to ensure that everyone is informed appropriately, thereby giving the project the best chance of success.

Human nature is a strange thing. It is usually the case that if someone believes you value their opinions, they will also value yours. If you hold them in high regard, they will also hold you in high regard. After all, you must be really smart to have noticed how smart they are, right? Thus, it is always good to ask for others' opinions and to pay attention to what you hear. You do not have to agree with them, but be respectful and thank them for their input. You do not have to comment on how useful or not useful it was! There will be situations where you will not be able to reach agreement. In these situations, you can agree to disagree as long as it is clear who the decision-maker is going to be. By listening and responding to input from your team members and stakeholders, you are empowering them to continue to contribute to the process. They will feel that they are adding value to the project and to the project team.

Presentations and Reporting

Creating and presenting various project presentations to clients, stakeholders, and team members is a very important and often a very time consuming part of a project manager's role. Throughout the project, there will be a lot of presentation work. Presentation meetings require careful planning and execution. During the design and development phases of the project, there will likely be weekly or monthly (or possibly even daily) project status meetings that will be much more informal. The overall length of the project and the stage of the project that you are in will determine the frequency of status meetings. For instance, if you are working on a year-long project, you may have monthly or biweekly status meetings during the development stage of the project and then increase this to daily meetings in the few weeks or days prior to the deployment (release) of the product.

Project Documentation

A project manager is often responsible for writing a certain amount of the project documentation. The amount and level of documentation you will be required to create will depend on your level, and areas, of technical knowledge or expertise and your knowledge of the product. Some of the documents are standard project management documents written by the project manager; the client, business managers, business analysts, engineers, or vendors will write others.

In addition to these documents, there will be numerous presentations and status reports created regularly throughout the project Life Cycle. If your project team is a permanent team (not created on a per-project basis), you may need to create a Team Charter or Mission Statement for the team. If you are directly managing people, you will also be responsible for documentation such as *Personal Development Plans*, individual team member goals and objectives, and annual (or project-related) employee reviews.

Appendix D includes a flowchart and a list of all documents required during the project Life Cycle. A template for every document is included on the CD-ROM that accompanies this book.

Even if you are not involved in the actual writing of these documents, you are very likely to be involved in the reviewing of some, if not all, of the documents. The first time you see the *Proposal Document* may be when you receive it from your sales department. Be aware that you might get a bit of a shock (sales people often oversell on the features of a product and undersell on what it will cost to develop). You need to read the documents and ensure that you understand what you are committed to. To fully understand your project you need a good, solid understanding of what your product is and what your product can (or will) do. Reading the technical and user documentation is a great way to get up to speed on these areas quickly.

The project documents are covered in more detail in later chapters. Sample documents are included on the CD-ROM that accompanies this book.

Estimation

The estimation of project tasks is a complex, and never exact, science. Project managers are responsible for working with their teams to produce the initial, high-level, detailed, and final estimates. Estimating complex projects takes a lot of coordination, and there is often a tight deadline for completion. Unless you are an experienced developer, you will need help from your project team to create realistic estimates. The rule of thumb is that engineers usually overestimate what they can accomplish by at least 20%, so be prepared to update their estimates accordingly. This will vary from person to person, and you will need to monitor their results with estimating to gauge what kind of adjustment you need to make before submitting your estimates. If you work on the same team or product for some time, you may be able to create the estimates yourself without additional technical assistance. It is great if you can do that, but remember to ask for a sanity check from someone else on the team before submitting estimates. You might have missed something really important that was not evident to you from the estimation request but will be to the engineer who will be implementing the feature.

Project Scheduling

The project manager is responsible for the creation and management of the project schedule. In this book, we will assume that you are using Microsoft Project software to manage your project. It is one of the more popular project tracking tools in technology project management. There are many other project tracking software programs available that can be used effectively. The basic principles of tracking project status are the same, or similar, in the majority of these programs. Some have better functionality and are easier to use than others. You may get to choose what tools you use on your project, or you may be required to use whatever the standard tools are at the company where the project is being implemented. Creating a project schedule can be relatively easy if you have a small project with few resources and minimum dependencies. It can also be very challenging, especially if you have a large, complex project with multiple engineers and skill sets and complex dependencies between tasks and features. For smaller projects, creating a schedule can be accomplished in as little as an hour or two. Larger projects can take anywhere from a few hours to a few weeks! Do a sanity check on your schedule with one or more of your team members before you finalize it. You may have missed something that will adversely affect the schedule.

Managing the ongoing schedule tasks and interim (or internal) as well as final releases is the most challenging part of scheduling. In your role as scheduler, you will need to recognize problems that will have schedule impacts and know what processes to follow if there is a problem. If you are a junior or assistant project manager, you will likely have a senior, or group, project manager to help you manage these problems. For smaller projects, or if you are the only project manager on the project, you will be required to manage this yourself.

Updating the schedule and ensuring that the implementation team is kept up to date on changes to the schedule are a part of the status reporting and management aspect of a project manager's job. Proactively getting status reports from individual team members and communicating this status to the relevant stakeholders, with the appropriate level of detail, is the responsibility of the project manager. Keep in mind that the frequency of status reporting should be appropriate both for the length of the project and the phase of the project that you are in. You do not want to ask for status reports from your team members on a monthly basis if the project is only going to be 4 months long. This will not give you adequate time to respond to issues. Similarly, it is unlikely that you will need daily status reports during all of the phases of a two-year project.

Managing the Project Team

There are various management structures, which will be covered in more detail in the organizational structure section in this chapter, and some of those structures require the project manager to also be a people manager. This has advantages and disadvantages, and you will form your own opinions about which method you feel is most advantageous as you learn more about the different approaches to managing projects and project teams.

Project managers who are responsible for the management of their project teams have a whole host of additional responsibilities related to managing people. These include coaching and development, personnel issues, tracking work hours, vacations, sick time, setting business and personal objectives, reviewing performance, technical training/development, team motivation, and individual performance management.

Conflict and Change Management

As a project manager, whether or not you are also a people manager, you will be required to manage relationships between your team members and your stakeholders. This will include managing conflict as well as managing change. Regardless of how well planned a project may be, unforeseen changes and project demands can take their toll on you and your team members. Managing the impact of these changes can be very challenging. Conflict resolution and change management are an important aspect of the project manager's core responsibilities.

Contributing to the Company's Management Team

As a member of the management team, you are likely to have additional responsibilities directly or indirectly related to your project. These can often involve numerous meetings; reporting, collecting, and analyzing business and productivity metrics; process improvements; project proposals for future projects; planning for the next project while implementing the current one; and budget tracking and reporting, to name but a few.

Dual Roles

On smaller projects or within smaller organizations, you may find yourself in the dual role of project manager and lead engineer, project manager and technical writer, project manager and product manager, and on and on; the list of combinations is endless. Being in the dual role of project manager and a contributing member of the development team can be challenging. You are, in effect, managing yourself, which means that you have to hold yourself as accountable as you hold the other members of your team. For smaller projects, there may not be enough work to keep a full-time project manager busy, so being in a dual role is the best way to accomplish at least some level of project management for the project. This can also be a good way to start the transition from engineer or engineering lead into a project management role. On larger projects, it can be much harder to split your time between two very different roles, and you can often find yourself trying to do two full-time jobs. This is where you must focus a lot of attention on your own personal time management and ensure that you are not overcommitted. Trying to do too much will result in you doing a passable job in each role but not excelling at either. This is not good for the project or for your own self-esteem.

Managing multiple projects is also very common. The likelihood is that you will be working on more than one project at a time. This may mean that you are managing more than one project team or that you have overlapping project teams. In this situation, you need to ensure that you and your team are giving each of your projects the appropriate amount of time and attention.

Being an Employee

So, let's imagine that you are employed as a project manager for a large company. The chances are that your manager will set formal goals and objectives that you need to accomplish over the following year. You will be required to keep your skills and knowledge up to date. You will have some personal objectives that require you to improve on some aspect of your job, such as communication. This is your role as an employee and as a team member. It is an important role for the project manager and one that is sometimes neglected in the rush to get the project implemented. This is an area that requires focused attention if you are to continue to grow and develop as a project manager. It is an essential ingredient in meeting your own career goals.

In conclusion, a project manager has many functions that comprise this "role" of project manager. It is hard to get bored in a project manager role when there are so many functions that need simultaneous, and possibly equal, focus. It is a highly critical position in a fast-paced environment. Consequently, it is easy to get burnt out. For this reason, it is very important that you manage your own time effectively and not feel pressured to set unrealistic deadlines or work consistently long hours.

Skills Required for Effective Project Management

To be an effective project manager you need a fairly diverse set of skills. To develop these skills you need a certain level of talent in quite a few areas. For instance, you need to be very organized. If you live your life in a totally chaotic way, never remember to pay bills on time, turn up late for everything, and hate having to live by a schedule, then this is probably not a good career choice for you! An important note is that being a great engineer or an accomplished technical lead does not necessarily mean that you will make an effective project manager or that you will enjoy being a project manager. Project management should not be seen as the obvious next step on the career path of an engineer who is looking for what he or she should be doing next. Project management is a career in itself, and though it requires some level of technical acumen, it is not going to be a good career choice for everyone whom possesses some technical knowledge.

You can develop the skills that you need to be an effective project manager as long as you have some basic talent or skill to build on. You need to be passionate about this career choice. It will be challenging and demanding. It is also going to be fun and very rewarding. It will require a lot of effort on your part to develop and hone the skills necessary to enable you to have a successful career in technology project management. This exciting career opportunity offers myriad opportunities for advancement.

Organizational Skills

Organizational skills are essential for a project manager at any level. Whether you are an assistant project manager, a junior project manager, or a senior project manager, you will not be able to function without excellent organizational skills. You will be juggling multiple tasks and dealing with lots of different people. You will be committing yourself to deadlines both personally and for your team, so you need to be sure you can deliver on them. This means that you need to have a really good sense of where you and your project team are with the project at all times. You also need to know how much "wiggle room" you have available to work on tasks not directly related to the development of your product. This could be reporting, budgeting, or attending planning meetings. A project manager constantly has a whole host of requests coming in from every direction imaginable.

You need to be able to organize your project, your own schedule, and those of your team members. Organizing your team is not telling them what to do; it is working with them to help them to manage their own time and to ensure that they have the time and resources to implement the tasks you have assigned to them. You are empowering your team members to achieve their objectives. You will be required to constantly prioritize and reprioritize tasks for yourself and your team members. You need to be able to respond to changes quickly and effectively.

Being "organized" means knowing where the file is that you need for your next meeting, arriving on time for your meeting, and being prepared. If you are hosting the meeting, you should ensure that you have prepared an agenda, that the agenda has been distributed to the attendees ahead of time, and that you have a clearly defined purpose and goal for the meeting. No one wants to spend time in meetings that are not productive or effective. If the meeting is not adding value, productivity, or effectiveness to your project, then perhaps you do not need to hold the meeting!

Engineers, developers, and technical staff cannot be expected to be the best organizers. It is a great bonus if they are, but the success of the project hinges on the project manager's ability to effectively organize all aspects of the project and the project schedule.

Without good organization, you will not be able to schedule effectively for yourself or for your project team(s). You will not be able to prioritize and reprioritize appropriately. You will be unable to communicate effectively and accurately to your stakeholders regarding the status of your project. You will also have no idea whether you can deliver your project on time, with high quality, and within budget. You should always know where you stand, and even in the early stages of the project, you should have at least an 80% level of confidence on whether you will be able to deliver your project on the specified completion date and within the specified budget.

Leadership

A project manager is a leader, not only for the project he or she is managing, but also within the organization for which the project is being developed. To lead effectively you will need to develop a high level of leadership skill. Organizational ability is a prerequisite for building effective leadership skills. Leading a project team can be a complex task. Unlike management in some other fields, technology management works a little differently. For instance, the manager is not necessarily the highest-paid person on the project team. It is not unusual for senior engineering employees to be on a higher salary than their manager. Unless you came from a senior engineering position before becoming a project manager, the chances are that your team members will determine *how* the project gets implemented. You will communicate what needs to be accomplished, and their job is to figure out the best way to implement a solution within the allotted time and with the required functionality. You have a responsibility to remove any obstacles that prevent your team members from spending the maximum amount of their working time on tasks directly related to the development and implementation of the product.

Respect for your leadership is not a right, it is a privilege, and it needs to be earned. Your team needs to see you demonstrating your contribution to the project and the team; this shows that you are adding value to the process. The team may not always agree with your decisions, but they need to have confidence that you know what you are doing. You need to demonstrate integrity and treat others with respect and dignity at all times.

People Management

In your role as project manager, you may also need to be a people manager. You may be directly managing some, or all, of your team members. An effective manager needs to be able to set work assignments and track progress. This is, basically, the project management part of your job. In addition, other very important skills are required to build and maintain a highly productive and high quality team. You will need to coach and develop your team members. You will need to help them create and achieve their individual training and technical development goals.

You may be responsible for goal and objective setting at the start of each year and for producing formal written performance reviews for each employee at the end of each year. Knowing what contributions each team member has made to the project or projects and to the team is essential to accurately and appropriately deliver performance feedback to your team members. Companies determine the level of salary increase, bonus, and other compensation given to each employee based on performance review feedback from their manager. Therefore, honest and constructive feedback is critical to both the company and to each team member. Knowing your team members individually and understanding their work styles and their career goals is essential to developing highly motivated and productive team members.

There is an old adage that states, "Treat others as you would like to be treated." That is a nice sentiment, but we challenge that this approach is not going to help you build a successful team. You need to treat others as *they* wish to be treated and not as *you* wish to be treated. We are all different, and we all have different needs. We are motivated by different assignments and by different rewards. Take the time to find out what those motivations are for each member of your team. Do not assume that you know what motivates and inspires someone. Ask them; you might be surprised at what you can find out. You might also be surprised at how easy it is to make adjustments to the way you manage each person that will prove to be mutually beneficial. We are all different, and diversity builds excellent teams. As a manager, you need to learn how to manage in a diverse environment and develop the ability to adjust your management style to fit the individual and the situation. These are important keys to successful people management.

Communication

Project managers need excellent communication skills, both written and verbal. You may not start out as excellent, but you must be continually striving to get there. Communication skills are like your golf game: You are never quite good enough; you can always improve your game, but just when you think you have attained excellence, you play a really bad game and end up back where you were a year ago. You must practice constantly to keep your skills honed. There is no such thing as too many lessons. You can learn from books, from classes, and from other people. One thing you will never be is a perfect, infallible communicator. If you misjudged how to handle a situation (just as you may have misjudged getting that golf ball onto the green), you need to put it behind you and continue without losing your confidence. Tomorrow could be an excellent communication day!

Being able to communicate clearly and effectively is fundamentally important. Knowing how to stay high level and not getting into the details is critical. Your role is to communicate what someone else needs to know, not to impress him or her with how much you know. Knowing what level of detail your stakeholders and team members need is a skill that you will learn to develop both from reading this book and from personal experience.

High-quality written communication is a necessary skill for any project manager. You will be required to write documents, reports, e-mails, and, possibly, employee reviews. These all require more than basic writing ability. If your writing is not very good now, we recommend that you brush up on that skill as soon as possible. One way to improve your writing ability is to read a lot of material similar to the documents you will be writing. This will give you a feel for the content and the style of the communication. Many companies have specific formats or templates that they use for documents and reports. This makes it a little easier to get started, and you can read some of the previously written material to get a feel for the style and tone that is commonly used at that particular company.

Time Management

Engineers are not generally known for having great time management skills. It is the project manager's job to help his or her employees accomplish their tasks in a timely manner regardless of how good each employee's time management skills are. You need your team members to be at meetings on time, and you need them to focus on the assigned tasks and not get distracted. Be creative when you come up with ideas for how to accomplish this. One project that we were involved in had a rule that if you were late for a meeting you had to tell a joke, sing a song, or dance for the team. After that rule was introduced, there were only two more latecomers to a meeting for the duration of the project. One habitual latecomer stated that the thought of having to perform in front of the whole team cured him of his tardiness. He figured out how to set reminders on his calendar and paid attention to them! This kind of rule may not work well in corporate settings, but it might be just the ticket in more informal environments, where the team members know each other very well! Another rule we have seen that works quite well is not allowing latecomers into your meeting unless they bring donuts for the team. This can work particularly well for the more thrifty members of your team. We have also seen projects where latecomers are not allowed into the room. The rule is to either turn up on time or not turn up at all. That can be rather harsh and may not always prove to be the most productive way to run your meetings, but in some situations, or for specific types of meetings, it may work. We would certainly not recommend that you put this rule in place for your weekly scheduled status meetings!

Your own time management also may be a challenge for you. Being an excellent organizer will not necessarily make it easy for you to manage your time. It can still be difficult. The nature of a project manager's business is to have more on your plate than you can manage. Prioritizing tasks in order of importance rather than just working on the easy ones first is the most efficient way to manage your time. If you are accomplishing tasks that are critical, those will have the most positive impact on your project. Noncritical tasks may never get accomplished, but there may be little or no effect on your project from not completing them.

In some project management jobs, you will find that you are interrupted from your work approximately every 10 to 15 minutes. Consequently, during the course of an hour you can be dealing with any number of issues. Remembering (and finding time) to get back to your original task can be challenging. As you get more comfortable with working in this way, you risk developing an inability to focus on things for more than 10 or 15 minutes. There will be times when you have to spend hours writing documents and reviews, or are in important meetings and have to focus on one thing for an extended length of time. You need to develop the ability to focus on one thing for a long period of time and also develop the ability to focus on many things at the same time. We never said that this job would be easy! Trying to hide out in meetings rooms and bathrooms or keeping your office door closed won't protect you from the onslaught! You have to be available at all times for your team members. They need you to be available so that they can continue to be productive. If any major issues come up, you need to be informed, and you need to make sure that your team members know this. You are the nucleus of the project; the team needs to be orbiting around you. You are the force that keeps them on track. When you feel the urge to bury your head in the sand, remember that at the end of the day, you are the one who will be held accountable!

Technical or Specialized Knowledge and Understanding

To manage technical projects, you need some knowledge of technology. You do not necessarily need to understand how to write code to be able to manage software developers. Additionally, you do not need to be able to install a network to be able to manage network engineers, but you need to understand enough about the technology that your teams are using to be able to understand what your team is working on. Without this knowledge, you will be unable to recognize whether your team is developing a high quality product. Having some experience in one or more areas of engineering work will be of great benefit to you and your team, but it is not a necessity to be an effective project manager. Most technology project manager positions require some technical training. Some require a bachelors or even masters degree in a technical discipline.

Domain or "subject matter" knowledge is also important. You can learn it on the job, but you will often need to get up to speed very fast if you are going to produce a good quality product and be able to communicate effectively with all your stakeholders. For example, if you are working on developing a financial product, you will need some knowledge of finance, banking, and financial terms. If you are working on a system for dental practices, you are going to need some basic understanding of dental procedures and dental terms.

Business Management

Project managers are the "middle people" between the technical team and the business team. You need to be able to translate technical terms to business terms and vice versa. To understand business requirements you will need some understanding of business and business management. Your world will often be completely technology focused, but the users of your products may not be technically adept at all.

Building the biggest product with the most features and using the most up-to-date technology that you can is not what a project manager is hired to do. Engineers usually want to build the biggest and the best and to have as much technical challenge in each project as possible. Your role is to ensure that you are meeting the business requirements of the project. You have a budget, a timeline, and a project scope. Your client, whether internal or external, will very likely have compromised on the features that they would have liked in order to make the project financially feasible. The product should be built to meet the client needs and not to fulfill the desire of your technical team to produce the most technically advanced product that they can. This is where your understanding of the business needs is necessary to make informed decisions. You need to be managing the scope of your project within your development team as well as with the client. You need to be sure that your team is not going above and beyond in areas that are not ultimately beneficial to the business or to the client. You are the voice of the business to your team members, and you need to ensure that you have a clear understanding of what is good for the business and what is not good, so that you can communicate this to your team and manage the scope of your project.

While implementing your project, you will have specific business objectives to meet. You will be accountable to the business for the project deliverables and for completing your project within budget. You may need to supply the business managers and administrators with data and reports. The business managers are paying for the project(s) that you are managing so you need to be able to work well with those folks and to have their trust and confidence in your ability to deliver.

Creating and Giving Presentations

Getting up in front of a room full of people and presenting your own (or other's) ideas is not everyone's idea of a great day at the office! Whether you love an audience or are shaking in your boots at the prospect, it is going to be a part of the job at some point. Initially you may help put together the presentations and a more senior project manager may present them, but as you move up the project management and corporate ladder, you will also be presenting. You can develop skills in presenting, meeting facilitation, and public speaking. The best way to improve your presentation skills is to give a lot of presentations. Volunteer to present as often as you can on subjects that you feel comfortable with. You will find yourself getting more and more confident as time goes by. You will stop being concerned about people looking at you and will be more concerned with the subject matter and ensuring that everyone understands the full impact of what you are communicating.

Tools

You will need to be proficient in PC computing and various project tracking tools to manage your projects. These include:

- E-mail
- Calendaring and meeting scheduling software
- Microsoft Word or equivalent
- Microsoft Excel or equivalent
- Microsoft Project or equivalent
- Microsoft PowerPoint or equivalent
- Microsoft Visio or equivalent
- Web browser

It is assumed that you have some basic experience with all these tools before you start.

The Characteristics of a Project

A project is an undertaking of any size, budget, or timeline that has a specific desired outcome. The most important characteristic of a project is its purpose. Unless a project team knows what the specific purpose of the project is, they will be unable to undertake it.

If the project must have a purpose, then it must also have a means of measuring how well it accomplishes the purpose. A project is designing, creating, building, developing, or constructing a building, product, or service. In this book, we will focus on managing projects for products and services in the technology and IT industries.

A project must have an owner, the person who has requested that the project is implemented. It must also have a project team, the people who will implement the project. It is possible to have a project without a project manager, but it is very difficult to have a successful project without a project manager. "Uncontrolled," "chaotic," "unscheduled," and "uncertain" are words that can be used to describe unmanaged projects!

How to Measure Project Success

To measure project success, you need to determine early in the process the desired outcome of your project and how the results will be measured. If your stated outcome is not measurable, then it should be revised so that it clearly states a measurable outcome.

Unless you know how you will measure your success at the start of your project, how will you be able to document the "before" data to compare to your "after" data? It is vitally important that you have clear and accurate "before" data documented and signed off on by your client before you start. You also need to agree on when and how you will measure success after the project has been implemented. There should be no room for differing interpretations of the results. If your measurement criteria are clear and precise, you can avoid a lot of problems later on.

Different Types of Organizational Structure

Traditional (Hierarchical) Management

The traditional organizational structure is a vertical management hierarchy. It starts with the CEO and the president and branches downwards and outwards, with every employee reporting to their (vertical) line manager. The organizational chart for a traditional management structure will look similar to the one in Figure 1.1. This system of management has worked well for many years and is still the most widely used management structure in businesses today.

An advantage of the traditional management structure is that employees clearly understand to whom they report. They report to one manager, and that manager is responsible for their career management, team management, and project management. This includes setting goals and objectives, managing performance, assigning tasks, and project scheduling.

A disadvantage of the traditional method is that development hours not used by engineers on one project cannot easily be transferred to another project. The projects are developed independently of each other. Each project team has specifically assigned team members. Project downtime cannot be used elsewhere, and any project shortfalls cannot easily be filled with members from other teams.

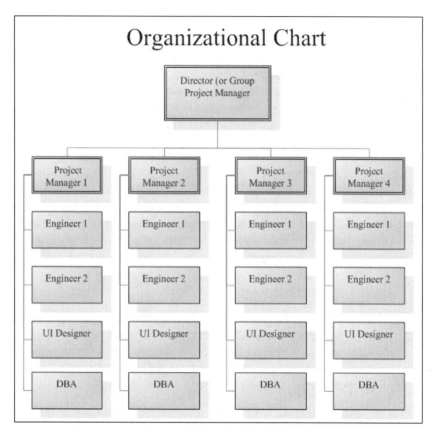

Figure 1.1: Traditional organizational chart.

Matrix Management

There are two schools of thought on the matrix management system, and they are directly opposed to one another. One believes that this method increases efficiency by decreasing development downtime. The other believes that it decreases efficiency by adding unnecessary management overhead.

This system appears to work more effectively in larger organizations that are working concurrently on large, complex projects.

The concept behind matrix management is that the team manager is the line manager for his or her team members. The team manager is responsible for day-to-day management of the team, which includes defining processes, procedures, and best practices for the group. The team manager is responsible for growth and development, coaching, and setting goals and objectives for individuals. Team members have dotted line relationships to the project managers for their assigned project. A team member may be assigned to one project or multiple projects at the same time. The project manager schedules the team member's time for the allocated amount of hours per week, and the team member reports his or her status to the project manager. In effect, this means that each team member has two (or more) managers and is a member of two (or more) teams. The team member has a specific role on each team and a specific responsibility to each manager.

The reporting relationships can be rather confusing, as shown in the example matrix management organizational chart in Figure 1.2.

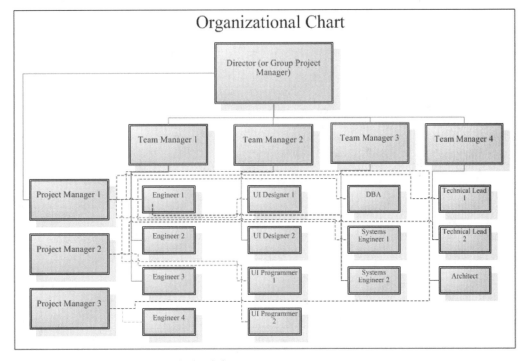

Fig 1.2: Matrix management organizational chart.

As you can see, the dotted line relationships are hard to distinguish after a few have been added to the chart.

Under this system of management, there are usually some departments still organized in the traditional way. HR and finance are good examples of departments where the matrix management system does not work well. IT departments often struggle with this type of organization because they are usually responsible for existing applications (operational support) as well as for new projects (development and implementation support). The matrix system is difficult to maintain in environments where multiple functions need to coexist within one department.

There is also a mixed organizational structure that combines aspects of the traditional and matrix organizational structures. Different project structures coexist simultaneously in the same project. With the mixed organizational structure, flexibility is an advantage; however, unclear lines of responsibility and increased communication complexity are major disadvantages.

Project Management Methodologies

A huge number of different project management methodologies are being used in organizations today. Some of the methodologies are homegrown *proprietary* processes, and some are more widely used and are available in the public domain. There are project management certifications available in some of the methodologies, whereas others are less formalized. It is not hugely important which methodology you use to manage your project, as long as you are using a documented process. The larger and more complex the project, the more defined and detailed the process needs to be for it to be effectively managed.

No matter what methodology is used to manage your project, you will need an understanding of the project Life Cycle. As with the methodologies, you will see variations in the phases, and the names of the phases, in the project Life Cycle, but they are all fundamentally very similar.

Project Life Cycle

The project Life Cycle describes the phases or steps that are completed throughout the project, from the initial concept through to post-deployment and project closure. The Life Cycle divides a project into six very distinct phases (see Figure 2.1):

- Planning
- Design
- Development
- Integration (including testing)
- Deployment
- Post-deployment

All six stages are critical to the success of a project. Trying to save time by skipping a phase or reducing the time needed to complete it successfully will result in either a substandard product or a completely failed project.

It is common to see the last of these phases, Post-Deployment, missing in some project life cycles, but we believe that it is a necessary phase. It is not often that a project is delivered to the client free of any defects and without the need for any operations support, technical support, engineering involvement, or communication after the project handoff. To guarantee client satisfaction, there must be a plan in place for managing any post-deployment issues.

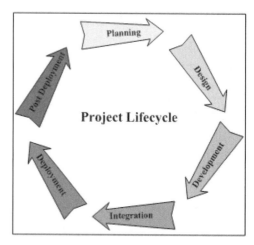

Figure 2.1: The project Life Cycle.

It is good practice to document your project Life Cycle or methodology before you start your project. In most companies, this Life Cycle is the same for every project, so it may well be documented as part of the company's processes and procedures. If it is an undocumented process or if there is no standard process in place, then this is the time for you to document the process that will be used for your project. Everyone on the project team should understand the process and be aware of what phase you are in as you progress through the Life Cycle. A project Life Cycle PowerPoint presentation is included on the CD-ROM that accompanies this book.

Planning

The Planning phase starts with the project concept and incorporates all the meetings, research, and reporting that are necessary to get the project approved. As a project manager, you may not be involved in all the pre-project planning, but you will be involved in a substantial amount of planning before your team starts developing or building any products. High-level estimates, selecting your team members, project definition, and kick-off meetings, for instance, are all part of the Planning phase. The Planning phase is complete after you have the *Project Definition*, *Project Plan*, and *Project Approach* completed, reviewed, and approved. The Project Definition describes *what* the project is; the Project Plan describes *how* it will be implemented; and the Project Approach describes the processes that will be used during the project Life Cycle.

During the Planning phase, it is extremely important to get the client to sign-off on all deliverables. Any changes must go through a predefined change control process. This ensures that both the project team and the client are on the same page and that there will be no misunderstandings about deliverables later on down the road. Verbal agreements are not worth anything. Make sure everything is in writing.

So how do you get the Planning phase completed? This is one of the most difficult phases of the project. You need to get it right the first time because your whole project will be scheduled and built in accordance with what you define and document in this phase. This is where your team builds the roadmap that will get the project from here to closure.

It is critical that the technical requirements are documented fully and completely. This document will serve as the template for the design specifications. If the project is very complex and comprises multiple features or components, then there should be a technical requirements document for each feature. If the project is very small, one technical requirements document will be sufficient.

The size, complexity, and scope of the project will determine how much detail is needed for the Project Plan and the supporting documentation. The time spent on putting the plan together should be proportional to the size and complexity of the project. The *Project Definition*, *Project Plan*, and *Project Approach* documents will be the roadmaps used by the project team to guide them to project completion. The project manager will create a high-level schedule for the team.

Design

The Design phase of the project is an area that is often neglected, at least to some extent. We have seen teams who implement their code and then write the design specification after the fact. This is not going to result in consistently high quality, reusable, and extensible code and systems. The starting point for writing a design specification is to review the *Functional* and *Technical Requirements* documents. If the project is very complex and comprises multiple features and components, there will be a functional and technical specification for each feature. There should be both a *Hardware* and a *Software Architecture Design*, which usually are documented by the lead engineer or architect. The Architecture will show all the features and components of the product or system and how they integrate with each other to constitute the final product. If you have multiple features in your product, you will need multiple design specifications. Either the technical lead or architect will write the designs, or each feature will be assigned to an engineer who will use the Architecture documents as a guide when creating the design specification. The design specifications often require that the engineer write test code or build a mini prototype to verify that the design will work. The design must include details on how the feature or component will be tested both by the developer (unit testing) and the quality assurance group (integration testing).

The *Design Specification* documents are used by the feature designer, technical lead, and project manager to break down each feature into tasks and subtasks. Any task that takes more than a week or two should be broken down into subtasks. These lists of tasks are called the *Detailed Task Lists*. The Detailed Task Lists identify dependencies among tasks that enable the project manager to schedule them appropriately. The Detailed Task Lists also include *Final Estimates*. The project manager needs to review the Final Estimates to ensure that the overall project can be completed within the proposed timeline and budget. Generally, you will find that some tasks come in under estimate and some over estimate, and as long as you have left some buffer time to allow for this, you should be pretty close to the estimates created during the Planning phase. If not, then this is the time to review the *Task Lists* with your team, and possibly your client, to make decisions about how to proceed.

The Design phase of a feature usually takes about 20% of the total implementation time for that feature. For example, if you have eight weeks assigned to implement one feature, approximately two weeks will be for design (including design meetings, necessary prototyping, design reviews, and all reviewing and updating of documentation). If prototype or test code is written, it is usual for this code to be used as a starting point for the feature implementation.

Development

During this phase, the project manager will create the detailed project schedule. The Development phase is when the code is written and the system is built. This phase includes unit testing of the features and components. It includes writing any test code or building any test systems that are needed for the Quality Assurance (QA) group to be able to adequately test the product. The project will have been broken down into releases or milestones during the Planning phase.

Once the detailed schedule is complete and the milestones and deliverable dates are finalized, the actual development of your product begins. The project manager's job is primarily to track and manage the project schedule and the project team. This includes managing the scope, resources, budget, change control, status reporting, and quality of the product. This phase may contain many internal releases and test cycles that continue until all of the features and components are completed. The developers will be unit testing their code before checking it in for a build; they will be tracking down and resolving bugs in their code. All of the code should be implemented, and all unit testing and bug fixing on individual features and components should be completed at the end of the Development phase.

Integration

The Integration phase is when the code or the system components are integrated into what will be the final product. For complex systems, whether hardware or software, the chances are that there will be some integration issues. Integration bugs will likely be found and need to be resolved before the product is ready for release. Applicable performance and stability testing of the product will be performed and changes made to ensure that the product or service meets the specified performance specification. This is not as simple as it sounds. This can be the most stressful phase of the Life Cycle. If you are running out of time and cannot track down that one critical, elusive bug that is a showstopper, you and your team could find yourselves working long hours and long, long weekends for some time until the issues are resolved. If the product is being deployed at the client's site, there could be some integration with the client's existing systems. Usability testing or beta testing programs will also take place during this phase of the project. The project manager will be working on the plans for deployment and post-deployment during the Integration phase. The operations plan will need to be completed so that the training plan can be completed and the training manuals and course descriptions created.

Deployment (Launch)

There are a few things that need to be accomplished during this phase before you will be ready to hand off the product to your client. The client training will take place during this phase. Any critical bugs found since integration will be fixed and verified. The final product will be delivered, whether that is physical hardware, a CD, or a product installed on Internet servers. The client will approve the deliverable prior to deployment. The client will perform client acceptance testing after deployment followed by a formal client acceptance meeting when final agreements are signed. The final product hand-off occurs when both parties have fulfilled all contractual obligations.

Post-Deployment

In most respects, your project is completed. Depending on the nature of the project, you will have somewhere between zero and many final tasks to complete before project closure.

During this phase, you and your team may continue to be responsible for some ongoing support to the technical support, customer service, operations team, and so on. This could include weekly meetings with technical support and customer service representatives to analyze data relating to how many calls and e-mails they are receiving on different issues and areas of the product. You may have regular meetings with the client to troubleshoot issues and to discuss bugs and schedule maintenance releases for the product. You may need to work with the technical writing team to update help screens, user guides, and installation and set up guides to either correct errors or to incorporate changes from maintenance releases. For Internet products, you may be responsible for some operations support for the system. You may need to analyze performance statistics to ensure that your product's performance in a production environment is in line with the results that your team achieved in the test environment. Will the system support the peak loads that were agreed to and confirmed in the contractual agreements? Time for these tasks must be included in your scheduling, and for many, or all, of the project team, this may overlap with new assignments and new projects. Even though your project has been handed-off, you can't necessarily wash your hands of it and move on without looking back!

Lessons learned, which are sometimes rather morbidly referred to as "post mortems," are an essential final step in any project. Do not be tempted to skip the lessons learned. They are very valuable and a great way for a project manager to get feedback on how the project went, any issues encountered, what things went well, and what things could be improved.

Managing Each Step of the Project Life Cycle

The steps of the project Life Cycle may not necessarily run consecutively. Often the steps will overlap and run concurrently for some period of time. For example, if the planning step is scheduled to last for 10 weeks, and the project will be a three-phase implementation, you may want to get your development team working on the designs for phase one before you have completed the planning for phases two and three.

If you are inflexible on overlapping the steps, you may find that you are wasting a lot of development time and that your development team is sitting around twiddling their thumbs waiting for something to do while you are tied up with hours of planning meetings each day! To maximize the effectiveness and efficiency of your team, you should always be looking for ways to keep everyone working at full capacity and minimizing project downtime.

Some features will need more design time than others. The time required will depend on the size of the feature. You should not stop your team members from moving onto the development step for features that have completed designs because you have other team members who are not finished with that step yet. The same can be said for moving from development to integration.

You will find at times that some of your team members are on a different step in the process than others. However, you should still have timelines for each step. You should document the start and finish dates for each step even though you know you will have a few exceptions to those hard dates.

You may be managing, or working in some capacity, on more than one project at a time, and this will add to the differing number of Life Cycle steps that you are required to manage at any one time. For the company to be consistently working on projects and keeping all the employees busy, they will very likely be planning the next project while you are still implementing the current one. This planning is also likely to require some of your time. If your project timelines are not too long, you may find that you are managing the post-deployment step of your last project while managing the deployment step of your current project and the planning step of your future project! It is all about juggling your time and setting priorities. It can be challenging, but it is also a lot of fun, and it certainly does not give you time to get bored!

In longer-term projects, it is often a cause for celebration to be moving from one Life Cycle step to the next. Just when you thought you had taken all you could stomach of daylong planning meetings, you move into the Design phase. Then again, just when you are feeling a bit less challenged by development when everything is running so smoothly, you switch to the Integration phase and find lots of issues that require your troubleshooting skills. Many teams celebrate meeting the milestones that move them to the next step of the project Life Cycle. It is easy to track progress using the Life Cycle wheel, and though you know that it starts all over again as soon as you finish, it is still fun to see yourselves getting closer to the end goal.

Industry Standard Methodologies and Processes

There are many project management, quality management, and business management processes being used in organizations today. It would be beyond the scope of this book to try to mention them all. However, we would like to briefly introduce four industry-standard processes that are widely used and recognized in companies worldwide today.

Project Management Institute (PMI)

The Project Management Institute (PMI) was founded in 1967, in Pennsylvania, USA. Today, PMI is an international organization that develops professional standards and certification programs in project management. PMI has *The Project Management Body of Knowledge (PMBOK)*, which is its project management "bible." PMBOK is a collection of best practices combined into PMI's nine knowledge areas that constitute the project methodology. PMI and PMBOK are not industry specific. They are focused on a generic methodology that can be used in any industry; for example, construction, pharmaceutical, automotive, software, and financial.

Six Sigma

The term "Six Sigma" came into use in the early 1990s. Motorola invented Six Sigma and later created the Six Sigma Technical Institute, where they collaborated with companies such as Allied Signal, IBM, Texas Instruments, and Kodak to further develop the process.

Six Sigma is designed to eliminate defects in any type of process, whether it's a product or a service process. Achieving Six Sigma means that the process has no more than 3.4 defects per million opportunities. Six Sigma is nonindustry specific and can be applied to processes in any type of organization. Six Sigma uses two methodologies: DMAIC (define, measure, analyze, improve, control), which is used to improve existing processes, and DSS (Design for Six Sigma), also called DMADV (define, measure, analyze, design, verify), which is used for designing new processes. Six Sigma has three levels of certification: green belt (GB), black belt (B), and master black belt (MBB).

Six Sigma is used in hundreds of organizations today, such as General Electric, Ford, Kodak, Texaco, the U.S. Air Force, and UPS, to name but a few.

Software Engineering Institute (SEI)—Capability Maturity Model Integration® (CMMI)

The Software Engineering Institute (SEI) is a federally funded research and development center sponsored by the U.S. Department of Defense.

The Capability Maturity Model Integration (CMMI) is designed to help organizations identify and improve the maturity level of their processes. There are five maturity levels:

1. Initial—Processes are ad hoc or chaotic.

2. Repeatable—Basic project management processes are in place.

3. Defined—Business and technical processes are standardized and documented throughout organization.

4. Managed—Processes and quality are measured, analyzed, and managed.

5. Optimized—Processes are predictable and effective, and continuous process improvement is part of the processes.

Some organizations require that vendors be at a specific CMMI level before they will consider them for contracts. Many government departments, for instance, have this requirement. Hence, many companies working on military and government contracts use and maintain the process standards required by CMMI.

International Organization for Standardization (ISO)

A group of representatives from 25 countries formed the ISO in 1946. Its goal is "to facilitate the international coordination and unification of industrial standards."*

ISO primarily focuses on technical standards for both products and services and is used in both the public and private sectors. The standards require a repeatable process that yields consistent results. The desired results include meeting client, quality, and regulatory requirements, continual improvement of processes and results, and high client satisfaction.

ISO 9000 and ISO 1400 are generally recognized generic standards for quality management and environmental management, respectively. These processes are used in many technology companies worldwide today.

*Source—ISO organization (www.iso.org)

CHAPTER 3

Project Initiation

In the mid eighties and early nineties, industries were jumping on the dot-com bandwagon. You may remember this as being a time when dot.com companies were popping up left and right, engineering salaries went through the roof, and the stock market was at an all time high. The dot.com era was making people millions. All you had to do was call yourself a dot.com startup company and you were worth a fortune. Most of those companies were not profitable, and many of them had no chance of ever being profitable. Their stock was hugely overpriced, and the companies often lacked the business leadership necessary for long-term success. Companies were launching projects haphazardly just to keep up with the competition and to show that they were being productive. Those projects were launched without clear business or technology goals and objectives, leaving the project without the strategic planning and direction needed for long-term business success. With this frameset, many companies were purchasing equipment and services that would work with existing systems—thinking that this would be conducive to faster time to market. This was not always the case. It took time to get projects up and running, it was often very difficult to integrate the old legacy systems with the new technology, and by the time the product was finally ready, a new product was introduced and the old one was already out of date.

In the midst of this dot.com madness, there was also the Y2K bug to contend with. Many of the old technologies were built many years ago, and no one was looking forward as far as the turn of the century and planning for how these systems would hold up. They probably never thought that the systems would be around that long. As a result, it became an engineering standard in many companies to write dates with a two-digit year. The default year (if the system could not recognize what year was entered) was usually 1984. Therefore, when we changed from 1999 to 2000, the system did not know whether it was the year 1900 or the default year—1984. There were thousands of projects being launched to address the Y2K bug, many of which were probably not needed. Nevertheless, there was a necessity to be seen doing something about this due to paranoia that companies could be sued if they did not show that they were addressing the year 2000 issues. This used up many of the market's engineering resources and created a technology boom. Many could not see that, at some point, the bubble had to burst.

It was a nice ride for a while, but the bubble did finally burst. Many dot.com's went out of business. Those investors who held onto their dot.com stocks for too long lost a fortune equivalent to those they thought they were going to make. Venture capitalists became much more savvy about technology businesses and were not throwing around anywhere near the many millions of dollars they had in the previous decade. The dot.com industry matured, and those companies that were left standing made serious changes to their business and technology strategies to enable them to compete in today's marketplace.

Today, companies are looking at the bottom line. They want to see the *return on investment (ROI)*, and they want to know exactly how long it will take to achieve the ROI. Anything longer than a couple of years is a pretty hard sell these days. Proposals for senseless products are no longer getting into the boardroom. They are being nixed much earlier in the process. Processes are being put in place to ensure adequate due diligence on project proposals. Executive-level management is taking the time to review the proposed projects and their long-term goals and objectives. Initiatives are not being given the green light unless a justification for overall business success is prevalent. However, this does not mean that companies have stopped thinking outside the box. In fact, this kind of thinking is even more necessary in today's marketplace. Differentiating oneself from the competition by coming up with creative and unique concepts is the key to initiating successful projects.

Once a project concept has been presented to executive management and accepted as a feasible idea, the project *proposer* will be tasked with creating a formal *Project Proposal*.

The initial Project Proposal is a high-level plan that includes estimates for resources required to complete the project. Once the Project Proposal is complete, a decision will be made whether to go forward with the project, to change the scope of the project, or to terminate the project. If the project is greenlighted, the proposal will continue to the project definition stage.

There is a huge amount of work that needs to be accomplished in the planning stage of a project. So much so that it is often a wonder that the project got started at all! If you want your projects to be completed on time, within budget, and with high quality, and if you want them to be successful, you need to invest the appropriate amount of time and effort in planning. It is an area that is often overlooked or rushed through very quickly. The eagerness to get started actually coding or building something can overwhelm common sense and cause companies to skimp on this phase. The more thorough the planning, the fewer problems you will encounter during the project creation. This will lead to higher productivity, higher team morale, and a higher-quality product.

The Planning phase of a project includes the following steps:
- Project Concept
- Request for Proposal (RFP)
- Project Proposal
- Project Greenlight
- Project Definition
- Project Approval
- Project Kick-off
- Project Plan
- Project Approach

In this chapter, we will cover the steps in the process from project concept through project greenlighting, the Project Initiation Process is shown in the Workflow diagram in Figure 3.1.

The project concept and proposal incorporate all the meetings, research, and reporting that is necessary to get the project greenlighted.

Project Concept

The *concept* is the idea or the reason that the project is deemed necessary. It can be a simple idea that can be implemented in a matter of weeks, or it can be a complex concept that will require a monumental engineering feat and a few years to accomplish. The concept describes either a problem that needs to be solved or a solution to a problem.

The concept should, ideally, contain the following elements:

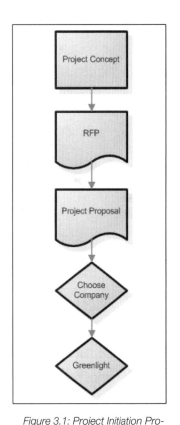

Figure 3.1: Project Initiation Process Workflow.

- Business Case—The business case describes the reason that the presenter believes the project is necessary. For example, the presenter could use facts about where the business is currently compared to where it needs to be in the future or financial statistics showing negative trends that can be reversed by implementing this project.

- Benefits—This is the value that the project will have to the organization. This should be described in terms of how it will help the company meet its business goals and objectives. If there is a company strategic plan in existence, the concept could be mapped to a specific goal. For example, increasing client satisfaction, reducing call center costs, and increasing development team productivity.

- Description (Problem or Solution)—A description of the problem that needs to be solved and the proposed solution (if there is one). At the concept stage, it is not always possible to know how a problem can be solved. If it is critical that the problem must be solved, it can be presented as a concept and the solution can be developed during the proposal stage.

- Initial Estimate—If the concept is still very vague, it may not be possible to include an estimate. If this is the case, it is good practice to decide on a "not to be exceeded" figure for what is considered a reasonable amount to spend to fix this specific problem. The estimates will be as vague as the description. Thus, if the description is really well defined, the estimates will be much more accurate.

Companies often use brainstorming techniques to come up with concepts for projects. Brainstorming is an excellent way for a group of people to bounce ideas and thoughts off each other and work on them to come up with well-defined concepts for projects.

The Brainstorming Process

Brainstorming is the process of formulating ideas that can be refined into a concept for a potential project. Brainstorming can be done with small or large groups of people. You can have a successful brainstorming session with as few as 2 or as many as 100 people. Ideally, for the best results, limit brainstorming sessions to groups of 5 to 20 people. Meetings with more than 20 people can be difficult to facilitate because there will be too many people wanting to contribute ideas and comments at the same time. If people are waiting too long to contribute, the conversation may have gone in a different direction by the time it gets to their turn. They will feel that it is too late for them to contribute to that particular topic so they pass or attempt to bring the conversation back to where it was previously, thereby losing the natural flow of the brainstorm for that topic.

There are many different techniques and tools for brainstorming. We describe one technique that works well. Experiment with the process, refine it, and customize it to fit your specific needs and the needs of the group that you are working with. You may decide to set the meeting up in a less formal way. If you have only two topics, and they are very clearly defined, you may want to skip some of the early steps in the process and jump right into the discussion about them.

You should use a facilitator for your brainstorming process. It should be a person (or persons) who will not participate in the brainstorming. The role of the facilitator is to run the meeting, keep time, and ensure that the brainstorming process is followed. The facilitator will keep things moving along so that the team does not get stuck on one point or digress into areas that are not relevant to the brainstorming session.

Define the Purpose of the Meeting

The purpose should include the goals and objectives of the brainstorming and, very importantly, the scope of the brainstorming. If the scope is too broad, you will find it almost impossible to focus in on a limited number of specific topics! If you have a lot of topics that you need to brainstorm about, divide them into categories and schedule separate meetings for each category. Some examples of brainstorming topics may be:

- Product A—increase revenue
- Product B—reduce costs
- Dept X—decrease run-the-business (RTB) costs
- New product ideas

Communication and Preparation

Tell the attendees what to bring with them. If you want them to think about the topics in advance, schedule the brainstorming session a week or two in advance to give them time to think and to prepare notes. If you want the team to brainstorm cold and to come to the meeting with no preconceived ideas or notions, then do not tell them the purpose of the meeting in advance. Tell them just before you start the meeting.

Rules

It is vitally important that you have rules for your brainstorming process. The following are some typical rules for brainstorming sessions, but you should customize them for your particular session:

- Both problems and solutions will be discussed.

- You do not have to have a solution in mind in order to bring up a problem that you believe needs to be solved.

- You cannot name people or blame people for problems.

- You cannot defend yourself or others when problems are being discussed.

- Everyone's opinions are valid.

- All comments are welcomed as long as they are relevant to the topics under discussion.

- Nothing discussed in this room should leave this room.

- The facilitator is running the meeting. If the facilitator asks the group to move on from a topic or discussion, they will do so. The facilitator will capture any ideas or suggestions that are important but not relevant to the session so they are not lost. Discussion around those topics will not continue in the brainstorming session.

Brainstorming Topics and Categories

This is where you start the actual brainstorming. You should have one or more brainstorming topics that you defined in the purpose. Use those topics to come up with a list of categories. You may already have a list of categories prepared, or you may wish to brainstorm with the team to come up with categories before you start. The brainstorming will not be limited to the categories you define, but these topics will help the group to get their creative juices flowing.

Using the examples of "Increase Revenues" and "Reduce Costs," for instance, you may come up with the following categories:

- Increase per-customer revenue
- Attract more customers
- Provide incentives for existing clients to order more product
- Expand product range
- Offer accessories and related products (one-stop shopping)
- Reduce call center costs
- Reduce facility overhead

Using the categories as a general guideline, you can either use a method where the group calls out problems or ideas and the facilitator lists them on a whiteboard or flipchart or you can use the "sticky note process" (as described in Chapter 14). For this example we will use the flipchart process.

Capturing the Ideas

There are a couple of different approaches to this. The first is to have a free-flow discussion where ideas and suggestions are captured as the discussion continues. You can also go around the room and ask each person to contribute any ideas or suggestion they have, or you can just ask people to call out ideas as they think of them. Regardless of which process you use, the facilitator will capture the ideas on the flipcharts. As we mentioned before, the ideas can be problems or solutions. Both are valid in brainstorming sessions. If you have a large brainstorming group or the discussion is expected to be fast moving, it is a good idea for the facilitator to have one or more assistants to help capture the ideas in writing. If there is only one person scribing, either the discussion will have to stop to wait for the scribe to catch up or the ideas will get lost if the scribe cannot keep up with the pace of the group.

Categorizing the Ideas

Once all the ideas have been captured in writing, they need to be categorized. Some will fit into the categories that you defined at the beginning of the meeting, and some will require new categories. If there are ideas coming up that are clearly outside of the defined scope, capture them in an out-of-scope category. Those ideas may be very useful later for meetings or projects where they fall within the scope.

Summarizing and Prioritizing Categories

Each category should be summarized by the facilitator or a group member. The out-of-scope category does not need to be summarized.

Selecting Categories for Further Brainstorming

The team will need to prioritize the categories and ideas to decide which ones will move forward into the next round of brainstorming. Prioritizing can be done using a voting system, or it can be accomplished by group discussion. Depending on how much time you have available and how many ideas have been chosen for further discussion, you may need to schedule additional brainstorming sessions to discuss them. If the team is brainstormed out, you may decide to end the initial brainstorming session and continue the discussion of individual ideas in a subsequent meeting or meetings.

It is advisable not to try to discuss more than two or three ideas in one session. Brainstorming is mentally a very intense process, and it is easy to get burnt out and start to lose the creative edge if you try to push the group too far in one session. For some brainstorming sessions, one idea per meeting will be sufficient.

Brainstorming Individual Ideas

Brainstorming on the individual ideas (problems or solutions) can either be done by the whole group or it can be given to separate subgroups (brainstorming focus groups). It may be that to fully explore a specific idea, the group will need some specialized technical or subject-matter knowledge that was not available in the initial brainstorming session. It may also be that the initial brainstorming group was a large group (of, say, 20 people), and it is usually a good idea to have much smaller subgroups.

The brainstorming focus group takes one idea at a time and has an open discussion about the idea. If the idea is a problem, the group will first need to come up with some potential solution ideas before they can brainstorm on the potential solution or solutions. If the idea is a solution, the team should ensure that it fully understands the problem that the solution is designed to solve before brainstorming on the idea.

The group should be assigned a team lead and a note taker. As the team works its way through various scenarios and comes to conclusions about what will and what will not work, it is imperative that the note taker captures the key points and accurately summarizes the discussions. The brainstorming focus group should conclude their meeting(s) with a fully documented concept that is ready to be presented to the authorized approver and decision-maker.

Prioritizing Concepts

Once all the ideas have been brainstormed and developed into project concepts, the concepts may need to be prioritized. The prioritization may be done by the original brainstorming group, or the concepts may go to a separate business or product management group for prioritization.

Finalizing Concepts

When the list of prioritized concepts is complete, the development team will most likely be asked to put some initial estimates on them. The business groups will then estimate ROI and other benefits before presenting them as concepts for approval to the senior management team.

Brainstorming can be used for more than just project and product ideas. It is a great tool for identifying process improvements, ideas for team events, and ideas on how to implement specific features or code for an approved project.

How Initial and High-Level Cost and Time Estimates Are Generated

The initial and high-level cost and time estimates for projects are generated using historical data and information gathered both internally and externally from employees and outside vendors. Initial costs are generally required when submitting project concepts for approval to move forward to the proposal stage. High-level estimates are needed at the proposal stage of a project. For outsourced projects, many of the initial costs are estimated during the creation of *Request for Information* (*RFI*) and *Request for Proposal* (*RFP*) documents.

To estimate time and cost resources for a project prior to a project definition or project plan being created, you will need specific pieces of information and preferably access to people with some historical perspective on development time and costs. Initial costs are used when deciding whether to propose a project. The estimates are not expected to be 100% accurate at this stage. It is likely that you will be asked for ballpark estimates, but bear in mind that the estimates need to be based on some realistic foundation. Alternatively, you may be required to submit an estimate with a low and a high threshold ($120,000–$160,000 for example).

To estimate project costs you will need the following information:

- Approximate development time (hours or weeks) for project and cost per hour per developer

- Management team required and costs

- Approximate size of project team required

- Approximate cost for hardware, software, development and testing equipment, and tools

- Approximate quality assurance testing time (hours or weeks) and cost per hour

- Support staff required (client support, technical support, operations team) and cost per hour

- Consulting or contractor time required and cost per hour

- Time needed for research, requirements, and design including costs for resources

- Deployment, delivery, and manufacturing costs

- Advertising and marketing costs

- Time and costs to produce estimates (initial, high-level, and detailed)

- Project kick-off and project completion parties!!

As a new project manager, you may have no idea where to start when trying to estimate these costs. With experience, you will find it becomes easier and easier to estimate the cost of a project. In fact, you can get to the point where you can do the calculations in your head and come up with a ballpark figure of say, $10,000 to $15,000 or $400,000 to $500,000. The closer you get to the project being approved, the more accurate the estimates need to be. You will continue refining the initial numbers as more information becomes available and as the project scope and definition become more developed.

If you have an experienced technical lead or senior engineer available to you, he or she will be able to furnish most of the above information. Your senior technical staff has in-depth knowledge of the technology, architecture, and design of the products as well as a great understanding of the skill sets of the other team members. Do not underestimate how useful they can be to you when you are trying to put together initial estimates for projects. They will often be hesitant to give you information if you have limited requirements (they are engineers, after all, and they like to have lots of details), but by presenting your questions in the right way (as hypothetical problems, for instance), you will be amazed at how much valuable information can be gleaned. Remember that no developer ever gets to spend 100% of his time on development tasks. Taking the estimate and adding a 20% buffer to allow for meetings, unit testing, technical issues, setting up equipment, support for other team members, design and code reviews, and so on, and ensuring that time has been allocated for writing requirements, specifications, and designs should give you a pretty good starting point for initial estimates. A sample

Estimate document is shown in Figure 3.2. An estimate template document is included on the CD-ROM that accompanies this book.

Feature No.	Feature / Task	PM	S/W Engineer	UI Designer	Technical Lead / DBA	Systems Engineer	Business Analyst	QA Manager	QA Engineer	Product Manager	Usability	Graphic Design	Consultant	Contractor	Vendor	TOTAL HRS
Estimate — OFIS																
1	Planning meetings	50				10			15		50					125
2	Project Documentation	80	35	10	80	10	10	50	50	20	10					355
3	Feature 1 Design		40	10	10								25			85
4	Feature 2 Design		40			50										90
5	Feature 3 Design		30													30
6																0
	TOTAL HOURS	130	145	20	90	70	10	50	65	20	60	0	25	0	0	685
	Charge to Client Per Hour	65	55	47	70	70	60	50	50	45	60		50			
	Total $	8,450	7,975	940	6,300	4,900	600	2,500	3,250	900	3,600	0	1,250	0	0	40,665

Figure 3.2: Estimate.

Business managers often create initial estimates. Sometimes they are realistic, and sometimes they are not. Do not panic if you see an initial estimate that you know is way off the mark. There will be opportunities to refine estimates before and after the project is formally proposed. It is possible that you will be asked to do a sanity check on an initial estimate. You may think that what you see is a complete joke and wonder how someone could seriously believe that they could develop the project with such a low budget. In this situation, it is not a good idea to be completely honest about your feelings. Remember to be tactful and respectful while being honest about the facts. It would be great if you could keep your job until the project is actually approved!

Concept Approval

A concept is presented either in written form or verbally. Regardless of the method of presentation, it must contain sufficient information for the decision-makers (typically, senior management and executives) to be able to determine whether the concept is viable and worth pursuing. The project concept will either be approved to move onto the proposal stage, declined, or postponed pending additional information being presented to support the request.

The Project Proposal Process

At this point, you will need to enter the wacky world of the three-letter acronym (TLA). You will find a whole host of TLA's in general use in the technology industry and a boatload more that are unique to individual companies. No matter where you work, you are going to have to learn a certain amount of techspeak (if you have not done so already). If you are working with outside companies, either as the client or as the vendor, you will experience the unique acronyms and technical (and sometimes not so technical) terms that they commonly use. Initially you will wonder what on earth everyone is talking about, but you will gradually begin to understand this new language. Then one day, you will hear yourself talking and realize that you have finally become proficient in the TLA dialect of the company for which you are working. Don't be fooled into believing that everyone understands what all the TLAs mean. Some people are too embarrassed to ask so they just pretend that they understand. Don't be embarrassed about asking the meaning of terms used. If someone uses an acronym or a term you are not familiar with, ask them what it stands for or what it means. You may see a look of relief on more than one other face in the room when you get the answer. Some people just make up their own acronyms, and often they are the only person who understand their meaning. It is a rather amusing trick that engineers like to play on management. They make up a new TLA to confuse the other team members, and then they wait to see how long it takes until someone asks what it means. Who said that engineers do not have a sense of humor?

Companies who are looking either to outsource a project or to procure software or hardware from an outside vendor generally use Request for Information (RFI), Request for Proposal (RFP), and Request for Quotation (RFQ) documents. It is possible, though not very common, that some companies will also use these documents for internal projects.

As a project manager, you may never write an RFQ, RFI, or RFP. The chances are that at some point in your career you will be involved in some capacity in responding to, or supplying information to someone else in your company who is responding to, an RFI or an RFP. For internal projects, the Project Proposal will be written based on the Project Concept; therefore, an RFI, RFP, and RFQ may not be required at all.

Even if you never have to write any of these documents, it is important that you understand what they are and the importance that they have to the initiation and approval of projects.

Request for Quote (RFQ)

An RFQ is used for requesting an exact quote for a specific service or an item of software or hardware.

RFQs are commonly used for ordering development equipment and tools. In smaller companies, or those that are decentralized, you may be required to complete and submit the RFQs yourself. Alternatively, your company may have a procurement department or an administrative assistant who will take care of requesting quotes on your behalf. In either case, you will need to supply the necessary information to whoever is submitting the request to ensure that the quote you receive is to the correct specification.

An RFQ is a much more straightforward request than an RFI or RFP. It is used to request a quote for a specific standard product or service. For example, you may need to purchase 10 development systems for your project engineers for which you have a specific set of hardware and software requirements. The vendor, in this case, should easily be able to respond quickly with an exact quotation of the cost for each system. RFQs are used for getting quotations for off-the-shelf products such as consumer software products or desktop computer systems.

An RFQ template is included on the CD-ROM that accompanies this book.

Request for Information (RFI)

An RFI is used to garner information for a project prior to sending out an RFP. Some examples of the information requests that you may see in an RFI:

- Verify the assumption that the software can be designed to interface with the accounting system that your company uses

- Ascertain whether the software can be developed to run on multiple platforms

- Find out whether the company has a Unix development environment

- Find out whether their engineers have the necessary security clearance required for working on special government projects

- Discover how large the development team is

- Find out whether X component can interface directly with Y component

- Discover the cost of X part

- Ascertain the approximate time to develop X component

The information gathered from the RFI can help the submitter whittle down the vendor list to a more manageable number prior to sending out the RFP. For example, the RFI may be sent out to twenty-five companies, and the RFP may go out to only ten of those companies. Alternatively, the RFI might be used to gather information such as input into a Project Concept.

The RFI is also commonly used as a sanity check for budget, timelines, and technical requirements that will enable the author to a creative a more realistic and comprehensive RFP.

An RFI template is included on the CD-ROM that accompanies this book.

Request for Proposal (RFP)

An RFP is a request sent out to a company (or companies) asking them to submit a proposal to develop a project as defined in the RFP.

The purpose of an RFP is to elicit high-quality and reasonable proposals. The proposals will be based on the information and requirements provided in the RFP, so it is imperative that this document contains accurate and detailed requirements. In an ideal world, the RFP will serve as the foundation for building a successful and mutually beneficial working relationship between the client and the vendor(s). Projects can be challenging, problematic, and expensive, so it is important that these early communications between the companies are an effective model for future communications.

It is very important not to underestimate the difficulty in creating a written document that expresses clearly what it is that the company is trying to achieve. Bear in mind that the person receiving the RFP may have no previous knowledge of the requester's company or products. Therefore, terminology needs to be explained and not left open to interpretation. The company sending out the RFP may not be clear on what exactly it is that they need, in which case the RFP may focus on the problem rather than on the desired solution. No matter whether the solution is predefined, the RFP must be clear, concise, and free of ambiguity. The must-haves must be clearly distinguishable from the nice-to-haves and the icing-on-the-cakes. The focus should be on what needs to be achieved rather than how it needs to be achieved. If the *how* is critical to the project, then it should be clearly stated (for example, if some or all areas of the project require that engineers have security clearance, if the solution must integrate seamlessly with existing systems, or if the solution must be written in a specific programming language). If a how is not critical to the success of the project but is desirable, then it should be listed as a nice-to-have, leaving the door open for the vendor to propose alternative solutions.

The information contained in an RFP will vary depending on the type of project. In addition to a detailed description of the company, the project, the market space, the end user, the project goal, detailed project requirements, and the budget range, it should also contain a high-level schedule of events. For example:

- March 1st—Request for Information (RFIs) sent out
- March 12th—RFI Information due
- March 15th—Short list of selected vendors
- March 23rd—Request for Proposal (RFPs) sent to selected vendors
- April 20th—RFP Proposals due
- April 23rd—Project Contract awarded to selected vendor
- April 24th—Purchase order for project issued
- April 26th—Project Definition (Charter) meeting

- May 21st—Marketing Requirements Document due
- May 24th—Kick-off Meeting
- May 27th—Project Plan due
- June 4th—Development begins
- September 6th—Phase One complete
- October 4th—Phase Two complete
- December 15th—Phase Three complete
- January 20th—Project end date

The RFP will contain information about the project concept and will ask for specific information that will constitute the proposal. The information requested will differ depending on the type and size of the project. The vendors must respond to the RFP with a Project Proposal by the specified deadline to be considered for the project.

The most important thing to remember about RFPs is that they need to be realistic, as do the proposals submitted in response to them. You cannot expect to get a $100 million project developed for less than $500,000. Similarly, you cannot submit a proposal for $100 million for a project with a budget of only $500,000. Requirements and proposals need to be in line with the budget range. If your requirements are unrealistic, the vendors who receive the RFPs will not respond. This is why it is important to use an RFI to confirm and verify assumptions, facts, and figures before creating and sending out an RFP to multiple vendors.

Sometimes companies will pay vendors to write proposals for large projects. It can take a significant amount of time to respond to an RFP, and if many companies are bidding on the same project, the chances of winning the contract may be rather slim. The cost of responding to an RFP for a large project can be high. Hours or weeks of work may be required to complete it. These factors can discourage some vendors from submitting proposals, especially if they believe that the company is only using the proposals for comparison and already has a vendor of choice. To get around this problem, some companies will offer to pay a fee to help cover the costs of preparing the proposal.

The RFP will include, but is not limited to:

- An executive summary of the client's company and market space
- A description of the problem and proposed solution
- Key business and technical requirements
- Proposed project phases and milestones
- Quality assurance requirements
- Budget
- Schedule of events
- Proposal template

An RFP template is included on the CD-ROM that accompanies this book.

What do you do if you are asked to respond to an RFP? Imagine that you receive an RFP from a client and are unsure why a particular requirement is necessary. The requirement does not make sense to you, which leads you to the assumption that perhaps the person who wrote the RFP did not really know what they were asking for. The company who sent you the RFP may not take inquiries from vendors, especially if they sent it out to many companies. If the RFP is not clear and you believe there is a better solution, then offer it as a second alternative in the proposal that you submit. Do not automatically assume that the client is wrong and they do not need what they asked for. They may not have explained very clearly why a specific requirement is important, but that does not mean that you can ignore it. Respond to the requirements that they give and offer alternatives where it seems appropriate. This way you are covering all your bases. If you fail to respond to the specific requirements, they may put your proposal aside, assuming that you are unable to meet the requirements. They are not likely to contact you to ask why you proposed a different solution if other vendors are able to offer solutions that met the specified requirements. You need to get the proposal right the first time because it may be the only opportunity you will get. A good-faith attempt to offer alternative solutions, especially ones that will save the client money, will be appreciated even if the alternatives turn out not to meet the requirements. The client will feel that you have their best interests at heart and that you are focused on the most cost-effective solution rather than on making as much money as you can. You are demonstrating integrity and a commitment to the potential client to read between the lines and to make the best possible recommendation that you can.

The Project Proposal Document

The Proposal Document explains the problem together with a description of how the problem will be solved, and it includes a high-level estimate of what it will cost to develop and deploy the solution. For an external project, the proposal planning will begin, for the development company, after they receive a Request for Information (RFI) or a Request for Proposal (RFP) from a prospective client. The client company will have completed the project concept and will have been through an internal approval process before sending out the RFI or RFP documents to prospective vendors. For an internal project, the Project Proposal will be based on the approved Project Concept.

The Project Proposal document will include a high-level description of the project and the proposed solution. The proposal will be submitted to senior management (or to the client) for greenlighting to move on to the Project Definition stage. A proposal can be a very detailed document, or it can be a very high-level, conceptual document with a lot of open issues that will need to be addressed during the Definition phase. The accuracy of the estimates and costs are contingent upon the level of detail contained in the proposal. An external project will require a much more detailed proposal than an internal project. The client will be unable to approve the project to move ahead into the Definition phase without a pretty good idea of the time, cost, and effort involved in the project. If you are asked to submit estimates for an RFP document, be sure to document the accuracy of your estimates and any assumptions used to come up with the estimates. If a disclaimer is necessary, then include it. For instance, if you are not sure how you will be able to solve a specific problem due to the immaturity of the technology being proposed, then clearly state this on the proposal. If the client is not told that no one else has solved this problem yet, they may go into the project with unrealistic expectations! Don't try to tell them what they want to hear just to get the contract. It will come back to haunt you. Remember that the key to keeping your clients happy is to under-promise and over-deliver.

The following information will typically be included in a Project Proposal document:

- Executive summary
- Corporate and cultural information
- Previous projects and clients
- Client references
- Development methodologies and processes
- Quality assurance and testing processes and procedures
- Development environment
- Assumptions
- The problem
- Proposed solution(s)
- Constraints, limitations, and risks
- Proposed project phases
- Milestones and deliverables
- The proposed project team
- Costs and payment details
- Terms and conditions
- Proposal submission and questions
- Proposal acceptance and approval

Executive Summary

For external projects where proposals are submitted in response to RFPs, an executive summary is very important. If the company requesting the proposal has never worked with your organization before, they will need some compelling data that compares you favorably with your competitors. The executive summary should include a brief history of the company together with some high-level financial information. The executive summary is a key input into the decision making process because many of the proposals are likely to be similar in solution and costs. If a company is investing a substantial amount of money in a project, they need to feel confident that they are working with a high-quality, reputable company.

Corporate and Cultural Information

This section will contain additional information about your company and the technical department(s) that will be involved in the project. It should include a corporate overview and some information about the company culture. For example, it could include operating values or mission statements for the engineering department. Explain whether the company has a casual, informal culture or a disciplined, formal one. This information could be very important to the client's selection of a vendor and will ensure that there are no misconceptions should the project be approved and awarded to your company.

Previous Projects and Clients

This section will contain descriptions of previous clients and projects that were similar to the project the client is proposing or that will demonstrate your organization's expertise and experience in project management and development.

For reasons of confidentiality, you may not be able to cite the names of some of your clients or too much detail about the projects you implemented for them. High-level information with a description of the market space that the client operates in, together with a synopsis of the success of the project(s), will be sufficient.

Client References

Here you should list some of your clients who have agreed to give references regarding projects you have implemented for them. Include contact names and titles as well as a brief description of the project(s) you worked on for each client.

Development Methodologies and Processes

This section will include an overview of the project Life Cycle and the documentation that is produced during each phase. It should also include information about processes and procedures for such things as configuration management, quality management, source control, security, and any other standard processes used during the development of projects.

Quality Assurance and Testing Processes and Procedures

Quality assurance processes, procedures, and methodologies should be outlined together with an overview of the documentation produced at each step of the Life Cycle. There may be testing outside of the quality assurance team that also needs to be accomplished, such as performance testing, security testing, or product verification and acceptance testing.

Development Environment

This section includes a brief description of the development environment. This will include details about the hardware platform for development, including operating system, design packages, programming software, unit test software, and so on.

Assumptions

This section should contain both organizational assumptions and technical assumptions. Organizational assumptions would include such things as the expectations the vendor has from the client as far as involvement in the project; client responsibilities, such as testing or documentation; and client representatives for the project (project manager, for example). Technical assumptions will include items such as the client's existing hardware, systems, and software that will be used for the project; specific technology that will be used in the development of the product; and consultants who will be engaged for specific areas of development requiring specialized knowledge or skill sets. A lot of assumptions will need to be made to create a Project Proposal document. It is important to document assumptions so that there are no misunderstandings later on.

The Problem

This section includes a brief description of the problem. This can be taken directly from the RFP or can be elicited from the client via phone conversations or meetings.

Proposed Solution(s)

This section contains details about the proposed solution or solutions. There may be more than one way to solve the specified problem and, if this is the case, give the client some alternatives. Different solutions should not be presented if they are just variations on the same theme. For example, do not present the same proposed solution with just one or two details changed. These specific options can be discussed and finalized later if the client decides to go ahead with the project. If you present 350 possible solutions, you will overwhelm the client with too much information, making it impossible for them to make a decision.

Constraints, Limitations, and Risks

Note any constraints, limitations, or risks that are currently known. This can include things such as the timeline for the starting the project. You may need to complete another project before you will be available to work on this one. Any limitations that your company has with regards to technology, knowledge, and skill sets should be identified together with a proposal for how you would manage them should you be awarded the project. Risks are things that should be obvious to you based on the information that the client has already furnished. It is important to ensure that you and the client are on the same page with what you consider to be constraints, limitations, or risks for the project.

Proposed Project Phases

The project may need to be developed and delivered in phases either because the client has requested it in the RFP or because you feel that the size or complexity of the project warrants it. For example, the project may consist of three distinct products that need to be developed consecutively because of dependencies among them. You may propose that the project be delivered in three phases, with one of the products being delivered in each.

Milestones and Deliverables

High-level project milestones and deliverables are detailed here. These would include the project phases, if relevant. At this early stage of the planning phase, the milestones may be confined to approximate dates for completion of specific documents for the planning phase and a high-level timeline for when each of the subsequent Life Cycle phases will be concluded. It should be obvious from the RFP and the solution section whether there are other key milestones or deliverables that should be specified.

The Proposed Project Team

The proposed project team will include the specific roles and positions needed together with some high-level qualifications and skill sets. Individuals do not need to be identified at this point. If it is known who the sponsor and the project manager will be, then name them. If you are not sure, you can specify that you have three project managers, all of whom have at least six years project management experience, and that one of those managers will be assigned as soon as the project contract is awarded and timelines are finalized.

Costs and Payment Details

This section will contain high-level estimates based on the initial estimates that were created during the concept phase or the budget information contained in the RFP.

Payment details will contain the payment terms. For example, payment for creating the Project Definition may be required prior to the project kick-off. Payment for development may be in installments. Some companies ask for 50% up front and 50% on completion of project.

Terms and Conditions

This will include some legal jargon that will most likely be supplied by the legal department. It will contain some disclaimers related the accuracy of the information contained herein, together with contractual requirements for the approval to move forward with the project.

Proposal Submission and Questions

This section will include the contact information of the proposal preparer, the date and time that the proposal was submitted, and the method of delivery. It will also include any questions the preparer has about anything in the RFP that was not clear. There may be some updates needed to the proposal before it can be finalized and approved if there are open issues or questions at the time the proposal is submitted.

Proposal Acceptance and Approval

By signing this document, everyone involved is in agreement that the proposal document is accurate and complete and is approved to move forward.

The client (or requester) will typically have a standard process for awarding the project contract to the chosen vendor.

Greenlighting

Greenlighting simply means that the project has been approved to continue. If the project is external, the green light will be given by the client. If it is internal, it will be given by a senior manager in your company. There is usually a standard process for greenlighting projects. In some companies, the CEO has to approve every project. In other companies, the CIO has an annual budget and can spend it on whichever projects she sees fit. Product managers may be responsible for greenlighting in some organizations. The process is typically a little different for high-dollar projects. They will usually require approval from a more senior executive than will the lower-cost projects. As a member of the management team, you may get to vote on which proposed projects you would like to see approved. The process is different in every company.

It is not unusual for there to be limited project management involvement in the initial planning stages of a project. Once the project has been greenlighted, however, the level of involvement is likely to increase significantly. The project may have gone through the concept and proposal stages, and the initial estimates may have been created, without any representation from project management or the development team. If this is the case, you will have quite a bit of catching up to do when the project is greenlighted and you are assigned as the project manager.

The Project Proposal may have been written in response to an RFP from an outside client or may have been written by someone working for your company who is proposing an internal project. The proposal may be as vague as a few ideas and a ballpark dollar figure that needs a lot of work to become a project description, or it may be a 50-page document that precisely details every aspect of the project and does not leave much to the imagination! Whatever the case may be, the project was greenlighted based on the information contained in the proposal. If you were not involved in its creation, it would be wise to get as familiar with it as possible without hesitation. Ask questions. Make sure that you understand the logic behind the problem, the description, the solution, and the initial estimates. If the project is for an outside client, the proposal may be seen as a template for a contractual agreement between the companies, so any discrepancies should be brought to the attention of the project sponsor as soon as possible.

It is important that you understand how projects are approved and greenlighted in your company. The more efficient the greenlighting process, the less likely that projects will be canceled part way through due to a change of heart, or change of direction, by senior executives. The more senior the managers that approve the projects, the less likely that someone will pull rank and cancel a project that is in progress. This can happen when someone on the management team "discovers" that projects are being worked on that do not fit within the company's business or strategic plan. If all projects go through a strict process for approval, this is less likely to happen. Many companies require that a Project Proposal clearly state how the project will move the company closer to its business and financial goals. A clear definition is required, specifying which company strategic objective the project is meeting and exactly how it is going to achieve it. It may seem at first sight that applying this kind of structured discipline to a creative process will result in inflexibility and the inability to get any projects off the ground. In fact, in the long term, more often than not, it results in the company being much more successful due to the fact that every department within the company is working towards the same company goals and objectives. This unified approach to strategic and tactical planning is the key to business success in today's competitive marketplace. However, if the company principals and employees are unable to make decisions, or are unable to stick to decisions once they are made, then things can get chaotic and unstable really quickly. Be aware that this will be the case whether you have a strict process or not. It is not the process that cannot make the decision: It is the people! Lack of effective decision-making is spreading like a virus in corporate America today. It is not the actual decisions that people struggle with; it is the reluctance of managers to take responsibility for a decision, so they refuse to make it. This is the reason why you must clearly identify and document all the decision-makers for your project during the planning phase.

The Different Kinds of Projects

Not all projects are created equal. There are large projects and small projects, complex projects and simple projects, short-term projects and long-term projects, top secret projects and open source projects, and on and on. There are many different perspectives on which projects belong in which categories. If a company usually works on projects with a duration of three to six months, they would consider a year-long project to be long term. An organization like NASA would likely consider a year-long project to be short term. A long-term project for them may be 20 or 30 years! Complexity is also subjective. What one company would consider complex another may consider simple. For these reasons, we are not going to try to specify what these terms mean. Each company will have their own definition for these terms and their meaning within their organization. If you are starting a new job as a project manager, you will need to ask for clarification on the terminology used within the organization. That way you can be sure that you are using the correct terminology and categorization for projects.

There are some categorizations of projects that are common across companies, such as internal and external projects, desktop and Internet projects, and software and hardware projects. These are explained in more detail in the following sections.

Internal versus External

An *internal project* is a project where the client is a person or department inside your organization. An *external project* is a project where the client is a person or company outside your organization. When we refer to the "client," we mean the person, department, or organization that is funding the development of the project. The end user of a product is not necessarily the project client or the customer.

Some companies almost exclusively develop internal projects. Technology, Internet, and software companies such as Microsoft, eBay, and Dell are primarily developing internal projects, where they are their own clients, and the end user is the general public. If your project is internal, it is important to remember that you do have a client and that you have the same responsibilities to that client as you would if you were working on an external project.

Let's assume that the company owns and develops an Internet product or service with product releases on a six-month project cycle. The client could be a product management group, a business development group or perhaps even the CEO. The client will provide requirements and will be the person or group who signs off on the deliverables. It can be trickier keeping the floodgates closed to midproject requests for additional features and enhancements when working on internal projects. If you do not have a contractual agreement, it can be harder to say "no" and to justify why you are unable to fulfill a request. Remember that a project manager has the same responsibility to her team members not to work them into the ground as she would if the client was an outside company. Project managers must not allow themselves to be bullied into taking on more work than the team can handle due to pressure from senior management. If there is a release due in six months, then there needs to be a project plan and schedule that can be accomplished in a six-month time frame. Believe us when we tell you that no project manager will enjoy working on a never-ending project. It can easily happen if the same discipline is not applied to internal projects as to external projects.

It is inevitable that if you keep adding more and more features and pushing out the delivery date, before you know it, your six-month project Life Cycle is going to be in its fifteenth month with no end in sight! If you see this trend starting to occur within your company and on your project, then you should meet with the project team and the sponsor to reevaluate the goals of the project. If the expected outcome of the project keeps changing, then you may be unable to deliver on it effectively. A disciplined approach to project management is a necessity for each and every project for them to be delivered on time, within budget, and with high quality. Having some flexibility with the completion date can also work to your advantage. If you do not have a legal responsibility to complete the project on time, both the internal client and the project team have the option of asking for more time to add or enhance features if it is going to add significant value to the project.

The quality of your product or service is a major success factor in both internal and external projects. The project manager of an internal project has the same responsibility to both define and achieve quality in the product as the project manager for an external project. Accountability may not be as formalized for an internal project. However, maintaining a high level of professionalism by ensuring that you are developing and delivering a high-quality project is of the utmost importance.

Another issue that can occur with internal projects is the lack of a standard budgeting process. If you do not know how much money is in your budget, how do you know whether the projects you are managing are cost efficient? Your internal client may assume that since you are not tied to a budget, you can just keep adding things to the schedule as you go along, with little or no impact on the project outcome. This is not the case. The resources required for projects are not limited to money. People and time are also limiting factors. You may have the funds to pay for more people, but it is not always possible to divide a two-week task for one engineer into two one-week tasks for two engineers. There is a limit to how many people can be working on the same piece of code at the same time. This looseness around budgets can work to your advantage, however. If you want to use new development tools or environments, it will be easier to get funding than if an outside client were being asked to foot the bill. You also may have more flexibility in your estimates. If you have underestimated costs by 40%, it may not be a huge problem if the costs were not tied to a strict budget in the first place. Regardless of these advantages, we would advise that you try to stick to a standardized process for your projects as much as possible. It is a good discipline to learn early on, and it will serve you well in the future, regardless of whether you are working on internal or external projects. Learning sloppy project management skills is not going to help you in the long term with your personal career development. It is very difficult to unlearn bad habits.

External projects have their own set of unique problems and advantages too. Working with outside clients, where you are restricted by very specific contractual agreements can reduce the flexibility that you have in how you implement and manage your project. Your accountability is going to be to a wider group of people and departments. There will be a more formalized process for reporting the status of your project, and it is likely that you will be expected to follow a standard reporting process. You may find that you have less autonomy managing an external project than you would have managing an internal one. Your milestones and deliverables will have high visibility. Client interaction can be time consuming. The client's company likely uses some different terminology than your company does, so miscommunication and misunderstandings are common pitfalls. Every detail of the project should be documented, including the definitions for terms used. The client may be very demanding and not sensitive to the fact that you have other clients and other responsibilities.

The benefits of working with external clients are that you must have a clearly defined and documented budget for your project. The client has a project completion deadline and a contractual agreement detailing exactly what is included in the project. Changes must go through formal change control because it is the only way to ensure that costs are kept within budget. Though the client might be a pain in the butt to work with, you always have your "contract" as ammunition to back up your reasons for denying a request or referring it to change control. Your relationship with a client is very different from your relationship with someone who works for the same company as you. The relationship is much more formal with an outside client, and communication will be subject to specific standards and guidelines as defined by your company. It is good practice to ensure that you keep your client relationships as formal and professional as possible. It will help you avoid situations where the client employs the use of emotional blackmail tactics when requesting additions and changes. By "emotional blackmail," we mean using personal friendships or favors as collateral. It is hard enough when you have to deal with this internally; do not fall into the trap of letting it happen to you with external clients, too.

If your company works primarily on external projects, they are very likely to have some internal projects too. For example, they must have business or desktop systems that employees use for development and administrative purposes. They may have a company Web site and an Intranet site. Some companies develop their own proprietary tools and applications for use by their employees. In addition, system and software upgrades are managed by internal support groups such as IT, IS, or desktop service teams. If you are working on these internal projects, ensure that you are using project methodologies the same as you would if you were working on a product development project. All projects must be managed effectively if they are to be successful. It is easier to hide inefficiencies when working on projects for internal groups that do not affect a product or service that is destined for sale to an outside client. Do not allow yourself to fall into the trap of embarking on projects with no real plan, with unrealistic timelines, or without an approved budget. It is your responsibility to set the standard for how your projects will be set up and managed. Set the bar as high as you can, and expect others to follow your lead. Lack of accountability is a poor excuse for executing substandard projects.

Desktop versus Internet

There are quite a few differences between managing desktop software and Internet projects. Internet projects have added complexity due to the number of different operating system (OS) and browser combinations that need to be supported. In addition, there is significant system and load-testing required to support a Web product. This additional coding and testing needs to be taken into account at the project planning stage to be sure that you have allocated sufficient time for the deployment tasks.

One of the biggest problems with developing for the Internet is coding the graphical user interface (GUI) to look and feel good and to be usable on different platforms and browsers. The same code will display very differently on a PC than on a MAC and differently in Internet Explorer and Netscape browsers. There are differences between the operating systems on the same hardware platform and differences between different versions of the same browser. Then there is the issue of screen resolution, affecting how the site displays and scrolls. Decisions have to be made concerning which platform-OS-browser-connection speed combination the site should be optimized for use on. It is almost impossible to optimize the site for everyone. These issues create a huge amount of work for developers, because they have to develop and unit test their code using many different system combinations. Quality assurance teams also have their work cut out testing the numerous combinations. Connection speeds can also be a problem. If a user is on a slow connection, they may time out on some CPU-intensive screens if the performance is too slow, which can make the product unusable for them. It is possible to get around these problems by supporting a very limited number of OS-browser-connection speed combinations, but this can sometimes backfire. If the majority of your prospective end users are using an unsupported system configuration, you risk losing a lot of business. The early adopters, who are generally also Internet users, are quick to upgrade to the latest OS and browser versions. As a result, if you release your product one month before a new OS or browser is released, you may find that your early adopter users are no longer able to use your product if the new browser is not supported. It could also be that the majority of your users are on slow connections. If this is the case, your site needs to be designed so that it will work for those users. Unless you specifically lock out users who are on unsupported systems from a Web site, you may risk bad publicity as well as losing customers if users are able to connect to the site but then find it unusable.

Load and stability tests are critical for Internet products and services. Desktop products are generally designed to run on one computer with one user at a time. Testing the performance of a system under those conditions is pretty straightforward. The performance of the product will depend on the computer system that the user has the product installed on. With Internet products, this is true to some extent, but there are many other bottlenecks that can be encountered over which the user has no control. For instance, network problems either with the user's ISP or at the facility where the site is hosted, a high number of users on the site, and reduced Web site capacity due to technical problems and system crashes can all degrade performance. Load testing is an art, and if the application is complex, it can be very hard to get the user models right for running the load tests. You need to know what percentage of your users is on which browsers, OSs, and connection speeds. If you have a large number of users on broadband connections, they will be moving through your site at a faster rate, which will increase load on the system. On the other hand, if they are getting through the site faster, the chances are that they will close their session sooner, freeing up bandwidth for more users. Therefore, with a large number of broadband users you may be able to support less concurrent users but more users per hour or per day. The more you get into the details of load testing, the more mind boggling it gets. Suffice to say, if you have an Internet product, make sure that you have adequate time for testing and that your load testers are experienced and knowledgeable in the tools and techniques for effective load testing.

If an end user is playing around with the product and either intentionally or accidentally crashes the system on a desktop product, they are going to crash their own computer, and it will not affect anyone else. If they are using an Internet product and manage to crash the application, however, it is possible that the server the application is running on will also crash. There is a potential that hundreds or thousands of other users could be impacted by a situation like this. The Internet application needs to be designed to handle these types of problems in a graceful way with minimum impact on other users. Security for Internet products is another critical area that needs adequate attention and a lot of specialized testing. A denial of service (DoS) attack could bring down your whole system and perhaps even your business systems if they are running on the same network. None of these are issues for desktop products. There is a lot more to developing products and services for the Internet than just writing a few lines of HTML. Your product plan should reflect this.

Remember that it is much easier to track down the cause of a critical problem before your Web site is live than afterwards, so check and double check your test plans for both functional and performance testing before you sign off on the project plan!

Desktop products have their own unique challenges. One of the beauties of Internet development is the ability to fix problems with the product for every user with one update to one product (the Web site). With desktop products, once the CDs are burned and the customer has purchased one and installed it on his system, the product is going to stay exactly the way it was when it left the manufacturer unless there is a way for the user to upgrade the product later. Each fix requires that every user update his product individually. Most companies offer upgrades and bug-fix releases for desktop products via the Internet. The biggest problem with this is that there is no way of ensuring that all users download the upgrades. Many of them will not. It also means that, even for desktop developers, there is some Internet programming required in addition to some testing of the Internet systems used as the download site(s).

Programming code to run on different hardware and operating systems can also be challenging. Different versions of the product will need to be developed for different platforms. Backwards compatibility is also an issue. If a user upgrades to a new version of the product, there is a possibility that her files from the old version may not work with the new one. If a user upgrades from Windows 98 to Windows XP, will the product still work? Should the product work with the new OS, or will the user be asked to download an upgrade or purchase a new product?

Your engineering team may be developing on Windows XP machines with 2 gigabytes of RAM, but most of your end users may be on Windows 98 machines with 256 megabytes of RAM. Do you have sufficient test systems for your developers to ensure that their code runs optimally on the older OS and much less RAM? There are many intricacies involved in developing a product that go beyond making sure that the product runs on the system that the engineers are using for development. Your product plan must take all these things into consideration.

Software versus Hardware

Many projects contain a combination of both software and hardware, but they will likely be focused primarily on one or the other. For instance, a hardware project may use software to support the hardware development and vice versa.

Examples of software projects include desktop programs (one user), enterprise software (multiple users on a network), Internet products and services, telecommunications, and databases. Examples of hardware projects include desktop and laptop computers, servers, networking, backup systems (tape drives), storage systems (flatfile and databases), consumer electronics and telecommunications, and aerospace.

Most of the examples we use in this book relate to software projects. There are differences between managing software and hardware projects. However, the similarities far outweigh the differences. The following table shows a basic comparison of the Life Cycle phases for software and hardware projects.

Table 3.1: Hardware and Software Life Cycle Phases

Life Cycle Phase	Software	Hardware
Planning	Planning can be a long and drawn out process. It can be challenging defining the problem to be solved. There are often multiple options on how to solve a problem. It can be difficult to define the scope.	Planning generally can be completed in a much shorter time frame. The problem is more tangible and less elusive. There are limited options on how to solve a problem. Scope is often implied by the nature of the project. It is not open to debate or interpretation as much as it can be in software development.
Design	There can be any number of ways to solve one problem. Ten different engineers or designers will likely come up with 10 different designs based on the same requirements. The project team creates the software and system architecture. They also create a product design along with individual component or feature designs. This phase is much more complex in a software project than a hardware one. If a software project is going to be canceled, it is most likely to be at this stage, when the true costs for the project are identified. As this phase ends, the very costly Development phase of the project begins.	Due to the use of standard components in hardware, there are usually only one or two ways to solve a specific problem. Ten different engineers or designers will likely come up with one or, at the most, two designs based on the same requirements. Different components may be designed by different teams or different companies. For instance, Power Supply Units (PSUs), Application-Specific Integrated Circuit (ASIC), Input/Output (I/O) Cards, and so on. For servers, the unit cases have to be a standard size to fit into standard racks. The standard rack sizes are used globally, and all rack-mounted electronic and computer equipment is built to standard rack size specifications. In the Design phase, the team will produce blueprints for the circuit designs, and technical writers will create precise specifications for the fabricator.

Table 3.1: Hardware and Software Life Cycle Phases

Life Cycle Phase	Software	Hardware
Development	This is one of the most expensive phases of the project and takes a large percentage of the overall project time. In this phase, the team uses the designs to create the technical specifications and to build the components and features that constitute the product. The features and components are tested with each build of the product. The entire product does not have to be completed for testing to begin. However, unlike hardware projects, software projects do not use standard components so there are no preexisting specifications. Each software component has to be tested individually as well as together. The complexity of this phase is much higher in software than in hardware projects.	This is a relatively inexpensive phase of the project. It takes up a small percentage of the overall project time. This phase is where the fabricator produces a working prototype from the circuit designs.
Integration (and testing)	This is the phase where the different components of the software are integrated and tested. The full QA test process is implemented and, for Internet products, stability and performance tests are run. The risk factor in this stage is fairly minimal. The product components will have been tested at regular intervals during the development of the product so the integration testing should identify integration-related bugs only. Issues that arise during testing at this stage are generally solvable. Usability and beta testing will be scheduled to occur during this phase.	This phase and the following one are the two most costly phases of a hardware project. In this phase, the prototype is tested and refined to produce a blueprint for the final product. The testing for hardware can be more complex than for software projects. For instance, reliability testing, EMF testing, stability testing, and environmental testing are completed. Some of these tests are regulatory and need to follow a clearly defined process. The physical product needs to be tested for durability as well as the functional product testing. For instance, what happens if the server is dropped or if it gets too hot? If a hardware project is going to be canceled due to issues, this is the phase where it will often happen—right before the costs start to escalate at a rapid rate.

Table 3.1: Hardware and Software Life Cycle Phases		
Life Cycle Phase	**Software**	**Hardware**
Deployment	This is where the final testing is done on the product. For desktop software, the master is sent to the CD manufacturer and the artwork is sent to the packaging manufacturer to produce the final product. Distribution deals are finalized. The major expense here is producing the master. If a problem is detected after the CDs have been burnt, the master can be recut and the CDs rerun. This is an additional cost but not one that is likely to lead to the project being canceled. Training for technical support and customer support groups occurs during this phase.	This phase is where the specifications and circuit designs are updated and sent to the manufacturer. The risk factor for this phase is very high for a hardware project. One mistake or undetected bug in the hardware can result in hundreds or thousands of defective units being manufactured at very high cost. Manufacture of spare parts for the product is also required for the actual hardware units. If the company is international, shipping and processing for spare parts can be a huge expense. Training for support (including repairs) is extensive and can be a global issue. If beta testing is required, it will happen in this phase—after the final product is released. Beta testers are usually the early purchasers of the product, and they often get discounted product rates for agreeing to be the guinea pigs for a new product line. It is not unusual for them to get free use of the products for an extended period.

Table 3.1: Hardware and Software Life Cycle Phases

Life Cycle Phase	Software	Hardware
Post-Deployment	Post-deployment for software usually involves some scheduled bug fix releases and updates that are delivered either via the Internet (download) or by the customer buying an updated copy of the software. Product support for software is usually about three to five years. It is usual for an updated version(s) of the product to be released during that time frame and support for the older versions to be withdrawn after a few years.	This phase is much more complex and long lived for hardware. The term "sustaining engineering" is used often to describe the process and the teams involved in post manufacturer and post sales support. This support is more complex than for software because it involves getting hardware out to clients who have faulty units. It is a lot more time consuming and costly than asking a user to download a software update. Spare parts need to be available quickly along with trained personnel to install them. With global distribution this can be challenging. A customer does not want to be told that their part will arrive in 6 weeks because it has to be shipped from Germany to the USA and it "takes that long to get it." The shelf life for hardware is much longer than for software—on average about 5–10 years. Hardware is more costly to upgrade so clients usually keep the same systems for a number of years before upgrading. The sustaining engineering department is kept busy for years testing new software releases and hardware component upgrades.

Hardware projects are generally less complex than software projects due to the use of standard components. For example, a company that manufactures servers will usually purchase the disk drives, power supplies, and some circuit boards from a manufacturer who specializes in those specific components. The components are built to standard specifications and meet the compliance criteria. These components may be less complex, but mistakes can be much more costly. If you burn 400,000 CDs and find that there is a bug in the code and have to recut a master and reburn the CDs, it is going to eat into the bottom line a lot less than if you have 400,000 high-availability servers just off the production line and find a design flaw that makes them low availability and they have to be rebuilt with newly designed components. That kind of mistake could bankrupt a company overnight.

One anomaly that is interesting to note about hardware versus software is the apparent inability of these two technology disciplines to work together effectively. We are not sure whether this is due to a rivalry between these two distinct disciplines or a lack of understanding of how much each one impacts the other. We suspect the latter. It is often the case that we think whatever we personally are doing is the best, the most important, the most challenging, and so on when, in fact, we just do not understand enough about what others are doing to truly appreciate their challenges and their achievements.

In our observations, it seems that hardware developers tend to be totally hardware focused despite the fact that their products usually require the use of software to work. The same goes for software developers. They are so focused on software that they often forget to take into account the different kinds of hardware that the product needs to run on. Neither can work without the other, but there is not much evidence of integration between these two groups in today's technology companies. Some companies may have both hardware and software departments or teams, but it is often the case that they do not work together on one project team for a specific product. The hardware is kicked over the fence to the software department (or company) and vice versa. What great strides could be made in this area if the project managers working in each discipline had a greater understanding of the challenges that the other faced! We could see a lot less install and set-up time for products if they were truly designed to work together.

The Different Kinds of Stakeholders

You might be wondering what exactly we mean when we refer to a "stakeholder." If you asked 10 people that question you might get 10 different answers! It is not unusual for members of the same project team to maintain their own lists of stakeholders that bear no resemblance to the lists maintained by other team members. Therefore, when discussing stakeholders, project team members are not necessarily talking about the same set of people.

We are going to give you a general definition of "stakeholder" that is designed to be used in conjunction with an identifier that is unique to a specific set of stakeholders.

A stakeholder is a person, group, department, or company who is involved in, or has an interest in, the project or the outcome of the project. For most projects, there will be different sets of stakeholders, each of whom will be interested in different aspects of the project. To really understand stakeholders and to manage communications with them effectively, you should analyze the list of all stakeholders that belong in the general stakeholder group and assign them to unique stakeholder subgroups according to their interest in the project. Many of the stakeholders will belong to more than one stakeholder subgroup.

It is very frustrating for the stakeholders, and the project manager, if there is only one list of stakeholders for a project. This means that everyone on the list has to either opt in or opt out for all communications about the project. What invariably happens in this situation is that stakeholders are bombarded with a lot of information that they have no use for. After a while, they will consider the communications to be junk mail and will delete or ignore everything that they receive concerning the project. The information that is really important to each person then gets lost in the noise. This could be disastrous for you and for your project.

Imagine that you have a stakeholder who works in the legal department at the client's headquarters. Additionally, you have a stakeholder who is a member of the data center operations team at your company. If you are sending out everything related to the project to every stakeholder, these two people are going to receive e-mails pertaining to the development environment for the engineering team; meeting minutes for your weekly development team meetings; team lunches and outings; decisions to cut features from the project; design review notes, and so on. As you can imagine none of these topics are going to be of interest to either of those stakeholders, and these e-mails could add up to many per week, especially if some of them turn into e-mail debates where "reply to all" is used on every e-mail. (You know this can happen!) You could have 50 people on your stakeholder list, and each one of them is going to be overwhelmed with too much information about details of the project that do not affect them in any way.

Therefore, split your stakeholders into subgroups and make sure that everyone on the project team is using the same subgroups to send out information and updates. You can group your stakeholders in many different ways and, of course, each stakeholder can belong to one or many of the stakeholder subgroups. Certain pieces of information will need to be sent to all stakeholders. For instance, if the project is canceled or postponed, or if there is a major change in the project team (a change of sponsor or project manager, for example), then this is information that all the stakeholders will need to be aware of.

Here are some examples of how you might subgroup stakeholders:

- Steering Committee—The steering committee comprises the key decision-makers on the project. Typically this group will include (but is not limited to) the sponsor, the project managers, the product managers, and the client.

- Internal development—Use to share information that relates to the internal development groups and quality assurance such as development environment, changes to requirements or specifications, design reviews, code reviews, and coding standards.

- Security—Use to share information about security concerns, breaches, and standards with relevant members of development, senior management, security, client, and operations teams.

- Project plan changes—Use to share information about proposed changes to the plan including additions and deletions of features. Members may include client, product management, legal, quality assurance, and project sponsor.

- Deployment—Use to communicate all deployment related information. Members may include operations team, client, and quality assurance.

Depending on the size and type of your project and how many stakeholders there are in total, you will need to decide how to subgroup the stakeholders based on who needs to know what and when. It would be wise to meet with the project team to discuss the process for defining stakeholder groups before finalizing the list of groups. Send the list of subgroups, including which stakeholders are included in each group and a description of the type of information that will be shared with each group, to all the stakeholders. This gives them an opportunity to ask to be added or removed from any of the lists. This validation of your communication plan for stakeholder groups ensures that everyone will receive the information that they need and that they have asked for.

The Different Kinds of Resources

Two of the main factors involved in project planning are resources and scope. If you manage your resources effectively, you will also ensure that your project stays in scope. Resources are the inputs for each task, and deliverables are the outputs. Resources can be categorized into four main areas:

- People
- Equipment
- Time
- Money (budgets)

Resources may be acquired, rented, or provided from within the organization; may come from the client; or may be contracted or purchased from outside the organization. This includes your project team, equipment and technology, and money. Time is intangible so it cannot be acquired or increased without affecting the outcome of the project in some way. Managing project resources involves more than people management; it includes the management of equipment, money, and time. The number and combination of resources needed to execute a project is determined during the Planning phase of the project Life Cycle.

Costs are a major resource, and they are determined and managed through budgets. The word "budget" often elicits groans and even feelings of near panic in some people. They are not as scary as you might think. You just need to learn how to create, track, and manage them. Your project schedule is your tool for tracking people and time resources; your budget is used to track your cost resources. Equipment resources are managed to some extent in both of these processes. For example, equipment purchases are tracked in your budget, but installing and setting up the equipment is tracked in your project schedule.

All four resource elements are interrelated and need to be balanced appropriately. Each of the four factors must be managed effectively and simultaneously for the project to be successful.

People

Your people resources include your project team, other company employees (operations staff, for instance), vendor staff, consultants, and contract labor. Assembling a project team (and identifying required support resources) with appropriate skills and availability is critical to your project. Resources must be identified in the planning phase of your project. You cannot commit to a project and a deadline if you have not yet found a vendor to supply necessary services.

When identifying your people resources you need to ensure that you have not forgotten anyone. Identifying and budgeting for your core project team should be fairly straightforward. Identifying other internal resources, such as quality assurance and testing, operations, technical support, marketing, and product management may not be as simple. If you identify these people or groups as resources, then you need a commitment of specified time that will be spent working on your project. Telling your operations team that you need some support and them telling you that is OK and to just let them know when you need them is not going to be sufficient. You need to have a plan, and you need them to sign off on the commitment of time to your project. This is also true of resources being supplied by the client. For instance, they may have agreed to take on some level of quality assurance or testing responsibility for the project. You need to ensure that they have adequate resources and that they will be available when you need them. You cannot afford to be waiting around for the client to start testing if your whole team is waiting for them to finish and sign on before proceeding. Contractor, consultant, and outside vendor resources need to be planned in the same way. For all of these different resources, you need costs. You need to ensure that you will stay within budget, so all these costs need to be documented and approved before you start.

It is vitally important that everyone understand his or her own roles and responsibilities, those of everyone else on the team, internal and client resources, and the roles and responsibilities of all contractors, consultants, and vendors who will be involved to any degree in the project. This information should be documented and shared with your team. Contractual agreements need to be in place with any external resources. Some kind of written agreement also needs to exist for any internal resources that are not part of your project team. The exact way the agreements work will vary from company to company, but be sure that you have them. External agreements will usually need review by a legal team. The company implementing the project will most likely have a process that you need to follow to ensure that this is done correctly.

The use of contract labor is becoming increasingly common in technology and IT projects. Some companies maintain a small staff of experienced people to serve as team leaders and employ staffing agencies to provide contract workers for the project teams. Other companies employ the majority of their staff full-time and use contract workers for specialized work. There are advantages and disadvantages to using contractors.

Some of the advantages are that the company doesn't have any obligation to the contractor after the completion of the project. When the project is finished, the contract staff member is bid farewell and thanked for a job well done. The company is paying a set hourly rate for the contractors and is not liable for benefits, bonuses, vacation and sick pay, or unemployment claims. Contractors are usually brought in to work on one specific project so the chance of someone stealing them from you midproject to work on something else is minimal. If you need a developer with specific specialized technical or domain knowledge for just this one project, then hiring a contractor is the most efficient way to fill that role. Because contractors are being paid hourly, they are not usually averse to working overtime when necessary.

On the other hand, there are also disadvantages to using contractors. Unless you have worked with the person before, you are really not sure what you may be getting or if their skills are really as advertised. Normally, when choosing team members, you have some previous knowledge of their work ethics and team interaction from observing or working with them on previous projects. With contractors, you have minimal information about their work ethics and personality types. When companies hire a new employee a rigorous hiring process usually involves multiple interviews and background checks. With contractors, you are relying on the staffing agency to have done this on your behalf. One big problem with using contractors is that once the project is finished, they take all the knowledge and experience that they gained from it with them. If their code is not well documented or their project documentation is not accurate or updated, it can take a lot of time and effort for another team member to come up to speed sufficiently to resolve any post-project issues or bugs.

Most companies will tend to use the same one or two staffing agencies to supply all their contractors. Once a good professional relationship has been established with an agency, it becomes much easier to find the kind of contractors that you need. If the agency understands the company culture and the team dynamic, it will try to find you contractors that fit well into your environment and have the appropriate technical skills that you need. If you are using contract staff, you must remember that they are joining your team as bona fide team members, and you need to treat them with the same dignity and respect as the rest of your team. You also need to hold them to the same standards as the rest of your team. They need to be fully aware of their own roles and responsibilities, those of the other team members, and additional project participants. They need to be aware of the company and the team processes and procedures and understand the goals of the project in the same way that the rest of your project team does.

Consultants may be hired for the duration of the project or for one specific part of the project. Consultants are usually experts in a specific field or fields. They may work onsite or offsite. Depending on the nature of their involvement in your project, they may act more as advisors than developers. Whatever their role, they will need to work closely with the project team and with you, the project manager, to ensure that information is flowing effectively in both directions. Consultants sometimes work for an hourly fee and sometimes for a flat fee. If they are charging an hourly fee, you will need to closely monitor this expense to ensure that you are not going over budget. Make sure that the consultants are staying on track and that they are meeting deadlines. Ensure that you have a contract in place that specifies *exactly* what you are engaging them to do. Let them know that no additional work outside of the contract can be approved without a new contract being drawn up. You do not want your consultants doing additional work that they "assume" you need and then billing you for it! You may need to keep a close eye on the time spent working on your project to ensure that they are not neglecting your project to work for other clients. If your consultants are working offsite, a weekly status meeting is essential to make sure that they are on track for their deliverables.

Managing outside vendors can also be tricky. You will need to monitor progress closely to ensure that they are on track to deliver exactly what you ordered and that it is delivered on time. Vendors often overpromise and underdeliver. If you have a drop-dead date for what you need from the vendor, ask for it two to four weeks earlier than that. This will give you some wiggle room if they run into problems or if they turn out to be unreliable. As with the consultants, ensure that you have a contractual agreement and that they have a schedule from you detailing the deliverables that they have agreed to.

Internal resources outside of your project team will often be required for certain aspects of your project. Your IT group, QA department, data center, or operations team may be needed to set up systems, order hardware, implement some parts of the project, conduct security reviews, test the product, and so on. The commitments to deliver or participate in these tasks should be documented together with timelines and costs. (Work completed by other departments within your company is not free; those people have to be paid, and it is likely coming out of your budget!)

Equipment

The project may require hardware or software to run on. This is especially true for Internet products. You may need servers, databases, backup and restore systems, test systems, operating systems, application server software, Web server software, database software, an so on. The list is endless! The project team will also require development hardware, software, and tools in addition to various materials and supplies that will be needed to complete their tasks. This equipment includes the facilities, computers, printers, desks, communication equipment, development and staging servers, CD burners, software, hardware, licensing for software and hardware, books. This list can be endless, too! It is the project manager's responsibility to identify all the equipment needs for implementing, testing, and releasing the final project. Some of the equipment will likely already exist and will not need to be repurchased. You should not be trying to get your company or the client to buy everything that your heart desires. The object is to make sure that you identify what you need for the project. The key to managing equipment resources, much like managing people resources, is to make sure you have the right equipment in the right place at the right time. Any necessary supplies, licenses, or operating manuals should also be provided. There is no point in having a lot of hardware sitting around if it is not possible to operate it due to lack of supporting materials or equipment. You may also need the right people resources to support the equipment resources. If they are not available to set up your equipment when it arrives, then you are going to have a scheduling problem.

Creating a desirable environment in which the project team can be effective and successful is the responsibility of the project manager. A factor that you have to consider when building your team and your development environment is whether the team will be working on their home turf, at the client site, or at another remote site. If they will be traveling or working offsite, they may need laptop computers. If they are working at the client site, is the client providing a development environment? Is the client providing this service free of charge, or do they expect you to pay for it? If your team is working at another remote location, do you need to pay rent for the facilities and equipment? You also need to consider what specialized tools your team may need to implement the project. If you have the tools at your home site, but your team will be working at the client site, will they have remote access to the tools? Do they have the necessary networking and Internet access that they need to connect to the home office? These are just a few of the funding questions that you will need to answer to accurately estimate your equipment resource needs. Equipment resource planning needs to be done early in the planning phase of your project to ensure availability when you need it. If you order equipment 1 week before you need it and discover that it will take 10 weeks to receive your order, then your project is going to be in trouble before you have even started.

Management of your equipment resources is a requirement for managing your people resources. Your team members rely on the equipment to be able to implement their project tasks. If you are not effectively managing your equipment resources, then your team could come to a standstill. You may need to get more creative when managing equipment resources than with other resources. If your project depends on it, then make sure you have a plan A, a plan B, and if possible, a plan C.

Consider this example: Your project plan specifies that the development team will be working on a new development server that was ordered during the planning phase of the project and is due to be delivered two weeks before development is due to begin. This task is on the critical path but is not considered to be a high risk because it is due to be delivered early enough to allow a week for installation and setup plus an additional week buffer zone before the team needs to start work. One week before the server is due to be delivered, however, you receive a phone call from the supplier telling you that the server is going to be two weeks late. So what do you do?

One option would be to try and push the start of development back a week and reschedule the setup of the server for two weeks later than it is currently scheduled. This is not a great option because you will start your project one week late and, if there are server issues, possibly even two weeks late.

Another possibility would be to see whether you can find a spare server in-house that you can borrow for a period of time until you receive your server and have the time to take the servers down and swap them out. This is a better option, but you still have some server downtime to deal with. You are also assuming a level of risk by making a midproject development environment change.

A much better solution would be to negotiate with the supplier to see whether they can offer you a substitute server that is comparable to the one you have on order. The chances are that the supplier will have a server either one step up or one step down that will still work for you. If you take one that is one step up, ensure that you are not charged any extra for it. However, if you take one that is one step down, negotiate a lower price. If neither of these options is available, you could ask the supplier for a loan server to use until your server is delivered.

As a very last resort, it might be possible for your team to start working on the project and saving all their work locally (on their desktop or laptop systems). They will need to be very meticulous about backing up the data every day, which could be tedious, and some level of risk is involved, but it is better than not doing anything for a week or two.

As we said, be creative, think of as many options and plans as you can, and be sure to have a couple of back up plans just in case your first one doesn't work. This is a good process to follow for anything that is outside of your direct control. By this, we mean any work or service being provided from outside of your core project team. You can prioritize and escalate issues on your own team, but you are relying on someone else to do that in other groups or companies. Always have a plan B just in case there is a problem. As you gain more experience managing projects, this kind of planning will become second nature to you. You will learn not to trust 100% that something being managed by someone else will definitely be completed on time. You should hope for the best and plan for the worst.

New technologies emerge so fast these days that you may find the original system you negotiated at the beginning of your project is no longer the latest or greatest solution available. Work closely with your suppliers and build strong professional relationships with them. If you are partnering with your vendors rather than just telling them what to do, they will be proactive in letting you know about changes or opportunities that may impact or benefit your project. They will work with you to get you the best price and proactively search for alternative or better solutions. Having said all this, you do need to be careful about using new technology on projects that cannot tolerate a high level of risk. If you are looking for stability and proven performance and reliability, then don't consider technology solutions that have been on the market for less than a year. No matter how long the technology or system has been on the market, ask for contacts at other companies that have implemented the same solution or are using the same technology and be sure to follow up with them. You can learn a lot by talking to the technical teams at those companies. Your supplier may tell you that ABC Company is using the same solution and it is working just great for them. When you call ABC Company you may find that, though they are using the same technology, they are using it for a completely different purpose and are not utilizing most of the features and functionality that you need for your project.

You will need time to work with your suppliers, and some of your technical staff may also need time to research technology solutions that they are recommending. Make sure that you allow time in your project schedule to accommodate this. You should also allow extra time for equipment installation, setup, and testing. You should never assume that your equipment is going to work without a bit of tweaking and testing. If you have ever received a new computer system, you are well aware of what we mean by this. There is always a lot more setup and troubleshooting than we anticipate! Remember, developing a high level of skill in managing equipment resources won't be of much use to you unless you can also stick to the project schedule. Schedule and time management is critical for successful project management.

Time

Time is intangible, but it still needs to be managed. You may think that as long as you have enough people to complete the work, the equipment you need, and the money to pay for it, where does time fit into this equation as a resource? You are assigned a set amount of time to implement your project. If you need more of it, you have to ask for it, and you will likely need more money to pay for it. So why can't you get more people and pay for them without asking for more time? That doesn't always work. For example, imagine that you are one week from your project completion deadline. You have 20 days of work that still needs to be completed and five full-time developers available. You cannot necessarily assign four engineers to work five days each or five engineers to work four days each to complete the task. The task may need to be completed by one person, sequentially, over the course of 20 days. This is true for all of your project scheduling. Some of your tasks may be able to be split between two people, but the majority of them will need to be implemented by one person. Throwing more people resources at the problem may not resolve it. If your development server arrives one week late and you need one week to set it up and test it, you cannot ask five engineers to work on it for one day each or ask the test team to work concurrently with the setup team to save time. You still need a week (or five days) to complete the task. Time is often the forgotten resource. If it is not managed appropriately, it can run out, and once that happens, it is inevitable that your project is going to be late or is going to be delivered with some functionality missing or compromised.

Money

Once you have your required equipment and people resources identified, you need to make sure that you have the money to pay for them. Managing money as a resource is not always an easy process, especially if you don't like finances. If the thought of managing money makes you break out in a cold sweat, you need to get over your fear and do so fast. Managing money and project budgets is a huge part of a project manager's responsibilities. Managing money includes all costs associated with the project. These costs include tools, people, equipment, testing, measurement, training, employee motivation, development environments, build systems, desktop environments, production environments, and travel. Depending on your project, you may need to budget for all or some of these. Depending on how the budgeting process is structured at the company implementing the project, some of these costs may be budgeted outside of your direct project costs. For example, if you are working on an internal project for a company that develops its own products, you may have separate budgets for all, or some, of your people- and equipment-related costs. The salaries, development environment, development tools, facilities, employee motivation, training, and training-related travel may all be included in your administrative or run-the-business budget, and only the costs uniquely and directly associated with your project may be in your actual project budget. Those costs would include special tools or technology required to support the project, contractors and consultant fees, vendor costs, travel related to the project, and project equipment. Different organizational and project structures organize budgets in different ways. You still have to manage all the costs, but you may be managing them independently of each other.

Each project feature or task will have a cost associated with it, whether it is for labor hours for your team members, or the purchase of your staging server. Within larger companies, a designated person (or department) usually is responsible for making the purchases on your behalf. There are pros and cons associated with this method of procurement. On the plus side, it saves you the time because you don't have to do all the legwork of working with suppliers. It also allows the company to negotiate special rates and discounts and to manage those costs closely. This may mean that they are managing the equipment part of your budget for you, which will save you a lot of time tracking it. The negative side of this is that you may be limited in who you can order from. Your company may have purchase agreements with a limited number of suppliers, and if you want to order from elsewhere, there may be a long and painful process to go through to get that approved. If it is not approved, you may end up having to order equipment that is not really what you want or need and may require some work-arounds to make it suitable for your project. (This happens more often than you would think in larger companies. The process is running the company and project rather than the company and project running the process.) You also lose the personal contact with the supplier, which can make it harder for you to follow up to ensure that your order will arrive on time and that the procurement department did not forget to order any accessory items that you needed. In smaller companies, you may be the person who is responsible for all the negotiation for your equipment.

CHAPTER **4**

Advancing Beyond the Green Light

The project has been greenlighted; what next? The flowchart in Figure 4.1 shows the workflow process from greenlighting through project approval. If the project is for an external client, it is standard for a contractual agreement to be drawn up between the two parties. The reason for this agreement is that in the event that the project is canceled after the Project Definition is complete, the vendor can charge the client for the time spent working with the client on the Project Definition. This can amount to a substantial amount of work for quite a few members of the proposed project team. The contractual agreement offers a level of protection to the development company by ensuring monetary compensation for time spent on the project, and it dissuades the client from working with multiple vendors on Project Definitions at the same time. If they are not charged for the time, then they have nothing to lose by wasting the vendor's time on projects that they have little, or no, intention of awarding them.

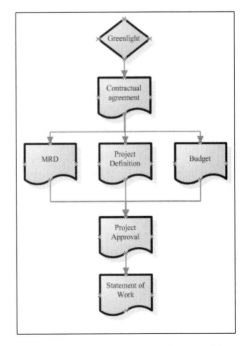

Figure 4.1: Advancing beyond the green light flowchart.

Project Definition

Subsequent to the greenlighting of a project, a client meeting will be held to create a Project Definition document. A Project Definition is also referred to as a "Project Charter." A client may be an external client, when your company is being contracted to develop the product or service for them. Alternatively, the client may be an internal customer, when, for instance, a technology company is developing a new product for their own product line. The key people involved in the project are defined in the Project Definition. The Project Definition is a must-have for all projects no matter how large or small they are. This document is the basis on which successful project plans are built. It provides specific agreements, including budgets and schedules, to which all team members will commit. It is used as a major input to the detailed resource and development plans that are created as each phase of the Life Cycle is planned (planning, design, development, integration, and deployment). The Project Definition document will be used in conjunction with the *Marketing Requirements Document* (MRD) as the foundation for creating the initial technical requirements documents for the product. The lack of a Project Definition document can lead to poor communication, misunderstanding, and potential confusion. The failure to have a formalized plan can put the project at high risk. Everyone involved in the project needs to have clear and specific goals outlined prior to the project being kicked off. The whole team needs to understand the big picture as well as the specifics for their individual contributions.

The clear and accurate definition of a project and its objectives is extremely important to a project's success. Defining the project, specifying the scope, and developing a common vision of the project objectives and deliverables are synonymous with effective planning.

Producing a quality Project Definition document requires following specific steps and involves a lot of attention to detail. The amount of detail necessary for the Project Definition document will depend on the size and complexity of the project. The document must include specifically what will and what will not be delivered. Prior to starting work on the Project Definition, it is imperative that you have written approval from the client (who can be an external company or an internal department or group). After all, they will be billed for the time, so they need to agree to pay for it!

The Project Definition comprises the following sections:

Project name	Benefits	Project constraints
Client name	Target audience	Project risks
Decision-makers	The problem	Time and costs
Project description and goals	The solution	Project organization
Business case	Project scope	Project definition approval
Key business requirements	Prerequisites	
Project objectives	Assumptions	

It is the project manager's responsibility to get the Project Definition document completed. In this chapter, we will lead you through each section of the definition document and give you the information and the tools you need to both understand and create it.

Creating the Project Definition Document

The Project Proposal document will contain some of the information needed for the Project Definition document. The amount of data that you can reuse will depend on how detailed the Project Proposal is. You can use this existing information as a starting point and then work to verify, refine, define, and elaborate on it until you have a complete, detailed, accurate, clear, and concise definition of your project. The following sections are designed as a practical guide to help you understand and create the Project Definition document.

Project Name

The official (and unique) name of the project should be documented to differentiate it from other projects. At many companies, multiple projects will be in progress at the same time, and the project name must differentiate it from other projects.

The client will likely have a name for the product that they want built. It is common practice for companies to call their projects by code name instead of using the actual product name for a project. For example, in our case study the product, OFIS, could have used a project codename of "Orange" or "Oliver." This use of code name for projects is especially important for companies that want to keep the nature of their development efforts confidential until they are ready to release the product. It also gives the company the opportunity to change the product name without it impacting the project name. It is possible that you may not be told the actual product name. It may not even have a name yet. Regardless of whether you are using the actual product name or are inventing a project codename, you must ensure that the name is unique to the project you are working on. Whether your company has 10 or 100 projects in progress, the project names must be easily distinguishable from one another. As the project manager, you may choose to use a codename for your project instead of the product name. As long as the client is not opposed to it, there is no reason that you should not choose an appropriate codename. Do not choose a name that is facetious or in bad taste, though. Be respectful at all times.

Client Name

In this section document the legal name of the client company along with any acronyms or nicknames that are used to refer to the client company. In this section, you should also document the names, titles, and contact information for each employee of the client company who will be involved in the project in any way. This will include their administrative assistant, legal reviewer, accountant, and so on, as well as the actual project team members.

Decision-Makers

It is critical that the project decision-makers be identified and documented and that those decision-makers are aware of their responsibilities. These are the decision-makers on the client team and the vendor teams as well as those on the development team. Having this information well defined and documented will prevent the project from grinding to a halt if a roadblock is encountered. In our experience, the lack of clearly defined decision-makers is a common cause for projects being left in limbo for some period of time when there is a problem. Everyone has to stop while the project manager is trying to figure out who has the authority to make the decision that will enable the project to move forward. This kind of situation can impact both the scheduled delivery dates and team morale.

To complete this section, you will need to identify who all the decision-makers are at each level, and for all aspects of, the project. You must document what kinds of decisions each person is responsible for and the contact information for each person. You may not have identified exactly who the team members are going to be yet, so this list will consist of names and titles for some decision-makers and just titles for others. The blanks will be filled in when the Project Plan is created after the project has been approved. For those decision-makers that are defined as a specific person, make sure that you have the work, cell, and home phone numbers. If it is not appropriate to put personal numbers in this document (due to wide distribution), then keep these numbers on a separate list and ensure that all the managers involved in the project have access to it. If more than one decision-maker is needed for some decisions, make it clear who is the primary decision-maker. This will be the person who will take responsibility for making the final decision and who is responsible for coordinating and communicating the decision to the project team. In the example shown in Figure 4.2, the name of the primary decision-maker is italicized.

Decision Makers

- Cancel or postpone project

Name	Title	Company	Workphone	Cellphone	Homephone
Paulette Green	*Project Sponsor*	*XYZ Corp.*	*555-555-5555*	*666-666-6666*	*777-777-7777*
Trudi Finch	CEO	ABC Inc.	555-555-5555	666-666-6666	777-777-7777
Robin English	Program Manager	ABC Inc.	555-555-5555	666-666-6666	777-777-7777

- Postpone or make changes to milestones or deliverables

Name	Title	Company	Workphone	Cellphone	Homephone
Daryl Johnson	*Project Manager*	*XYZ Corp.*	*555-555-5555*	*666-666-6666*	*777-777-7777*
Cal Smith	Project Manager	ABC Inc.	555-555-5555	666-666-6666	777-777-7777
Jeff Sterling	QA Manager	ABC Inc.	555-555-5555	666-666-6666	777-777-7777

Figure 4.2: Decision-makers.

The more kinds of decisions you can identify in this section of the Project Definition, the more quickly decisions will get made and the more smoothly the project will run. If everyone on the team knows who is authorized to make decisions about what, it avoids misunderstandings and confusion when direction is coming from more than one direction. It will be clear that decisions about a specific part of the project are valid only if they come from the person designated as the decision-maker.

Project Description and Goals

The *project description* describes the project in terms that are understandable to everyone on the project team. Avoid the use of technical or industry-specific terms whenever possible. Keep the description simple, accurate, and unambiguous. For example:

> *"The goal of the OFIS (Order Fulfillment and Inventory System) project is to port ABCs existing internal enterprise order management software system to the Internet."*

The *project goals* are what the project must achieve at a high level. These are not the same as the objectives. Goals are high level and are not measurable (broad focus). Objectives are precise, detailed, and measurable (narrow focus).

How to Determine the Goals

To determine the goals of the project, you should ask the client the following questions:

- What would you like to achieve?
- Why would you like to achieve it?

Here are some examples of what you might learn:

- We would like to move our company to the Internet sometime in the next year.
- We want to improve our call center operations.
- We want to offer our retailers more ways to contact and connect with us.

Business Case

As the project manager, it is unlikely that you will be required to define the business case unless you are the person proposing the project. It is common for a business case to be presented during the concept phase of the project, and if this is the case, you need merely to copy and paste the business case directly into this document.

The business case typically includes some historical data about the company that defines how and why things have been done in the past, together with data showing current trends and changes in the marketplace, or organization that make the project necessary. The detail and complexity required for the business case will be directly proportional to the size of the proposed project. At the very least, it needs to include a high-level and compelling overview of why the business needs to move in the specific direction that the project proposes.

How to Determine the Business Case

To determine the business case for the project, you first need to understand the goals of the project.

Using these example goals, which we defined earlier:

- We would like to move our company to the Internet sometime in the next year.

- We want to improve our call center operations.

- We want to offer our retailers more ways to contact and connect with us.

Ask your client these questions:

- Why are these goals essential to your company?

- How will it change the way you do business?

- How will it benefit your company financially?

Here is an example of the kind of information you are trying to extract from your client:

- Over the past seven years, the company has grown from having a relatively small retailer customer base in a few states to having a distribution network of over 2,000 retailers in 50 states. We are in the process of securing wholesale distribution contracts with a number of international businesses. Our call center has grown significantly over the last few years. Due to the multiple time zones we are servicing, the call center needs to be operational for approximately 12 hours per day. Our overhead is out of control, and we need to reduce costs.

- By integrating the current order management system with the inventory system and moving it to the Internet, the company could offer access to retailers to place orders, get status on current orders, get quotes, view the current catalogue, and check available inventory 24/7.

- We believe we can reduce costs by 60% in the call center, by 20% in the sales department, and by 60% in marketing.

Key Business Requirements

The client will have some very precise requirements regarding what is necessary and how it is to be implemented. This section should document each and every requirement that the client has in respect to this particular project. For example, they may require that the coding be done in a specific programming language or that the product be designed to run on a particular hardware platform. Other examples could be that some existing systems must be used in the solution or that the project must be completed before a specific date, even if that means reducing the project scope to meet that date. In addition requirements may relate to specific processes and procedures or security concerns. The client may have identified some, or all, of these in the RFP. It is your responsibility to work with the client to ensure that this information is complete and accurate so there are no surprises later on. You don't want to implement and test a product with an Oracle database (because you know the client uses one) and then find out that the client will be using this product with their proprietary database and not with the Oracle database that they use for accounting.

Ensure that you capture the low-level as well as the high-level requirements. The more you know about what the client specifically wants and specifically does not want, the better positioned you are to deliver a quality product with high value to the client. Anything that is critical to the business needs of the client should be documented clearly and concisely in this section.

How to Determine the Key Business Requirements

To get insight into key business requirements, ask the client these questions:

- How many users do you need to support?

- What technologies and processes cannot be changed?

- What technologies and processes must be changed?

Using our previous examples, here are some examples of what you might hear:

- We need to significantly increase our distribution network without increasing headcount.

- The system must be implemented to support 4,000 retailers and have the scalability to support 8,000 retailers.

- Order management, back orders, inventory, and account information must be seamlessly integrated.

- The call center screen must have ability to show all account and order information on one screen.

- The existing Oracle database must be used for back-End.

- Retailer account numbers must not change.

- Product numbers must not change.

- The system must integrate with the billing and accounting system.

- The warehouse system must support bar codes.

- Processes need to be created and documented for sales, warehouse, and shipping.

- Functional training will be needed for sales, warehouse, shipping, and accounting.

- Technical training will be needed for the onsite webmaster, systems administrator, and database administrator.

Project Objectives

This section should clearly define the objectives of the project, including a description of the problem to be addressed and the proposed solution. Remember that objectives are precise, detailed, and measurable (narrow focus). Goals are high level and are not measurable (broad focus).

The objectives define precisely what it is the project must achieve. The objectives must be clear, concise and unambiguous, achievable, and most importantly, measurable. The objectives should include a high-level description of how the objectives will be achieved, together with a clear definition of how the success of the project will be measured. None of this information should be based on assumptions or verbal agreements. Objectives should always be documented and reviewed with the client and the project team to ensure that all team members clearly, and commonly, understand them. If you find that team members have different understandings of the written objectives of the project, you should rewrite them to remove the ambiguity to ensure clarity.

Understanding the project objectives is vitally important to the successful launch, implementation, and completion of a project. It is the destination that your project journey is taking you to. Your project will not be successful if the team members are traveling to different destinations, even if they are only a short distance apart. Everyone must be focused on exactly the same outcome. Understanding what you are trying to achieve as well as how you are going to achieve it is critical to the final outcome of your project.

How to Identify the Objectives

To identify the objectives of a project, you first need to understand the goals, the business case, and the key business requirements for the project. You may already have some objectives defined in the Project Proposal, if so, you can use that data as a starting point to complete this section of the document. To define objectives you need to understand the goals, business case, and key business requirements for the project. The objectives should be consistent with the goals, business case, and key business requirements. If those the client has stated are not, you need to work with them to find out why and to resolve the inconsistencies.

Using the information contained in the previous sections, you may conclude the following to be some of the project objectives:

- Change the order management system from an in-house enterprise system to an online Internet system that is available to retailers to place orders, get status on current orders, get quotes, view the current catalogue, and check available inventory 24/7.

- Decrease costs in the first year by 60% in the call center, by 20% in the sales department, and by 60% in the marketing department.

- Support 4,000 concurrent users and be scalable to 8,000 users

- Implement seamless integration among order management, back orders, inventory, accounting, call center, warehouse, and shipping.

Remember that your objectives must be concrete statements that describe precisely what the project is trying to achieve. The objectives should be clear, concise, and easily understood by all team members, and they must be able to produce measurable results. Though it is possible to pull the necessary information from the data you get from the client and use it to define objectives, the client must agree that the objectives are complete and accurate. They are their objectives for the project, after all.

Benefits

This section should describe the value that the project will bring to the organization. Though the business case may have been high level and intangible, the benefits are practical and tangible. The benefits section identifies and describes all the benefits of the project and not just those specific to the business problem that it is addressing. For example, a project to improve customer satisfaction may also have the benefits of increased employee satisfaction and productivity, increased revenue per customer, and a decrease in customer support calls.

Understanding the benefits of the project is as important as understanding the objectives. The two go hand in hand. Benefits will be different for every project, and it is unlikely that you will ever see two projects with identical benefits. However, in corporate America, the benefits can usually be boiled down to two distinct areas:

- Increased revenue
- Decreased costs

An increase in revenue is achieved by offering more value to customers so that they buy more products. It can also be accomplished by offering more products for sale. Alternatively, it can be attained by building or selling products more cost effectively, thereby increasing revenue per unit or revenue per customer. Projects that lead to increased productivity, efficiency, or effectiveness decrease costs, which more often than not, leads to higher profit margins. In summary, most projects aim to make money.

We say that *most* projects aim to make money because there are exceptions to this rule. For example, some projects are launched for humanitarian reasons, others to meet legal or security standards or obligations, and yet more for defense or national security reasons.

Understanding and being able to explain the benefits of the project is essential for any project manager. The benefits, along with the objectives, are used when making decisions during the project Life Cycle that will affect the outcome of the project. As long as the objectives are met and the benefits are realized, it is possible to make changes along the way that can still result in a successful project outcome.

How to Determine the Benefits

The benefits are how the end results of the project will positively impact the organization. They can include organizational, human resource, and financial benefits, and they are not confined to the documented objectives. It is common for a project to have benefits that result from a domino effect of the project on the organization.

Some specific questions you can ask your client to determine benefits are:

- How will the end result of this project benefit the company financially?

- How will the end result benefit the employees?

- How will the end result benefit your customers (the retailers)?

- How will the end result improve processes and procedures?

- What other areas of the business will be positively impacted by the outcome of this project and in what way?

Using the information contained in the previous examples, here are some example benefits:

- Decrease call center, marketing, and sales costs by 60%, 60%, and 20%, respectively

- Provide 100% Return on Investment (ROI) within one year

- Improve coordination and productivity throughout the organization

- Improve retailer experience

- Provide competitive advantage by giving customers real-time access to product information and simplifying the procurement process, making it easier for retailers to do business with ABC

- Increase productivity and efficiency in accounting department by removing many manual steps in the billing process

- Improve accuracy of invoices by removing the need to manually reenter order data

- Improve employee satisfaction because increased profits mean increased profit sharing bonuses for staff

- Reduce the size of the call center, meaning that the company can stay at the current premises for another four years instead of moving to a larger building in one year.

It is important to document as many positive benefits as possible. There could be cost savings in many areas of the business that are not directly related to the project. The more you can draw this information out of the client and document it in a compelling way, the better chance you (and the client) have of getting the project approved to continue.

Target Audience

The client will define the target audience for your product. The target audience incorporates anybody and everybody who will be an end user of the product. The exact demographic information required depends on the type of product or service that the project will produce. The definition of the target audience will be influential in both the design and the specification of the project, and as such, it is vital that it is accurate and complete.

Understanding the demographics of the audience, or end users, is a requirement for successfully designing and implementing a solution that will fit their needs. Demographic data on the end users are also vital to sales, marketing, and media teams.

A product would be designed very differently for children than it would for adults. It would also be designed differently for expert computer users than for novices. The gender or geographical location of users can also be a factor that needs to be considered both for development and marketing of the product. Global products need to be designed in a different way from national or regional ones. Understanding the competitive marketplace for the product is also an important key to producing a high-quality and highly desirable product.

The target audience may, to some extent, also impact the scope of the project. If the project is going to be designed for a specific user group, the scope must explicitly include that user group and exclude all others. For example, if the project is a Web site for a fashion distribution company, the target audience would be limited to retailers and would explicitly exclude other groups, such as the general public and resellers.

How to Identify the Target Audience

If the client does not already have the demographic data for their potential and desired end users, you can help them define the user by asking them to answer some direct questions. For example:

- What percentage of the end users has a proficiency level in the use of computers, technology, and the Internet of advanced, intermediate, or beginner?

- What percentage of the end users orders goods and services via the Internet often, sometimes, or never?

- What percentage of end users is in each time zone?

- Are there any cultural or language factors to consider?

- Are the users consumers or businesses?

- What is the age and gender of users (if applicable)?

- Will the end users be adults or children or both?

- Are there any disabled users that the product needs to be specially designed to work for?

The product or service may need to be designed for the lowest common denominator, or the client may need different versions, or different paths through the product, for different demographic groups of users (different target audiences). Once the potential user groups have been defined, the client can make the decision on what the target audience(s) will be for this particular project. It is often the case that the client has to choose for which target audience to optimize the product or service. It may not necessarily prevent other types of users from using the product, but they may not get the optimal experience.

Here are some example demographics for the users of the OFIS system used in our previous examples:

- End user proficiency in using computers:
  - Advanced 15%
  - Intermediate 50%
  - Beginner 35%

- End user proficiency in using Internet:
  - Advanced 10%
  - Intermediate 30%
  - Beginner 60%

- Users who have never ordered goods or services online: 85%

- Users that are retailer outlets whose staff have expert fashion knowledge: 100%

Even with this limited amount of information about the target user, it is possible to start getting a picture of the end user needs that the project must meet. For example, there is a high percentage of users with no Internet experience, and most of the users have never ordered anything online before. Therefore, the site should ideally be easy to use and intuitive and should contain help and demo screens to assist users in negotiating their way around the site and the ordering screens. The better you know the target audience, the better you are able to design a product or service that will fit their needs.

The Problem

This section clearly and accurately describes the problem, or problems, that need to be addressed, in whole or in part, as part of this project. It is not necessary for every problem to be solved. It is common for some of the problems identified for a project to be later defined as "out of scope" due to complexity or financial reasons. The problems should still be captured in this section, and those items should be listed as specifically out of scope in the scope section of the document. Problems should be described in detail and should include examples, where possible, to ensure that the project team fully understands the implications of the problems.

The proposal document will have contained a problem section. That information should be used as a starting point to complete this section of the document. However, as you work your way through completing the Definition, it may become clear from conversations with the client that other problems were not clearly identified in the Proposal. Those problems should be captured and added to the existing problem description in this document.

Documenting the Problem

Describe the problem or problems in as much detail as possible. Do not leave anything to the imagination or open to interpretation. It is critical to the success of the project that the project team has a clear understanding of every aspect of the problem(s) that the client is trying to solve. Any problems that are deemed too large, too difficult, or too expensive to solve must be explicitly listed in the scope section of the document as "out of scope."

Here are some example statements for the problem section based on our OFIS example project:

- The current system requires that retailers phone or fax their orders into the call center during business hours only (no after-hours support).

- Catalogues are updated every two months, but it is expensive to design, print, and distribute them to all customers and potential customers. Thus customers often use old catalogues when placing orders.

- Order entry is a manual process and apt to operator and key entry errors.

- The order management and the inventory system are not seamlessly integrated.

- The operator cannot see all data on one screen.

- Shipping and warehouse departments use manual processes for updating inventory. They are often a day or two out of date and apt to operator and key entry errors.

- Retailers are often told that items are in stock when they are out of stock, due to system not being updated.

- Operators do not know the expected date of delivery of incoming stock or how many other back orders are in the system for that particular item.

- Back orders are not always processed in the order in which they were received.

The Solution

The solution describes how the problem(s) will be solved. The information contained in this section is the foundation for producing accurate time and cost estimates for the project. Therefore, this information must be comprehensible, unambiguous, and very specific. This section should address every problem so that it is clear exactly how each one will be solved. If only one solution solves all the problems, make sure that it is 100% clear why and how all the problems are addressed.

Documenting the Solution

Describe the solution in as much detail as required to produce feasible estimates (for time and costs). Explain how the solution will solve each problem. Describe the high-level components of the solution (physical or logical) and how they will integrate with each other. The solution should contain high-level functional and technical requirements that are detailed enough to produce good-quality time and cost estimates.

Using our example, you may break the solution down into three specific areas with detail in each area:

- Front end
  - A business-to-business order management system utilizing shopping cart technology and requiring that users be registered and authenticated is implemented.
  - The online catalogue is available to anyone on the Internet (in a nonsecure section of the Web site).
  - The call center continues to use the existing desktop PC computer systems.
  - The solution utilizes the existing Oracle database on the back end.

- Back end
  - The solution is implemented on the Unix platform.
  - The system supports automated e-mails that notify retailers that an order has been received, processed, or shipped.
  - The warehouse and shipping departments utilize bar code scanners for checking inventory in and out.
  - The shopping cart is integrated with the existing accounting system.
  - Operator screens have full GUI interface.
  - Retailers' order histories are stored in the database.

- Processes
  - Training programs will be created for functional and technical users who are employees of the client.
  - The business analyst will create a workflow process for warehouse, shipping, and accounting departments.

- Functional requirements

- Technical requirements

Project Scope

The scope of a project is defined by specified boundaries that separate what is included in the project from what is not included in the project. If the scope of a project is too broad, it is going to be almost impossible to complete it successfully. To clearly define what is in scope, it is important to specifically document what is out of scope. This will help to avoid misunderstandings and disappointments as the project progresses.

The scope includes the departments, locations, and products that will be involved and included in the project. It also includes what features or functionality will be delivered in each phase of the project, the technical specification, the target audience for the project, and each phase of the project. The target audience further defines the scope of the project. Any features or functionality that are not required by the target audience will be clearly identified as out of scope.

Understanding the scope, both what is in scope and what is out of scope, is vitally important. The project manager is responsible for the timely completion of a high-quality project that meets the specified requirements. Those requirements cannot be met if the scope of the project is vague or open to interpretation. A high-level scope diagram is shown in Figure 4.3. This method of defining what is in and what is out of scope can be very useful and can be easily be created on a whiteboard or flipchart during the planning sessions.

The project scope may need to be defined multidimensionally. For instance, it could include which internal departments are affected by the project, which platforms will be supported, if it is for Internet or desktop or both, whether the target audience is business or general public, whether the final product will be scalable (and if so, to what extent), and on and on. The more specific you are about what is not included, the more common understanding there will be about what is included in the scope of the project.

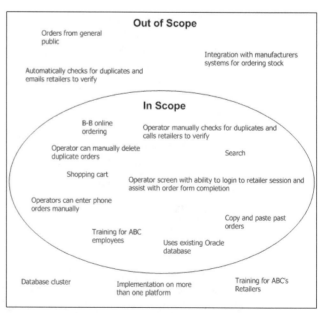

How to Determine What Is In and What Is Out of Scope

How do you determine what is in and what is out of scope? Ask the client a lot of questions about how the product will be used and about systems and processes

Figure 4.3: Whiteboard scope diagram.

that the product will integrate or interact with in some way. Make sure that those systems and processes are either included in the in-scope or the out-of-scope section. No matter how much you talk about these things, there will be misunderstandings later if you do not accurately document where the boundaries of the project lie. What often happens is that the client does not fully understand the implications of not including something in the project. No matter how much you try to explain, they are adamant that they do not need to pay for that extra widget or upgrade. As you near the end of the project, the client starts to realize that they really do need that upgrade or widget. If you have documented it as out of scope, the client cannot argue because it was discussed and specifically and purposely omitted from the project. If it is not documented, they may conveniently "forget" that you talked about it, or they may say that you did not fully explain the consequences of not including it. The client could try to make a case for getting it included in the project at no cost. They may go to your superiors and imply that you were negligent in your duties. Do not underestimate how often this happens. It happens even when you have documented it.

Once the scope has been well defined, you need to ensure that it is documented in a way that is understandable to everyone involved in the project. The use of a *system diagram* (see Figure 4.4) depicting the boundaries of the project can help to add clarity to the scope description. This diagram will clearly show the boundaries of the project. It shows that the project is limited to writing code for an existing order management database and supplying and writing code for an order management system and a Web site. Though the call center operators and the

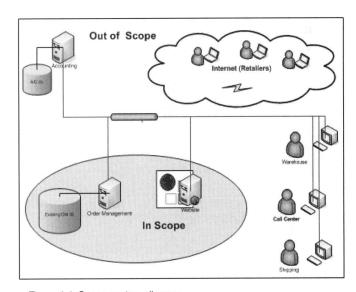

Figure 4.4: Scope system diagram.

Internet retailers can access the Web site, the project team is not responsible for writing any code specifically for their computer systems or supplying any equipment or hardware for their use.

Prerequisites

Document any specific prerequisites for the project. This can include third-party software or hardware versions that the client has agreed to have installed prior to delivery of the first release, and subsequent releases, of the product. It can also include any testing that the client has agreed to perform on the product. Client testing will usually involve integration testing with their existing systems. For various reasons, this testing cannot always be performed by the team developing the product. For instance, the client systems may be proprietary, they may be high-cost systems that are nonstandard or unavailable at the development site (making purchasing them specifically for this project unacceptably expensive). Security or privacy issues may exist with an outside company or department having access to the data on the client systems that would be necessary for testing purposes. Anything that you assume the client will be providing, or will be responsible for, should be clearly documented in this section.

How to Determine the Prerequisites

Use the project scope as a starting point for your prerequisite list. Anything not being supplied by the development team will be a prerequisite for the client team. In our example for scope, that would include:

- The database server
- The network
- The desktop systems for call center, warehouse, and shipping departments
- The accounting system

The client may also be required to have specific operating systems (OSs) and versions installed on their servers and desktop systems. It may be required that the employees being trained have a minimum level of experience in specific software programs. The client may be responsible for some of the testing of the product and for supplying the test environments for that testing. Anything at all that the client is required to do or to supply should be listed here.

It may be helpful to the client if you also list the person at the client company who is responsible for each item. It is not your responsibility to determine who that person should be, but the client may need some help identifying which technical group would ordinarily be responsible for such an item. For instance, if they need to install an Internet router or a T1 phone line, you can advise them that their data center or network team would most likely be the group that would take care of it. Do not assume that the person from the client company has any technical knowledge. What may seem obvious to you could be a complete mystery to your client. By the same token, do not assume that the client knows nothing. Be respectful and tactful when offering help or assistance so as not to offend.

Assumptions

This section of the document must clearly define any assumptions being made about the project, the technology, the project team, roles and responsibilities, and so on. It will be understood that all information contained in the Project Definition document, including time and cost estimates, are based on these assumptions.

It is common for many assumptions to be made about the project, the team, and the roles and responsibilities while creating the Project Definition. It is not possible to have all the answers that are needed to produce a 100%-accurate document, so assumptions are used to fill in the gaps. It is important to document those assumptions, whether they are assumed to be true or are known to be inaccurate. Document any verbal agreements between the client and the project manager. For example, the client may have agreed to be responsible for some of the quality assurance testing, or they may have agreed to an access schedule for the project team to have use of the database outside of normal business hours. Assumptions may be made about technology being compatible or about the client's domain expert being available to review design documentation with a set time period.

How to Identify the Project Assumptions

As each section of the Project Definition is completed, ask yourself what assumptions were made to complete that section of the document. Even if the assumptions seem obvious to you, make sure that they are explicitly stated. Never assume that everyone on the team is making the same assumptions.

Some examples of assumptions based our previous examples are:

- The client will ensure that the existing database server is upgraded to the most current version of Oracle.

- The client is responsible for setting up their data center and network to accommodate the project.

- The client will continue to use existing desktop systems for call center, warehouse, and shipping departments. The development company is supplying no hardware or software for any desktop systems.

- The accounting system already exists, and neither the OS nor the accounting software version will be upgraded between now and project completion.

- A subject matter expert will be available on day one of the design phase of the project.

- The client is responsible for all communications and support with the end users (retailers) of the project.

Project Constraints

Project constraints are anything that limits the project, the project team, or the client in any way. Resources (people, equipment, time, and cost), scope, and requirements are the most common areas where constraints will be evident. Some constraints will be identifiable at this stage of the project, and others will not become clear until the project plan is created later in the planning phase.

For example, if the client has a fixed budget for the project that is nonnegotiable, that is clearly a constraint. If the development company has a team of only 10 developers and the client will not pay for any more, that is also a constraint. If the project team can program in Unix but not in Windows, that is a limit on how the product can be developed, so it needs to be documented here. Some constraints may be related to physical space. For example, the client may have only 10 units of rack space available in their data center, which limits the physical size and number of pieces of hardware that can be used in the solution. The scope of a project can also be a constraint if it specifically excludes something from the project. You can find most of the information you need to define the constraints in other sections of the Project Definition. Present those constraints to the client and the project team and ask them to verify that the list is correct and complete. Having a group discussion about the constraints should lead to other constraints being identified.

Project Risks

Risk is the probability that something may happen during or after the development of the project that will have an adverse effect either on the project or the organization. Risks are events or unknowns that are beyond the control of the project team.

Identifying as many risks as possible early in the Life Cycle can save you a lot of headaches later on. Being aware of the risks means that you can plan for them and manage them. With forward planning, you can have contingency plans in place for any number of what-ifs that will help you to minimize risk as much as possible. The more you do to ensure that surprises do not creep up or jump out at you, the more organized and the less chaotic your management of the project will be. Predictability is a project manager's friend. Embrace it.

Recognizing and evaluating project risk starts at the project concept and continues throughout the entire Life Cycle of the project. Identifying and managing risks will not be completed until the project is signed off and delivered to the client.

Unfortunately, risk has quite a bad reputation, one that is largely undeserved. Risk is seen by many as a terrible thing and something to be avoided at all costs. However, viewed from a different perspective, risk is intrinsic to anything that involves change or progress, both of which often have very positive outcomes. Risk is also inherent in exploration, adventure, travel, and many sports, and most people would not consider these things to be negative. Risk is one of the things that makes life exciting and fun. We take risks every single day, in almost everything that we do. We plan for some, try to avoid others, and purposely go in search of a few more. Risk is neither good nor bad. It just is.

Millions of people love to surf. The freedom and excitement one gets riding the waves is unbelievable. The risk of shark attacks, being hit on the head by someone else's surf-board, or crashing into the reefs or rocks does not appear to be of much concern to the die-hard surfer, who is totally focused on looking for that perfect wave. Appearances, however, can be deceptive. Most surfers take precautions prior to, and during, their time in the water. By doing so, they are managing risk. A surfer will usually check the surf report to find out how high the surf is before they go in to ensure that they are not surfing in conditions that are beyond their capabilities. If they are surfing in a new loca-tion, they will find out where the hidden reefs and the rocks lie so they are not sur-prised by a sudden (and dangerous) impact. While waiting for a wave, they may put their feet up on the board rather than let them dangle in the water. If a shark sees a leg dangling in the water covered by a shiny black wetsuit, it can mistake it for a seal and think "Mmmm breakfast"; you can imagine what could happen next! Surfers keep their eye on other surfers while in the water, so they are aware of any runaway surfboards (or the runaway novice surfer). Many surfers will surf with a friend so that they have some-one to help them if there is an accident. Some will make sure that they know where the nearest phone, and the nearest hospital, is—just in case. Surfing is a high-risk sport, but the risks are known, so they can be planned for. Being proactive and identifying, evaluating, and planning for the known risks helps a surfer to stay safe and be success-ful in the water.

Just as any good surfer will check the surf report and make sure she is aware of any po-tential hazards before going into the water, the project manager should perform a risk evaluation of the project with the client and the project team. To manage risk success-fully, you must manage risk proactively. Managing risk reactively leads to project man-agers running around like chickens with their heads cut off, screaming for help when something terrible happens. OK, that might be a bit of an over exaggeration, but you get the point!

Identifying Project Risks

The definition of "risk" as something unavoidable or unpredictable and that may ad-versely affect the outcome of the project is rather a broad description and could lead to any number of things being identified as risks. Therefore, the key things to consider when identifying project risk are:

- The probability of it happening

- How critical the impact on the project could be

If the either the probability or the criticality of any risk is low, it does not constitute a project risk. It must be high probability and high criticality to make it onto your risk list. (See Figure 4.5.) If the potential problem falls into the top right square, it should be documented as a risk.

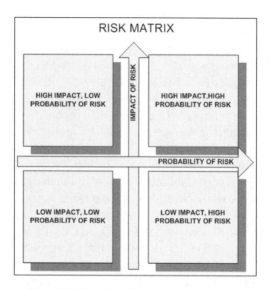

Figure 4.5: The risk matrix.

You can imagine how big the risk section would be in your project documentation if every tiny little thing that could possibly go wrong were included. You might see entries like this:

- An earthquake may cause the building to fall down.

- One of the project manager's relatives may get seriously ill, requiring that he take a leave of absence.

- A developer's computer might crash.

- Someone on the team may have an accident and be out of the office for a few weeks.

- The "x" feature may be finished a few days late.

- The testing systems may be delivered a day late because of a public holiday that week.

- The client may be unavailable for a status meeting.

- The engineers may not update their documentation on time.

- Someone on the team may leave the company.

Though all of these situations would impact the project in some way, they are either extremely unlikely to happen or would have a minimal and manageable impact on the project.

To help you in defining appropriate risks for your project, consider the three main areas of impact.

- Project risk—Scheduling or other nontechnical issues that threaten the successful completion of the project

- Business risk—Risks that threaten the client's business in some way (financially or organizationally)

- Technical risk—Technical risks that have the potential to negatively impact the outcome of the project

Most risks will fall into one of these three main categories, all of which are important to the successful outcome of the project. The second of these areas of risk is most often overlooked. Understanding business risk is necessary for the client to make informed decisions about the project. If they do not consider business risks during the planning phase of the project, they may start to make sudden direction changes during the course of development to try to mitigate unexpected risks as they become apparent.

Taking all this information into account, the kind of items you would expect to see listed in the risk section of the Project Definition are:

- The existing database it is very old, and it is unknown whether it will work effectively with the new technology being used to develop the project.

- The estimate for the barcode technology is based on a lot of assumptions so the estimate could be highly inaccurate.

- We have been unable to find a Subject Matter Expert (SME) for the project. If we do not find someone soon, we could create a lot of rework by making incorrect assumptions during design and development.

- A very short time is allocated to staff training on the product. It might not be enough time and could result in major teething problems after the new product goes live.

- One of the developers on the team is shared between two project teams. He may not have adequate time to support this project effectively. He is a key contributor to the project, and his work cannot be done by anyone else.

- Deployment date for new site is set for two weeks before an important client conference where they want to demonstrate the new Web site. If the launch is late, the client will miss the opportunity to demonstrate the site live to retailers.

- The conference scheduled for two weeks after deployment is expected to generate an unusually high volume of orders. If system is not stable, a huge increase in traffic is very risky to the stability and reliability of the OFIS system.

It is important that all team members be aware of the risks that exist both for the project team and for the client.

Time and Costs

This section will contain information on the expected time frame of the project and the associated costs. This is where the initial and detailed estimates that were created during the concept and proposal stages of the project are refined to become detailed estimates. The estimates will go through one more round of review after the technical designs are completed, at which time final estimates will be produced. The accuracy of the detailed estimates needs to be pretty close to where the final estimates will be. The information contained in the solution section of the document will be used as the basis for the detailed time and cost estimates.

Creating Detailed Estimates

The Project Definition should contain sufficiently detailed information about the project and the scope of the project to enable the various development groups to create detailed estimates for the project.

Each company will have its own process for how estimates are created and its own definition of "detailed" as compared to "high level" or "initial." Some companies expect that estimates will have a variance factor of up to 50%, and others expect only 20%. The accuracy required by the client for the detailed estimate will determine whether the development team needs to produce high-level designs before creating the detailed estimates for each feature.

Similar to the high-level estimates, the following information will be required to produce the detailed estimates. We have broken this into two lists: The first contains the estimates typically supplied by the project manager, and the second contains estimates typically supplied by other departments.

Project Manager Estimates

- Development time (days or hours) required to meet project requirements, including total cost per developer

- Cost per feature based on high-level design (if required)

- Time and costs to produce estimates, including high-level design if required

- Project management time (days or hours) required and total costs per manager

- Costs for hardware, software, development, and testing equipment and tools for each team member

- Development consultant or contractor time required and cost per hour

- Development time needed for research, requirements, and design

- Development deployment, delivery and, manufacturing costs (including equipment)

- Development team employee motivation and training costs

- Other project-related costs

Estimates Supplied by Other Groups or Departments

- Quality assurance testing time (days or hours) and cost per hour per tester

- Support staff required (customer support, technical support, operations team, etc.) and cost per hour

- Nondevelopment management time (days or hours) required and total costs per manager

- Nondevelopment consulting or contractor time required and cost per hour

- Nondevelopment time needed for research, requirements, and design

- Nondevelopment deployment, delivery, and manufacturing costs (including equipment)

- Advertising and marketing costs

- Employee motivation and training costs

- Other project-related costs

The detailed estimates are used to verify that the project can be completed within the specified budget. It should be relatively clear at this point whether the project requirements are in line with the budget. If they are not, three courses of action are available to the client:

1. Scale back the requirements

2. Increase the budget

3. Cancel the project

The development time estimates may be supplied per feature and may contain variable estimates based on the different complexity levels that are possible for the feature. The client, or the business team, will use the variable estimates to decide whether the added complexity is worth the additional cost (value). It is not always possible to make those decisions without understanding the difference in the costs—hence the need for variable estimates. Final decisions on which features are approved and the scope of each feature are usually made before the start of the design phase of the project. However, if the high-level estimates require a small percentage of variance from the detailed estimates and actual costs, a high-level design may be required from the development team to complete detailed estimates and the planning phase of the project.

Typically, the detailed estimates are used by the project manager to create a high-level project schedule prior the start of the design phase of the project.

If the detailed estimates come in exactly on budget, it is unlikely that your project can be completed within budget without making trade-offs during the Life Cycle. There are always differences in the estimated versus actual costs, and it is highly unusual for the actual costs to be lower than the estimated ones.

Project Organization

A well-defined and appropriate organizational structure for the proposed project team is essential to the Project Definition. At this stage it does not have to include specific names, but it should include titles (or roles) so that the size of the team is clearly understood. This information is required to estimate costs.

The organizational structure for the team can be supplied as an organizational chart. (See Figure 4.6.) The project organization may also include high-level information regarding roles and responsibilities for the project. Roles and responsibilities will be described in detail in the project plan.

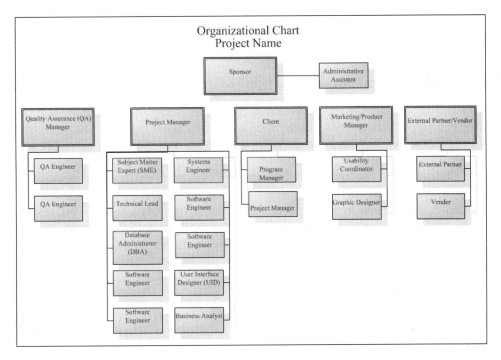

Figure 4.6: Project organizational chart.

Project Definition Approval

This section should document the approval process and authorized signatories for the Project Definition document. The client project approval process and timeline should also be contained in this section.

The names, titles, and companies of the Project Definition approvers should be clearly stated. If the names of the actual managers are not known at this time, their titles and companies will be sufficient. The approvers will most likely be one or two managers each from the client company and the development company. For example:

- Daryl Johnson, Project Manager, XYZ Inc.
- Project Manager, ABC Corp.
- Paulette Green, Sponsor, XYZ Inc.

The designated approvers must have the authority to sign off on the document because their signatures act as final approval that the Project Definition is complete.

The client will provide a process, including timelines, for their internal approval process of the project based on the Project Definition. The approval means the go-ahead for contracts to be signed and the project to continue. The development company will provide a timeline for how soon the project can start based on the approval date given by the client.

Finalizing and Approving the Project Definition

Does everyone agree to start this project? It is essential that all parties understand and agree on the Project Definition and the assigned responsibilities. A commitment from the decision-makers must be made that this project should be initiated and that there will be absolute support from the team for the project. This includes having the support of senior management. Without senior management support, your project will be more of a challenge. It is not always necessary to have full consensus on a project. It is always necessary to have agreement from the identified decision-makers or the percentage of decision-makers needed to carry the decision, as defined by the client or the project team. As long as a documented process is being followed, then this step can be accomplished without necessarily having 100% consensus on the initiation of the project. Each company will handle this differently but will likely have the same process for every project.

The Project Definition must be as complete and accurate as possible. It is the foundation on which the entire project will be built and the yardstick against which all project decisions will be made.

Marketing Requirements Document (MRD)

The product manager or the marketing team is usually responsible for writing the *Marketing Requirements Document (MRD)*. If detailed Project Proposal and Project Definition documents have been created, an MRD may not be necessary. It may be written by someone in-house or may be supplied by the client. It defines the product and how it will work from the end-user perspective. It will identify inputs and outputs for the product, the user interface (UI), security and privacy requirements, a selling price for the product (if applicable), special requirements like disabled access to the product, the usability testing requirements, beta program details (if applicable), registration or product activation requirements, a Service Level Agreement (SLA) if applicable, and so on. It will also identify where the final product should be delivered, who will be producing artwork for the packaging (if applicable), and any business partners or contracts in place for the product (perhaps it will be bundled with a product from a third-party company). This document is very important to the project team. This information will be used together with the Project Definition to create the technical requirements and specifications for the project.

A typical MRD will contain some or all of the following sections:

- Strategy and Overview
  - Description of project
  - Goals and objectives
  - Project scope
  - Target audience
  - Competitive strengths and weaknesses
  - Cost analysis and strategy
  - Budget
- Business Model
  - Value proposition and benefits
  - Market space
  - Cost structure
  - Competitive strategy
- Affected Groups
  - Internal
  - External
  - External partners and vendors
- Hardware, Equipment, and Tools Requirements
  - Development
  - Support
  - Operations
  - Sales
- Product Requirements
  - Performance and stability requirements
  - Backward compatibility
  - Physical and logical architecture
  - Platforms and protocols
  - Uptime and quality of service
  - Security
  - Benchmarking
  - Special requirements
- Functional Requirements
  - Must have
  - Highly desirable
  - Nice to have
  - Usability requirements
  - GUI
  - Usability testing
  - Beta program
- Service Level Agreements (SLAs)
- Deliverables

- Future Requirements
  - Extendibility
  - Scalability
  - Upgrades and enhancements
  - Desired future features
  - Out of scope or specifically not being implemented

An MRD template is included on the CD-ROM that accompanies this book.

Understanding Budgets

A budget is the tool that you use to manage the costs associated with your project. You, or whoever is proposing the project, will usually come up with a ballpark estimate of project costs when you are working on the Project Proposal during the planning phase of your project. After project approval, an initial budget will be drawn up, detailing each cost and identifying which costs are known and which are still uncertain. This initial budget will need approval, and any constraints should be identified. For example, the company may have decided that your project may not have more than five engineers at a maximum total salary cost of $250,000 for the project duration. The number of engineers will often be specified because the costs per person are greater than the total of the salary payments. The company has to pay benefits to each person and also supply office space and equipment for each engineer. You may not have the option to hire more staff at lower salaries. Your initial budget may have come in at over $1 million, but your company may feel that this project is not worth more than $850,000, which means if you cannot implement it more cheaply, the project will be canceled. You should always get your initial budget approved before starting to work on your final budget. You could end up wasting a lot of time on a budget that will need to be completely redone or for a project that gets canceled because it is too expensive. You will have a date to submit your final budget for approval. This is usually before the start of development, but it can sometimes be later than that. Bear in mind that if you start your project development without an approved budget, there is some risk.

You may not be the person creating your budget. It could be that you will be asked for a lot of information and someone else at your company will put together a budget for you. You may not have much input into some parts of the project. For instance, training and travel may be a set per-person amount determined by your organization. Whatever process is used to create your budget, it is beneficial and smart to ensure that you have a firm understanding of it, and the many elements that are included, before you start working on your project. Budgets can be quite complex, and trying to understand and analyze every single detail could take up so much of your time that you will not have time left to manage the rest of your project. It would be wise to identify what the most critical elements of your budget are and to focus primarily on those.

Most companies have a system or process for tracking your project costs against your budget. This is done by using financial codes for everything that you do and everything that you spend. The hardest part of tracking your budget often is figuring out which costs go into which category. It is not always black and white. If you do not categorize your costs in the same way you categorize your budget, then it will not balance. Try to make notes for yourself about what you include where so that you do not forget when you start to track expenses. The accounting department will often ask you to submit paperwork with all costs categorized and, on a monthly basis, they will give you a budget report. Budget reports vary from being very useful to completely useless and everything in between! You may need a secondary system for yourself if you really want to stay on track. Some companies do not offer reports at all, so it is up to you to manage the costs day to day. If you are responsible for this, give the process some serious thought before proceeding. If you mess it up, it will be really hard to go back and recreate and recategorize everything.

Some companies will determine certain budget categories for your team or your department based on historical data. You may not be able to negotiate on those. You may, however be able to add some of those costs into the project cost if it is appropriate and can be justified. For example, say you are allowed to send your team members to one week of training per person, per year. Your entire team needs to learn a new technology that the company will be implementing this year, and they are scheduled for one week of training each in that technology. Then you find that you need to use another new technology for your upcoming project that will need a week of training for one of your team members to get up to speed. This training cost might well be a justified project cost that can be added to your project budget. If the alternative is to hire a consultant to do the work, the training cost may well be a much more economic option, and it also keeps the knowledge in-house. You pay for training once, but you can use the knowledge over and over again.

Many projects begin without realistic timelines or budgets. Without adequate project planning, this is inevitable. Deciding on a budget or timeline for a project before creating a project plan is going to cause problems down the line. If you track your budget by adding up the costs as you go and then declaring that you have run out of money when it has all gone, you are hardly likely to end up with a successful project! If you managed your household expenses in this way, you might well end up with one week per month when you had no money left for food.

By monitoring your costs and tracking them against your budget, you will start to see warning signs that your project is starting to overrun. First, you need to ensure that this is not due to a tracking error (for instance, you tracked training-related travel as a business travel cost and so that category is over budget and the other is under budget). If you really are over budget you need to find places to make some cuts. These cuts may need to be made in the same category as the overrun, or you may be able to make cuts in other areas. It is always tricky finding places to cut costs. With equipment you can downgrade servers or continue to use the old version of the development platform. In the area of people, you can cut some of the contractor hours or find a lower-cost contractor.

Sometimes cuts are not due to your costs exceeding your budget but are due to the company needing to make cuts for business reasons. They may be concerned about meeting their quarterly earnings estimates, or they may have already come in low and want to make some cuts to help increase shareholder confidence. Compaies decide that they need to make cutbacks for lots of reasons. Sometimes they will tell you why and sometimes they will not. You have no control over these cuts; you just have to learn how to manage and deal with them. These kinds of cuts are usually made in the personnel-related categories, such as training, employee motivation, books, and bonuses. It is unfortunate when cuts are made in areas that serve as motivation for your team members. Developers generally look forward to training and keeping their skills up to date. They may need the training to be able to move to the next version of development tools, and by cutting the training, you have to cancel the upgrade. Your team will be unhappy about using out-of-date tools to develop the project. Cutting employee motivation budgets is tough on the team but especially so on the project manager. You may need to cancel your team celebration to mark your first milestone or cancel the thank-you gifts that you ordered to thank the team for working through an entire weekend to fix a critical problem, or you may need to stop buying bagels or donuts for your weekly team meetings. These are all great motivational and team-building tools, and managing a team without them will be more challenging. Cutting bonuses is also very hard on team morale. Last year, they looked forward to their bonus if the project was successful, but this year they will not receive a bonus even if the project is successful. Some of these perks could be key reasons why some employees chose to work on your project in the first place. It is a project management challenge to manage budget cuts and keep a team motivated and enthused.

If you have the control to move budgeted money from one category to another, bear in mind that these easy-to-cut expenses might end up being the most critical to your project success. Your team must be happy and motivated, or you will not be getting their best performance. All aspects of the project are important, and starting to run over on certain categories in your budget does not necessarily justify taking money from other components to balance it.

Expenses never track exactly to a budget. There will always be some differences, and your company will likely have a policy on what percentage over or under is acceptable. Having a *percentage variance allowance* is advisable. This is also referred to as a "contingency budget." A contingency budget is a cushion that gives the project manager some breathing room if some tasks go beyond schedule and over budget. This budget also allows for any unplanned tasks or equipment (i.e., added software and hardware, or any team changes). The contingency budget is usually in the region of 10% contingency for a project budget. However, keep in mind that this doesn't give you any leeway for schedule slippage. It only pays for additional costs, and those will need to be justified. The contingency budget is usually restricted to project-related costs only. You will not be able to use the excess to pay for things like employee motivation or training costs, for instance. Your responsibility as the project manager is to try to keep the actual costs at, or below, the estimated costs. You need to be in control of all the costs for your project. You cannot let other people spend money from your budget without your prior approval. If you allow that to happen, you will not be in control of your own budget, and before you know it, you will find that you have overspent. There are no ifs, ands, or buts about this. You need to reserve your contingency budget for emergency use only and to try to use as little of it as possible.

In some organizations, management bonuses are tied to managers' performance with budgets. In other words, if you come in under budget, you get a larger bonus. This can be both good and bad. It is a motivation to manage costs closely, but it can also be a motivation to cut corners. Some managers start to cut perks for their team members to keep their costs under budget. This is not the behavior of an effective and highly skilled project manager. You should *never* try to take things away from your team members to benefit you personally. It is a bad habit to get into, and it will not make your projects successful. If you have ever known a manager who is more focused on coming in under budget than she is on successfully implementing the project, you will know that these are not good managers to work for. They are penny pinching at every opportunity. They make you share books rather than having your own copy. They never take the team out to lunch. They make you keep your old computer that you have to reboot every 45 minutes because they do not want to spend budget money on a new one. None of these actions will result in a motivated or productive team. They are counter productive and very demotivating. So be warned—this bonus rule can be dangerous. If it is in place at your organization, focus on the project and the team, and forget about the bonus until later on. Never allow money to lead you to compromise your integrity. If the right thing to do is to spend the whole budget and get a lower bonus, then do it.

Staying on schedule and meeting, or beating, your scheduled milestone deadlines is the best way to maximize your chances of completing your project within budget. Even though this will significantly increase the probability that you will meet your budget goals, there is obviously no guarantee. The two usually go hand in hand, so make sure that you are managing both very closely. In project management, the only guarantee you really have is that every day will bring new challenges.

When the project is initially budgeted, costs are sometimes uncertain, so the project budget will usually include an allowance for such cases. The budgeted amounts may include *variable* costs (development server $25,000–35,000, for instance) that will be finalized as you move through the planning phase of the project. You will have a deadline for finalizing your project budget, and this may be anything from a week to a few months.

It may be that the actual costs come in lower than the estimated costs, which leaves you with a budget surplus. The company may allow you to use this money for some other project-related cost (more labor hours for schedule slippage, for instance). However, this is quite rare, especially in larger organizations. The money is usually only allowed to be spent on what it was budgeted for. You cannot buy a cheaper server and use the surplus to hire additional developers, or use it to "top up" your employee motivation budget. Most companies track budget in separate *buckets*, which are coded categories that are often also used for revenue-, cost-, and tax-reporting purposes. Putting costs into one bucket and then spending the money in another may well be grounds for dismissal, so make sure that you check with your senior managers (and get approval in writing) before you go off and start spending any budget surplus. Having a job is a really important aspect of successful project management!

Creating a Budget

The budget should summarize the planned expenses and revenues related to the project. Each project task will have a cost associated with it, whether it is your engineer's labor hours or the price of the testing database. In preparing the project budget, all project costs need to be categorized, estimated, and totaled. You may need to prepare multiple budgets for your project. As we discussed earlier, you may have both a project budget and an administrative or "run-the-business" budget. Monies from separate budgets are not usually transferable across budgets.

Most companies have set rates for estimating staffing costs. They use an average that they calculate based on the salaries for those positions across the company. A software engineer, for instance, may have a different cost than a database engineer or a UI designer. The costs for full-time employees usually include additional amounts that cover the employer cost of the employee. This covers office space, equipment, taxes, workers compensation, medical benefits, vacations, sick time, bonuses, and so on. Contractor rates will be different again.

Project Approval

Project approval does not necessarily require consensus and agreement from the whole project team. The team will review the final document, and the team members will have a lot of input into the contents. However, the document requires agreement from the identified, authorized decision-makers that the Project Definition is complete and meets the needs of the client. When the decision-makers have agreed that the definition is complete, accurate, and acceptable, the Project Definition will be signed by the documented approvers as complete.

The client representative will agree to get the necessary authorization to continue with the implementation of the project. This may be approval from a senior manager, or for an external client, may necessitate a contractual agreement being drawn up between the development company and the client, where the client agrees to pay the costs for the development of the project. The agreement may include a contingency for update after the project designs are complete. The client may agree to no greater than an $x\%$ increase in costs at that time, or it may be left relatively open ended. At the very least, the client will agree to pay for time and costs incurred during the creation of the functional and technical designs. The contract will be based on the Statement of Work that the development company presents to the client detailing what the project entails and what the development company is agreeing to deliver.

Statement of Work

From the Project Definition, a comprehensive Statement of Work (SOW) is generated. The SOW sets the rules for the project once the key stakeholders agree to the content in the Project Definition. The SOW includes the purpose of the project, milestones, project scope, deliverables, any constraints or assumptions, and acceptance criteria for project closure. The Statement of Work should be clear, concise, and as complete as possible.

A Statement of Work template is included on the CD-ROM that accompanies this book.

CHAPTER 5

The Project Plan
and Project Approach

The Project Definition, Marketing Requirements Document, and budget have been approved; contracts are signed, and the project is ready to be kicked off! Before you rush off and schedule your project kick-off meeting, there are a few things that you need to do. You must identify and secure the project team members for your project, and you must prepare a first draft of the Project Plan and the Project Approach. Both of these documents will be updated to incorporate additions and changes after the kick-off meeting and will be finalized soon thereafter.

The Project Definition will be used as the foundation for these two new project documents. No changes may be made to the Project Definition document after it has been approved. Any required changes to what is contained in that document must be documented in the Project Plan, issued as an addendum to the Project Definition document, and signed off by the client.

The *Project Plan* is a living set of documents in which many areas of the plan will be changed, updated, and expanded as the project progresses. The *Project Approach*, generally, will not change after it has been finalized following the project kick-off meeting.

The project manager is responsible for creating the Project Plan and Project Approach documents. It is important to be aware that in some companies, and for some projects, the documents that constitute the Project Plan and Project Approach will be combined into one or two documents. Regardless of how this information is organized and presented, it needs to be created by the project manager with input from the client and the project team.

Understanding Quality Management

Before getting started on creating the Project Plan and Project Approach, it is important to consider how you will ensure that the quality of your project meets the quality standards and best practices required by the client and your organization. Even if neither organization has a formal quality management process, do you know how you and the client will determine the quality of the end product?

To determine whether a project has been completed successfully, it must meet three requirements.

1. Completed on time
2. Completed within budget
3. Completed with high quality

The first two requirements are relatively easy to measure. You have a delivery date, and you have a budget. Either you meet them, or you do not. High quality is not as easy to measure, so you need to ensure that you do not leave the criteria for measuring it open to interpretation.

You cannot wait to start to thinking about quality until you are in the integration or deployment phase of your project. You need to define quality during the planning phase. It is a critical requirement of any project and one that you cannot afford to leave undefined. The project team and the client must have a common understanding of the term "quality" and how it applies to your project. You also need clearly defined criteria for measuring and evaluating the quality of your project.

To determine the quality of the outcome, you need to be able to compare the start point with the end point. You need consistent measuring techniques and a consistent way of documenting the results. Your client must agree to, and sign off on, the process for measuring quality. If this is not done, you may find yourself in a situation where you have total confidence that you have delivered a high-quality product, but your client feels that you have delivered a substandard project.

Quality planning is all about achieving measurable results. How do you do that? First, you must ensure that what you deliver to your client meets the specification. To meet specifications, it is imperative that you first accurately document them. The initial requirements and specifications should be reviewed and finalized before each feature is designed. A formal design review must be held for each feature, headed up by a technical lead or senior engineer. The design reviews should ideally have quality assurance involvement. When each feature is completed, a formal code review and a security or compliance review should be done. Without the reviews (the *checks and balances*), it is unlikely that you will achieve a high-quality result. You will never know what level of quality you have achieved if you have nothing against which to measure the results. To be successful you need to communicate, document, review, and finalize each requirement. This is the key to producing high-quality results.

One of the most important things to remember about measurable results is that they must include timelines. Stating that a project will increase sales by 20% is not measurable because no timeline is associated with it. Increasing sales by 20% by the end of the first quarter is measurable. You must state clearly what you will measure, how you will measure it, and when you will measure it.

Some examples of measurable versus nonmeasurable outcomes are shown in the following table.

Measurable	Not Measurable
Increase sales by 20% in first quarter following project completion	Increase sales by 20%
Increase Web site concurrent user capacity by 500 users per server during peak hours of 7pm–9pm PST Monday through Thursday	Increase capacity by 500 users
Increase volume of technical support calls handled per hour by 10%; decrease average call length from 5 minutes to 3 minutes	Increase efficiency of technical support personnel

Let's discuss in more detail the example of increasing sales by 20% in the first quarter. You need to determine whether the 20% is a measurement of the number of customers that will be increased or the total revenue from the customers. Will the revenue measurement be limited to new customers, or will it include revenue generated from existing customers? Are you measuring only for specific products or for the company's entire product range? From what source will you get the data that you use for measurement? Various systems may contain this information available at the client site. You need to specify which system will be used, and what specific data you will use, for measurement. For instance, will you measure the revenues prediscount or post-discount? Are you measuring data for all sales persons, or just the top performers or the lowest performers? By now, you are probably beginning to realize the complexity of measuring success. It is not as simple as merely completing the project on time, within budget, and without too many bugs.

Your client may be responsible for some, or all, of this measurement. How much you are involved in the quality management for your project will depend on the nature of the project and whether your team responsibility ends when the project is handed-off to the client. Even if your responsibility were to just hand-off the product, it would be wise to familiarize yourself with the expectations of the client in regard to quality. The client may have asked your company to help them increase sales by 20%, in which case someone at your company came up with the solution based on their own Project Proposal. If this is the case, make sure that you understand the rationale behind the decision. Without the background information on what the project is designed to do, you will be hard pressed to make the most effective decisions on how to implement the solution most effectively. You will also need to ensure that the capability to measure the performance of the product or service exists. It will be your company's responsibility to show that the project meets the client's requirements.

On the other hand, the client may have a goal of increasing sales by 20% but may have come up with their own solution to the problem that they have asked your company to develop. They will still need to measure the success of their project after you have delivered it to them. Unless you understand what the client is ultimately trying to achieve, you will be unable to make suggestions about how they can most effectively achieve their goals. You may not have the time to come up with a measurement process for the client, but you should at least ask them how they plan to measure their success. This way you can confirm that their assumptions about what the product or service will do are correct. They may assume that they can run reports from the system because they know that certain pieces of data are used by the system. It could be that the system you are developing uses those pieces of data for specific calculations and then discards them because there is no requirement to save them or there is no database functionality to store those specific pieces of data. It could be that some of the data they want to use for reporting are personally identifiable information and that they are not compliant with the client's privacy policies to store the information for further use.

There could be any number of reasons that the client's assumptions are incorrect. Where will it leave your client if they are not aware of these issues until after project completion? Not in a good position and possibly with the prospect of having to spend a lot more money to get what they really want. If this happens, is it your fault? No, it is not your fault in the sense that your client received a project that met their written requirements. However, the art of successful project management is not just giving someone what he asks for; it is ensuring that what they are asking for is really what they need. You want your client to be happy and to come back with more projects. You want them to feel that they are getting added value from working with your company. You want them to feel that they need you to be successful. Having quality-related conversations during the planning phase of your project will ensure that you and your client really understand each other. Do not assume that your business, sales, or marketing team will understand that what the client is asking for may not be what they really need. They do not understand the technology to the level that you and your team do, and they will not be implementing the solution.

Take the time to talk to your client about their measurement process and their assumptions about how they will gather their measurement data. It is possible that they will need to get some of their measurements from the product that you are developing. You and your team need to be aware of these requirements so that you are including those tools and capabilities into the product plan, thereby ensuring that it is included in the contractual agreement. You must ensure that the client is not assuming anything that is not an explicit requirement in the specification.

Let us assume that you are going to be responsible for some measurement either of your project or perhaps for one of the processes you are using to manage your project(s). At what intervals should the results be measured? Measuring only once may not be a good indication of success.

In our 20% increase in sales example, you may want to consider measuring success every quarter. Perhaps as time progresses and the team get more familiar with the new process, they will increase sales by 30% or 40% per quarter. Then again, perhaps after their initial training on the new process or tools, the sales people will slip back to using the old process, and sales will decrease again. This happens more often than you would imagine. The failure of a team to continue using a new process after the initial enthusiasm has worn off is the single most common reason for process improvements to fail.

It is possible to write an entire book on the subject of how to measure project success or quality. Many scientific and nonscientific methodologies and techniques exist for quality management. You may remember that we mentioned some industry-standard quality management processes in Chapter 2 (Six Sigma, SEI CMMI, and ISO). These are examples of scientific methodologies used in many companies to manage quality and ensure consistent results.

When you are measuring project success, you are measuring the quality of the project. Completing the project on time and within budget are yes or no answers. Completing the project with high quality is the area that requires a clearly defined process for measurement. "Quality" is subjective. It could mean a hundred different things to a hundred different people. To ensure that your project team has a common understanding of what it means to your project, you need to define and document it in as much detail as you can. You can learn the basics of measuring quality fairly quickly. You will become much more experienced in this area as you complete more and more projects. Paying particular attention to this area will set you apart from many project managers, who assume that delivering the project on time, within budget, and without too many bugs is the definition of "quality" and "project success." We believe that as a project manager you have a responsibility to be much more concerned about the quality and appropriateness (for the purpose) of the projects you are managing. This is an area where you can add value and really shine as a leader within your organization.

The Project Plan

The project manager creates a draft Project Plan incorporating all the known information prior to the project kick-off meeting. Any unknown or undefined areas will be defined during the project kick-off meeting.

The Project Definition document describes what the project is (strategic plan); the *Project Plan* will detail how it will be accomplished (tactical plan). The Project Plan will reference the Project Definition document in addition to a number of other documents required to complete the Project Plan.

The Project Plan and its related documents are living documents that will be subject to changes and updates during the Life Cycle of the project.

It is possible to combine some or all of the Project Plan documents into one document if required. This may make it simpler to track documentation for smaller and less complex projects.

The Project Plan contains the following sections (the italicized items are separate documents referenced in the Project Plan):

- Project Definition Overview
- Changes Since Project Definition Was Approved
- *Staffing Plan*
- *Development Environment*
- *High Level Schedule*
- Deliverables and Milestones
- *Functional Requirements*
- *Technical Requirements*
- *Decision Support System Plan*
- *Quality Assurance Plan*
- *Communication Plan*
- *Deployment Plan*
- *Operations Plan*
- *Training Plan*
- *Risk Management Plan*
- *Measurement Plan*
- Client Acceptance Criteria
- Project Plan Approval

Creating the Project Plan

The following sections are designed as a practical guide to help you understand and create the Project Plan document.

Project Definition Overview

The Project Definition overview section should contain a high-level, brief overview of the project including client name, project name, and a brief description of the project. The Project Definition document should be referenced.

Changes Since Project Definition Was Approved

The Project Definition document cannot be updated or changed after it has been approved so any changes made to the definition of the project since the definition document was finalized should be clearly documented in this section. Anything in the Project Plan that contradicts the Project Definition, requires additional resources, or affects the outcome of the project must be documented, clearly and accurately, in this section. The client will be required to sign off on these changes after the Project Plan is complete and before the project can proceed to the next step.

Staffing Plan

The project team as specified in the Project Definition is verified and finalized in the Staffing Plan. The Project Definition may have had some open positions listed that will now need to be assigned to a real person. If a significant time lapse has occurred between the Project Definition and the approval, some of the team members specified in the document may no longer be available, so you will need to reassign those roles to someone else. You will be unable to move into the next phase of the project unless you have your project team in place. Getting the right people can take time, but you need to move fast if there is a tight schedule to meet.

In this document, identify each of the team members, departments, and companies that will be assigned a specific project role and individual project responsibilities.

A *project role* is similar to a job description. Where an employee job description will include details of every single aspect of a job, the project role will identify the job description as it applies specifically to this project. For example, an employee may have been hired to perform the dual role of software engineer and UI designer. If, on this particular project, she is functioning purely as a software engineer with no UI design responsibilities, the project role will reflect only the software engineer role as it applies to this project. Some of your team members may be assigned to more than one project, or they may be assigned to more than one feature or component for the project. Be sure to document what percentage of time they should be spending on each and, if applicable, which project or feature will take priority in the event of a critical situation. It is more common for project team members to be multitasking than not. Depending on the project and the size of your team, one person may fill more than one role and be covering a broad range of tasks.

A team member's project role may last the entire length of the project, or it may change with each phase of the project. In either case, the specific roles and responsibilities should be clearly defined with relevant timelines. The level of responsibility, authority, decision-making, and ownership for each team member should also be clearly outlined. These can be described in broad terms; however, you must ensure that team members understand the scope of their responsibilities. When in doubt, of course, they should always consult with the project manager to ask for direction.

The following sections should be included in the Staffing Plan:

- General Information
- Skills Assessment
- Staffing Profile
- Organization Chart
- Outside Resource Profile
- Project Roles and Responsibilities

General Information

This section will contain the name of the project, the client, the project manager, and the project start and end dates.

Skills Assessment

In this section, you will describe the types of personnel/project roles required to complete the project milestones from Planning through Post-Deployment. Include the timeline and duration, title, source, project role, and skill level. See the example in Figure 5.1.

Staffing Profile

This section will show the people resources required for the project, including required hours per week and duration of tenure. See Figure 5.2.

Milestone/Objective	Title	Source	#	Skill Level /Special Requirements
Milestone # 1	Project Manager	Internal		Experienced PM with at least 10 years experience with system integration
	Technical Lead	Internal	1	6-8 years of experience in a functional/technical leadership role. Experience with leading, planning, design, and implementation activities.
	Business Analyst	Internal	1	Knowledge of Application Development, business analysis, data modeling,
Milestone #2	User Interface Designer	Internal		Requires the ability to critically review user interface designs from a user-centered design perspective. Possesses thorough experience and understanding of research practices and HCI/User-Centered design principles and applies them in innovative ways. HTML, Java

Figure 5.1: Skills assessment.

Calendar (month or quarter)	Title (personnel category)	Resource Name	Level of Commitment (utilization rate)
Period #1	Project Manager	Daryl Johnson	1 – Full time
	Technical Lead	David Moss	1 – Quarter time
	Business Analyst	Susan Chen	1 – Half time
Period #2	Project Manager	Daryl Johnson	1 – Full time
	UI Designer	Matsu Liu	1 – Full time
	QA Engineer	Mark Terry	1 – Half time
	Software Engineer	Roger Brady	4 – Full time

Figure 5.2: Staffing profile.

Organizational Chart

The organizational chart produced for the Project Definition should be updated to include individual names of project team members. See Figure 5.3.

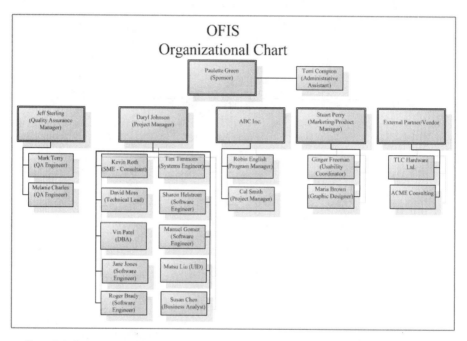

Figure 5.3: Organizational chart.

Outside Resource Profile

This section details information on client and vendor representatives and consultants or contractors assigned to the project. See Figure 5.4.

Calendar (month or quarter)	Title (personnel category)	Resource Name	Company	Level of Commitment (utilization rate)
May-July	Project Manager			1 – Full time
	Technical Lead			1 – Quarter time
August - October	Project Manager			1 – Full time
	Quality Assurance			1 – Half time

Figure 5.4: Outside resource profile.

Project Roles and Responsibilities

Here, the roles and responsibilities for each team member, client representative, and vendor representative are described in detail. It is important that this section be very clearly defined and understandable to everyone on the project team. The chart in Figure 5.5 shows some example project roles and responsibilities for technology project personnel.

Resource Name	Title	Project Role	Responsibilities
Paulette Green	Project Sponsor	Has ultimate responsibility and accountability for the project.	Provides overall strategic direction, assists project management and business management with issues when necessary. Is usually in a support role (not a decision making role). Liaises with senior level management on executive level decisions.
ABC Corporation	Client Role	Is the outside company or internal group that the product or service is being developed for. The client is the person paying for the project.	Provides requirements for the project. Attends planning meetings and client sign off meetings. Is available to answer questions and clarify requirements. Pays for the product or service. Has specific contractual obligations. For example the client may have agreed to be responsible for some on site testing of the product or they may be responsible for supplying hardware that the product will be installed on.

Figure 5.5: Project roles and responsibilities.

Development Environment

This document describes the development environments used by the engineering and development team(s), the client (if applicable), and the vendors and consultants. It describes the platform, the operating system and version, the development tools (editors, compilers, and debuggers), design tools, unit test tools, and any other special equipment or tools. This information is necessary to ensure a consistent environment. The Development Environment document will include the following sections for each development environment being used:

- Platform
- Operating System (and Version)
- Development Tools (editors, compilers, debuggers)
- Design Tools
- Unit Test Tools
- Other Equipment or Tools

High-Level Schedule

The high-level schedule shows detailed task assignments through the design phase of the project and high-level task assignments for development through deployment. The high-level schedule can either consist of a list of assignments and resources in the Project Plan document, or it can be created using a project scheduling software, such as Microsoft Project. After the design phase is complete, the full project schedule will be developed with detailed and accurate assignments through project completion.

Deliverables and Milestones

All projects have *deliverables*, and it is vital to the success of the project that everyone on the project team understands what each of the deliverables is and who is responsible for them. The deliverables encompass a lot more than the delivery of the final product, though, of course, that is the most important deliverable of all. The deliverables define what each group is responsible for outputting (delivering) during the course of the project and when those deliverables are due. As the project proceeds through each phase of the Life Cycle, the project manager is responsible for managing the completion and hand-off of specific deliverables as well as the receiving of deliverables from the client, vendors, and internal departments. The client will have responsibility for some deliverables, as will any outside vendors working on the project. Those deliverables may be documents, information, hardware, or software that is required for the successful implementation of the project. Pretty much every company, department, and individual will have responsibility for deliverables during the project Life Cycle. There will be thousands of deliverables during the course of the project, but the critical deliverables must be identified, documented, and understood by the project team. Many of the documented deliverables will also be identified as project milestones. Milestones do not necessarily have deliverables associated with them. The successful outcome of the project is dependant upon the milestones being met and deliverables being delivered on time and with high quality.

Each major deliverable will be documented and will contain the following information:

- What specifically is to be delivered
- What the dependencies are
- Who is responsible for delivering it
- Who the receiver is
- The delivery method
- The delivery location
- The delivery date (and time, if relevant)
- What the receiver needs to do to prepare for the deliverable

Most of these are self explanatory. However, the last of these items warrants some further explanation to ensure it is fully understood. Here is an example of "What the receiver needs to do to prepare for the delivery." Let us say that the vendor, TLC

Hardware, has a deliverable to supply three servers to the project development team by August 12th for production-like testing. The development team will need a location where the servers can be set up and installed. The team will need an engineer scheduled to do the set up and installation of the server and will need to ensure that adequate space, ventilation, power, and network is availabile for the servers. If the vendor delivers the hardware and the development team is not prepared for it, then the deliverable will be useless to them.

Deliverables are not always tangible items. A deliverable can be information. For example, the client may have a deliverable to make a decision on a specific user requirement. Understanding each deliverable, and what its importance is to the project, is essential to a smoothly running and well-organized project.

Milestones, on the other hand, may or may not have deliverables associated with them. Milestones mark major achievements and checkpoints throughout the duration of the project.

Some example milestones:

- Project Plan Document finalized and approved
- Planning phase complete
- Database integration with order management front end complete
- First successful lab test complete

Functional Requirements

This document should describe the intended behavior of the system, including the tasks, services, or functions that the system is required to perform. It should clearly describe anything that clearly differentiates the product from other similar products.

The Functional Requirements document should contain the following sections:

- Features
- Performance
- Speed
- Ease of Use
- Use Case
  - Define different types of users
  - Interaction with product
  - Workflow diagrams
  - Alternative workflows
- Usability
  - User interface
  - Look and feel

- Legal Requirements
  - Regulatory requirements
  - Security
  - Privacy
- Decision Support Requirements
  - Data requirements
  - User requirements
  - User Interface
- Access requirements
  - Remote (VPN, Internet, etc.)
  - Local
- Backup Requirements

Technical Requirements

Technical requirements are also called "nonfunctional requirements." The Technical Requirements document should define all requirements necessary for technical designs and specifications to be developed.

The Technical Requirements document should contain the following information:

- Network Requirements
  - Hardware
  - Software
  - Server requirements
  - Hardware
  - Software
- Workstation Requirements
  - Hardware
  - Software
- Database Requirements
  - Hardware
  - Software
- Error handling
- Error logging, reporting, monitoring
- Redundancy
- Capacity
- Reliability
- Interoperability
- Scalability
- Stability
- Extensibility
- Flexibility

- Portability
  - Security
  - Authentication
  - Monitoring
- Decision Support
  - Logging
  - Data collection
  - Data storage (database)
  - Reporting mechanism
- Systems Monitoring
- Monitoring mechanism
- Reporting and alert system
- Backup technical requirements

Decision Support System (DSS) Plan

Decision Support Systems are computer-based information systems that are used by companies to assist them in decision-making. These systems are used frequently by marketing and product management groups to collect demographic and usage data about the end users of the products. Using database-logging techniques, it is possible for companies to collect and store huge amounts of customer data. Many of them make good use this functionality and have databases full of lots of useful and insightful information. At least, it would be useful and insightful if they had a strategy for mining and analyzing the data. Collecting the data is the easy part. Knowing what to do with them and how to mine them can be a lot more challenging.

Every company needs a Decision Support System strategy. The strategy to collect every single piece of data is not necessarily a good way to go, though many companies opt to go this route. If you have an Internet product, every single time you log some data, you use up system resources to do so. You are using up CPU capacity on the Web site's host server every single time you log data. After you collect the data, you need to store them somewhere. That generally means moving them from the server that it originates on to a database somewhere in the system. Moving your data can use up network bandwidth. If you are logging a lot of data for each user, by the time you multiply the system overhead per user by the number of concurrent users, you could be severely im-pacting the performance of your system. To your users, this can mean a significant slow-down in the responsiveness of your Web site. Unfortunately, many companies have used the "log everything" approach, have ended up with vast amounts of data locked away in various disparate systems around the company, and have no strategy or process for using it. The volume of data becomes overwhelming very quickly, and every-one is scared of trying to figure out what to do with it.

The key to successful Decision Support System planning is applying a systematic approach to data logging, data mining, and knowledge management. The users of the decision support data need to define the requirements for the data before any data collection takes place. These requirements serve as the basis for a Decision Support System plan. Decision Support data can be sampled, or they can be collected for each user. If they are sampled, what is the sample rate? Does the analyst or statistician agree that the sample rate is going to give accurate results? Does the DSS plan fall within the budget range allocated for it? The more data you need, the more it is going to cost you to get them. Data collection, storage, and retrieval all cost money. Data mining is not as easy as it might sound. It entails using the data requirements to write reports against a database, run the reports at regular intervals (as defined by the client), design a user interface for the reports, analyze the data, and then decide what to do with them. The analysis of Decision Support data sometimes requires the services of a trained and qualified statistician. We touch on Decision Support in this book but we could write a whole book, or perhaps even a series of books, about it.

Suffice to say that you need a plan for the collection, storage, and retrieval of the data, and it needs to have been accounted for in the budget. A typical Decision Support Plan will contain the following sections.

- Demographic Information Required
- Accuracy of Data
- Data Collection Strategy
- Data Storage Requirements
- Data Mining Tools
- Reports and Analysis
- Network and Hardware Requirements
- Backup Requirements
- Roles and Responsibilities
- Privacy Policy

Quality Assurance Plan

The *Quality Assurance Plan* will be provided by the quality assurance manager. It will include a description of the testing methods to be employed for this project. It will identify the percentage of code coverage expected from testing and the types of testing that will be performed. It will also include a high-level schedule. The following sections will be included, or the separate documents referenced, in the Quality Assurance Plan:

- Introduction
  - Project Overview
  - Project Scope
  - Testing
  - Completion Criteria
  - Schedule

- Test Matrix
  - QA methodologies
  - Test summary report
- Test Plan
  - Activities
  - Resources
- Traceability Matrix
- Test Cases
- Test Scripts
- Defect Reports
- Quality Risk Assessment
- Performance and Stability Test Plan

Any additional testing, such as performance or security testing, will also be detailed or the relevant documents referenced in this section.

Communication Plan

Communication is an important success factor in any project. To ensure that the communication is appropriate, timely, and effective, it is good practice to have a Communication Plan tailored specifically for each project.

Knowing when to communicate, what to communicate, and to whom should be clearly defined in a detailed and thorough Communication Plan. Depending on the complexity of the project, a Communication Plan can range from a simple document consisting of one or two pages to a more comprehensive documentation containing detailed guidelines on each type of information and action. The plan is designed to identify all formal communications that will occur throughout the Life Cycle of the project and to define the process for how they should occur. The plan should also include general guidelines for managing informal communication. The Communication Plan can be used in conjunction with the status reporting process contained in the Project Approach.

The Communication Plan will contain the following:

- List of Steering Committee and Stakeholder Group Members
- Formal Communication Schedule and Plan
- Informal Communication Plan
- Communication Rules

List of Steering Committee and Stakeholder Groups and Members

List the steering committee and all stakeholder groups, including a description of the purpose of each group and a list of the members. See the example in Figure 5.6.

Stakeholder Group Name	Description	Members
Steering Committee	Decision Makers, Approvers and Client for the project	Paulette Green. Daryl Johnson, Cal Smith, Stuart Perry, Jeff Sterling
XYZ Internal Development Team	Engineering Team	Daryl Johnson, Kevin Roth, David Moss, Vin Patel, Jane Jones, Roger Brady, Tim Timmons, Sharon Helstrom, Manuel Gomez, Matsu Liu, Susan Chen, Maria Brown

Figure 5.6: Stakeholder groups.

Formal Communication Schedule and Plan

The formal communication schedule and plan will contain the following information and may be presented as text or as a table (see Figure 5.7):

- Communication—This is a brief and descriptive title of the communication.

- Content—Give a brief overview of the type of information to be communicated.

- Objective—What does the communication need to achieve? What is the desired result?

- Owner—Who is responsible for creating and delivering the information to the audience?

- Audience—Define the target audience. Here you can name the stakeholder group or groups that need to receive this particular information or attend this particular meeting.

- Communication method—How will the information be communicated? For example, meeting, video conference, e-mail, memo, presentation, reports, and so on.

- Frequency or Date—How often will the communication occur? For one-time communications, what is the date for the communication?

Communication	Content	Objective	Owner	Audience	Method	Frequency / Date
Client status meeting	Milestone and deliverable status updates. Schedule and budget status. Communicate and update on any important issues	To ensure that steering committee are aware of status on key milestones and issues	Daryl Johnson	Steering Committee	Meeting - with powerpoint presentation	Monthly
Client status meeting minutes	Minutes of status meeting - including presentation	To ensure that team members are aware of status, issues and concerns	Daryl Johnson	Steering Committee, Internal Development Team	Email	Monthly within 2 days of status meeting

Figure 5.7: Formal communication schedule and plan.

Informal Communication Plan

The informal communication plan should contain the following information:

- Issue
- Content
- Objective
- Owner (escalate to)
- Audience
- Communication Method
- Timeline

This information can be displayed in a table, as shown in Figure 5.8.

Issue	Description	Action	Owner (escalate to)	Audience	Method	Timeline
Cannot meet scheduled deliverable	Any technical or non-technical issue that will impact a deliverable to the client	Escalate to project manager who will try to resolve issue. If cannot be resolved, ensure that all affected stakeholders are aware of problem	Escalate to: Daryl Johnson	Steering Committee, other impacted groups	Initial email or phone call (if late discovery) followed up with Meeting	Within one week of due date or asap if discovered with less than one week notice
Security problem	Critical security issue	Escalate to Project Manger who will inform security team	Daryl Johnson	Security Team	Phone call or meeting - must not discuss security or privacy	Within 2 hours

Figure 5.8: Informal communication plan.

Communication Rules

Here you should list any rules, either company or regulatory, that exist at your company, the client company, or the vendor's company on what and how things can be communicated. Many companies prohibit any communications regarding security or privacy via e-mail. Many companies also prohibit the distribution of confidential documents via e-mail—for example, Technical and User Interface Design documents.

Deployment Plan

This document will identify the steps required to deploy or hand-off the product to the client. It will include roles and responsibilities for the deployment of the product, the location the project will be deployed from and to, timelines, and a schedule of events.

- Introduction
  - General information
- Network Deployment
  - Network setup
  - Network test
- Server Deployment
  - Directory structure
  - Deployment steps
- Workstation Deployment
  - Directory structure
  - Deployment steps
- Database Deployment
  - Directory structure
  - Deployment steps
- Database Access
- Data Conversion
- Security
- For Software Project
  - CD mastering and duplication
  - Artwork and packaging
  - Printing
  - Assembly
  - Distribution
  - Shipping
- Deployment Schedule of Events and Timelines
- Roles and Responsibilities
- Verification and Test
- Acceptance Criteria
- Project Hand-Off

Operations Plan

The *Operations Plan* is also referred to as the "Post-Deployment plan." It consists of the following series of documents:

- Operations Document
- System Administrator Guide
- User Guide
- Technical Support Guide
- Customer Support Guide
- Release Notes

Training Plan

The *Training Plan* will define the training needs and the training schedule for all project-related training. This applies to user and technical training for project products, services, or processes. The Training Plan will include the following sections:

- Introduction
  - General information
- Purpose and Goal
- Objectives
- Scope
- Assumptions
- Training Requirements
- Training Strategy
  - Training resources
  - Hardware environment to be used
  - Software environment to be used
- Dependencies, Constraints, and Limitations
- Types of Training Manuals Required and Number of Each
- Course Description (for each course define):
  - Course outline
  - Target audience
  - Goals and objectives
  - Content
  - Learning methods and activities
  - Attendee prerequisites
  - Training resources
  - Training environment
  - Training materials
  - Training evaluation
  - Certification

- Constraints and Risks
- Roles and Responsibilities
- Training Schedule
- Training Log

Risk Management Plan

The *Risk Management Plan* describes how risks will be identified, evaluated, analyzed, prioritized, and managed.

The Risk Identification and Evaluation Process

- Identify—This is the first step in the risk management process. Identify exactly what the risk is, how it will manifest itself, and where it will occur.

- Evaluate—Evaluate the potential risk to determine its level of criticality to the project and the likelihood of it happening. Potential risks with low criticality or low probability should be tracked as *issues* and not risks. They should be reevaluated as risks if more information becomes available or if the status of the problem changes.

- Analyze—Using the risk evaluation, determine how high on the priority list it should be. Separate risks from issues, but continue to track both.

- Risk Action Plan—Specify what steps need to be taken to reduce or control the risk and the timeline in which these actions need to occur.

Prioritization of Risks

You will need a process for comparing risks to one another and evaluating the importance of each. For example, if the definition of "critical" has resulted in hundreds of critical risks, you need an additional level of prioritization to determine which are the most critical, or you need to reevaluate the feasibility of the project based on the risk level. The higher the risk level, the less likely the project will be completed successfully.

Management of Risks

The easiest and most common way to manage risks is via a *Risk Log*. The Risk Log is explained in detail in Chapter 10. See Figure 5.9 for an example of a risk log. Risks should be managed on an ongoing basis, and a standard reporting process should exist for updating the steering committee and team members on the status of risks. It is typical for status updates to be given only on the highest-priority and most critical risks. The steering committee does not want to sit through a four-hour meeting while you drone on about every single risk (or issue) that has been identified for your project and provide a synopsis of the action taken for each and every one of them. They would probably last about 20 minutes before all falling asleep!

No	Description	Originator	Date Found	Assigned To	Criticality	Probability	Priority	Action Plan	Status	Date Resolved
	Risk Log					**OFIS**				
1	Unexpected technical problems	David Moss	04-Apr	David Moss	High	High	High	Evaluate the technical problem and make appropriate suggestions for workarounds.	Open	
2	Tim Timmons is out ill and expected to be out for 2 weeks	Daryl Johnson	10-Apr	Daryl Johnson	Medium	High	Medium	New team member to continue with the work.	Closed	20-May
3	Bug in code	Daryl Johnson	13-May	David Moss	Medium	Medium	Medium	Fix bug in code	Closed	21-May
4	Main graphic grainy	Paulette Green	18-May	Matsu Liu	Low	Low	Low	Graphic needs to be redesigned with more clarity	Open	

Figure 5.9: Risk Log.

Measurement Plan

The Measurement Plan defines how the results of the project will be measured and by whom. It is vitally important that you have identified what the expected results are and how you plan to measure them. For example, if the client is looking for a 20% reduction in customer support phone calls, how will they measure that? Does the development team need to add reporting functionality to the system? Do they need to supply the client with instructions for a DBA on how to write queries or run reports? You may find more items that need to be added to the Technical or Functional Requirements documents after completing the analysis of how to measure results. See Figure 5.10 for some sample items in the Measurement Plan.

Measurement	Reason	Method	Frequency	Expected Results	Person Responsible
Customer support call volume	To determine call volume per hour and per day	Using automated call system tracking. Results logged to SQL database. Run reports weekly and analyze daily, weekly & monthly results	Hourly and Daily. Start 4 weeks prior to launch and continue indefinitely	Reduction in calls (20%) after deployment	Customer Support Manager
Customer support call length	To determine average call length per hour and per day	Using automated call system tracking. Results logged to SQL database. Run reports weekly and analyze daily, weekly & monthly results	Hourly and Daily. Start 4 weeks prior to launch and continue indefinitely	Reduction in average call length time of 40%.	Customer Support Manager

Figure 5.10: Measurement Plan example entries.

Client Acceptance Criteria

List here the criteria, as specified by the client, that the project or product must meet to make it acceptable as "complete" and "meets requirements" by the client.

Project Plan Approval

This section should document the approval process and authorized signatories for the Project Plan document.

Project Approach

The *Project Approach* is also referred to as the "project methodology" or the "project process." It describes all the processes and procedures to be used during the project Life Cycle to accomplish the successful development and completion of the project. The Project Approach includes internal processes and procedures as well as external processes and procedures. There may also be some additional information that needs to be documented that is unique to this particular project. There may be some areas of the standard project processes that are not relevant to this project. These will be clearly identified in the Project Approach.

It is not common for the Project Approach documents to be changed or updated during the Life Cycle of the project. If changes to the Project Approach are made during the life of the project, it is vitally important that all team members who are affected by the process changes are aware of those changes. Process changes must be adopted by everyone on the team, and sending them out as updated documents in e-mail is not the way to communicate them. If the change impacts the whole team, an all-hands meeting should be called to discuss them. If the changes affect only the development team, such as the internal build process, a meeting should be called that includes the development and quality assurance teams. The Documentation Process section of the Project Approach will clearly identify the process for updating, tracking, and communicating changes to project documentation.

It is possible to combine some or all of the Project Approach documents into one document if required. This may make it simpler to track documentation for smaller and less-complex projects.

The Project Approach contains the following sections (the italicized items are separate documents referenced in the Project Approach):

- Project Life Cycle
- *Change Control Process*
- *Technical Processes*
- *Organizational Processes*
- *Client Processes*
- *Vendor Processes*

- *Defect Tracking Process*
- *Decision Support Process*
- Status Reporting Process
- *Monitoring and Reporting Process*
- Special Processes or Considerations
- *Escalation Processes and Procedures*
- Project Documentation Process

Project Life Cycle

The project Life Cycle describes the six distinct phases in the life of the project. In this section of the Project Approach, the Life Cycle will be described exactly as it pertains to this particular project. The standard Life Cycle process is described in detail in Chapter 2.

The standard project Life Cycle comprises the following six phases:

- Planning
- Design
- Development
- Integration (including testing)
- Deployment
- Post-Deployment

Change Control Process

Successful change control requires a commitment to sound project management methodologies and the tools to implement those methodologies. Having a well-structured change control process to request and document changes to the project is essential. Your process should be designed to handle all changes no matter how big or small, including the addition or removal of features or functionality, major specification changes for all or a piece of a system or product, and changes to milestones or other delivery dates. The process must include defining and analyzing the impact of proposed changes on the project resources, timeline, and budget. The goal of the change control process is to ensure that the impact of any change is well understood, carefully considered, and consciously approved before it is executed. See Figure 5.11 for the change control process workflow.

Everyone involved with the project, including stakeholders, client, and contractors, should have access to the Change Request Form and the Change Control Process documentation so that they can submit requests. Remember, any change that will affect the project resources, timeline, cost, or quality must go through a change control process. A sample Change Request Form is included on the CD-ROM that accompanies this book.

There are a number of different reasons that change is requested. For example:

- The client requests additions, deletions, or changes to one or more features or specifications.

- Internal technical or business issues require changes to be made to the project.·

- Business requirements or strategies change.

- Changes to support performance or stability improvements for the product are necessary.

The Change Control Process document identifies who "owns" the change control process. It needs to clearly define the different kinds of changes and at what point in the project Life Cycle those changes need to go through the formal change control process. For example, bug fixes on interim releases will likely be approved and assigned to team members by the project manager without the need to go through a formal change control process for each one. As the project gets close to completion, after the feature complete or code complete date for instance, this process may change, and bug fix requests may need to go through the change control process to ensure that only critical fixes are being approved. Without this control, the project will never be ready for release to the client. The person(s) who is responsible for receiving the change requests needs to be identified along with the members of the change control board, if one is being formed to consider change requests.

The change control board comprises representatives of the various groups impacted by changes. Typically, this would include the project manager(s), the quality assurance manager, and the program manager(s). It is good to keep the team as small as you can, or you will never make any decisions. The change control process owner is usually the project manager but, in some larger companies, this process is managed and facilitated by a separate group. The frequency of the meetings should be defined in the Change Control Process document. These meetings are usually held once a week or once a month. The frequency may change depending on the Life Cycle phase of the project. There also needs to be a process for dealing with critical issues that arise that cannot wait until the next change control meeting.

The process owner will meet with the change control board on the regular schedule to review the change requests and to make decisions on next steps. The change control process is split into two rounds. In round one, the change control board decides whether to approve the request for further analysis or whether to reject or defer it. After this first round of change control, the change requester must be notified about whether their request was approved to go through to round two or whether it was denied or deferred. The requester should have the opportunity to appeal a denial or a deferral decision, especially if it is problem that will need a work around if the requested change is not implemented.

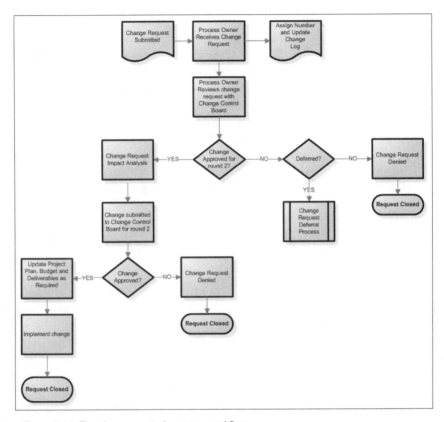

Figure 5.11: The change control process workflow

The Change Control Process document needs to define the process for deferred changes. The requester needs to be aware of what "deferred" means for this request. Often, deferred requests are reevaluated for inclusion in a subsequent release. Some examples of why changes may be deferred rather than approved or denied include:

- The change may not have been considered critical enough to be included in the current release.
- The impact of the change may have been considered too risky at this stage of the project.
- The change could be more suited to a subsequent releas,e where new features will increase the need for it.
- The cost to the client may be rather high, and they do not have the budget for it at this time.
- The change could cause schedule slippage that is unacceptable, so it is being considered for a point release.

There are many reasons for deferring a change. A clear "yes" or "no" is not always possible. If a change is approved in round one, the project manager will work with the project team to complete an impact analysis. This analysis will identify both the positive and the negative impacts that this change will have on the various stakeholder groups, including the project timeline, cost, and quality. Once the impact analysis is complete, the project manager will once again present the change request, with all supporting documentation, to the change control board for a round two change control decision. The additional information presented will enable the change control board to make an informed decision on whether to approve, defer, or deny the request. As with round one, the requester may appeal any denied or deferred request. If the request is approved in round two, the project manager needs to:

- Incorporate the change into the project work plan and schedule.

- Make any necessary changes to the resources and schedule.

- Review the change with the team members to ensure that it is properly understood.

Change requests are managed and processed using the change request form. The change request form is described in detail in Chapter 10.

As change requests start coming at you left and right, you may feel overwhelmed and worried about keeping track of everything. It is important to ensure that your change control process is followed and that you have a watertight process for tracking all change requests that come in. All requests need to be logged whether or not they are approved. All related documentation needs to be kept for all change requests along with the actions taken, decisions, and final resolution on the change request. This log should be kept in a single location and will contain all the data on all the changes received during the Life Cycle of the project. It must be simple to use and maintain.

The log should list each change request by number, a brief description of the change request, date received, date reviewed, decision, status, and actions required. The log should also reference all related documents. The change log then can be used to track the various changes to the project requirements. By using an Intranet system that all team members can log into, they will be able to verify what changes were approved, denied, and deferred and who is responsible for the changes.

It's human nature to resist change. As creatures of habit, we prefer the security of familiar surroundings and often don't react well to changes in our environment, even when the changes are positive. This holds true for our workplaces and the security and identity that a familiar job provides. Changes in the work environment trigger fears and apprehensions that are deeply rooted in the human psyche. Insufficient information about the impulse for a change and its sought-after benefits is likely to cause considerable distress among those affected by the change.

Technical Processes

This document includes all the technical processes that will be used during the project Life Cycle. Some examples are:

- The Build Process
- Source Control
- Versioning
- Configuration Management

Build Process

The process for building the product (for software development projects) should be defined here. Some teams build the product daily and others build weekly, monthly, or on a set build schedule. An example of some of the information contained in the build process is as follows:

- Build Schedule
- Time Builds are Kicked Off
- Approximate Completion Time
- Who Kicks Off the Build (if it is not automated)
- Who Is Responsible for Ensuring the Build is Done
- Who Is Responsible for fixing Problems that "Break" the Build
- Which Builds are Given to QA for Testing

Source Control

No self-respecting project manager would preside over a project that has no *source control*. It is a recipe for disaster. Source control is used for many reasons. First, it prevents engineers from stepping on each other's toes. It prevents more than one person from making changes to the same piece of code at the same time by using a process of checking out and checking in code before and after it is worked on. Source control also acts a rollback mechanism. If code is checked in and subsequently breaks a build, the code can be rolled back to the last working version. In fact, it can be rolled (or reviewed) back to any saved version. This is useful if previously deleted code now needs to be added back or if a feature that was added earlier needs to be removed.
It also allows engineers to experiment locally with the code without affecting the last saved version. A developer can see at a glance all the changes that he has made since the last check-in or between two check-ins of code. This is really useful for identifying where bugs were introduced into the product. The source control acts as a backup for the code because there are copies of all versions stored on the source control server. It

allows a developer to work on more than one development system and always have access to the latest copy of the code.

The process should define the source code used, the process for checking in and checking out code, who is responsible for the source code system, and procedures for dealing with problems that require the source code to be restored or rebuilt.

Versioning

Versioning is used for component-based systems. Versioning "stamps" a build with a numeric code (a version number and date), and any additions or changes to that build need to be created with the next numerical version. The versioning tracks what version of each component in the source code has been used for a particular build and timestamps the build. This helps track who is using which version, both during development and out in the field once the product has been released. It avoids confusion related to defect tracking because all defects can be tracked to a build or release version. It will be clear whether a defect has been reported on an older release of the code that may have been fixed in a later version. Versioning is good housekeeping. When working with large, complex code bases, you need as much process control of your code as is feasible so that you can track down and fix issues as quickly and efficiently as possible.

The process should define the versioning method and who is responsible for tracking the current version.

Configuration Management (CM)

Configuration management makes use of source control and versioning and is a way to control how a full product is built and released. For example, there may be three different levels of the same product, with each product containing some of the same and some different feature sets. Basic, intermediate, and advanced could be levels, for instance. On the other hand, perhaps a product has different versions based on the type of user. Maybe there is a different version for different industries, such as pharmaceutical, construction, and automotive. If you have an Internet product, it may be updated every day, week, or month, and it is vital that all new components be updated on schedule. Configuration management is a way to control which components and features are included in each build of the product. It is especially useful if there are multiple development teams working on a project. The configuration management system will always have the latest (verified and tested) copy of each component from each development team. It avoids confusion over which copy of which code should be used and ensures that only fully tested and approved code is included in a product release.

The configuration management process should be defined: who owns it, who uses it, and what the process is for using the CM system for building the final products.

Organizational Processes

These processes refer to any nontechnical internal processes used by the development team. They could include time-tracking processes, the internal build and release process (how a build is handed off to QA, for instance), the process for requesting time off, and the process for getting technical information from the engineering team (via the project manager for instance, or during weekly meetings). There could be any number of important processes used by the team in relation to the project; these need to be documented and communicated to the rest of the project team.

Client Processes

Any processes that are used by the client company or the client team assigned to the project should be described here, or the relevant document should be referenced. It is important that the various teams and companies involved in the project both use and understand the processes and procedures in place for each group.

Vendor Processes

Any processes that are used by the vendor companies or the vendor representatives assigned to the project should be described here, or the relevant document should be referenced. It is important that the various teams and companies involved in the project both use and understand the processes and procedures in place for each group.

Defect Tracking Process

It is critical to the success of a project that there is a standard procedure for tracking, evaluating, and monitoring bugs. The project manager and the quality assurance manager will need to work closely together to ensure that the process is clearly defined and followed by all team members. Failure to follow the process can lead to disaster. For instance, if an engineer finds a bug in the code and decides to just go ahead and fix it because it will only take about half an hour to do so, what impact might this have on the product? The project manager should be the person who decides what bugs should be fixed and what bugs should be deferred or not fixed at all. The engineer should not be making that decision.

The quality assurance team does not know that the bug fix is in the code, so they will not test it. It is possible that the bug fix has broken something else in the code, and that code may not have been tested either because there was no indication that anything had changed that could possibly have affected that particular area of the code. Months later, a problem may be found with one of the features that was caused by this very same bug fix, but five or six builds have been done since then and hundreds of other things have changed. It could take weeks or months for someone to figure out what changed and caused the problem. They may be reading through developer release notes and finding nothing until finally they have to start stepping through the code line by line (a long and arduous task). When the culprit is eventually found, it is discovered that a lot of code has been written on top of that code, so it all has to be re-written to support a new bug fix to remedy the initial bug fix. We could go on, but we are sure you get the idea. A small fix can turn into a huge problem if a standard process is not followed. Most companies use standard bug tracking tools and will have a process for approving, assigning, resolving, and closing bug reports. The defect tracking and resolution process is often similar to the change control process, though it is managed at the development team level.

The Defect Tracking Process document should include the following sections:

- Definition of Defect
  - Defect bug
  - Enhancement
  - New feature
- Who Can Submit Defects
  - How to complete a defect report
- Defect Process
- How to Reopen a Defect Report If the Defect Is Not Fixed
- How to Appeal a Decision to Defer or Close a Defect Report
- Roles and Responsibilities

Decision Support System (DSS) Process

The department that owns and manages the DSS data should use the *Decision Support Plan* to design a process for managing and analyzing the DSS data. The owner may be a marketing department, a statistics group, or the client. If the owner is the client, you do not need to take responsibility for defining this process and can mark this section "N/A." However, you will need to ensure that you have a detailed DSS Plan included in the Project Plan because the client will be unable to collect any DSS data without your team implementing the functionality that enables them to do so.

Status Reporting Process

There are different kinds of status reports. One type of status report is the one that you give to your clients and stakeholders. This *Status Communication* contains information about the high-level milestones, risk factors, and budgets. These Status Communications are often combined with formal Project Review meetings. Then there is the *Status Report*, which you need to share with your development team. They need to know more of the details of what is happening in each phase of development. They need to be aware of dependencies and whether someone else's schedule issues are going to affect their ability to get their own work completed on time. This status is typically given at a weekly team status meeting. Your team members need to give you regular Status Reports on how they are doing with their scheduled tasks so that you can manage your project schedule. The information in these Status Reports is used together with budgeting and risk factor analyses to compile the Status Communications and Project Review Presentations for your stakeholders.

Written Status Reports are excellent checkpoints for development team members. They require that the team members review their assignments, evaluate their own progress, and submit a formal progress report on a regular basis. Status Reports are generally required on a weekly basis. The Status Report often includes a time-tracking report, where each team member documents how much time was spent on each task. This information can be used for billing, where the client is billed for development time hourly rather than being billed a set price for the whole project. The time tracking is also used for the company to track how much time was actually spent on project work and how much time was spent on other organizational or run-the-business tasks.

Formal project reviews are great opportunities for sharing high-level status about the project. These are the meetings that are scheduled every month or so between the project manager and specific stakeholder groups. These meetings are scheduled in advance to occur at regular intervals in accordance with the communication plan. The content of these meetings includes high-level status on the major project milestones, overview of any critical issues that have arisen, and updates on identified project risks. These meetings are generally run by the project manager and include a formal PowerPoint presentation and a detailed agenda.

Designing a Status Reporting System

When designing and implementing a status reporting system, you need to first identify the data outputs required. Once you have determined what those are, you can identify the data inputs required to produce those outputs. The reporting frequency and methods also need to be determined.

Review the communication plan and discuss the reporting system with your sponsor and other project stakeholders, to determine what *data outputs*, or information, your stakeholders are going to need from you during the course of the project. Make sure that you can answer the following questions:

- What information have the client and stakeholders asked for?

- How much detail have they requested?

- What do they want to see, how frequently do they want to see it, and how do they want it delivered?

- Do they want a narrative style report (word document), or do they want a visual presentation (graphs, PowerPoint)?

You also need to identify what outputs you need for your team members. They need to be aware of the status of the project at a more granular level than the stakeholders. They need to be aware of technical issues and major technical decisions being made by team members during the course of the project. Discuss this with your team to ensure that you have not missed anything.

Finally, you need to determine what inputs you, the project manager, need to manage the schedule, the team, the project, and the status-reporting process.

Once you have determined specifically what needs to be included in the various status reports, you can start designing a flexible and multipurpose reporting system for your project team. You most definitely do not want to implement three different systems to satisfy three different needs. You should be able to have one standard set of inputs that can be used to produce different sets of outputs. You can liken this process to designing a database. You would not have one database for each group of people that needed to get data out of it. You would have one central database where all the data is stored and that has the ability to run different reports for different groups.

Monitoring and Reporting

Monitoring and reporting is the management of the error logging and reporting system that the development team builds into the product for use by the operations team for monitoring and maintaining the system. The network and system administration teams will also log system errors. It is usually a common, shared monitoring and reporting system. This document defines the process for collecting, categorizing, reporting, and sending alerts for errors on the system.

Errors are usually categorized according to severity and frequency. The process needs to define the action that is required based on the severity and frequency of the error. The process should also identify who is responsible for managing each type of problem and the timeline in which it should be dealt with. This process is most often handed off to the client at the conclusion of the project, or it is created by the client for its own use.

Special Processes or Considerations

Any special processes or considerations not covered in other sections should be covered here.

Escalation Procedures

It is critical to define and document *Escalation Procedures* as early as possible in the Life Cycle of your project. There are two main reasons problems should be escalated. The most important is when a critical problem is encountered that could severely impact the ability of you and your team to complete the project on time, within budget, and with high quality. The second reason is when someone does not respond to a question in an appropriate amount of time or when a response is unacceptable or inadequate. In this situation the escalation is usually to speak to one's manager, who will escalate to that person's manager. The Escalation Procedures for critical, technical, or business issues are not always as straightforward and need to be documented precisely. The kick-off meeting is the ideal time to have these prepared, reviewed, and finalized. The project manager owns the Escalation Procedures, and it is the responsibility of the project manager to ensure that they are followed. Clearly defining both the escalation path (see Figure 5.12) and the notification process (Figure 5.13) will ensure that there is no confusion about what to do if the project runs into problems.

Level	Definition	Expected Response	Call Intervals
Priority 1	Critical Security Issue	Security Team take ownership of problem and implement security emergency plan. No alerts or discussion of issues allowed via email. No details to be discussed outside of security team	Immediate
Priority 2	Major Impact - Impact to the Client's Business	Problem is worked on continuously until the problem is resolved.	Immediate
Priority 3	Large impact - significant inconvenience to customers where a workaround might be implemented	Work is expected to continue on a workday basis until a more permanent solution is in place.	2 hour maximum
Priority 4	Small to Minor Impact - Minor to small inconvenience	Resolution is worked into a planned project list and schedule or it can be deferred until there is time allowed in the project schedule.	24 hours maximum

Figure 5.12: Escalation path.

You may need to hold a follow up meeting to finalize the Escalation Procedures because you will need to have your Project Plan and organizational structure finalized to define who the decision-makers will be for each situation. It is important to the success of your project that all team members know who the decision-makers are and what kinds of decisions they are responsible for.

Sequence	Contact/Name	Work Phone#	Home Phone#	Mobile/Pager #	Title/Description
Priority 1	David Moss	222-222-2222	333-333-3333	444-444-4444	Technical Lead
Priority 2	Tim Timmons	222-222-2222	333-333-3333	444-444-4444	System Engineer
Priority 3	Jane Jones	222-222-2222	333-333-3333	444-444-4444	Software Engineer

Figure 5.13: Notification process.

Project Documentation Process

In this section you should define the update and communication process for each project document. (See the example in Figure 5.14.)

Document	Owner	Update OK	Authorized Updaters	Reviewers	Communication Method	Approver
Project Concept						
Initial Estimates						
Request For Quotation (RFQ)						
High Level Estimates						
Marketing Requirement Document (MRD)						
Budget						
Project Definition						
Statement of Work						
Project Plan						
Staffing Plan						
Quality Assurance Plan						
Communication Plan						
Deployment Plan						

Figure 5.14: Project documentation process.

Project Approach Approval

This section should document the approval process and authorized signatories for the Project Plan document. (See the example in Figure 5.15.)

Project Approach Approval

The project approach draft documents will be reviewed by the client and the project team within one week of completion. Changes will be incorporated and the updated documents redistributed within 3 days. All changes will be clearly marked. Any additional comments must be sent to the document owner within 3 days of the finalized document being distributed. Any unresolved issues will be managed by the project manager who will make the final decision on how the issue will be addressed. The client, sponsor and project manager must sign the project approach approval. Subsequent proposed changes to the project approach must be approved by the client, the sponsor and the project manager. The changes must be distributed to all team members and stakeholders and the changes will be clearly marked in the documents.

Client Representative:	Signature:	
	Print Name:	
	Title:	
	Date:	

Sponsor:	Signature:	
	Print Name:	
	Title:	
	Date:	

Project Manager:	Signature:	
	Print Name:	
	Title:	
	Date:	

Figure 15.5: Project approach approval.

Project Kick-Off

As soon as the project has been approved and the project manager has prepared the draft copies of the Project Plan and Project Approach documents, the project can be kicked off. The project manager will not personally create every single detail of each project document. She will work with various members of the project team and the client organization to produce the documents. The documents will be reviewed in the project kick-off meeting, at which time a lot of the blanks will be filled. The project manager will complete the Project Plan and Approach documents in as much detail as possible following the kick-off meeting. Some of the Project Plan documents will not be able to be completed until later in the project Life Cycle. Many of the documents will continue to be updated throughout the project. The Kick-Off Process Workflow Diagram is shown in Figure 6.1.

The Project Kick-Off Meeting

The kick-off meeting takes place after the project has been approved and funded. The kick-off meeting is the first time the entire project team will meet. They will gather in one room to review and finalize the plans for what the project is and how it will

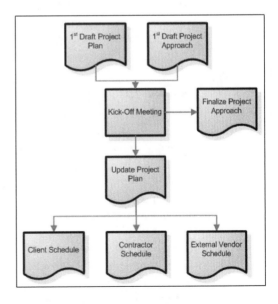

Figure 6.1: The Kick-Off Process Workflow Diagram.

be implemented. It will be the first time that you will be asking for a commitment to the project from the project team. The goal of the kick-off meeting is for each team member involved in your project to leave the meeting with a clear understanding of the project's goals and objectives and the roles and responsibilities of each team member. The kick-off meeting will include all key members of the project (i.e., product development, programmers, graphic designers, database administrators, etc.), and a client representative.

It is possible that you will not have been involved in all the meetings that happened prior to the project being approved. This is more common in larger corporations than smaller ones. Smaller companies generally have smaller project teams, fewer projects, and a much smaller number of decision-makers. This makes it much easier, and in some cases, more important for team members to be involved in a much greater proportion of the project planning. In larger corporations, if you are lucky, there may have been one or more project managers involved in the proposal and definition stage of the project. However, do not assume this will necessarily make your job any simpler. The project manager involved in the meetings may not be familiar enough with your technology, your team members, and your other commitments to have been able to effectively represent the interests of your team in those planning meetings. If you are working on a project for an outside client, you may find that a salesperson, to close the sale, has promised the world to a client and now expects you to deliver on those promises. Before you slash the tires on the salesperson's brand new sports car, or decide to go on a three-month vacation, you should first schedule your kick-off meeting. Here, you will get the opportunity to review the Project Definition with the client and to raise your concerns so that they can be addressed and incorporated into your final Project Plan.

Preparation for an Effective Kick-Off Meeting

You know the necessity of a kick-off meeting, but how do you prepare an effective presentation and agenda that will result in the highest-quality outcome in the shortest period of time? Preparation for an effective kick-off meeting is the key to success. As the project manager, you will be responsible for staffing the project. By now, you should have a draft of the Project Plan and the Project Approach documents. You should also have a pretty good idea of the skill sets that are required to staff your project appropriately. The more projects you have under your belt, the easier it will be to staff your projects with exactly the right people. It takes time to get to know the specific skills and work habits of individual team members. As you get to know them better, you will gain a better understanding of their personalities and the kinds of team dynamics you will create by adding certain groups of people to your team. This understanding of the dynamics of your team will enable you to be a more effective manager. All teams are different, and changing just one team member can alter the dynamics and the personality of the whole team. The selection of the right team members for your project can have a significant effect on the project's chances of success. A project's success or failure will reflect heavily on the project manager. You cannot blame your team if you fail to deliver on time or if you fail to deliver a quality product. You are responsible for ensuring that your team has what it needs to be successful. That means the right skill sets, a feasible schedule, and appropriate resources.

With this in mind, you need to be very meticulous in your choice of team members. You need to ensure that you are not choosing team members just because you like them or because you think they will be easy to manage. You need to choose them because they are the right fit for your team and the specific project, or projects, you will be assigned to. You will most likely have you're a-list individuals whom you really want to have working on your project.

Be careful when creating your list of potential team members. You do not want two team members on your project who do not get along and refuse to communicate (childish as it seems, this will happen from time to time). You do not want a programmer who has a terrible work ethic and no enthusiasm for the project, no matter how talented and accomplished a programmer he may be. You want the best team possible for project success. You want to select team members who are willing and, hopefully, excited to be working as part of a team and who have demonstrated previous project success in a team environment. If you have prospective team members who have worked with success on projects similar to yours, you should be considering them for your team.

You may need to use your negotiation skills and powers of persuasion to get the right people on your team. You may resort to begging, pleading, and bribery, but remember that keeping your integrity (and that of your team members) intact is critical so make sure that you know where to draw the line! You will often need to offer something on your team that other teams are not offering. Great teamwork and an exciting project can be very compelling. A great project manager can also help swing them in your direction.

Don't make the mistake of trying to recruit only senior people to your team. Work on every project that is appropriate for junior and intermediate team members. You need a good balance. You are also creating your future senior team members while you are coaching and developing the junior and intermediate ones. With the right choices, you can be setting yourself up for success now and for the next few years.

Once you have decided who you want to engage for your team, speak with their supervisors to confirm that those potential team members have the time to be engaged on your project. You will also need to ascertain whether there is an interest in working on your project. Engaging a programmer who has been dragged to your team kicking and screaming is not really a great indicator that this is going to be a successful partnership. There is also nothing worse than having a team member who is really interested in your project but who has stretched herself too thin by committing to too many projects and who will be unable to meet her objectives and commitments.

Once you have your team members identified and confirmed, you will be ready to schedule your kick-off meeting. As the project manager, you will be responsible for reserving an office or a conference room that will be large and comfortable enough to accommodate all your team members. If your project is for an outside client, it will probably be more convenient to hold the meeting at the client's site, provided they have the necessary space and equipment to hold an effective and productive meeting.

Scheduling your meeting can often take a lot of time. You will be working with multiple people's schedules, and you will be trying to reserve an appropriate meeting room and equipment for your meeting. You may have to juggle things around a few times before you have things scheduled so that all your team members are able to attend. One suggestion is to give your team members a window when the meeting needs to take place. Have each team member give you two dates that work for them, and go from there. This will eliminate running back and forth constantly trying to get team members to change their schedules. Some team member's schedules will be more flexible than others.

At this point, you may be thinking to yourself "Why can't an administrative assistant do this? Is this really the role of a project manager? Should I not be spending my time on the millions of other things I have to do prior to the meeting?" If you are lucky enough to have an administrative assistant assigned to you, and if they are highly competent and know exactly what you need for your kick-off meeting, then the answer is "yes," he or she can do this for you. However, an administrative assistant may not fully understand the criticality of everyone being available, the room being large enough, the right equipment being there (and being there ahead of time so you have time to set it up), and how important it is that everything goes right for this meeting. If you are unsure, then schedule it yourself. It is important to get your project off on the right foot and you cannot afford any uncertainty about the arrangements. It is the project manager's responsibility to make sure that the location is equipped with all the necessary materials needed to have a successful meeting. You are the one everyone is looking at and looking to. You are the leader for this project and this project team. Your leadership is what is going to make this project successful. You need to gain the confidence and the respect of all your team members starting on day one, so leave no loose ends and no room for surprises.

The equipment and props include, but are not limited to:

- Overhead Projector
- Tables
- Chairs
- Computer, if applicable
- White boards (Recommendation: Interactive White Boards if applicable)
- Dry-erase markers
- Dry-erase erasers
- Easels
- Paper
- *Lots of caffeine, water, and snacks*

On a side note, you may have the occasional *virtual employee*. It is very important that all team members are involved in the kick-off meeting. However, your project may include one or more team members who are located in different time zones. It is important to the success of the project that these virtual employees be involved in the meeting via video conference or, at the very least, phone conference. Employee's time zones must be taken into account when scheduling the meeting so that they are not being asked to attend in the middle of the night. Depending on which time zone they are in, though, scheduling during work hours for all participants may not always be possible.

The initial kick-off meeting can last anywhere from a couple of hours to a couple of days. Smaller projects may take only a couple of hours. Larger projects could be between four and eight hours, whereas more complex projects can take as long as two days. No matter how long the meeting(s) need to be, they should be held during the client's normal business working hours if at all possible.

If the meetings are going to be all-day events, ensure that you have the appropriate budget to keep your team members fed and watered. It is not conducive to a productive meeting to have your team members falling asleep or dying from hunger or thirst halfway through! Have something for your team members to eat in the morning—doughnuts, bagels, fruit, juice, and coffee. This will ensure that the energy levels start off high.

You should also include lunch and afternoon snacks. You should try to avoid having your team members leave the group to have lunch off-site, though. You will be on a tight schedule and don't want to have to wait for team members to return or figure out what happened to them if they do not. It is always good to keep the team together for the social parts of the meeting as well as for the working parts of the meeting. This gives the team members time to interact on a personal level and is a great first step to team building.

Try to avoid starchy, heavy foods for lunch. You do not want your team members falling asleep right after lunch. Make sure you ask if there are any dietary needs when ordering the food for your meetings and ensure that this information is communicated to the person who will be preparing the food. You may have people with food allergies or who are unable to eat certain foods for personal or religious reasons. There is nothing worse than inviting a vegetarian to an all day meeting and discovering the only thing on the menu they can eat is the lettuce or the chocolate brownies. This happens more often than you probably think.

You will need to create an agenda for the meeting. An agenda will give you control over the direction and tone of your meeting and will ensure that the meeting is kept on track and takes place within the allotted time. Provide the agenda to all meeting attendees ahead of time so that they can come prepared to discuss the topics on the agenda. Ask them to inform you, in advance, about any additional items they would like added to the agenda. This way you can have an updated agenda prepared for the day of the meeting. The agenda will let your team know what time they will get breaks so that they can arrange to call into their offices for phone messages or e-mails during those times rather than having to leave the meeting during the discussion to attend to those things.

It is very important to have someone assigned to document the action items during the meeting. It may be difficult for the project manager to be taking notes on action items at the same time as facilitating the meeting. This is especially true for a large meeting to discuss a complex project. Make sure that you assign this task to another team member or an administrative assistant prior to the day of the meeting.

Meeting Agenda

The agenda can include, but is not limited to, the following list of items. A meeting agenda document is included on the CD-ROM that accompanies this book.

- Welcome and agenda—The sponsor welcomes everyone to the meeting, and the project manager briefly reads the day's agenda.

- Introductions—Team members introduce themselves and briefly describe their professional and technical backgrounds.

- Purpose of the meeting—The sponsor presents to the team the purpose of the meeting and the desired outcome of the meeting (goals and objectives).

- Project background—The sponsor gives a description of the project's background and the high-level needs and expectations of the client.

- Presentation of Project Plan—The project manager presents the Project Plan, including:
  - Project Definition Overview
  - Changes Since Project Definition Was Approved
  - Staffing Plan
  - Development Environment
  - High-Level Schedule
  - Deliverables and Milestones
  - Functional Requirements
  - Technical Requirements
  - Decision Support System Plan

- ◆ Quality Assurance Plan

- ◆ Communication Plan

- ◆ Deployment Plan

- ◆ Operations Plan

- ◆ Training Plan

- ◆ Risk Management Plan

- ◆ Measurement Plan

- ◆ Client Acceptance Criteria

- Presentation of Project Approach—The project manager presents the Project Approach, including:
  - ◆ Project Life Cycle

  - ◆ Change Control Process

  - ◆ Technical Processes

  - ◆ Organizational Processes

  - ◆ Client Processes

  - ◆ Vendor Processes

  - ◆ Defect Tracking Process

  - ◆ Decision Support Process

  - ◆ Monitoring and Reporting Process

  - ◆ Special Processes or Considerations

  - ◆ Escalation Processes and Procedures

  - ◆ Project Documentation Process

- Open discussion—This is an open forum for discussing any additional issues or questions that the client or project team members have about the project or the staffing of the project.

- Action items—The project manager, or the meeting's note taker, reads the list of action items that were taken throughout the meeting. The team verifies that all actions have been captured and that they are documented accurately. Any changes are made at this time.

- Next Steps—The project manager summarizes what has been discussed in the meeting and schedules the next meeting, if a follow up meeting is necessary.

- Adjourn—The project manager adjourns the meeting.

Figure 6.2 shows an example meeting agenda.

Document Name Template

OFIS Kick-Off Meeting

Agenda

Date: Wednesday, March 3, 2XXX
Time: 8:00 AM PST – 5:00 PM PST
Location: XYZ Corporation Board Room #5

8:00 Welcome and Agenda - Paulette Green & Daryl Johnson
Paulette Green will welcome everyone to the meeting and Daryl Johnson will read the agenda.

8:15 Introductions - All attendees
Each team member will introduce themselves and briefly describe their professional and technical background.

8:30 Purpose of the meeting - Paulette Green
Paulette Green will present the purpose of the meeting and identify the goals and objectives that are pertinent in order to have a successful outcome.

8:45 Project Background - Paulette Green
Paulette Green will describe the project's background and the needs and expectations of ABC Incorporated.

9:00 Presentation of Project Plan - Daryl Johnson

- Project Definition Overview
- Changes Since Project Definition Was Approved
- Staffing Plan
- Deliverables and Milestones
- Functional Requirements Overview
- Technical Requirements Overview
- Decision Support System Plan

- 15 minute break

- Quality Assurance Plan - Jeff Sterling
- Communication Plan
- Deployment Plan
- Risk Management Plan
- Measurement Plan
- Client Acceptance Criteria
- Questions & Answers

12:00 LUNCH

1:00 Presentation of Project Approach Daryl Johnson
- Project Lifecycle
- Change Control Process

Page ▇ of ▇
Created by "Author"

Figure 6.2: Sample kick-off meeting agenda.

Setting the Tone and Staying on Track

The day of the kick-off meeting will be a very nerve-wracking experience for most project managers. It is the first time that you will meet formally with your new project team, so you will not be comfortable with each other yet. It may be the first time that you will be meeting your client. It is very important that both the team and the client are impressed with your performance in the meeting and your demonstration of leadership ability. Arrive early to ensure that you have everything you need. Check that the room is large enough and has enough seating to comfortably accommodate the group. Make sure that the equipment, tools, and supplies you need are in the room, set up, and operational. Check that the temperature in the room is comfortable, and make sure that your refreshments have arrived and that any further refreshments are scheduled for delivery at the specified time. Ensure that you have enough copies of the agenda, the PowerPoint presentation, and any other documentation pertinent to the meeting. Do not assume the attendees will print out and bring the ones that you e-mailed to them earlier. This early preparation will set you up for a successful and relatively stress-free meeting. An example Kick-Off Meeting PowerPoint Presentation is shown in Figure 6.3, and a copy of the full presentation is included on the CD-ROM that accompanies this book.

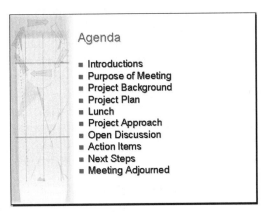

Figure 6.3: Kick-Off Meeting PowerPoint Presentation.

Once everyone has arrived and sat down with their cup of coffee and bagel, it is a good idea to ask your team members to turn off their phones and pagers or to put them on vibrate or silent mode during the meeting and step outside the room quietly before answering them. This will avoid disrupting the whole meeting and losing the focus and attention of the rest of the attendees when someone's phone starts ringing. It is very irritating to be in an all-day meeting where other people's phones and pagers are constantly ringing and beeping.

As soon as everyone is settled, with phones and beepers turned off, the sponsor will explain the reason for the meeting. This includes why the team is here, what the team is trying to accomplish, and how it will be accomplished. Next, team members will individually introduce themselves with a brief description of their backgrounds. The project manager will then communicate to the team the specific roles and responsibilities of each team member.

It is very important to stick to your agenda as closely as possible or your meeting will get out of control and very likely run over schedule. Enthused people love to hear themselves talk, and if you did your job correctly in staffing, you will have a very energetic and enthusiastic group. However, technical people sometimes go above and beyond the call of duty when answering questions. They can often go into excruciating and painful technical detail that is neither relevant nor understandable to most of the people in the room. Your technical resources may have some brilliant ideas that are outside the scope of the project or the contract that they decide to discuss with the client in this meeting. The client may ask to have that specific feature or functionality added into the Project Definition, which will mean having a discussion with the client about revising the project scope and the contract.

You can avoid these distractions by keeping the meeting on track. You should politely interrupt if someone is going into too much detail or is diverging into other areas that are not relevant or specific to this project. As the project manager, you must be the person in control of the meeting. Do not let it take on a life of its own. Be firm and be an assertive timekeeper. Do not let the attendees run amok and, in effect, dictate how the meeting should be held. If you feel comfortable with having another team member do most of the talking during the kick-off meeting because of their technical experience, then make sure this is worked out prior to the meeting. You do not want to look disorganized or incompetent in front of the client. You are the contact person for this project, so they must trust and respect you at the end of this meeting.

There may be times when the meeting gets out of control, and you are finding it hard to get it back on track again. If you are worried about this happening, enlist the help of your fellow team members in advance. Ask them to help you keep the meeting on track if they can see it getting out of control. The chances are that one of them will turn to their teammate and say, "That is not relevant to this project and is out of scope, so let's move on," and they will likely apologize and shut up!

Make sure that no promises are made during the meeting that you know cannot be kept or are out of scope. You can let a technical person do most of the talking, but you can step in and state that something they just mentioned is out of scope. You can let the client know that if they want it included in the project, you will need to have a separate meeting, offline, to discuss changes to the contract. The chances are that the client will not want to do this and will be keen to move on. If they do want to discuss those contract changes, you can move on in this meeting and agree to discuss that item in the second meeting that will be scheduled after the contract has been revised and additional costs agreed to.

Throughout the meeting, you should be taking personal notes even if you are not the person capturing the minutes. Some of these will be action items that you agree to follow up on and some will be notes on items that have come up that you want to ensure you do not forget or you want to follow up on for your own benefit. Make sure your designated note taker is present at the beginning of the meeting to start taking the minutes. The minute taker may be the same person that documents the action items, or you may decide to assign this to someone else. As the meeting progresses, the Project Plan will become better defined, and the important milestones will be agreed upon and documented.

Documenting Meeting Minutes

Was the kick-off meeting a success? We certainly hope it was. It is now up to you to do the necessary follow up to ensure that everyone left the meeting with a common understanding of what was discussed and agreed to. You should type up the meeting minutes along with the action items and distribute this to all attendees and team members within three days (see Figure 6.4).

Ask the recipients to let you know whether they feel you have missed anything or misrepresented anything. Give them a deadline for getting this feedback to you—a couple of days are acceptable. Without a deadline, you may get comments coming back weeks later, at which time it is far too late to be making changes. Asking for feedback lets your team members know that you consider them all to be part of the process and that their opinions count. It is a great way to open up the lines of communication and let them know that you are leading the team and not dictating to them. If you get feedback that something was missed or misrepresented, be sure to thank them for their feedback and send follow-up amended minutes to the whole team as soon as possible after your feedback deadline (this way you can incorporate all feedback into one follow-up memo or e-mail). This two-way communication ensures that all your team members are on board and committed to the project. A Meeting Minutes template is included on the CD-ROM that accompanies this book.

Fundamentals of Technology Project Management
Project Name

Document Name Template

OFIS Kick-off Meeting

Minutes

Date: Wednesday, March 3, 2XXX
Time: 8:00 AM PST – 5:00 PM PST

- Paulette Green welcomed the project team
- Daryl Johnson presented the agenda
- Attendees introduced themselves and briefly described their backgrounds.
- Paulette Green explained that the purpose of the meeting was to introduce team members to the project and to each other as well as to officially kick off the project.
- Paulette Green gave a brief description of the background of the project. The project was initiated in .... by .... The company became involved when .....
- Daryl Johnson presented the Project Plan and the Project Approach to the group (presentations attached).
  - Project Plan included:
    - Project Definition Overview
    - Changes Since Project Definition Was Approved
    - Staffing Plan
    - Deliverables and Milestones
    - Functional Requirements Overview
    - Technical Requirements Overview
    - Decision Support System Plan
    - Quality Assurance Plan - Jeff Sterling
    - Communication Plan
    - Deployment Plan
    - Risk Management Plan
    - Measurement Plan
    - Client Acceptance Criteria
    - Questions & Answers
  - Project Approach included:
    - Project Lifecycle
    - Change Control Process
    - Special Processes or Considerations
    - Escalation Processes and Procedures
    - Project Documentation Process
    - Questions and Answer

Page 1 of 3
Created by "Author"

Figure 6.4: Sample meeting minutes document

For every single meeting that you hold for your project, make sure that the minutes are documented and distributed to the relevant team members. Even if you have a phone conference or receive a call from the client asking questions, follow up with an e-mail clarifying what you discussed and what was agreed to. You do not need to copy the whole team on every single communication. There are times when it will not be appropriate. It important to establish a paper trail for all the meetings and discussions held during the course of your project.

CHAPTER 7

Project Design

The planning phase of the project involves a lot of meetings and a lot of documentation. Once the kick-off meeting is concluded and the Project Plan and Project Approach documents are updated, it is time for the development team to spring into action and start designing the system, features, and components that constitute the product. The Design Process Workflow is shown in Figure 7.1.

A building, or a product, is only as good as its design. A building contractor would not start construction on a house without an architectural design. Who knows what the building would end up looking like or how functional it would be if the design specification were written after the building was constructed?

We have one example of this happening, and the results are interesting to say the least! About 40 years ago, a European gentleman bought some land on a hillside, a stone's throw from the house that his father had built many years before. The house that the father built did not have a bathroom, so he decided to build a new house on the land that he had purchased that would have its own bathroom. He couldn't wait to get started pouring concrete and building his new house, so he enlisted the help of some friends and family and started building his house. It was quite a long process because he had not planned how he would build the house and had only a vague idea of what it would look like when it was finished. He was no builder, so he decided to build a square house that would not be too complicated to complete. As the house was on a hillside, the back of the house had two stories and the front, only one. He built the bathroom in the back (downstairs) and had it plumbed with a flush toilet, a sink, and a shower. Upstairs he built two rooms. He put in some windows and a front door and declared the house built.

However, there were a few problems. He had not put in any stairs to get from the main floor of the house to the lower floor where the bathroom was located. The only way to get to the bathroom was to go out the front door and walk around to the side of the

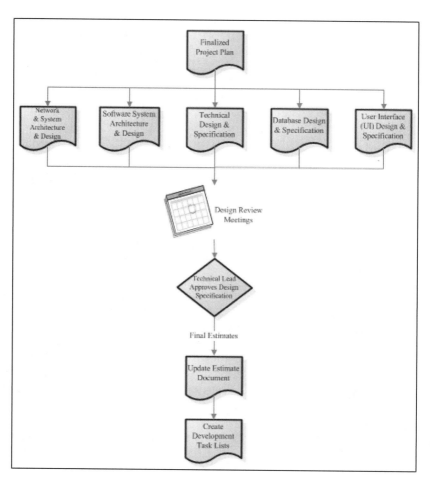

Figure 7.1: Design Process Workflow.

house, where one had to negotiate down a very steep muddy slope covered with brush and trees. Luckily he had put in a bathroom door to the outside. A trip to the bathroom was challenging during daylight hours but was positively dangerous when it was dark because there was no outside lighting and no street lights along the nearby road! He had also forgotten to put in a kitchen and had not plumbed the upstairs for running water so it was not an option to quickly add one later. After the house was built, he decided to use one of the upstairs rooms as a living room and the other as a bedroom, but he had not built a door between the two rooms. The rooms were open so he had to put a curtain up to separate the two rooms. He could not afford to spend more mone,y so the house remains the same to this day. If only he had spent some time on requirements and design, he could have built a very functional house for about the same as he spent on his barely functional house.

The same can happen with your software development projects if you do not spend the necessary time on the requirements and design for your product. Many companies, even today, build the product first and then write the design specs later, when they have the time! This is not good project management, and it is not the most efficient or effective way to build products.

There is a still a lot of work to be done before the team can start programming so don't let those itchy fingers start writing any code just yet. It is important that sufficient time be given to the design of the product before it is built. The Functional and Technical Requirements documents produced during the planning phase will give the designers the data they need to design a high-quality product that meets the needs of the client. Remember, you have a budget and a timeline for the product. Though the schedule will be finalized after the designs are complete, and there may be some renegotiation of costs and timelines with the client based on the designs, it is important that the team try to keep the costs and timelines in line with the estimates produced for the project plan. Those estimates should be very close to the final numbers.

This is where project managers start managing scope. The engineers and designers will often design the Cadillac version of the product when the client has asked for the Pinto! They may tell you that this is the only way the product can be built so you need more time and money to accomplish it. Your technical lead should be working with you to ensure that all the designs are appropriate and within scope as opposed to being the best they can be. The client may not need the best, and they may not be able to afford the best, which is why they did not request the best. Work with your team and ensure that they understand the requirements. Be sure that you are giving them very clear and specific direction on how to match the design to the requirements and the approved estimates.

Designing a product or component that is out of scope is like assuming that everyone who needs to buy a new car cannot live without a Ferrari, Rolls Royce, or Lamborghini. For most people those cars are far beyond what they need and what they can afford, so they opt for the Ford Focus or the Toyota Four Runner instead and are very happy with the end result.

The following documents are created during the design phase of a project:

- System and Network Architecture
- Software Architecture and Design
- Technical Design Specification
- Database Design Specification
- User Interface Design Specification
- Final Estimates
- Detailed Task Lists

All these documents are included on the CD-ROM that accompanies this book.

Designs and Specifications

All the design and specification documents are based on the technical and functional requirements documents that were created during the Planning phase of the project and included in the Project Plan document.

Network and System Architecture and Design

This document details the physical architecture of the network, servers, database, and so on. If the project has a systems architect assigned to it, she will create this document. It is common on many projects for different sections of this document to be created by different people or groups that include an architect and technical lead, a systems engineer, a network engineer, and a database engineer. The document should contain system diagrams and clearly state which group is responsible for implementing each part of the system in accordance with the documented architecture. This is a very technical document and, as such, should not be written by the project manager.

Here is an example of what may be included in a Network and System Architecture and Design document:

- Introduction
  - General information
  - Related documents
- Overview of the System
- Requirements Overview
  - Servers
  - Capacity
  - Connectivity
  - Storage
  - Availability
  - Backup
- Network and System Management
  - System monitoring
  - Logging
  - Notification engine
- Security
- Current Architecture
  - Overview
  - Network diagram
  - Hardware diagram
- Proposed Architecture
  - Overview
  - Network diagram
  - Hardware diagram

- Required Changes
  - Identify gaps
  - Define change plan
- Quality of Service
- Nonimplemented Tasks
- Summary

Software System Architecture and Design

This is the architecture and design of the whole system from a software perspective. Each feature or component within the system will have its own design specification. This document is typically created by the technical lead or architect for the project. The document will contain software system diagrams and file hierarchies that will serve as the software structure for the whole development team. It shows the interoperability among the separate features and components of the system to ensure that the individual designers create designs that will meet those requirements. It is important for the technical team and the quality assurance team to understand the goals of the project from a technical perspective and know how the whole system fits together. This is a technical document and, as such, should not be created by the project manager.

Here is an example of what may be included in a Software System Architecture and Design document:

- Introduction
- Overview of the System
  - Purpose of the system
  - Related documents
- Design Goals
  - Features and components
  - Connectivity
  - Performance, capacity, and optimization
  - Backup and restore
  - Disaster recovery
  - Deployment
  - Installer
  - Launch application
  - Monitoring and notification system
  - Code reuse
- Security
  - Authentication
  - Remote Access
- Current Software Architecture

- Proposed Software Architecture
  - File hierarchy
  - Component map
  - Data management
  - Links to other systems
- Platforms and protocols
- Nonimplemented tasks
- Summary

Technical Design and Specification

The *Technical Design and Specification* document may be one document for the whole project or product for smaller projects, or it may be a collection of documents for each feature or major component for larger projects. The designs must follow the guidelines and rules as set out in the Architecture and System Design documents. The Technical Design and Specification documents are usually authored by the technical lead, the software designer, or the engineer who will be developing that particular feature. This is a technical document and, as such, should not be created by the project manager.

Here is an example of what may be included in a Technical Design and Specification document:

- Introduction
- Design Overview
- Detailed Design
- Components and Processes
- Interfaces
- Security
- Reuse
- Test Plan
- Extensibility
- Nonimplemented Tasks
- Summary

Database Design and Specification

The *Database Design and Specification* document will contain the physical and logical database design specifications. The designs must follow the guidelines and rules as set out in the Architecture and System Design documents. The Database Design and Specification document requires specialized data modeling knowledge and is typically authored by the database engineer or database administrator (DBA) for the project. This is a technical document and, as such, should not be created by the project manager.

Here is an example of what may be included in a Database Design and Specification document:

- Introduction
- Design Overview
- Detailed Design
  - Logical design
  - Physical design
- Data Diagrams
- Database Structure
- Process Flow Diagrams
- Test Plan
- Extensibility
- Nonimplemented tasks
- Summary

User Interface (UI) Design and Specification

The *User Interface Design and Specification* describes the workflow of screens and defines exactly what the user will see on each screen. It illustrates the visual components of each screen, including, graphics, buttons, menus, dialog boxes, help screens, and so on. It defines behavior based on user interaction, including user exception handling and error messages. The document should contain mockups of online demos of the product (if applicable) and help screens. If the product has different interfaces for different users, for example, the call center employees may have a different view of the product than the users. These different views and workflows need to be clearly defined. The User Interface Design and Specification is usually authored by the user interface designer. Although this is not as technical as the other documents, it is recommended that this document not be created by the project manager.

Here is an example of what may be included in a User Interface Design and Specification document:

- Introduction
- Design Overview
- Detailed Design
- Site Structure and Navigation
  - Describe different types of users
  - Workflow diagrams
  - Alternative workflows
  - Site map

- User Interface
  - Graphic design
  - Look and feel
  - Screen mockups
  - Form mockups
  - Report mockups
  - Tabbing order
- Online Demo Prototype
- Help Screens
- Test Plan
- Nonimplemented Tasks
- Summary

Design Reviews

After the design documents are completed there is one more step before development can begin. It is a critical step in the process but one that is often overlooked or skipped due to the urgency to move on and start coding. The design review is a formal meeting that includes, at the very least, the architect, the technical lead, the DBA, and the person who wrote the design. Ideally, a design review should also include the whole development and engineering team and representatives from the quality assurance team. The goal of the design review is to ensure that the design is accurate and complete and meets all the documented requirements. The reviewers are also there to make comments and suggestions on the design that can improve it. It is important that the team work together and commit to designing the best and most appropriate features and components by allowing and encouraging all team members to have input into the designs. It is important that the designer is able to justify and defend his design decisions, but he should not be put on the defensive. Everyone needs to be open to feedback and suggestions and to be prepared to discuss ideas that could lead to a better-quality design.

The design reviews serve two purposes: The first is to ensure the highest quality designs for the specific project that is being designed. The second is to increase the knowledge and expertise of team members in designing projects. The team members can learn a lot from one another during the review process. If good quality teamwork starts here, it will continue throughout the development of the project.

The design needs to be approved by the technical lead (or whoever is responsible for the final approval on designs) for technical appropriateness before the final estimate is submitted for approval to the project manager.

It is possible that not all the designs will be finished at the same time. Some features may be much larger and more complex than others and will require more time to complete. Features may move into the development phase as they are approved, or you may have a process that requires that you wait until they are all completed so that the designs and final estimates can all be approved together.

Final Estimates

Once the final design is completed, the detailed estimates will be updated to become the final estimates. As with detailed estimates, the final estimates will need to be within budget and, depending on the standard budgeting process used, often need to be at 10 to 20% below the budget to give the contingency (buffer) required to allow for unforeseen costs that arise during the course of the project.

If the final estimates differ greatly from the detailed estimate, the project manager will need to revise the estimates and get the appropriate approval before the designs can move into development. Alternatively, she can direct the designer to come up with a solution that can be implemented in less time. What often happens is that some designs come in a little under estimate and some a little over, which leads to the final estimates for all work being about the same. The project manager will need to use her discretion, or standard company guidelines (if there are any), when deciding what needs further (more senior manager or client) approval, what needs a revised design and lower estimate, and what can be approved as-is. For instance, if you had a feature that was estimated to take 8 weeks and the final estimate comes in at 8.5 weeks, the project manager may decide that this is OK because he expects another estimate to come in a bit lower, and if not, the 20% schedule buffer would probably cover it. Thus it is a low enough risk to approve it as-is. On the other hand, if all the final estimates are coming in much higher than approved, a lot of redesign or a lot of extra budget is going to be necessary. This is an area where we cannot tell you the best solution. As the project manager, you will have to make the decision based on what you know and perhaps, to some extent, on your gut feeling. If a lot of the designs need rework, you could run into the problem of the designs taking much longer than estimated, which will also push up the costs of the project and pose a budget risk.

The final estimates are documented using the same estimate document that was used for the detailed estimates in Chapter 3, Figure 3.2.

Development Detailed Task Lists

Once the final designs and estimates are completed, the developers (or technical lead) should produce detailed task lists for the project manager to create the final schedule. Each feature or component should be broken down into a list of subtasks that can be tracked on the project schedule. An example detailed task list is shown in Figure 7.2.

Without this breakdown of tasks, identifying potential schedule problems is very difficult, and the project manager will not be alerted to problems until it is too late to resolve them. For example, if you have a feature that will take 8.5 weeks to develop, and you track this as one 8.5-week task, you will not be able to track the developer's progress on the feature. You will get to 8.5 weeks and find out whether it is on track. To produce an estimate, the designer must have estimated how long each part of the design would take and would probably have had a series of tasks that would last a few days to a couple of weeks.

Detailed Task List

		Bar Code Scanner							**OFIS**					

Prepared by: Sharon Helstrom   **Estimate:** 50 Hrs

Task No.	Task	Planning	Design	Coding	Unit Test	Bug Fix	Update Docs	Integration	QA Support	Other				TOTAL HRS	Dependencies
1	Task 1		10	5										15	
2	Task 2			8		1								9	
3	Task 3			8		0.5								8.5	
4	Task 4			12		0.5								12.5	
5	Task 5				2	0.5	1		1	0.5				5	
6														0	
7														0	
8														0	
	TOTAL HOURS	0	10	33	2	2.5	1		1	0.5	0	0	0	50	

Figure 7.2: Detailed task list.

You must track these tasks, together with dependencies. You do not need to understand exactly what the task is, or what the description means (if it is very technical), but you do need to understand what feature it pertains to, how critical it is, and what dependencies are associated with it. These task lists will be the meat of your schedule, and they are critical to your success in managing the schedule. Managing the schedule effectively is critical to your success in managing the project, so do not skip this step to make the schedule smaller or because the developers do not want to come up with the task lists. If they are unable to define the tasks required to implement the design, then they have not given you an accurate or complete estimate, because it would need to have been based on the work required to implement the design. This is where you can identify weaknesses in your technical team early on. If an engineer designed a feature but does not have the technical ability to implement it, you have a problem that you need to do something about before that person starts to write code.

CHAPTER 8

Creating the Project Schedule

The architecture and design documents are completed and finalized, the final esti-mates are finished and approved, and the development team has created detailed task lists based on the feature designs, so you should have everything you need to create the project schedule.

Project scheduling is a core function of project management. Without it, you cannot track the project progress, which means you will be unaware of whether you are behind schedule, over budget, or missing features or functionality. The success of a project is depends on the project manager knowing the status of the project, and being able to effectively manage it at all times.

Project scheduling is *not* project management. The project schedule is a tool used by a project manager to manage certain aspects of a project. A high level of skill in schedul-ing is a great asset for a project manager, but it is not a replacement for high quality project management and leadership skills. Your choices of tools in managing your pro-ject are, however, important to the success of the project. You need high-quality tools, and you need to know how to use them. Having high-quality carpentry tools will not turn a plumber into a carpenter. By the same token, a carpenter with low-quality tools will not be able to produce the high-quality work that she is capable of. These things are as true for project management as they are for carpenters. You need a high level of skill combined with the right tools to be able to manage a technology project effectively.

Project Scheduling Tools

Developing a comprehensive, realistic, and manageable project schedule is a time-consuming and complex process. However, it is one that is well worth the effort. You will be more than compensated for time spent on good schedule planning as you progress through the project Life Cycle.

Time management, for the whole project team, is an important and necessary part of a project manager's job. The success of the project depends on the project manager not only managing time, but also managing project resources and costs. Luckily for all project managers, many project scheduling software packages are on the market that are designed to assist the project manager in managing and tracking the project schedule, resources, and costs.

It is not hugely important which project scheduling software package you choose to use for your project as long as you are using something that meets your tracking and scheduling needs. It is important to bear in mind that the scheduling tools available vary a great deal in functionality and ease of use. Many tools on the market will allow you to track tasks but will not track dependencies. Some will track dependencies but will not manage or track resources. And some will track time, dependencies, and resources but are lacking in the cost-tracking department. You could easily spend months or years researching the various tools available. It is likely that the company for which you are implementing the project will have standard scheduling tools that they use for every project. If not, you should make sure that you get some scheduling software as soon as possible. Trying to manage a project using a collection of Excel spreadsheets and manual reporting processes is going to be very inefficient and extremely time consuming.

The goal of using a project-scheduling tool is to have at-a-glance insight into the status and progress of your project. You can produce visual reports quickly and easily for specified stakeholder groups that include time, people, costs, milestones, and deliverables. The development team members are able to see individual schedules and track which of their tasks are completed, in progress, or outstanding and whether they are on track or behind schedule.

Although this chapter does not aim to teach you everything there is to know about scheduling software, it is going to show you how to develop a project plan, starting at ground zero, using one of the more popular scheduling software packages, Microsoft Project.

Microsoft Project is a great tool and offers the user the following benefits:

- Cost effective
- Easy and convenient
- Manages tasks, resources, and costs in one package
- Automatically recalculates costs and timelines after each new schedule input
- Resource leveling, task conflict resolutions, and task filtering
- Comprehensive and flexible views and reports so you can find the information you need when you need it
- Built-in templates to get you started (you can also save your own schedules as templates for future use).

Developing a Project Schedule

A project schedule is a list of every single resource and task required to complete the project successfully, from the initial concept, through all Life Cycle phases, to the client handoff and post-deployment tasks. It incorporates technical tasks, functional tasks, and documentation. Your people resources will be assigned to the project along with their availability and associated costs. The Work Breakdown Structure will be developed as you enter your tasks into the schedule. You will create high-level tasks, which will be divided into subtasks and possibly broken down again into sub-subtasks. You need to ensure that you have included all the agreed-upon deliverables and milestones in your schedule. Dependencies will be identified and entered into the schedule. Critical tasks will be defined and flagged to reveal the critical path for your project. Resources will be assigned to tasks and the milestone, and deliverable dates will be verified and finalized. When these tasks are completed, you will be ready to start managing your project schedule. A schedule creation workflow diagram is shown in Figure 8.1.

In Microsoft Project, the schedule is referred to as a "project plan." It is important that you be aware of this difference in terminology so that you understand such things as the help screens in MS Project. In this book we will refer to it as the "schedule" so as

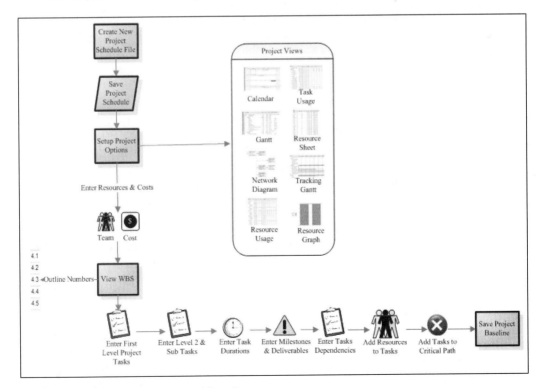

Figure 8.1: The schedule creation workflow diagram.

not to confuse it with the Project Plan document that is created during the planning phase of the project.

Creating a project schedule can be a complex process, especially if you have a large project with a lot of developers and a lot of interdependent tasks. The creation of a project schedule requires attention to detail and a flair for problem solving. Its usefulness to you in managing your project will be proportional to the time and effort you put into the creation of it.

Information You Need before You Start

Before you start to build your project schedule, you will need a certain amount of information about your project and the project team. As you progress with building your schedule, you will need to add more and more detail.

The basic information you need to start building your schedule is:

- Project Information
  - Project name
  - Project start and end dates
  - Milestones and deliverables with agreed-upon dates
  - Phases and release dates (if applicable)

- Project Team Members (Resources)
  - Names
  - Titles
  - Hours per week assigned to project
  - Hours per day
  - Cost per hour or per week
  - Vacation time scheduled
  - Company holidays (bank holidays)

- Estimates
  - Features and components list from detailed design
  - Detailed task lists for each feature and component
  - Final estimates for project and feature timelines
  - Accounting codes for tracking costs to your budget

Creating the New Project Schedule File

Once you have the basic information about your project, you can start to build your schedule. You may decide to start creating your project schedule while you are working on the project plan by entering the basic project information and adding to it as the designs and final estimates are completed and approved. Remember to save your project at regular intervals during the creation process.

The project schedule will be your primary tool for monitoring the project's progress. You will make adjustments and updates to the schedule as you progress through the Life Cycle.

The first step in creating your new project schedule is to create a new schedule file. Click **File** from the menu toolbar and click **New**, as shown in Figure 8.2.

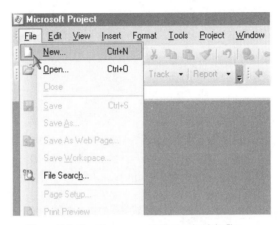

Figure 8.2: Creating a new project schedule file.

Figure 8.3 shows how the navigation pane changes to the New Project task pane.

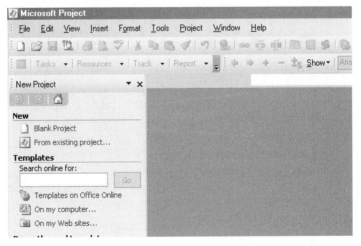

Figure 8.3: New Project Task pane.

Click on **Blank Project** in the left navigation bar to open a new blank project. You will notice that the right hand pane changes to display a blank project template.

Click on the Project menu on the toolbar and select Project Information (Figure 8.4).

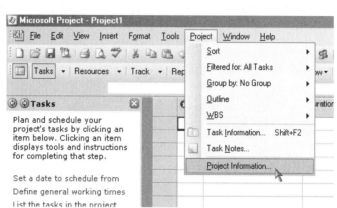

Figure 8.4: Opening the Project Information dialog.

The Project Information dialog appears (Figure 8.5)

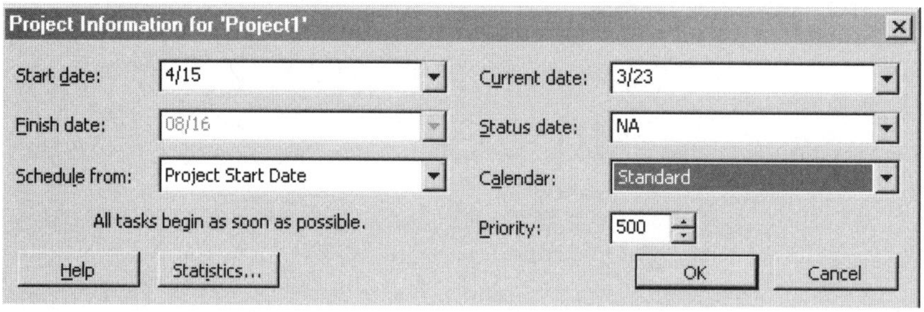

Figure 8.5: Project Information dialog.

You need to enter the following information into this dialog:

- Start date—The start date of your project.

- Finish date—You will notice that the finish date is grayed out. You enter a specific Finish Date in this field only if you have a drop-dead finish date that you can't go beyond. If this is the case, you will need to update the **Schedule from** field first.

- Schedule from—In this field you can choose to schedule from either the project start date or the project finish date; you cannot choose both. Depending on which one you choose, you will be required to enter a date either in the **Start date** or the **Finish date** field. Your schedule will work forward from the start date or backward from the finish date, whichever one you specified. The former is the more common approach.

- Current date—You can fill in the current date according to your computer's calendar or choose another date.

- Status date—You use status date when you are tracking the progress of your project at regular intervals.

- Calendar—You have three choices: Standard, 24 Hours, and Night Shift. Most likely you will use **Standard** because your resources usually work 8–5 or 7–4. IT resources are not generally put on night shifts. However, if your company uses flex-time, there may be resources working in three shifts a day. If this happens, your calendar must be set to **24 Hours**. This is not usually necessary for IT projects because you seldom have a programmer working in the day and then another programmer taking over at night where the day programmer left off. They will more than likely be working on their own scheduled tasks and not sharing the same tasks. Setting the calendar to **Standard** does not mean that all your resources are working the same shift or the same hours. One engineer may work from 6–3 and another may work from 9–6. As long as they are not sharing work, the calendar should be standard. Later, you will set up individual calendars for each resource on your team that will specify their work hours. This is a nice feature in MS Project.

- Priority—Assigning a priority to your project is useful if you are sharing resources across multiple projects. This setting will determine how tasks are delayed if you use the *leveling* feature to level resources across projects. If you are not sharing resources across projects, this setting does nothing.

Once you have entered all the relevant project information, click the **OK** button.

You will be taken back to the blank project schedule screen.

Click on the File menu on the toolbar and select **Properties**. The Project Properties dialog is displayed (see Figure 8.6).

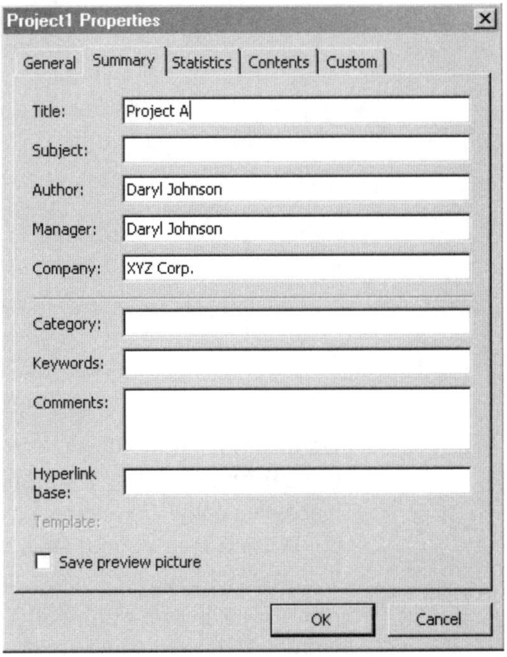

Figure 8.6: Project Properties dialog.

Click on the **Summary Tab** to enter additional project information. Click the **OK** button to save your changes.

Saving Your Project Schedule

If you have not done so yet, you should save your new project file by clicking on the File menu and selecting **Save As** (Figure 8.7).

Before you save the file, click on **Tools** and select **General Properties** (see Figure 8.8).

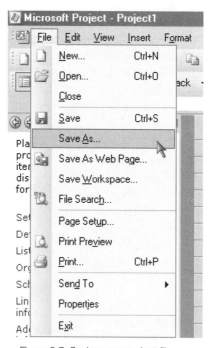

Figure 8.7: Saving your project file.

We recommend that you check the **Always Create Backup** check box as shown in Figure 8.9. This is so that if your file ever becomes corrupted, you have a backup of the last saved copy. We also recommend that you password protect your project file using the **Write Reservation Password** so that you are the only one who can make changes to it. It is not usually necessary to password protect your project for read access. In fact, you will most likely want others to be able to have read access to the file. We also recommend that you check the **Read-only Recommended** box, as it is good practice not to open your file as write enabled unless you are planning to make changes to it.

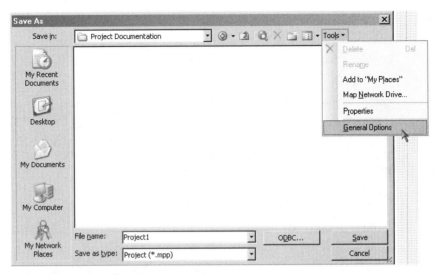

Figure 8.8: General Options.

One of the great features of Microsoft Project is how easy it is to update the schedule and to have Project update all related tasks automatically. This functionality can, however, also make it very easy to accidentally make a change to the schedule, that, in turn, updates many of the successor tasks and, if not noticed before you exit and save the file, can take a lot of time to track down. This is plain and simple good housekeeping for your project schedule.

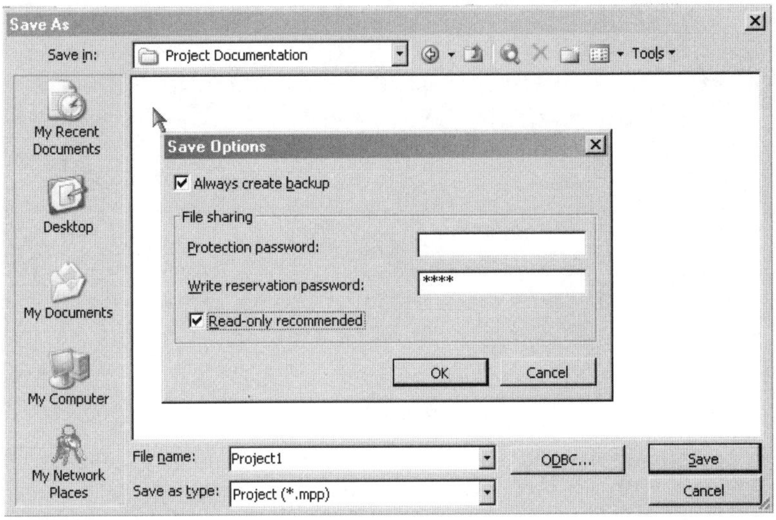

Figure 8.9: Save Options dialog.

Setting Up Project Options

There are many options that the user can set in Microsoft Project. To change the default options, click on the Tools Menu and select **Options**

The Options dialog is displayed in Figure 8.10. The Options dialog has 10 tabs: View, Interface, Schedule, General, Security, Calculation, Edit, Spelling, Calendar, and Save. There are a numerous options that you change or set using this dialog. The view shown in Figure 8.10 shows the View tab. We recommend that you look at all the options available and make any changes that you see fit. You should consider returning to this box later, after you are more familiar with MS Project.

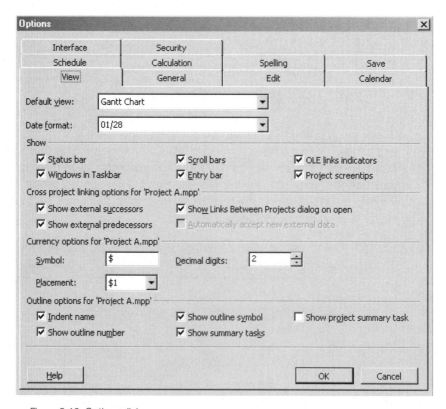

Figure 8.10: Options dialog.

The Many Views of Microsoft Project

The project view that you have been working in so far is called the "Gantt chart." MS Project 2003 comes with 24 different project views. The eight most common views are listed in the **View** drop-down menu by default. The eight default views are:

Calendar	This view looks like a regular calendar that shows the tasks by their dates.
Gantt Chart	The Gantt Chart is shown on a split screen. The left side is a list of the project tasks and subtasks (and, depending on what columns you have chosen to display, with durations and timelines, etc.). The right side is the Gantt Chart that displays as a bar going across the screen indicating the start and end dates for each task and the dependencies among them.
Network Diagram (PERT)	A diagram showing all the tasks and the relationships among the tasks.
Task Usage	A list of tasks showing the resources assigned to each task.
Tracking Gantt	A list of all tasks with the percentage complete for each task.
Resource Graph	A graph showing resource allocation. It identifies whether each resource is under- or over-allocated for.
Resource Sheet	A list of all project resources, both human and material resources, together with the costs for each.
Resource Usage	A list of resources and each task associated with each resource.

We will mainly use the Resource Sheet and the Gantt Chart while setting up your project schedule.

Entering Resources and Costs

As you have already learned, resources are not just people; they are also equipment, time, and money. In Microsoft Project, however, the term "resource" is generally used to describe people resources (team members).

The people resources for your project are defined in the project staffing plan. Each team member will have a specific cost associated with her, based on skills, experience, and seniority.

The people resource costs for a software project generally account for quite a high percentage of the overall project cost. To effectively track and manage your budget, it is imperative that you accurately track and report on costs using your project schedule. We will use the Resource Sheet to enter resources into the Project Schedule. The Resource Sheet allows you to enter both people and material resources. For this project, we will be entering only people resources.

Click the View menu on the toolbar, and select **Resource Sheet**. This displays the Resource Sheet, shown in Figure 8.11.

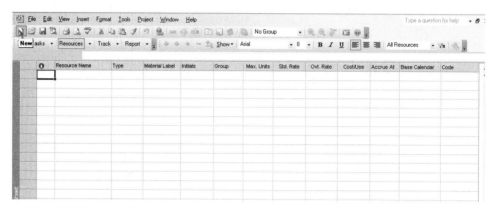

Figure 8.11: Resource Sheet.

Enter the following information into the resource sheet for each team member assigned to your project. You can also add the client, vendors, and other resources that you need to add to your schedule but that you do not need to track costs for. Add them here, but leave the rate columns blank or set to "0."

- Name—The team member's name.

- Type—This is the type of resource—Work or Material.

- Material—This defines the unit of measurement for a material resource (for example, pounds, tons, or cubic yards).

- Initials—These are the unique initials that each resource can be tracked by, in addition to using the full name. MS Project will track costs using initial or name to the same resource.

- Group—This allows you to group your resources (for example, you may group all project managers as PM, all software engineers as SE, and all business analysts as BA).

- Max Units—The percentage of time that the resource is available to work. The default is 100%. You may have a resource assigned part time to a role, in which case you could set this to 50% or 60%.

- Std. Rate—This is the standard rate and refers to the standard hourly rate for the resource.

- Ovt. Rate—This is the overtime rate and refers to the hourly overtime rate for the resource.

- Cost/Use—This is a "cost-per-use" field. The cost is charged each time the resource is used. (It is not calculated based on time.) It can be used if you have a resource that charges a set fee per task rather than an hourly rate. This field is also used for material costs for projects that are tracking materials as well as resources.

- Accrue At—This field is used to describe how and when costs are accrued for a specific resource. The options are Start, Prorated, and End. If you select the Start option, costs are accrued as soon as a task starts, as indicated by a date entered in the Actual Start field. If you select the End option, costs are not accrued until the remaining work is zero. If you select the Prorated option, the costs accrue as work is scheduled to occur and as actual work is reported and are calculated by multiplying unit costs by work.

- Base Calendar—Here you can select which base calendar to use for each resource. We chose Standard as our default calendar earlier. Here you can override that on a per-resource basis.

- Code—This field is typically used to track cost center codes for resources in projects. This can be really useful when tracking your resources against cost center codes for your budget. This field allows you to filter the resources to show only those resources assigned to a certain cost center.

Figure 8.12 shows an example of what your completed Resource Sheet will look like.

		Resource Name	Type	Material Label	Initials	Group	Max. Units	Std. Rate	Ovt. Rate	Cost/Use	Accrue At	Base Calendar
1		Paulette Green	Work		PG	SP	100%	$55.00/hr	$0.00/hr	$0.00	Prorated	Standard
2		Daryl Johnson	Work		DJ	PM	100%	$45.00/hr	$0.00/hr	$0.00	Prorated	Standard
3		Jeff Sterling	Work		JS	QAM	100%	$38.00/hr	$0.00/hr	$0.00	Prorated	Standard
4		Mark Terry	Work		MT	QAE	100%	$25.00/hr	$0.00/hr	$0.00	Prorated	Standard
5		Melanie Charles	Work		MC	QAE	100%	$25.00/hr	$0.00/hr	$0.00	Prorated	Standard
6		Kevin Roth	Work		KR	SME	100%	$45.00/hr	$67.50/hr	$0.00	Prorated	Standard
7		David Moss	Work		DM	TL	100%	$42.00/hr	$0.00/hr	$0.00	Prorated	Standard
8		Vin Patel	Work		VP	DBA	100%	$42.00/hr	$0.00/hr	$0.00	Prorated	Standard
9		Jane Jones	Work		JJ	SE	100%	$35.00/hr	$0.00/hr	$0.00	Prorated	Standard
10		Tim Timmons	Work		TT	SYS	100%	$40.00/hr	$0.00/hr	$0.00	Prorated	Standard
11		Sharon Helstrom	Work		SH	SE	100%	$38.00/hr	$0.00/hr	$0.00	Prorated	Standard
12		Manuel Gomez	Work		MG	SE	100%	$36.00/hr	$0.00/hr	$0.00	Prorated	Standard

Figure 8.12: A completed Resource Sheet.

Using the Work Breakdown Structure (WBS)

A *work breakdown structure* (WBS) presents task information in a hierarchical, numbered form. There are two basic approaches to creating a task list: the top-down approach and the bottom-up approach. The *top-down approach* starts by listing all the major phases of the project and then breaking each one down into a list of subordinate tasks. The *bottom-up approach* is accomplished by identifying as many specific tasks related to the project as possible and then organizing them according to the WBS.

The most commonly used WBS process is the top-down approach. It is a more methodological approach to building the project schedule, it minimizes the chances that you will forget something, and it will most likely be faster because you will minimize the time you spend reorganizing required tasks. You can use the standard line numbers on your schedule for numbering your WBS, or you can use WBS codes to organize and track your tasks in more detail. Figure 8.13 shows a simple WBS using the standard line numbers in Project to identify tasks.

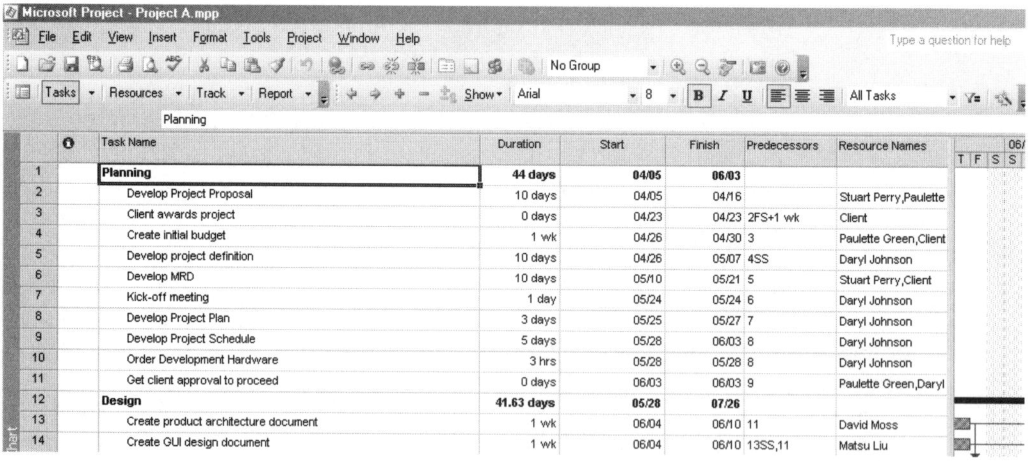

	Task Name	Duration	Start	Finish	Predecessors	Resource Names
1	**Planning**	**44 days**	**04/05**	**06/03**		
2	Develop Project Proposal	10 days	04/05	04/16		Stuart Perry,Paulette
3	Client awards project	0 days	04/23	04/23	2FS+1 wk	Client
4	Create initial budget	1 wk	04/26	04/30	3	Paulette Green,Client
5	Develop project definition	10 days	04/26	05/07	4SS	Daryl Johnson
6	Develop MRD	10 days	05/10	05/21	5	Stuart Perry,Client
7	Kick-off meeting	1 day	05/24	05/24	6	Daryl Johnson
8	Develop Project Plan	3 days	05/25	05/27	7	Daryl Johnson
9	Develop Project Schedule	5 days	05/28	06/03	8	Daryl Johnson
10	Order Development Hardware	3 hrs	05/28	05/28	8	Daryl Johnson
11	Get client approval to proceed	0 days	06/03	06/03	9	Paulette Green,Daryl
12	**Design**	**41.63 days**	**05/28**	**07/26**		
13	Create product architecture document	1 wk	06/04	06/10	11	David Moss
14	Create GUI design document	1 wk	06/04	06/10	13SS,11	Matsu Liu

Figure 8.13: Using standard line numbers.

MS Project includes functionality that allows you to apply outline numbering to the WBS. For example:

1. Phase One
   1.1. Feature 1
      1.1.1. Task 1 of feature 1
      1.1.2. Task 2 of feature 1
   1.2. Feature 2

Using this method, MS Project will update the numbering automatically if you delete or move a task.

You can also choose your own WBS numbers, which you enter manually. This option is useful for companies that use a standard WBS for all projects or if you need to use the WBS numbering for tracking specific metrics or for reporting purposes. This method of numbering the WBS does not automatically update if you delete or move a task.

To display the WBS column, right-click on the Task Name column, and click **Insert Column** (see Figure 8.14).

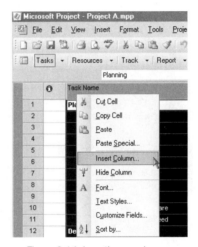

Figure 8.14: Inserting a column.

The Column Definition dialog is displayed Figure 8.15. Click on the Field drop-down menu, and select **WBS**. Click the **OK** button.

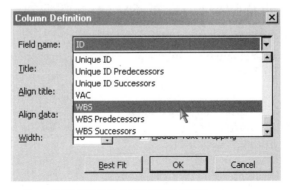

Figure 8.15: The Column Definition dialog.

To add WBS codes to your project schedule, click on the Project menu and then select **WBS** and **Define Codes**.

The WBS Code Definition dialog, shown in Figure 8.16, appears. Here you can enter a project code prefix for your WBS codes to differentiate them from linked schedule line items. You can choose to automatically number your tasks using one of the first three options, or you can choose "Characters (unordered)" to enter your own WBS codes. If you choose this option, the WBS field will display as an asterisk for a task until you manually enter a code for it.

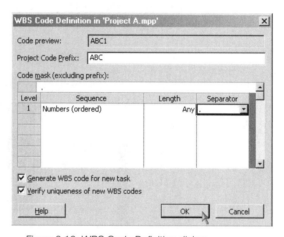

Figure 8.16: WBS Code Definition dialog.

Outline Numbers

In addition to using the WBS column, MS Project gives you the option to number your tasks using outline numbers in the Task Name column. This can help with the organization of your tasks if you decide not to use the WBS codes for tracking purposes. To display automatic outline numbering of your tasks, you will need to set the standard tabular numbering system.

Click the Tools menu on the toolbar, and select **Options**. This will display the Options dialog, as shown in Figure 8.17. Check the **Show Outline Number** box, and click the **OK** button to save your changes.

The task name column will then contain outline numbers (see Figure 8.18).

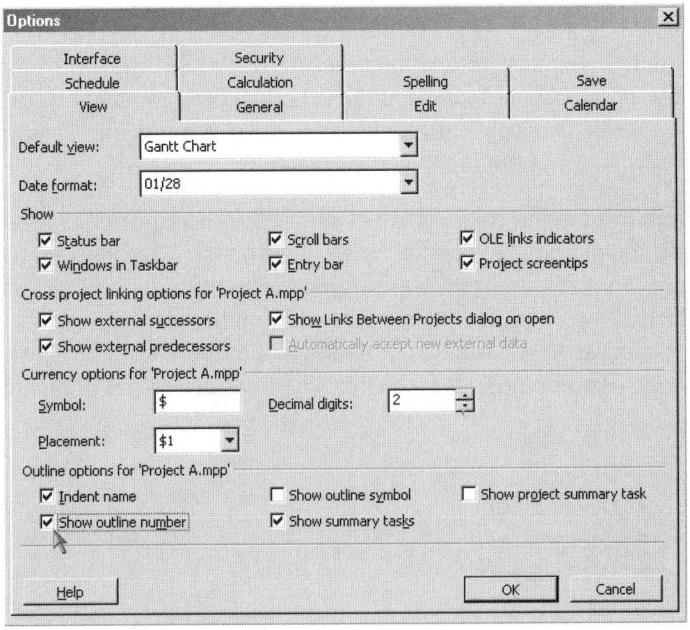

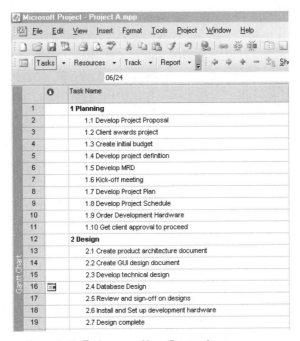

Figure 8.17: Options dialog.

Figure 8.18: Task name with outline numbers.

Entering First-Level Project Tasks

Now that you understand the theory of the Work Breakdown Structure, you are ready to start entering your tasks into the schedule. You can use any method that you choose to do this, but we would suggest that you take a methodical approach and build your schedule using the top-down approach.

Start by entering your highest-level tasks. These are your "Level 1" tasks. For example, you could group your tasks by Life Cycle phase. This is a very useful approach that allows you to do analysis later to ascertain what percentage of time your team spent in each of the Life Cycle phases. This information can be very helpful when trying to identify process improvements or finding the root cause of project issues. Taking this approach, you would enter the Life Cycle phases into the project schedule, as follows:

- Planning
- Design
- Development
- Integration
- Deployment
- Post-Deployment

Click in a cell in the Task Name column, and type in the name of the task (Figure 8.19). If you have the WBS column displayed, it will automatically enter a WBS code for each line item.

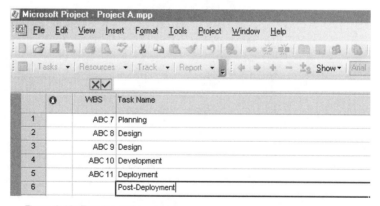

Figure 8.19: Entering tasks.

To enter additional task information, either double-click on the task name, or select the task that you want to update and then use the Task Information button ⬜ on the toolbar to access the Task Information dialog.

There are six tabs on the Task Information dialog (Figure 8.20). Using this dialog, you can enter various information pertaining to the task. After entering your updates, click the **OK** button to save your changes.

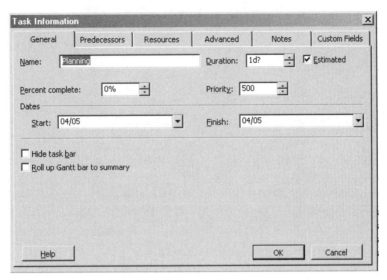

Figure 8.20: Task Information dialog.

Entering Level 2 and Subtasks

After entering your Level 1 tasks, you are ready to move onto Level 2, Level 3, and so on. To enter a lower-level task, click on the task below where you want to insert a blank line and hit the **Insert** key, or right-click and select **New Task** from the menu. Enter the task name information, and then use the Indent button ⇨ on the toolbar to indent the task and make it a subtask.

You will notice that the WBS codes are automatically updated (Figure 8.21).

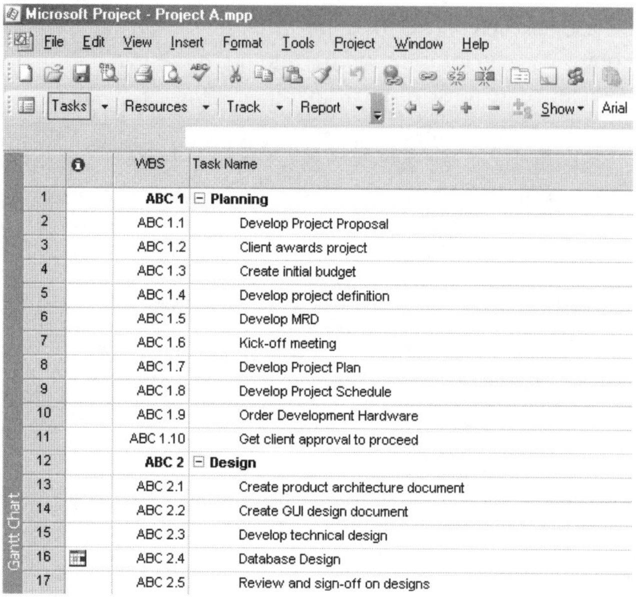

Figure 8.21: Level 1 and Level 2 tasks.

Any tasks that have subtasks associated with them are shown in bold. These are called "Summary Tasks." Summary tasks can be collapsed and expanded by clicking the **Expand/Collapse** button ⊟Planning next to the task.

Entering Task Durations

You will notice, when you enter a task into your schedule, that MS Project enters a default of "1 day?". To change this, enter the actual duration for all subtasks. You should not enter durations for any of the Summary (bolded) tasks. The duration for those tasks will be automatically calculated by MS Project by totaling the duration of all the subtasks associated with it. See Figure 8.22.

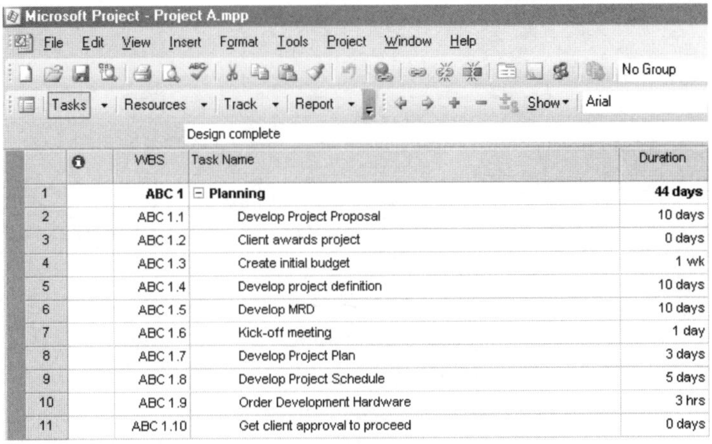

	WBS	Task Name	Duration
1	**ABC 1**	**Planning**	**44 days**
2	ABC 1.1	Develop Project Proposal	10 days
3	ABC 1.2	Client awards project	0 days
4	ABC 1.3	Create initial budget	1 wk
5	ABC 1.4	Develop project definition	10 days
6	ABC 1.5	Develop MRD	10 days
7	ABC 1.6	Kick-off meeting	1 day
8	ABC 1.7	Develop Project Plan	3 days
9	ABC 1.8	Develop Project Schedule	5 days
10	ABC 1.9	Order Development Hardware	3 hrs
11	ABC 1.10	Get client approval to proceed	0 days

Figure 8.22: Entering durations for subtasks.

You can add durations in days (d), weeks (w), hours (h), minutes (m), or months (mn). You need to manually type in the duration for each task. For example, "3w" represents 3 weeks, "15d" represents 15 days, and "120h" represents 120 hours. If you have tasks in your schedule that require no work—for example a milestone, deliverable, or reminder task—then set the duration to "0".

Entering Milestones and Deliverables

You have all your tasks entered into the schedule using a logical WBS, so the tasks and subtasks are arranged in a somewhat chronological order, and you have entered in the duration for each task. The next step is to ensure that you have all the milestones and deliverables entered and identified in your schedule.

You defined the project milestones and deliverables during the planning phase of the project. It is important to add them to the schedule and flag them as Milestones to make them trackable. You will use this data when reporting status to your client and stakeholders.

Milestone tasks should be set to a duration of zero. This is because the milestone is not a task in itself. It merely signifies that a task or a series of tasks have been completed.

To set the Milestone flag for a task, open the Task Information dialog by double-clicking the task or using the Task Information button. Select the Advanced tab, and check the **Mark task as milestone** check box. Click the **OK** button to save your changes and exit (see Figure 8.23).

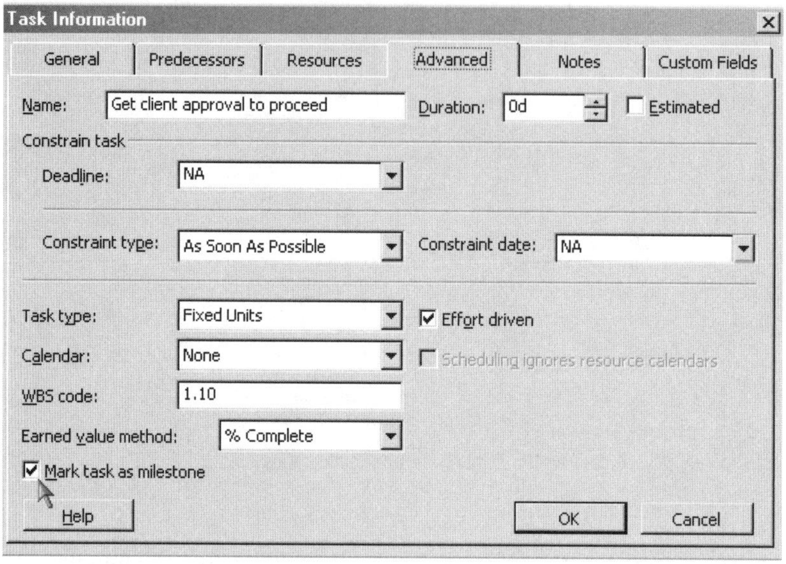

Figure 8.23: Setting milestones.

You can add milestones anywhere in the project schedule that helps you to track progress and report on status. It does not have to be restricted to the predefined milestones and deliverables identified in the planning phase of the project. For example, you can add a milestone to the end of the design phase to signify that all designs are finalized and approved.

Milestones are set to zero duration, so the only way to know when they are completed is to identify and link the tasks that need to be completed for the milestone to have been reached. These links, or relationships, between tasks are called "dependencies."

Understanding and Identifying Dependencies

Identifying task dependencies is one of the most challenging aspects of creating and managing a project schedule. You will need to enlist the help of your technical lead and developers to identify the task dependencies for your project. It is likely that you will have multiple dependencies, and until you have figured out what they are, you are not going to be able to assign resources or schedule start dates for any of the tasks on your schedule. Dependencies dictate the sequencing of project activities or tasks. Dependencies can be categorized as tasks, people, or a combination of both.

When creating dependencies, it is crucial that only the dependencies that represent real constraints be entered into the schedule. Otherwise, there will be so many dependencies that you could end up with thousands of them in your schedule, resulting in a very complex system of linked tasks that is almost impossible to update or manage.

What is a valid dependency? If task B depends on the start or finish of Task A to start or finish itself, then there is dependency between Task A and Task B. In most cases, a dependency signifies a chronological constraint—for example, Task B cannot start until Task A is completed. The task that depends on the other is the *successor* and the task that is depended on is the *predecessor*. In our example, that would made Task A the predecessor and Task B the successor.

You may need to add *lead time* or *lag time* to a task when setting dependencies. For example, you may need a lag of two days after Task A is completed before you start to work on Task B. Alternatively, you may want Task B to have two days lead time (or overlap) before Task A ends for maximum efficiency.

There are three different types of dependency:

- Mandatory dependency—Some activities must happen before another activity can begin. For example, you cannot test code until the code has been written.

- Discretionary dependency—These dependencies are defined by the project manager or the project team. They are not critical to the completion of tasks, but they may be used to make scheduling more efficient. For example, you may enter dependencies for a resource stipulating that he finishes one task before beginning another. Neither task depends on the other, so the dependency is discretionary.

- External dependencies—These are dependencies that exist external to your project schedule. You can add dependencies to tasks in other Microsoft Project schedules that will show as external dependencies in your project schedule.

When developing your project schedule, you have a choice of four different ways of scheduling dependencies:

- Finish to Start (FS)—This is the most widely method used. Task A must finish before Task B can start.

- Start to Start (SS)—Task A can't start until Task B starts.

- Finish to Finish (FF)—Task A must finish before Task B finishes.

- Start to Finish (SF)—Task A must start before Task B can finish.

Entering Task Dependencies

You should, by now, have met with your technical lead and your project team members to verify the mandatory dependencies between tasks that were identified in the Detailed Task Lists. These are the first dependencies that you should enter into the schedule.

You can enter dependencies into the schedule using the Gantt Chart View, the Calendar View, or the Network Diagram View. If you want to add lag or lead times among the tasks, use the Gantt Chart.

Linking Tasks Using the Gantt Chart View

There are three different ways of entering dependencies in this view:

1. If you do not need to add lead or lag time, this is the fastest method.
   - Hold down **CTRL** and click each task that you want to link.
   - Click the **Link Tasks** button.

2. You can manually enter the dependencies in the predecessor or successor column for each task. This method defaults to the Finish-to-Start dependency.
   - If you want to set a dependency other than FS (Finish to Start), you will need to type in the appropriate suffix: SS (Start to Start), FF (Finish to Finish), or SF (Start to Finish) following the dependency task number.
   - If you want to add lag or lead time to the dependency, you will need to type in the necessary suffix followed by a positive or negative number of days. For a dependency on task 2, with a lead time of one week, you would enter "2FS-1 w". For a lag time of 2 days you would enter "2FS+1 w". See Figure 8.24.

Duration	Start	Finish	Predecessors
44 days	**04/05**	**06/03**	
10 days	04/05	04/16	
0 days	04/23	04/23	2FS+1 wk
1 wk	04/26	04/30	3
10 days	04/26	05/07	4SS
10 days	05/10	05/21	5
1 day	05/24	05/24	6
3 days	05/25	05/27	7
5 days	05/28	06/03	8
3 hrs	05/28	05/28	8
0 days	06/03	06/03	9

Figure 8.24: Linking tasks in Gantt Chart View.

3. The third way of creating task dependencies is to use the Task Information dialog. Double-click the task to display the dialog and then select the Predecessor tab. You can either enter the task number in the ID

box, if you know it, or you can select the task by using the Task Name drop-down menu. You then choose from the four types of dependencies to add a lag time or lead time. Use a minus sign to signify a lead time. See Figure 8.25.

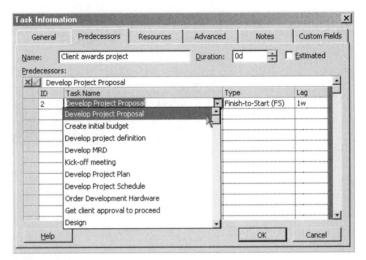

Figure 8.25: Linking tasks using the Task Information dialog.

Linking Tasks Using the Calendar View

- Hold down **CTRL**, and click each task you want to link.

- Click the **Link Tasks** button on the toolbar. See Figure 8.26.

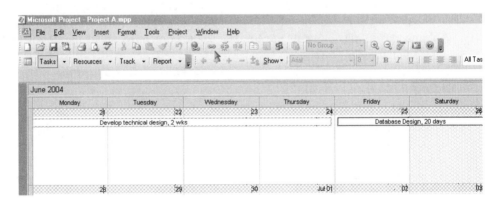

Figure 8.26: Link Tasks in Calendar View.

Linking Tasks Using the Network Diagram View

There are two methods for linking tasks in this view:

1. To link two tasks:
   * Position the mouse pointer in the center of the Predecessor task box. Click and hold the mouse button.
   * Drag to the task box. See Figure 8.27.

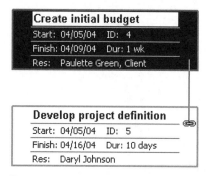

Figure 8.27: Linking tasks in Calendar View.

2. To link multiple tasks:
   * Hold down **CTRL**, and click each task you want to link.
   * Click the **Link Tasks** button on the toolbar.

Ensure that you have set the dependencies for all your project milestones. For example, if you have a milestone called "Design Phase complete," you need to ensure that this task is set to zero days and that it is linked (FF) with every single task in the design phase. You will not be able to set this task to complete until all the design tasks are complete.

Adding Resources to Tasks

Now that you have all your tasks and dependencies entered into the schedule, you need to assign resources to all the tasks. If you have a small team, this will not be very challenging. If you have a large team, it can be a bit hairy trying to get everything scheduled so that everyone is busy all the time, but is not over-allocated. You need to avoid too much downtime in your schedule or you will have bored team members sitting around with nothing to do.

You should have already entered your resources and the resource costs into the resource sheet. Before you assign your resources to the schedule, you need to update the Working Time for the both the project team and the individual team members to reflect any scheduled time off. Use the standard calendar to enter in any public holidays when the whole team will be off work (Christmas and Independence Day, for example). Use individual calendars to enter vacation time for team members. Entering this information will ensure that you do not schedule work for team members when they will be out of the office.

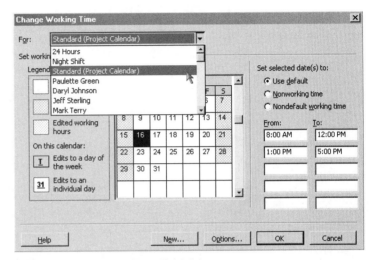

To update Working Time, click on the Tools menu on the toolbar and select **Change Working Time**.

In the Change Working Time dialog, you can select the standard cal-

Figure 8.28: Change Working Time dialog.

endar or the calendar of individual team members. (See Figure 8.28.) Update the calendars by clicking on the day that you want to change and then selecting the appropriate radio button on the right side of the dialog. Using this dialog, you can schedule team members to work on nonworking days, you can schedule them to not work on working days, or you can set the day back to whatever the default working time is.

Once you have the Working Time calendars set correctly for the project team and each team member, click **OK** to save your changes.

You can enter resources directly into the schedule by using the "resource names" field, as shown in Figure 8.29.

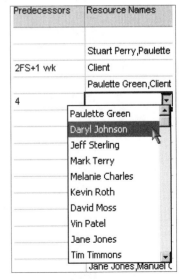

Figure 8.29: Entering resources into the Resource Name column.

Alternatively, you can use the Task Information dialog. Using the Task Information dialog, you can easily assign a task to more than one person and indicate the percentage of each person's time that will be spent working on the task. See Figure 8.30.

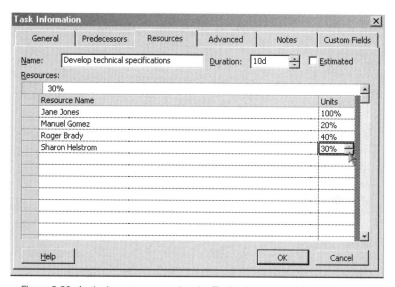

Figure 8.30: Assigning resources using the Task Information dialog.

You can also add resources by using the Assign Resources dialog to add resources to a task. Click the Tools menu on the toolbar and select **Assign Resources**. The Assign Resources dialog appears (Figure 8.31). Select the resource(s) you want to assign, and enter the percentage of their time assigned to the task. Click the **Assign** button to save your changes.

The finish date for the task will automatically update to reflect the percentage of time you have allocated for each person assigned to the task. For example, if you schedule a 10-day task and have one person working on it at 50%, it will take 20 days to complete the task.

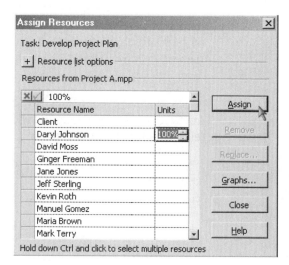

Figure 8.31: Assign Resource dialog.

Once you have all your tasks assigned to resources, you need to verify that none of your resources are over or under allocated. You can do this by using the Resource Usage and Resource Graph views.

The Resource Usage view will indicate whether there is a problem with a specific resource. The exclamation sign in the information column will alert you to problems. See Figure 8.32 for an example.

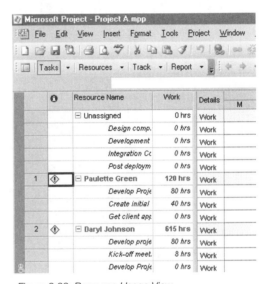

Figure 8.32: Resource Usage View.

The Resource Usage View shows that there are over-allocation problems with both Paulette Green and Daryl Johnson. We can look more closely at what is causing the problem by using the Resource Graph View.

In Figure 8.33 you can see that the Resource Graph View shows Daryl Johnson over-allocated by 100% (at 200% utilization) each day during the week of April 25th. The following week (May 2nd), he is not allocated at all.

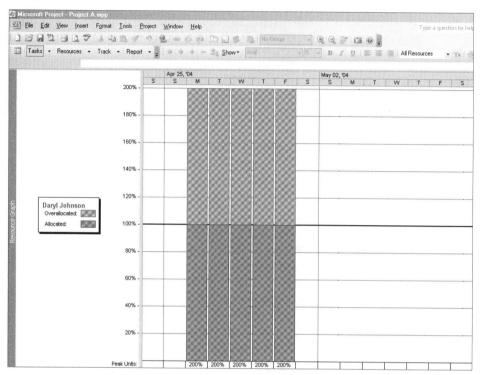

Figure 8.33: Resource Graph View.

In this case, it looks relatively easy to solve this problem by moving half of Daryl's tasks to the following week. Easy it may be, but effective perhaps not. If there are dependencies on the tasks that you want to move, that could affect other team members being able to start their scheduled tasks. You can level your resources by using the Resource Leveling tools, accessible via the Resource Leveling dialog or by updating your project manually. To use the leveling feature built into MS Project, click the Tools menu on the toolbar and select **Level Resources**.

This displays the Resource Leveling dialog (Figure 8.34) where you can choose to manually or automatically level your resource allocation.

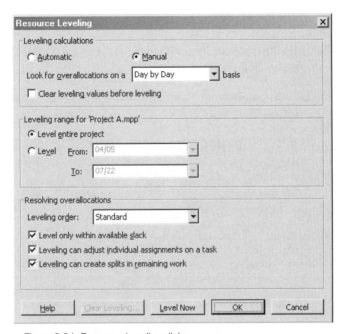

Figure 8.34: Resource Leveling dialog.

Having got this far, you should have a project schedule that is in really good shape. Your team members should have assignments that will take them from here to the end of the project, and you should be well set up to track costs and resource usage

Identifying and Adding Tasks to the Critical Path

So let's talk about the critical path. A critical task is defined as a task that *must* be completed as scheduled for the project to finish by the required finish date. If a critical task is delayed, it may delay the project completion date. The critical path identifies and links all the tasks critical to the success of your project. Some of the tasks on the critical path may not be critical in themselves, but they need to be accomplished for the critical task(s) to be completed. For example, driving to work is not necessarily a critical task for a heart surgeon, but if she is needed in ER to perform surgery, the drive to work is on the critical path for her to be able to perform the critical task (the operation). The operation will have its own critical path, as will the patient. As with projects, there is one major critical path that links the critical tasks that must be completed to complete the project. Each critical task will have a critical path leading to its completion. The high-level critical path will change as critical tasks and subtasks are completed throughout the course of the project. By default, MS Project identifies any task with zero days of slack as critical. You can change this definition using the Options dialog.

- On the Tools menu, click **Options**, and then click the **Calculation** tab.

- In the **Tasks are critical if slack is less than or equal to** box, type or select the amount of slack.

- Click **Set as Default** if you want this setting to be the default for all your projects. See Figure 8.35.

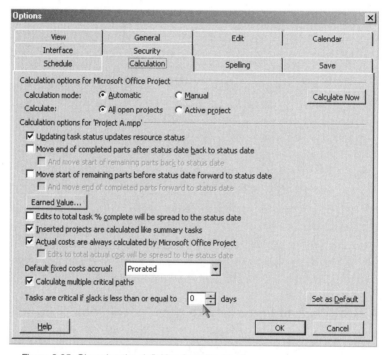

Figure 8.35: Changing the definition for critical tasks.

The Gantt Chart has been designed so that it is obvious which tasks are on the critical path. The default setting shows the critical path tasks in red and the noncritical path tasks in blue. These settings can be customized by right-clicking over the Gantt Chart and selecting the **Bar Styles** option. Figure 8.36 shows the critical path tasks as outlined boxes and the noncritical tasks as solid boxes.

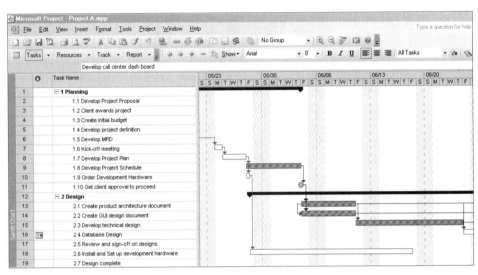

Figure 8.36: Gantt Chart showing the critical path.

You can also analyze the critical path using the Network Diagram View. In Figure 8.37 you can see how the critical tasks are displayed as square-edged boxes and the non-critical tasks as round-edged boxes.

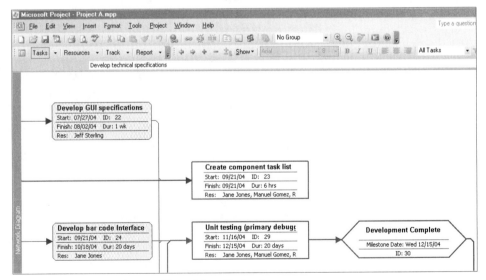

Figure 8.37: Network Diagram View of the critical path.

Saving the Project Baseline

A baseline is a project schedule comprising the original final estimate information for the project. This includes the original tasks, duration, dates, and costs. By saving a project plan with a baseline, you can track your schedule "actuals" compared to the original baseline schedule. By comparing the variances between the baseline and the current schedule, you will be able to track and identify where changes have occurred in your schedule during the course of the project. Using the baseline to do comparisons can alert you to slippages and delays that may not be so obvious when tracking the schedule on a day-to-day basis. For example, if a task is slipping a little but often, it may not be obvious that it is a big problem. When you compare with your baseline, however, you may find that the task is 20% over on the original plan.

When you initially begin building your project schedule and perform a save on the file, you will be asked if you would like to save the project with or without a baseline.   It is *very* important that you do not save it with a baseline. You should save your first baseline after you have entered all the data for your first project schedule. It is good practice to save the baseline at the end of each project phase. You may also want to save the baseline at specific, major milestones. MS Project allows you to save up to 11 baselines per project.

To save a baseline, click on the Tools menu, select **Tracking**, and select **Save Baseline**. The **Save Baseline** dialog is displayed as shown in Figure 8.38.

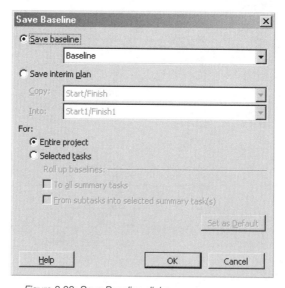

Figure 8.38: Save Baseline dialog.

Using this dialog, you can save the whole schedule, or you can save specific tasks.

You can track your schedule against the baseline by displaying the baseline on the Gantt Chart along with your critical and noncritical tasks. To display the baseline, right-click on the Gantt Chart and select **Gantt Chart Wizard**. The wizard will take you through the steps to display the baseline.

If you wish to view baseline versus actual statistics to track the progress of your project, you can view the information in the Project Statistics dialog. To display the box, click on the Project menu and select **Project Information**. The Project Information dialog appears (see Figure 8.39).

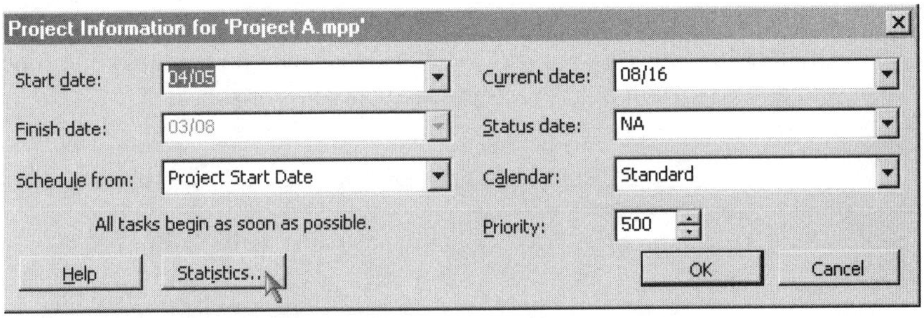

Figure 8.39: Project Information dialog.

Click on the **Statistics** button to display the Project Statistics dialog as shown in Figure 8.40.

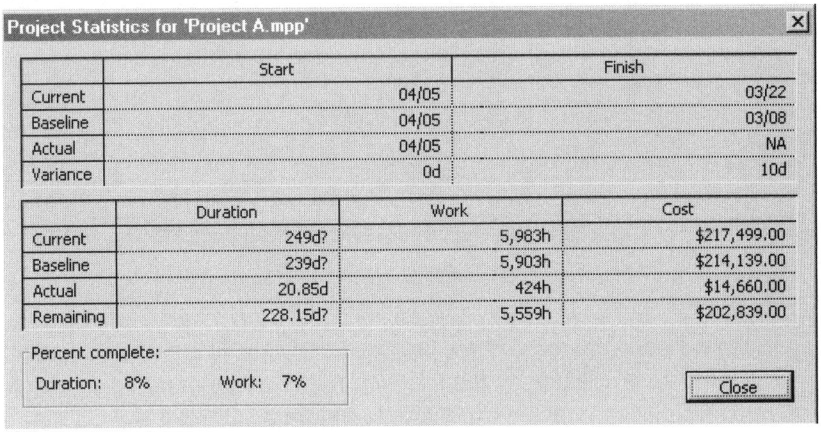

Figure 8.40: Project Statistics dialog.

Here you can see the baseline versus actual start and finish dates along with the variance. You can also see the variance in duration, work, and cost as well as the percentage work complete versus the percentage time elapsed.

Using Templates

Why reinvent the wheel when MS Project has been gracious enough to provide some very useful project templates? Depending on the nature of the project, you may or may not find these templates useful. If the tasks are similar to the ones you need, you could save a lot of time entering text into the Task Name field by utilizing one of these templates and updating it for your specific needs.

To use a project template, Click the File menu on the toolbar and select **New**. On the New Project task pane, select the **On my computer** option to access the Templates dialog (see Figure 8.41). Click a template to preview in the preview pane. When you find a template you like, select it and press **OK**. The template opens as an .mpp file, and you can update it as you wish. You will have all the same features and functionality that you would have if you had created the file yourself from scratch.

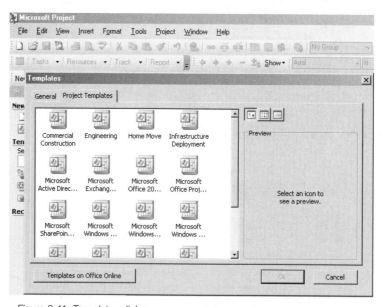

Figure 8.41: Templates dialog.

If you choose, you can save a project that you have created as a template for future use. Do so by clicking on the File menu on the toolbar and selecting **Save As**. Change the type in the pull down menu to **template** (Figure 8.42).

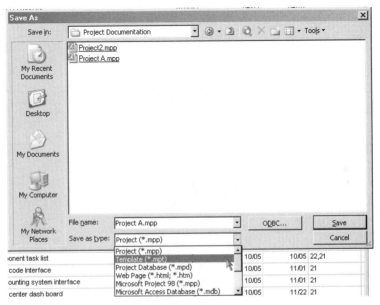

Figure 8.42: Saving a project schedule file as a template

Schedule management is an ongoing process that lasts throughout the project Life Cycle. Each time the project plan or the project schedule changes, the project manager needs to update the project schedule to reflect those changes.

CHAPTER 9

Project Development

By now you should have a well-defined project schedule with lots of team member assignments. So, what do you do now? Do you distribute the schedule to your team, wish them luck, and ask them to let you know when they are done? If you are nodding your head, yes, this could be a good time to start considering a career in another field! Creating the schedule is a major milestone accomplishment, but you have only just started on the road to project development. It is your responsibility to make sure that the project stays on track and that your team does not fall behind schedule. Your project schedule could well be a masterpiece on the grandest scale. You may think that you have exerted a lot of effort to plan your project with just the right amount of buffer time so that, no matter what goes wrong, you will still complete the project on time. Well, remember the old adage, "The best laid plans of mice and men often go awry"? We would like to update this to, "The best laid plans of mice, men, and technology project managers often go awry"! Expect problems. If creating the perfect schedule guaranteed a project's success, projects would not need project managers at all; they would need schedulers.

You have your schedule, and you have begun the development phase of your project. During this phase, you need to manage your schedule, your project, and a whole lot of issues. Remember that the schedule is not the project; it is a tool that you use to manage certain aspects of the project. This phase is all about management, management, management! The more, the better. A Project Management Process workflow diagram is shown in Figure 9.1.

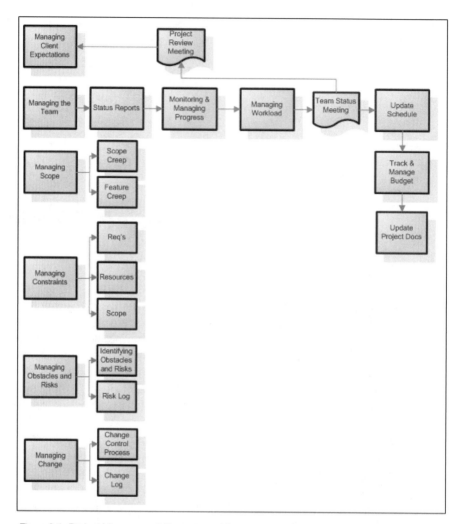

Figure 9.1: Project Management Process workflow.

While the project manager is managing the development of the project, the development team is implementing the development of the project. A Project Development Process workflow diagram is shown in Figure 9.2. The project manager needs to ensure that both these processes, and all the subprocesses, are being followed and that the milestones and deliverables are being met on time, within budget, and with high quality. This is where you truly start to juggle a lot of balls, and it is almost impossible to keep your eye on them all at exactly the same time. You need to figure out how to switch your attention between them so that you are not dropping things left, right, and center. It is critical at this stage of the project that you manage your time effectively and allocate time appropriately to the many areas that need your attention. This is a very challenging, but also very exciting, phase of the project.

Setting and Managing Client Expectations

To manage client expectations, you first need to set them. Setting client expectations means ensuring that you and the client are on the same page about what the project is and what processes will be used to implement it. There should be a common understanding of the proposed methods for implementing and managing the project. There should be agreement on the communication plan, including the methods and each party's responsibilities. This means that the client needs to be aware that they are responsible for informing you about changes and vice versa. You will need shared vision on the milestones, deliverables, and the scope of the project. If you set realistic expectations up front by ensuring that everything is documented, understood, and signed off by your client, you will have built a solid foundation for managing client expectations going forward.

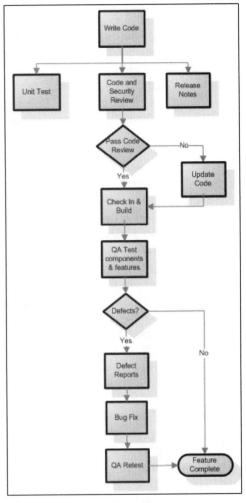

Figure 9.2: Project Development Process workflow.

The Project Definition, the Project Plan, and the Project Approach documents are your project guidelines and rules, and they ensure that the client and the project team know what to expect. This collection of documents is a must-have for all projects, no matter how large or small the documents are. They provide specific agreements, including budgets and schedules, to which the client and team have committed. All of these documents should have been created, reviewed, and agreed to by the client and the team during the Planning stage of the project.

Managing Client Expectations

You may be wondering why you need to manage expectations if you have set realistic expectations that both you and your client have agreed to. Making the assumption that the expectations are set and will manage themselves because all parties agreed to certain things at the start of the project will lead to disaster! You can set the stage for a theatrical play, but without effective stage management and direction, the performance is unlikely to be cohesive, enjoyable, or successful. The same is true for your project. Setting expectations is like getting the stage settings and props ready for the evening's performance. The real work will begin once all the actors are in their places and ready to deliver their individual contributions.

The ongoing management of expectations goes hand-in-hand with the ongoing management of your schedule and resources. You are responsible for keeping your client informed about the project's progress. This includes any required changes that will have client impact. Your client is equally responsible for informing you of any changes they require that will affect you, your team, or the project. If those changes require changes to contracts, resources, or timelines, then it is your responsibility to work with the necessary people and departments to ensure that the changes are approved and documented. Your team members must also be made aware of any changes going on behind the scenes. A change that you may not think impacts them very much could make a huge difference to what or how they need to implement part of the project. This continual multiway, or circular, communication will ensure that the team's vision and expectations are constantly aligned with those of the client.

In today's marketplace, does the phrase "The client is always right, no matter what they want" still ring true? Yes, it does. In the world of ever-changing wants and needs, the client is in control of their own destiny and, to some extent, yours! The client can get whatever they want, within reason, as long as they are prepared to pay the price in both money and time. It is the responsibility of the project manager to carefully manage the client's wants and needs and to deliver on those that have been agreed to. Managing client expectations is an art form. It will be one of the most challenging communication tasks that you undertake as a project manager. You will likely encounter a few problems and will need to use some negotiation skills while managing the client, but it will be rewarding, and it is very important to the outcome of your project.

It is unlikely that you will work on any project that does not have some changes to requirements at some time during the project life cycle. If you get to work on a project that never changes, the chances are that it will be a small project with a short timeline. It is very unusual to find a technology or IT project that does not change from the original requirements. The requirements and specifications can change for various reasons. Sometimes the client requests the changes, and sometimes they are due to technology changes or issues encountered by the project team. It is of the utmost importance to keep your client and your team aware of any requirement changes as well as the project's overall progress

If client expectations are managed well, your project has a much greater chance of being successful than if they are not. If all parties involved feel good about the progress and confident about the outcome, they will be motivated to work together to resolve any issues that arise. Every project experiences challenges from time to time. What is important is how those challenges are approached and managed.

If you are not managing client expectations on an ongoing basis, you may well be in for a rude awakening and more problems than you can ever imagine. If you have ever had surgery and been given pain medication by your doctor afterward, you will know that the rules are to manage the pain on a continual basis because as soon as you get "pain breakthrough," it can be almost impossible to get it back under control again. Taking the pills an hour after the pain has broken through will not make it go away. Taking a double or triple dose may not be effective either.

Remember this when managing your client's expectations. Once you have that pain breakthrough, there is not much you can do to get it back under control again. You may be dealing with the consequences for the remainder of the project. If you and your client have different goals or visions regarding the project, you are definitely in trouble. You most definitely do not want to be receiving angry or confused phone calls from your client on a daily basis. If there has been a problem or a change, they should have heard it from you first and should not have to call you to find out what happened. If your client is calling you to ask for a progress report for the project, you are doing something wrong. They need either more frequent updates or more appropriate updates. If you are doing your job as a project manager, you will be anticipating their needs and fulfilling them before they ever think about calling you.

Your communication plan should specify how often you will meet with your team and your client to give status updates. It will also determine how often you send written updates out to the team and the client. Your client will not normally be invited to your weekly team status meetings. It is more usual for your development team to be present and for the client to be sent the minutes of those meetings. You will need to meet periodically with your client for formal status and progress reporting—the *project reviews.* Those meetings should be held separately from your regular team meetings. It is common to schedule project review meetings to occur on a monthly basis or to coincide with major milestones.

Do not make these review meetings the only time you have contact with the client, though. You should set up a regular time to have a face-to-face or telephone meeting with the client to discuss the project. The client will likely have some deliverables that your team depends on, and these meetings are a great time to discuss progress and delivery dates for those tasks. Those tasks may be the responsibility of the client, but you need to be monitoring progress and ensuring that anything your team depends on to complete their tasks is being tracked along with the rest of your project tasks. A weekly phone call or meeting with the client will help you to build a strong professional relationship with them. It will build rapport and mutual respect. Set up a regular time to meet with your client rather than making a haphazard phone call whenever you think about it or being at the client's beck and call continually throughout the week.

These meetings are also great opportunities for your client to let you know about new upcoming projects or to involve you in the planning phases of projects that they are in the process of proposing. You should always be open to discussing new projects; it is a great way to start building partnerships with your clients and to keep them working with you on a long-term basis. The longer you work with the same client, the easier it is to set and to manage expectations. You can discuss any aspects of the project in these meetings. You may want to discuss those areas of the project that you feel are most risky technically, and they may discuss the areas that they feel are most critical to them. By having these conversations, you are avoiding any unpleasant surprises and are ensuring that you both understand each other's priorities. Hopefully, those priorities will be the same.

Additionally, you will need to set expectations with the client regarding when and where it is OK to contact you. For instance, unless it is a dire emergency that will result in serious damage to the project, the client should not be contacting you during your personal time. The hours that you are not in the office are your personal time, and they need to respect that. Calling you at home at 3 a.m. because they just had an idea about an additional feature they might want to add to the project is not acceptable. Your client needs to be made aware, in advance, of where those boundaries are. Do not assume they will know where those lines are drawn. What seems acceptable to one person is considered totally unacceptable to another. You are not responsible for managing your project 24/7. You should definitely make yourself available for emergencies, and having a company mobile phone is an ideal way of managing those calls. Giving out your home phone number to a client is not a good idea. Once they have that number, they could be calling you for years, even if you are not working on a project for them any longer. There is no reason that a client should need to call you outside of office hours for something that can wait until the next business day. Once you start responding to the client at all hours, you will start losing control of your project and your personal time. Once they have your home phone number, you could be in serious trouble!

Speaking of emergencies, you must be sure that your understanding of what constitutes an emergency is the same as your client's. You should document the meaning of the word "emergency" in your escalation procedures. Make sure your client understands exactly what it means and what it does not mean. You should be managing your client. Don't let the client start managing you.

You will be eager to please your client, but do not be tempted into promising the client too much. You may think that doing a little change here and there will please the client and will keep things running along more smoothly. It is going to have the opposite affect. Once your client believes that they can make changes whenever they want to, with no documentation or process, you are going to have a difficult time trying to convince them otherwise. If you keep changing the rules on the client, they will start to get confused and will eventually lose confidence in your ability as a project manager. You need to manage with consistency and appropriateness. Trying to win respect by being nice and saying "yes" a lot is not going to make you a successful project manager.

What happens if, after the project is completed, the client calls and reports that the project has not been implemented correctly, and they want something done about it? No amount of excuses is going to get you off the hook if you have a project that does not meet the documented specification. It is going to cost the company money, and depending on how costly it is going to be to fix the problem, it may cost you your job.

If you are unable to resolve issues with the client and keep the project on track so that the original contract can be satisfied, you may need to work with your senior managers, and perhaps your legal team, to review, and possibly to renegotiate, the contractual agreement. Renegotiation of contracts can be pretty tough, especially if you are already quite a way down the road with development. Hopefully, any anomalies will have been found early enough in the project life cycle so that you can make changes to scope and direction without too major an impact. It can be rather demoralizing for your team if you have started on a project with the usual gusto and enthusiasm only to get a time-out after a week or two and then have to wait around while the contract is renegotiated. The more thorough the planning phase of your project, the more unlikely it is that you will encounter these kinds of problems.

So what happens if you are in the midst of a project, and you suddenly realize that you most definitely do not have shared vision? You may think that the client has changed their mind and is asking for a lot more than they contracted for and perhaps you feel justified in being a bit miffed with them about it. However, the client may feel that what they are asking for is part of the project agreement and is, therefore, totally justified. How did this happen? You see it one way, and they see it another.

Consider the following scenario: The project manager working for the client's organization has a really clear idea of what the project is. In fact, he was a member of the team that initially proposed the project, and he was heavily involved in the early concept meetings. After his concept team had achieved project approval, it was handed over to their outsourcing department and their legal team to find a technology company to implement it. The company they decided to use was your company. Their legal team negotiated the contract with your company's legal team, and to keep within budget, they made a few changes to the feature list. The contract was finalized and signed by the senior executives at each company. This is where you came in and started working with the client. It is possible that the client's project manager has not seen the legal agreement between your companies. Although he has a specification from his manager, he is still working from the specification he has in his head from a few months ago. He does not realize that a number of features were dropped to make the project cost effective. He thinks he is asking for features that your team is supposed to deliver. He does not think that they are out of scope. We are not saying that this project manager should not have read the contract or reviewed the specification; of course he should have. We are just pointing out that sometimes misunderstandings and misconceptions arise about what constitutes the project.

You can minimize these kinds of instances with effective kick-off meetings and really clear and precise discussions with the client about scope. If the client has a different manager attending the planning meetings than the one who is ultimately assigned to manage the project, you will have your work cut out for you to bring the development project manager up to speed. If she tells you that she knows all about the project because she has been involved since the beginning, it may not mean that she has the same information that you do. Sometimes clarification is all that is needed to resolve the misunderstanding, not renegotiation.

What do you do if the client continually makes unrealistic and unreasonable demands on you and your team? Do you continue to make changes and keep pushing out the schedule? You could do this, but it is not going to result in a successful project. The client may be very intimidating, and you may be scared that they could make things difficult for you. No matter how you feel about the situation, you must take control and do something about it. If the situation is becoming unbearable, and you cannot reason with your client, then you need to take the problem to someone higher up in the organization.

First, make sure that you have documented everything. You need copies of e-mails, notes detailing phone conversations, meeting minutes, and any other supporting documentation. You need to go prepared with a recommendation. It may be that you are recommending that the project be assigned to a different project manager, due to personality clashes with the client. Be careful with this one: You may be talking yourself out of a job. However, if you feel that the project is important, but that you and the client are never going to be able to resolve your differences, then this may be your only option.

Another option is to recommend that the client be "fired." This sounds rather drastic, certainly, but if it is going to end up costing your company more to implement this project than they are earning from it, then you really would be better off pulling out of the contract right here. The final decision to fire a client will not likely be yours. It is a fact that, from time to time, clients are fired. Sometimes clients refuse to adhere to contractual agreements; they try to use bullying tactics to get more than they are paying for, and generally they are just a big pain in the butt and a drain on a company's resources and patience. Not all clients are ideal clients. Working with the wrong clients can do your company more harm than good. If it is getting really ugly, it could be the best thing to get out sooner rather than later. The severing of client relationships must be carried out with the same level of professionalism and respect as your other duties. You need to do as much damage control as possible to minimize the impact on your company and your team.

Establishing a process for requesting and communicating change will be your most valuable tool in managing client expectations. You will not be able to manage your client's needs if you do not have an effective process to manage change.

Managing Project Scope

Project scope needs to be managed on two levels:

- The high-level, overall scope of the project

- The lower-level, detailed scope of individual features

Both these areas can lead to your project getting out of control, so you need to make sure that you are focusing the appropriate amount of attention on each. It is common for the feature-level scope management to fall by the wayside. The scope changes seem so small that they are considered to be almost insignificant. However, those small changes soon add up and can result in a lot of extra time required to complete the project. We call these two areas of project scope "scope creep" and "feature creep."

Scope Creep

The words "scope creep" send shivers up the spines of even the most talented and experienced technology and IT professionals. *Scope creep* is the insidious growth or change of project requirements. Scope creep happens for various reasons. One reason is that project sponsors and project managers cannot always anticipate and identify all project requirements up front. Another reason is the client wanting to add a little here and change a little there, resulting in a lot more work. Sometimes scope creep is due to overzealous developers wanting to build the Cadillac version when the Pinto was ordered. Scope creep is the addition to or growth of a project's features and tasks, after the budget and specifications have been finalized and approved. In the technology and IT world, systems are very complex, and technical environments are ever changing. This can lead to a lot of retroactive changes being made to project definitions.

So, you may be thinking, "The client knows what they want. What does it matter if I do a couple changes here and there? They are not big changes and I want to make the client happy."

Imagine this scenario: You make an appointment with Mike, your mechanic, because your brakes are squeaking. He goes over a list of questions about the car and the symptoms you are experiencing and, based on this information, gives you a written estimate for the work. You sign the estimate; Mike takes your car into the workshop to start working on it and says that he will call you when it is ready to pick up later in the day.

A couple of hours later, you remember that the button to turn on your air conditioner is broken, so you call Mike to tell him about it. He says it won't be a problem, he has the part in stock and he can fix it if you want him to. HMMM....do you begin to see the scope creeping a little? Is Mike going to fix that button without making an amendment to the estimate? Of course he is not. He is going to need a new part, and he is going to need to spend some time replacing it.

You get back to work and forget about the car for a while, and then Mike calls you a couple of hours later to tell you that the squeaking is due to your car's brake pads being worn and that the damage is so bad the rotors also need replacing. The original estimate had included replacing the pads only, so replacing the rotors as well is going to be more expensive. Mike also tells you that due to the additional work and the extra parts he needs for the brakes, he is not going to be able to get your car finished until the following morning. You agree to the additional charges and time, and Mike fixes the car and has it ready for you in the morning. A mechanic gives an initial estimate based on some assumptions, but with a clearly defined scope. In this instance, the assumption was that the brake pads were worn, and the scope was limited to replacing the brake pads.

Mechanics, among other service professionals, have the right idea about how to handle scope creep. Although Mike may not have charged you for the broken air conditioner button (which costs about $2.00), he does charge you for the hour that it took him to disassemble and reassemble the a/c unit to replace the button. He also charges the $800.00 to fix the brakes. Would you have expected him to do this additional work without charging you or without it taking more time? Of course you would not. You would, however, have expected him to clear the additional costs and time with you before he started working on those things so that you were aware of how much each additional item increased the scope.

So can the customer always get what they want? Within reason, absolutely, but remember: Time is money! Even the smallest changes cost something, and those costs can soon add up. If Mike sat down and added up the costs for fixing all the little broken buttons, he would discover that the $2.00 turns into $200 over a period of time, and that doesn't include the hour of labor required for each one. If he had done this work free of charge, he would be losing money. His customers would start complaining that he was not getting things finished on time; he would be starting other jobs late because he spent an extra hour on each one. His customers would start to expect more and more work to be performed at no cost. They would assume that there was little or no cost to the mechanic for what they considered "small fixes," so they would feel that they should not be paying for those things. Mike would need to start cutting corners to make up for the lost revenue and the lost time. The quality of Mike's work would suffer.

The same point applies to technology projects. Even if you feel that making changes for your client is more important than nickel and diming them, a cost is associated with every change. Every minute your team members spend on making small changes is time not spent working on their assigned tasks. Your schedule will slip, your costs will increase, and your quality will decrease. It is a downward slope, and it is imperative that you set the ground rules up front and manage every change.

Another danger of scope creep is the unknown domino affect of changes. One team member may make a change for the client that takes them only five minutes. For instance, perhaps she added an additional button to a form for an Internet product. It was easy for her to copy and paste an additional button and change the text on the button, but what is the button supposed to do? Someone else needs to update the back-end programming to add the functionality for the button. Perhaps that function will add load to the server, which means that the system will no longer support the required number of users. The test plans may have already been created and the automated test scripts recorded. They will not work with additional functionality, and it could take hours to record them again. This one five-minute change could add up to hours or weeks more work for other team members as well as increasing the hardware costs for both the testing and production environments for the project. It is the project manager's responsibility to understand the impact of these kinds of changes and to ensure that all the changes through change control. That button may not have been just a small change to one feature, but a new feature in itself.

The project manager must manage scope creep closely. If you allow scope creep, you will increase costs and the need for additional, or different, resources. Your team members, as well as your client, may be big contributors to scope creep. The way you handle these situations will determine the project's chances of success or failure. Though your client probably understands that any big changes made in a project (like new brake rotors) require a new estimate, your client may not understand that a small change (like a new AC button) is also a new feature that can have a ripple effect on your production cycle.

What causes scope creep? There are a number of different factors, and it is usually a combination of these that can lead to serious damage to your project in a really short time span.

Scope creep can happen when:

- Features and other aspects of the project are left out of the original plan.

- You or your client has acquired a better understanding of the project or better awareness of the required, or desired, solution.

- The client or project sponsor requests additions to the project scope.

- Requirements change due to market forces or newer technologies.

These are some steps that you can take to minimize, or even avoid, scope creep:

- Features or other aspects are left out of the original plan—This is to be expected because you can't have 100% certainty about exactly what you will need until you have completed the planning and design phases of the project. Unless you can see into the future, it is almost inevitable that some things will change. If you can see into the future, you are probably in the wrong profession! It is important to have a formalized process for reviewing and updating the project plan at specific points during the early stages of the project. It also is important to incorporate any changes to the project definition and project plan and schedule as early as possible in the process and to make sure that your client and other stakeholders have signed off on the changes. These changes are not necessarily new features; they may be changes to tasks needed to support implementation requirements or changes to hardware to support the required technology. Allowing a contingency buffer for extra time and costs that arise for unexpected additions is a great idea as long as your client will sign off on this. Just make sure you aren't making modifications all the time. There should be a reasonable cut-off date for changes.

- You or your client has acquired a better understanding of the project or better awareness of the required, or desired, solution—This is related to the previous point and is really a case of the plan and scope becoming better defined as the project planning and design are finalized. Your client should be made aware at the beginning of the project that the proposed (and estimated) solution is based on assumptions and that those assumptions may change somewhat as the team learns more about the project and the various solution options. It might be that the initial proposal would work, but the client wants to go with a newer technology or more extensible solution. In this case, you must present the pros and cons of both solutions and let the client decide what they want to do. The client must feel confident that the solution will work. If they opt for a more costly solution, however, they will need to agree to the higher costs.

- The client or project sponsor has requested additions to the project scope—This is an old favorite. This is when your client is asking for something that is completely different from what is currently in the project plan, or they are asking for significant additional features or functionality. First, ensure that the project plan is clearly defined and agreed upon by both you and the client at the start of the project. This plan is your project blueprint, so make sure that it is not ambiguous in any way. You can refer back to it each time your client asks for additions and point out that the changes are out of scope. If your client wants to proceed with estimating the changes, then use the change management process. It will serve you well in these situations. Make sure that all changes are approved and all necessary contracts are amended before making any schedule changes.

- Requirements have changed due to market forces or newer technologies—If business requirements have changed due to new market trends, it is important to sit down with the client and discuss these changes with them. The changes may have been proposed by your project team or by the client. For example, a newer server may have been introduced to the market that will allow better functionality for the project. In this case, you would inform the client of your findings and any additional associated costs so that they could make an informed decision about whether to request a change. The change would go through your standard change management process. Your client may also instigate a market-driven change. There may have been changes in their market space that they are eager to respond to as quickly as possible, which will require changes to the project plan.

Your project can easily get out of scope due to a number of smaller and seemingly insignificant issues. Individually, these changes or issues will not affect the overall outcome of your project, but together they could add up to a significant impact. Thus, constant monitoring of progress is required to meet project deadlines.

Feature Creep

When dealing with software projects, you are very likely to experience feature creep. In *Feature creep,* a specific feature starts to get out of scope. There are various reasons that this can happen. Sometimes it is due to those little tweaks here and there that the client is asking for. Quite often, it is due to overenthusiasm on the part of the developer. Feature creep needs to be managed in the same way as scope creep. If your features get out of scope, it is only a matter of time before your whole project is out of scope and running late.

Software projects can be very complex, and more often than not, a few unexpected things happen during the project life cycle. As the project manager, the onus is on you to keep track of what your team is working on. One overenthusiastic developer could mean disaster for your project.

Consider the following scenario: One of your team members learns about a new way to code something and is really excited about it. He cannot wait to try out this new coding concept for himself. He starts to implement one of his assigned features using this new coding technique. He does this without consulting the project manager or the technical lead. It takes him an additional four hours to implement the feature, and it does not work exactly as in the specification. He is now behind schedule, and he has a feature that does not comply with the specification. This creates the domino effect that we discussed earlier, where test plans need to be rewritten, other coders have to reimplement their code to make it work with this new specification, and so on. The end result is often that the engineer is made to throw out the code he wrote and to reimplement the code according to the specification. This creates even more delays but is usually less of an impact than changing the specification, having the new specification reviewed and approved, and then asking everyone else to update their work to meet the new specification. If the decision is made to use the new code, you may run into problems further down the line. With new technologies, there are usually a few surprises. The limitations are unknown, work arounds have not yet been identified, and anything can happen. Like the old saying goes, it is "better the devil you know than the devil you don't." This is especially true in technology development.

You need to be aware of what your team members are doing, and you also need to ensure that the ground rules for following specifications and for using new techniques are clearly documented and understood by your team members. It is a programmers' and engineers' dream to continually find new ways to do things and to be able to experiment with new theories while implementing tasks. Working with new technology or new techniques for implementing technology is not always a bad thing. If you have planned for it and if you have allowed additional time to research and test the result, then it can be great for your project, especially if it is successful. New technology does have to be incorporated into your projects at some point, but it needs to be planned and managed carefully. You need to estimate the task appropriately, conduct a risk assessment, and have a plan B in place detailing what you will do if the new idea does not work. Jumping in feet first and assuming you will not sink is not the way to move forward and successfully implement new ideas. Each new technology or innovation takes time and adds a level of risk to your project. A project can assume only a certain level of risk, or it will quickly get out of control. You need to limit how many new things you are working on for your project. If your team members are assuming this risk outside of the project plan and without your knowledge or consent, they are seriously jeopardizing the success of the project.

Some clues will alert you to some unauthorized innovation occurring on your team. If an engineer's work quality starts to decrease, her work is not tested adequately, and she is continually behind schedule, it could be that she is focusing her attention on a new discovery. Alternatively, she could be adding a lot more functionality to the feature than was originally specified. For instance, the engineer thinks it would be cool if this feature could also do these other great things, and the client would love it! It can become an obsession for her to make every feature the best it can be. If the client is not paying for the best it can be, however, your team should not try to deliver that.

The end result of this kind of thinking is that the engineer ends up spending more and more time trying to get the feature working and getting further and further behind schedule. Before you know it, she has dug herself into a hole that just keeps getting deeper and deeper, and there is no way to salvage the situation without severe schedule impact. Restraint, self-discipline, and a strict adherence to the specifications are the only way to avoid these kinds of problems. It doesn't matter how experienced, talented, or innovative an engineer is; if she cannot deliver on time, according to specification, and with high quality, she is going to be a hindrance and not a help to you on your project team.

Your team members should all understand the change control process. If they feel that an additional feature or functionality is so compelling that the client will not want to live without it, they should follow the change control process. The client will be paying for the functionality in both money and time, so they should be the ones to decide whether to go ahead with the changes.

In conclusion, make it a personal as well as a team goal to implement every feature according to the specification. If the client ordered a bicycle, deliver a bicycle and not a Harley Davidson!

Managing Project Constraints

Managing project constraints requires an awareness of the resources (people, time, and cost), the scope, and the requirements for a project. If these *triple constraints* are not managed effectively, the project's risk factor will increase.

The triple constraints (see Figure 9.3) need to be appropriately balanced to ensure that the project is completed successfully (on time, within budget, and with high quality). When a change occurs in one of these areas, the other two areas will be affected. The limits, or constraints, around each of these areas will determine the limits and constraints of the other two. Constraints are interdependent. As a result, they need to be managed holistically to avoid creating unnecessary problems with the project.

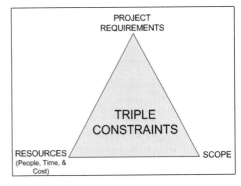

Figure 9.3: Triple constraints.

Here are some examples of managing the triple constraints:

- Let's say that the client has added some new requirements to the project. You decide to respond to this by hiring more developers to meet those requirements. This solution to one problem has the potential to create two more problems: an increase in cost (salary, office space, equipment, etc.) and an increase in the scope of the project.

- If the client wants to change the completion date of the project to a month earlier than scheduled, you will need to reduce the number of days (time) required to complete the project, change the requirements, or reduce the scope. If the scope and requirements of the project remain the same, the only way to accomplish the earlier completion date would be to increase people, either by hiring more developers or outsourcing some of the tasks to outside developers. This may solve the problem of the earlier completion date, but it will increase costs and may also increase complexity (and, therefore, risk).

- If you increase or decrease the scope of the project, a lot of work can be involved to reassign the workload, redesign the product, rewrite test plans, modify the project plan, update documentation, and so on. If you increase scope, you are increasing required resources. If you decrease scope, you are not necessarily decreasing resources. You may still need the same number of developers and skill sets to complete the project on time. You may increase costs with rework by the same amount (or more) than you decreased them by reducing the scope. There could be code dependencies that require a lot of code to be rewritten to support to the removal of part of the functionality.

If you add something to a project, you need to either take something away to maintain the balance (if that is possible), or you need to add to other areas of the project too. Managing project constraints requires skill and a lot of attention to detail.

Understanding the constraints of the project and knowing why you cannot easily change them is crucial to effective project management.

Managing Workload

If you asked multiple project managers what they consider to be the most difficult or challenging aspect of project management, you are likely to get a high percentage of answers that relate to managing people or managing time. If your project team is unhappy, overworked, or both, no one is going to be having much fun during the life cycle of your project.

Microsoft Project is one of many software tools that can assist you in not only scheduling work assignments, but also in alerting you when a resource has become over allocated. During the creation of your project schedule, you ensured that none of your resources were over allocated. You need to continue monitoring and managing your schedule to ensure that resources do not become over allocated due to additions to the schedule or work taking longer than estimated.

Matsu Liu works an eight-hour day. You assign him to create a GUI design document that is allocated 40 hours to complete. How long would it take Matsu to complete this task? If you said five days, you may be correct, or you may not be correct. This will depend on how you allocate time to tasks. It is almost impossible for a developer to accomplish eight hours of coding in an eight-hour day. They will be required to attend meetings, read and respond to e-mails, talk to their manager, assist other developers, answer questions from the client, read technical documentation, and so on. The project manager needs to define how many hours of coding are equal to an eight-hour workday. For example, let's say that in an eight-hour day, the average developer accomplishes six hours of real project development work. The project manager can allow for this time difference in one of two ways:

- She can submit technical estimates for the actual time it will take to complete each task and add a fixed amount of time (equal to 25%) to account for the nonproductive time. In this case, the project manager would schedule a 40-hour task to take 6.7 days. Alternatively, she could schedule 5 days for the task and an additional 1.7 days for project-related noncoding time.

- She can create and submit the estimates, assuming that 1 day is equal to 6 hours of coding or 1 hour is equal to 45 minutes of coding. In this case, the 40-hour estimate would take 5 days.

It does not matter which approach you take, as long as you do something to account for the nonproductive time. You need to be aware that you will quickly get behind schedule if you assume that your team can spend 100% of its time working solely on development tasks.

Even with this planning and scheduling for nondevelopment time, schedule conflicts will occur. These are not the conflicts that occur when two people are fighting or gossiping behind each other's backs, but the schedule conflicts that result when a resource is over allocated. Let's say that you schedule Jane Jones to work on several eight-hour tasks that must be completed on the same day. For example, the Resource Graph histogram in Figure 9.4 shows that, for the week of June 13th, Jane is allocated at 200% for five days. This means that she is 100% over allocated × 5. If Jane normally works 40 hours per week, she would need to work an additional 40 hours, a total of 80 hours, to accomplish her tasks for that week.

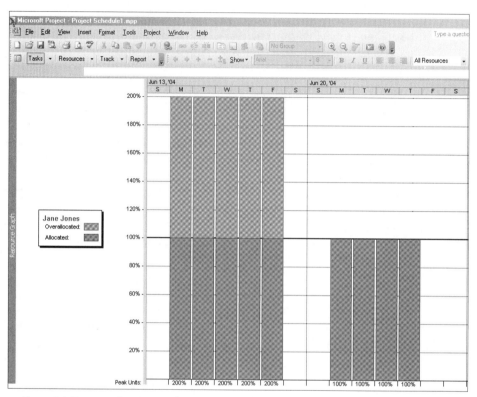

Figure 9.4: Resource Graph histogram.

Assuming that you have scheduled your resources while assuming 75% to 80% of time to be productive time, what can you do if you find you have a resource over allocated? You can panic and do the headless chicken impersonation, or you can ask your team member to work later every night and come in on the weekend so that the tasks are completed on schedule. These are both options, but they are not very good ones, especially if you happen to be the team member with the 100% over allocation for the week. There is an alternative, however, one that should satisfy both the needs of the project manager and the needs of the team member: You need to "level" your resources.

Use the resource sheet, resource graph, or calendar to identify problem areas. If the over allocation is small, and limited to one or two tasks or team members, you may choose to make adjustments to the specific tasks or resources manually. This gives you the option to switch resources for tasks so that they can be accomplished in the desired time frame.

When using the Calendar View, use resource filtering to see individual team member calendars. To filter for resources, click on the Project menu on the toolbar, select **Filtered for: Using Resource**, and then select **Using Resource**. See Figure 9.5.

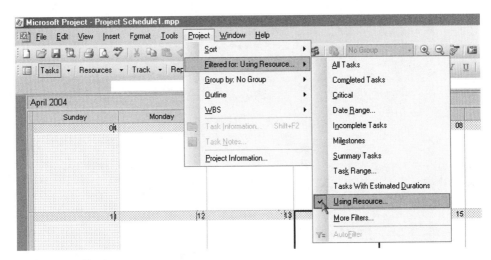

Figure 9.5: Filtering resources.

The Using Resource dialog will be displayed (Figure 9.6).

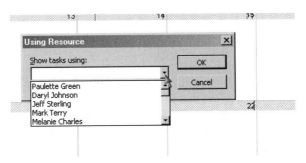

Figure 9.6: Using Resources dialog.

You can clearly see in Figure 9.7 that Jane Jones is over allocated during the week of June 13th.

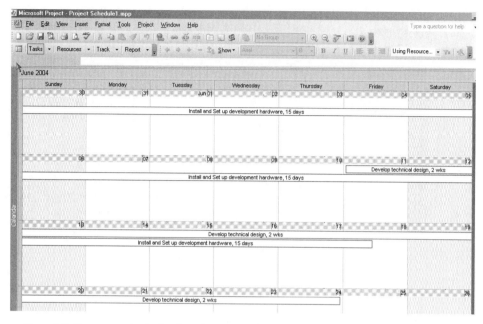

Figure 9.7: Resource calendar for Jane Jones.

You can drag and drop tasks in this view by clicking and holding the task and dragging it to where you want it to start.

You learned about the leveling feature in Chapter 8. If your goal is to keep the same assignments for each team member but to reorganize the assignments so that the resources are not over allocated, then this feature will be very useful. However, it cannot decide to move a task from resource A to resource B, so it is limited in its ability to find the best solution. If you have a lot of interdependencies among tasks, it may get difficult leveling resources without pushing out a lot of tasks, which could result in a delay in the project completion date.

It is beyond the scope of this book to teach you all there is to know about resource leveling. If you wish to learn more about this subject, we would advise that you take a class on or purchase a book about MS Project and resource leveling.

If you just can't find a way to move tasks around so that you are not overloading a team member, the project completion date may have to be moved out. You should look at every option prior to taking this route. This action should always be your last resort. Other options are available: you can reduce scope, increase resources, increase budget, or ask team members to work extra hours. Though we want you to focus on not overworking your team, there will be times when you may need to ask them for additional time. Bear in mind that the more hours a team member spends at work, the more personal things they will be taking care of while they are at the office. If your team members are working an extra couple of hours per day (10 hours instead of 8 hours), the chances are that they are taking longer lunch breaks, reading personal e-mail, shopping online, running errands, paying bills, reading the newspaper, and so on during work hours because they do not have time to do those things outside of work hours. You may find that you are still getting the same number of development work hours from each employee as you would if they were working a standard 8-hour day. If you are paying for overtime, make sure that the employee is actually working. Otherwise, you could be increasing your project costs without increasing productivity.

Status Reports

You know the importance of keeping your schedule up to date, but how do you do it? You need to know how your team members are doing with their assignments. This does not mean that you have to micromanage your team members by hounding them every 20 minutes to tell you where they are on their tasks. It means eliciting regular status reports from your team members, which occur on a set schedule and follow a documented process.

The data contained in the status reports will be your main input to updating your project schedule. Though it is very important that your team follow the standard process for updating you on their tasks, it is even more important that they are encouraged to inform you as soon as possible about any potential problems that could cause the project to slip. The sooner you know, the sooner you can take action to resolve the issue. It is very important that the project manager is informed and the project schedule is updated whenever any changes or issues come up.

The following is an example of the information contained in a status report. A Status Report form is included on the CD-ROM that accompanies this book.

- Contact Information—The team member's name, phone, and e-mail (so you know who the status report is from).

- Reporting period—The start and end date that the status report encompasses.

- List of tasks worked on during this reporting period—A list of both the scheduled and unscheduled tasks that the team member has worked on, the length of time spent on each task, and the percentage of each task that is now complete.

- List of issues—Issues with completing or starting assigned tasks. Special note should be made of any tasks on the critical path. List the reasons for any delays and the recommended steps to resolve each issue. Specify whether any task needs to be rescheduled to a later date because it is dependent on another task that is running late. State any issues with the task or feature being able to meet the requirements—for example, if it is not functioning as expected or there are unanticipated technology limitations.

- Plans for next period—Planned work during the next reporting period and overview of planned work to reach next milestone. Document any recommended changes to milestones since the previous plan.

- Project recommendations—Overall project recommendations that are not just confined to individual tasks and issues or concerns that team members feel should be raised with the project sponsor or stakeholders. These could be anything from potential issues with final product functionality due to technical problems to requests to use newer technology or to add additional resources (money, equipment, or people).

Figure 9.8 shows a sample status report form.

Getting Status from Your Team Members

The frequency you receive status reports from your team members is going to be based to some extent on the length of the project, the number of milestones, and how much time you have between each milestone. You do not want to ask for status reports from your team members on a monthly basis if the project is only going to be four months long. This will not allow you time to respond to issues in a timely manner. Weekly status will work better in this instance. For larger projects, every other week may be acceptable. This will depend on the complexity of your project, the frequency of your milestones, and which phase of the life cycle you are in. You may have a year-long project with monthly milestones, in which case you will need weekly status reports to effectively track progress. When you get to the integration and deployment phases of a project, more frequent status reporting will likely be necessary. At very critical points in the project, status may be required multiple times per day. You need status from your team members for two reasons: The first is to enable you to manage your schedule (and thereby your project); the second is to enable you to provide status communications to your stakeholders.

You should never be caught by surprise or be unaware of project performance or scheduling problems. However, you are walking a fine line when it comes to gathering status reports from team members. Without a consistent, documented process for status reporting, team members may perceive the requesting of status as a lack of confidence in their ability to get their work done. Status reporting should not be difficult, but when you spend unnecessary time tracking down elusive team members to get updates, it can end up becoming so. The project team should be made aware of the process, and individual roles and responsibilities, early on in the project life cycle.

Your team members need to understand the importance of status reports. If your team expresses concern about providing status, then address their concerns rather than just

Fundamentals of Technology Project Management   Document Name Template
Project Name

Status Report Form

Project Name:	OPIS
Project Manager:	Daryl Johnson
Date:	May 26th
Contact Name:	Maten Liu
Phone / E-mail:	555 555 5555
Reporting Period:	May 12st - May 26th
Are All Tasks:	

	Yes		No	
On or Ahead of Schedule?	Yes		No	X
Meeting Requirements?	Yes	X	No	

CURRENT STATUS

Scheduled Work

WBS #	Task	Hours spent on task	Percentage complete
23	UI for Call Center Screens	24	50

Unscheduled Work

Task	Time spent on task	Work Requested By
Working with graphic designer (new employee) to explain UI design	10	PM

Page ▌ of ▌
Created by "Author"

Figure 9.8: Status Report form.

brushing them off. Explain that requesting status updates is part of the process to ensure that the project is completed on time. You are not concerned about every single task being completed in exactly the time allocated to it, but you need to understand the big picture at all times to manage the schedule and the dependencies. This is not about trusting them or having confidence in their abilities; it is about successful project management and teamwork.

Your team must understand that you all have responsibilities to the client and the stakeholders and that providing status is one of those responsibilities. If the project manager is aware that something is taking longer than expected, then they can manage the risk and avoid a potential problem. Everyone on the team needs to understand that the project manager may, at times, have to move tasks from one team member to another. There are dependencies among tasks, and staying on schedule may require changes to resources assigned to certain tasks. Ensure that they understand why this may happen. You do not want your team reporting incorrect status so that they can keep all their assigned tasks. This happens often, so you must keep an eye on it.

There is pride in completing all assigned tasks, and developers can sometimes feel that they have failed if they have to give one up. Reinforce the message that successful projects are based on teamwork, and teamwork means sometimes having to give something up for the good of the team (and, ultimately, the project). Let them know that if they tell you a task is completed that means that it is implemented, unit tested, checked in, and ready for the quality assurance team to test. There is no such thing as "just about completed," "will be completed at the end of the day," or "as much as we need is completed." It is either completed at this time, or it is not. Ensure that your team understands that you are giving stakeholders an overview of the project, not telling them that, "John did not complete task Y on time, but Judy did complete task Y on time." Give them an example like "We have run into a few unanticipated problems and are a few days behind with feature 1 for our first milestone. We may be able to make up the time with some other features that are ahead of schedule right now, and our contingency plan is to release the first milestone without that feature, which has minimal impact, and to include it in the second milestone."

Giving and receiving status is the only method the team has to verify that the project is going smoothly. It is the only way that stakeholders and clients can be kept in the loop and aware of important issues. It is the only way to avoid surprises. By letting the stakeholders know that you may reach the first milestone minus one feature, you are making them aware of the risk and letting them know what you plan to do about it. If it is your first milestone, it will likely not be a big deal. If it is your last milestone before project completion, it will be more serious.

To maintain simplicity and structure, establish a regular reporting and communication system. The reporting system should be implemented as soon as the project starts and should be consistently enforced. If you let one team member slip, then it will only be a matter of time before the others start slipping as well, and then gathering status reports becomes a project management nightmare. Set a specific day and time for reports to be due, and give your team members a template or outline for how to report their status.

Ensure that your team members stick to the schedule. If you are using Microsoft Project Server or other interactive project tracking software, your team members will be able to update their status directly to your project schedule, and all you have to do is review and approve it. If you are using a standard version of MS Project or other noninteractive tracking software, you will need to collect status and manually update your project schedule for each team member. Asking your team members to send you regular status reports may also help reduce the number of team meetings you need. Be wary of eliminating status meetings completely because there could be more impact from a task being overdue than you realize. The project team collectively will be able to point out risks that you may be unaware of from reading individual status reports.

Urgent Issues outside of the Status Reporting Cycle

If an important deadline is missed or a catastrophic failure of some kind occurs, the news should not wait until the next status report is due. Your team members need to understand that they must report these issues to their project manager as soon as possible so the project manager can take immediate action. Policies and guidelines should be established at the start of the project to ensure that emergency communication and problem escalation are well defined. Just because your team report a big issue to you does not necessarily mean that it needs to be reported to the stakeholders or the client immediately. It may be that you can resolve the issue before the next status communication or project review meeting. If you alert them every time you have a problem, they will think that the project is one major disaster after another. It is common for projects to consistently run into problems that need project management intervention to resolve. That is the project manager's job and why project managers are needed to run successful projects.

Use your judgment wisely when deciding to involve others in issues if you have not tried very hard or explored every avenue to resolve it yourself. You might be opening up a can of worms. You don't want to be seen as a hysterical project manager who freaks out every time there is a problem. Worse still, you do not want to be seen as an ineffective project manager who is unable to work independently. Only involve others if you really need them to help you solve the problem. Explain the problem calmly and without too much drama. Do not focus on all the horrible things that could happen if this is not fixed or whose fault it is that it happened. Focus on solutions to the problems. Be factual, not emotional. This is what transforms a good project manager into an excellent project manager.

Development Team Status Meeting

A weekly project status meeting is a perfect venue for development team members to gather, share, and discuss progress with each other. These meetings are informal and should involve just the development team. All team members should be encouraged to be honest and open about any issues or problems they are encountering with their assigned tasks. This forum is a great opportunity for the team to discuss the impact of specific issues on other aspects of the project. For example, one team member may be experiencing a problem implementing a particular task. To get around the problem, he may be considering a different approach than that outlined in the design specification. Other tasks may be dependent on that task being completed on time and in a specific way, or the proposed change in the design may impact the design of other features or components. This information may not be obvious to the developer working on that particular assignment, and without a group discussion about the proposed change, the developer could implement a task in a way that has a huge impact on the ability of the rest of the team to complete their assignments with high quality and in compliance with the specifications.

A regular team meeting is an ideal venue for discussing project status. It is imperative that your team members understand what the other team members are working on and what issues they are running into. They can help each other resolve problems, and they can help prevent others from running into the same problems. You have to remember that some team members may not be working onsite together. You may have team members spread throughout the city, or even spread throughout the nation, working at different locations or telecommuting. Each team member needs to aware of what the others are working on. There are dependencies among tasks, and one team member's work can often impact another's. The project manager is responsible for ensuring that this communication occurs and that the team members are working together to solve problems and to help each other learn and grow.

The project team status meeting is also a great place to discuss technical approaches to tasks. The team can discuss the ins and outs of certain technologies or techniques for achieving specific outcomes. The technical lead for the project will typically have the final OK on technical decisions, but the whole team should have the opportunity to have input before major decisions are made. The reason that the project status meeting is limited to just the development team is so that the group will be able to concentrate on the most important issues that affect the functional or technical development of the project. The team can discuss critical problems, emerging issues, the status of the project with regards to any new requirements or timeline issues, and general development team items of interest without the client or other stakeholders being involved. Without status meetings or status reports, the team members could just keep working on their own tasks until they are done, without any real awareness of the impact that their progress has on the rest of the project schedule.

Status Communication to Stakeholders

Regular communication on the status of your project to your client and stakeholder groups will add value to your project by ensuring that no surprises occur for any of your stakeholders. Producing the right kinds of status communications will help you achieve the right kind of support from the client and stakeholders You may need to produce different status communications for different groups of stakeholders. Over communicating can be as fatal to your project as under communicating. If you give too much information, your readers (or listeners) will get bored and not bother to pay attention to it. If your reports are always long winded, people will just hit the "delete" button when they see your status communications in e-mail or tune you out in a meeting.

To produce effective and informative status communications, hit the most important issue you are addressing in the first sentence. Give a brief explanation of all the key issues (the highlights) in the first paragraph. If you need to add more detail for one or more issues, then write one paragraph on each issue giving more in-depth information. This gives your readers the opportunity to get just the highlights and to have access to more information if they need it. It is vitally important to always cover the most important issues first. It is not a novel; you do not have to write two chapters setting the scene and then spend four chapters building up to the point of the story. Just tell them what the issues are and then explain at a high level and in a nonmelodramatic way.

The frequency of status communications to your stakeholders may or may not be tied to the frequency of retrieving status from your team members. You are retrieving status so that you can manage your project effectively. This may require that you get status updates every week, but you may only need to report status to your stakeholders on a monthly basis or to coincide with project milestones. Do not tie these two events together. Just because you get status weekly does not mean that you need to report it weekly, and just because you only need to report monthly does not mean that you should wait a month to get status from your team. Your primary responsibility is to manage your project and ensure that it is completed on time, within budget, and with high quality.

Whatever the frequency of your written status communications, you must remember that formal Project Review meetings need to be regularly scheduled to discuss the status of your project. Status communications are very important, but do not make them your sole method of communication. At the very least, you should schedule Project Review meetings around key milestones. As always, give your team members prior notification about the meetings, including the purpose of the meeting and the date and time so they can plan to be available to attend. If you have a set time to meet each month or every few weeks, that would be ideal; this may not always possible, however, due to the timing on milestones or other things that are going on within your organization. A Project Review Presentation is included in the CD-ROM that accompanies this book.

What Do the Stakeholders Need to Know?

Remember, the technical level and granularity of information that you give to team members will be different from what you give to stakeholders and clients. You will be taking individualized status reports and consolidating them into a summary or overview of the project. Team members will need very detailed and very specific information, but the client and stakeholders need a high-level overview.

It is important, when writing a report, not to focus on the percentage of work completed but to focus on the milestones. A milestone is a progress marker that is used to measure progress during the project life cycle. A milestone can be set for when a specific functionality has been implemented, or it can mark a significant accomplishment, such as the successful integration of hardware and software. If milestone slippage is occurring, this is a danger sign that the project may be heading for trouble, which could culminate in the project not being completed within the specified time frame. Milestones are a project manager's best friend. They are an easy way to track progress over time and a great way to spot the molehills before they turn into mountains.

Be careful not to set too many milestones or artificial deadlines in your schedule, especially if you are doing this to make your status communications more meaty. It is OK to send out a status report that says that everything is on track to reach your next milestone, period. Your team needs to focus attention on completing the project and not waste time agonizing over reaching unnecessary weekly or monthly deadlines just to make your status communications look more interesting. If they are working on a feature that will take three months to complete, they cannot deliver anything for a milestone in six weeks without trying to engineer a way of showing that they are making progress. This will add time to the schedule and switch the focus from building a quality product to impressing the stakeholders. Set realistic, achievable, and meaningful milestones. They do not have to be evenly spaced throughout the project. You will likely have more milestones that are closer together around project completion than you will have in the middle of the development cycle. Figure 9.9 shows a sample Status Communication.

An added bonus for you when writing regular project status communications is that they provide you with an ongoing history of the details and progress of the project. This information will be very useful in terms of tracking progress and performance for your whole project. It also serves as a reminder of issues that you ran into along the way; this will be ideal input into the lessons-learned meetings that you hold at the end of each project. If your project is more than a few months long, it will be hard at the end to remember a lot of what happened in the early days. If you cannot remember issues, how can you improve processes to ensure that you do not encounter them again?

A sample status report form, status communication document, and Project Review Presentation are included on the CD-ROM that accompanies this book.

Fundamentals of Technology Project Management — Document Name Template

Project Name

Status Communication

Project Name:	OFIS				
Project Manager:	Daryl Johnson				
Phone / E-mail:	555 555 5555				
Today's Date:	June 1st				
Reporting Period:	May 1st - May 31st				
In the Project					
Meeting Milestones and Deliverables?	Yes	X	No		
On track for an ontime completion	Yes	X	No		

Overall Status

Project is on track. No major issues

Progress since last update

Milestone One is complete

Issues, Concerns & Changes

Have hired a new engineer for the development team. Will need 2 weeks ramp up time.

Risk Update

Risk one and two are now closed.
2 new critical risks added to risk log concerning potential incompatabilities between technologies

Budget & Costs

Project is at 20% complete. Budget is at 22%.

Milestones & Deliverables for next period

Milestone Two

Page 1 of 1
Created by "Author"

Figure 9.9: Written Status Communication.

Updating the Project Schedule

The schedule should be updated and distributed to the team members on a regular basis. While updating the schedule, it is important to identify both completed and uncompleted tasks that are running late and to determine the effect that these may have on the overall schedule. It is possible to recognize delays while the tasks are still in progress. For example: if a 20 day task has 10 days schedule time remaining but the work is only 30% complete, it should be clear to you that there is a problem. This problem should be dealt with as soon as possible rather than waiting until the task is complete.

It is important to ensure that you have a clearly defined definition of what "complete" means. You will be surprised at how many different interpretations there are of what that actually means. The project manager may define "complete" as "the coding is completed, the documentation is updated, the unit testing is completed, any known bugs in the code (found during the engineer's unit testing) are resolved, the code is checked in and ready to be built, and the release notes are updated." This definition could also include the code and security review. An engineer may think that "completed" means that she has finished writing the code, end of story! The other tasks that are necessary for the task to really be complete, however, could account for hours or days of additional time. Don't assume that you are all thinking the same thing. When creating your schedule, make sure that you have line items for every single task that you want each developer to complete before they can call a task or a set of tasks "complete." If tasks are marked as 100% complete on your schedule, no other work should be required on them. It is important that your team members give you accurate and honest updates. If they don't tell you the truth because they are afraid you will get upset that they are behind, you will never have an accurate schedule. Your team members need to feel safe about telling you the truth, whether it is good or bad. You need to have a status reporting process that does not allow for ambiguity or misinterpretation. Make it clear and specific.

MS Project has some great features, but you need to be aware that sometimes it is too clever, especially if you have added a lot of discretionary dependencies. If you have every task in the schedule linked together from start through completion, when you update one task to add an additional one day to it, your entire project schedule may be updated, and some of those updates may be unnecessary. Be aware of this, and keep an eye on what MS Project is doing when you make changes to your schedule. You need to be managing it, not letting it manage you!

Once you have updated your team members' tasks, it is equally important to update your cost analysis so that you can see where you are with regards to estimated versus actual costs versus remaining costs. By using a project-scheduling tool like MS Project and entering the resource costs into the schedule, you will automatically recalculate actual costs as you update the schedule. You will easily be able to see whether you are going over budget on resource costs and will be able to take action immediately.

Monitoring and Managing Progress

Active monitoring of your project is essential to the early detection of problems. The earlier you detect problems, the faster you can take action to fix those problems and keep the project on track. The more attention that was given to developing the Project Definition, the Project Plan, and the Project Approach during the planning phase of the project life cycle, the fewer problems you will experience during development. The project schedule should be reviewed and updated on a weekly basis. The project plan documents should also be reviewed and updated as necessary during the implementation of the project.

Although the project work is completed and delivered by the project team, the project team needs leadership and direction from the project manager to ensure the project keeps moving in the right direction. Leadership, guidance, and organization are the primary functions of the project manager during the development and integration phases of the project.

There is a lot more to monitoring the progress of the project than merely receiving status reports from team members. A project manager needs to be monitoring and managing the following aspects of the project:

- Use of Resources—Monitor the use of resources, and make sure that no team member becomes over allocated. When tasks are added to the schedule or the durations of tasks are extended, this can impact the use of resources.

- Tasks and Milestones—Tasks should be updated with actual time so that you can see the scheduled versus actual project progress. The project should be monitored against the baseline. Milestones should be monitored to ensure that they are being accomplished on schedule.

- Status Reports—Status reports are used by development team members to communicate status to the project manager and by the project manager to communicate status to the client and stakeholders. Status report frequency and content should be defined in the communication plan.

- Budget—Your project schedule and other costs should be regularly reviewed against the budget to identify any anomalies. Regular monitoring of costs will alert you to potential budget overruns early in the process and allow you to take action to avert them or minimize their impact on the project. It is typical for most companies to request monthly budget reports from their project managers. You will need to be prepared to explain any discrepancies, so make sure you can account for all the costs.

- Quality of the Product—The quality of the product is vitally important, and it needs to be monitored on an ongoing basis throughout the development cycle. The quality includes the look and feel of the product, the functionality, the performance, and the stability. There should be regular reviews with the project team and the quality assurance team to ensure that the quality of the product is meeting expectations.

- Builds and Releases—Most software projects will have a regular build and release schedule during the development phase. The project manager is responsible for creating the schedule and for monitoring the progress. The quality assurance team needs builds and releases to test the product throughout the development phase.

- Defects—Along with monitoring quality, you need to monitor and manag product defects together with the quality assurance manager. Unless your project is really small with a very short time frame, you should not leave defect tracking or fixing until after the development phase is complete. This is especially important if you have a lot of dependencies in your schedule. If a predecessor task has a defect, the successor task may not be able to be completed on time.

- Documentation—Some project documents require regular reviews and updates. Ensure that you are monitoring the progress of documentation and that your team members are producing the appropriate documentation.

- Communication—Regular communication between the project manager, the team members, and the client and stakeholder groups needs to be managed on an ongoing basis. Ensure that you are following your communication plan. Update it if necessary.

Without effective monitoring and tracking of the progress and status of the project, the project manager will be unable to make judgments and decisions about necessary actions.

Tracking and Managing the Budget

It is important to be able to effectively track and manage your budget if you are to ensure that you stay within it and complete your project with a successful outcome. The following section contains some information on tracking your budget that may seem rather complicated at first sight. Once you start using the formulas, though, you will find that they are nowhere near as complicated as they look. So, please, persevere with us on this one and be open to trying a few simple calculations. You might be really surprised at the results!

When tracking your budget, you should use two principal tools:

1. Gantt Chart—This provides a graphical view of the project timeline. You can see which tasks are complete, the variance between planned and actual schedule time, and the dependency relationship between work

units. The x-axis is time, and the y-axis shows the tasks to be performed to complete the project. Each task is displayed as a horizontal bar spanning the time period during which it is expected to take place. Microsoft Project and other project management software programs make it easy to create and maintain Gantt charts.

2. Earned Value Analysis—Three fundamental measures are needed to perform Earned Value Analysis on a project. These are based on estimated, as well as actual, costs.

   ◆ Budgeted cost of work scheduled (BCWS)—This is the total of all budgets for planned work that is scheduled to be completed at a specific point in time. This shows how much of your budget you should have spent up to this point if the project is on schedule.

   ◆ Budgeted cost of work performed (BCWP)—This is the budget total for all work that is marked as complete on your schedule.

   ◆ Actual cost of work performed (ACWP)—This is the total actual cost for the work that is marked as complete on your schedule.

Once you have performed the measurements and collected the data for the Earned Value Analysis, you need to analyze the data. You do this as follows:

- Schedule Variance (SV)—If BCWP is less than BCWS, you are behind schedule. This is called "schedule variance" (SV). The formula is BCWP – BCWS. A negative number indicates that you are behind schedule.

- Schedule Performance Index (SPI)—This is the ratio of work performed to work scheduled. The formula is BCWP/BCWS and is expressed as a percentage. If you are below 100%, you are behind schedule; if you are above 100%, you are ahead of schedule. The percentage will indicate how far ahead or behind schedule you are.

- Cost Variance (CV)—If BCWP is less than ACWP, you are over budget. This is called "cost variance" (CV). The calculation is BCWP – ACWP. As with SV, negative numbers indicate a problem. If the number is negative, you are over budget, and if it is positive you are under budget.

- Cost Performance Index (CPI)—This is the ratio of budgeted cost to actual cost. The formula is BCWP/ACWP and is also expressed as a percentage. Below 100% you are over budget; more than 100%, you are under budget. The percentage will indicate how far under or over budget you are.

If a project does run into trouble and your costs are exceeding your budget, several techniques are available to try to get things back on track. At the very least, these techniques should help minimize the overrun.

- Crashing—Project crashing is a method for shortening the project duration by reducing the time of one or more of the critical project activities to less than its normal activity time. The object of crashing is to reduce project duration while minimizing the cost of crashing. You accomplish this by adding resources to tasks on the critical path in an effort to shorten the project schedule. Effective crashing is difficult to achieve because there will be a resource learning curve that could slow things down and may counteract any time savings you achieve by implementing this method.

- Overtime—This is an effective way of adding people without adding a learning curve. If your team is salaried, the costs of overtime will be minimal. With this method you can add people for an extended amount of time. However, if you push your team to work too much overtime, they will start to get fatigued. This could backfire and cause even more development problems. Your team may also get a bit fed up with working overtime for no additional pay if you try to implement this method for long periods. Mistakes start happening when a team is tired, burnt out, and unhappy. Productivity decreases along with team morale.

- Fast track—Fast tracking is a project management technique used to ensure that projects are completed within the shortest time possible. When projects are fast-tracked, it usually indicates that tasks have been arranged to take advantage of nondependent activities that can occur simultaneously, thus shortening the overall project timeline. An example might be to have your programmer start coding for a software project before the requirements and design are 100% complete.

- Phased implementation—Sometimes the most critical need for the client is to get their hands on something with limited functionality that is available now and works quickly, delaying full functionality to some time in the future. This can work well if you have the option to go back to add additional components later. However, if this means reimplementing code—coding it twice in other words—it will cost more in the long run. At times, the demands of the schedule may make this an attractive option because shorter phases can be implemented more quickly and benefits will be realized sooner.

All of these techniques trade cost for time. If budget is the problem, you will need to reduce scope or allow more time. Increasing the budget or extending the schedule can help with scope and quality problems.

How to Stay within Budget

Tracking costs can be more complicated than tracking the schedule. With the schedule, you know right away whether you missed a date, but with costs, it is not always immediately apparent that you are going over budget. You might be thinking, "If I manage my resources effectively, I should know whether the costs are exceeding the budget, shouldn't I"? This is sometimes true, but it is not always the case. There is always lag time when dealing with financials. You may think you are on schedule and within budget because you recognize the expenses you are signing off on and know that they were budgeted. But then you receive a pile of invoices from the previous month, and it is hard to know where you stand. If you rely on expense or budget reports from your accounting department, you will see expenses showing up 30 to 60 days later. This is due to a few reasons. Accounts are closed out at month's end, so they usually wait about five days after the end of the month to start reconciling. It could be a few days to a few weeks before you receive your budget reports.

You also need to remember that most expenses do not show up on the books, or your reports, until they are paid. It is not unusual to have a NET30 or NET60 on your invoices, which means they are due 30 days or 60 days after receipt. If you are working with contractors, they will often submit their invoices for payment at the end of the month; likewise, your team members will usually submit their monthly expenses at the end of the month. So what does this all mean to your budget tracking? It means that you will not have the financial information in real time, which means that managing your budget probably falls somewhere between being a little frustrating and a living hell! But it can be done. Probably not quite in the way you would like it to be, but it can be done and with success.

You can do some things to help with tracking your expenses so that you do not have to wait until they are paid and reconciled before you know about them. These techniques may not get you the exact numbers that you need, but they should enable you to see whether you have more invoices coming in than you were expecting. Here are a few tips on managing expenses:

- Ask vendors, consultants, and contractors to send invoices directly to you, and tell them you will submit them to your accounting department for payment. If your accounting department insists on invoices being sent directly to them, ask for your suppliers to send you a copy for your files, too.

- Set up a process where all expenses are approved by you before being submitted for payment. Then you can check them off against your budget, making sure there are no surprises. You should also make copies so that, if you see on your budget reports that your costs are significantly lower or higher than you expected, you have some data to analyze to find out why.

- Try to do most of the ordering yourself rather than delegating this to your team members. Get written quotes and keep them on file.

- Set up a process with your consultants, contractors, and vendors that they may not bill you for anything that was not approved by you before they did the work. For instance, contractors may not put in any overtime until you have approved it in writing first. Ensure that it is clear that the only person on your team authorized to approve additional costs is you.

These methods will help you track incoming expenses, and those will ultimately map to your budget. You do not need to do in-depth financial analyses of your expenses each month, but you can be on the look out for any red flags or surprises. Budgets require a more creative management approach than schedules. With a few good solid processes in place you should be able to keep your project costs under control.

Defining measurable objectives that enable you to know that the project is on target is another huge factor in staying within budget. If you have determined the development hours that are required to complete each task and are proactive in monitoring and managing progress, you will have a pretty good idea when you might be heading for trouble even without financial reports. It is important that you stay on top of what is happening with your project and your team. You do not need to panic every time a task runs over by two days, but you do need to panic if it has run over by two days and the developer states that he still needs twice the originally scheduled time to complete it. This is indicative of a problem, and you will need to do something about it fast. At any moment, you should be able to give an overview of where you are with the project and what the highest risks are for that week or month. If your schedule is slipping, your budget will likely be following right behind it down that slippery slope to living hell! You need to be able to determine quickly whether additional resources, people, or equipment are needed to head off a potential disaster. Your budget is affected by any resource issue on your team, be it people, money, time, or equipment.

Once you know for sure that you must cut costs either because you are over budget or because some organizational budget cuts have been imposed, here are a few suggestions on some actions that you might consider:

- Team members—It may be possible to switch out some or all of your highly paid team members with those who can do the work at a lower cost. While it is important to try to keep your team intact, it is also important to make sure that your project is not canceled due to the costs being too high. It might be that some of your team members are overqualified for some of the tasks they are performing. You may be able to trade them for resources on other projects who are paid at a lower rate but who could implement those tasks just as effectively.

- Improve processes—Talk to your team for suggestions on how to cut some costs. Let them know that there are budget issues and that you need their help to figure out the least intrusive way of getting the project back on track. Your team will likely come up with some great suggestions. There might be a cheaper equipment solution that you had not considered, or perhaps they might be willing to work some overtime without charging it to the project.

- Scope change—Do not allow any scope changes to be implemented that have not been documented and signed off by the client. Sometimes you find out that your team members are working on additional functionality that was not approved by you or the client and this is why you have a schedule and budget overrun. It is critical that you monitor what your team is working on and that both you and they understand the scope of their tasks. If they are working on nonessential or nonscheduled tasks, they will not have time to work on their scheduled tasks.

- Dependencies—Ensure that you have the dependencies documented and scheduled appropriately. Check in with your team members regularly, and ask them whether any unanticipated dependencies have arisen. If an engineer is waiting for something from another engineer and is unable to continue without it, they may be sitting around not doing much at all. If you were unaware of the dependency, you may not have factored this into the schedule. If you are aware of these issues immediately, you can reschedule tasks to ensure maximum productivity at all times.

- Revisit nonlabor costs—Revisit nonlabor costs and see whether there may be hardware that can be negotiated at a lower rate or even a cheaper substitute that may be suitable. You may even want to look into renting staging servers or cohabiting a development server with another project to cut costs. You may have to consider looking into the training aspects of the project. Instead of formalized training, can team members do computer-based training, or can one of them take a training class and then train the rest of the team? When you get creative, it is amazing what you can come up with!

- Budget contingency—If none of the other options work, you may have to start using your contingency budget to get the project back on track. If it is early in the project, be very careful about using this as a solution. A whole host of other surprises may be just around the corner waiting to jump out and eat up more of your budget money. If you have used your buffer zone in the early stages of the project, you know that you are just delaying the inevitable. It is much easier to solve issues early in the project life cycle than later on, so try to save this contingency budget for last-minute emergencies that cannot be resolved in any other way.

- Reduce work—If all else fails, the worse-case scenario is that you raise the problem of escalating costs as an issue with your senior managers and work with the client to find an alternative. Maybe there is a way to reduce the work. Perhaps you could trade system performance tasks for additional hardware. Sometimes it is cheaper to buy more servers than spend the time trying to squeeze an additional 500 users out of the original number of servers.

So, what are the most risky areas of the project that are likely to lead to budget issues? This is a good question. These are some high-risk areas to be aware of:

- Technology costs—The initial estimated costs for technology may have been based on limited information and may have been way off target. Sometimes unforeseen issues occur. For instance, you based your equipment estimate on published performance data supplied by the manufacturer. You discovered after you started testing the equipment that your program was running about 10 times more processes than the test programs the manufacturers were using for their performance tests. Even with performance tweaking of the system, you may find that you need three times as much hardware as you had originally estimated.

- Requirements changes—Changes to requirements can occur for many reasons. Some of them arise due to misunderstandings, some because the client changed their mind about what technology they wanted to use, and others due to previously unknown technology limitations coming to light. Requirement changes can create a lot of additional work for your team and can be a major contributor to schedule slippage and budget overrun.

- Organizational changes—When any organizational change occurs (layoffs, mergers, organizational shake-ups, etc.), it can cause uncertainty in your team members. They start to doubt the stability of the organization, and when this happens, panic can set in. Insecurity and frustration will affect the productivity of your team. Fear will decrease productivity even more. If your team feels uneasy in the workplace, it is going to take a lot of effort on your part to try to keep your schedule on track.

- Poorly developed budget—If the budget is poorly developed and not properly reviewed, approved, and managed, then no matter how successful you are at staying on schedule, it is likely that the initial budget will prove to be insufficient.

With all that said, and perhaps with your head spinning trying to understand the difference between BCWS and SPI, let us just reiterate that monitoring the tasks and the costs together is what will keep your project on track and on budget. You do not need to memorize all the acronyms for financials to be able to manage your budget. As long as you are proactively managing your project, you will identify issues before they become issues and will not be blind sided by a disaster. It is a good idea to have a basic understanding of budgets because it will assist you tremendously with managing and communicating status for your budget, but don't get too overwhelmed with all the financial terms. Just remember that the most important thing is that you need to have more coming in than going out!

The more you work with budgets, the better and easier it will get, and the more comfortable you will feel with the process.

Code and Security Reviews

It is important during the development phase of your project that you conduct code reviews and security reviews for the features you are implementing. They are as important to the success of your project as the design reviews. If bad code is being written now, you will have a lot of work to do during the integration phase to remedy the issues. Code reviews are a great way of ensuring that code standards are being followed and met. The team members should be writing high-quality and efficient code and should be commenting the code neatly, clearly, and understandably. The same developer may not always be assigned to working on the code later on so it is vital to the success of your project that another engineer be able to view the code and quickly understand what it is supposed to do. The technical lead or architect should be heading up the technical reviews and taking responsibility for defining and enforcing coding standards.

Security in software design and development is vitally important. If you do not pay attention to the security aspects of software development, you could be creating a whole host of problems, the least being that someone may have to spend the rest of their lives managing the process of getting daily, weekly, or monthly security updates to the end users of your product! At worst, your company could be left open to lawsuits, which could have serious consequences for the success and longevity of the organization. On a personal level, a serious security hole in your project could mean that some heads have to roll; one of them could be yours. Either the technical lead or the security officer should head up security reviews for the relevant features, components, or products.

Feature Complete

"Feature Complete" is an important project milestone that signifies all the individual features and components of the project have been completed, unit tested, and checked in. It assumes that all known bugs detected during the development phase of the project have been resolved and that all parts of the code are functioning as designed. At this point, the quality assurance team will take delivery of the product to start testing the product's functionality from end to end.

CHAPTER 10

Managing Obstacles and Risks

No project manager wants to find himself working on a project and suddenly realize that it is three months behind schedule, over budget by 35%, and of a quality that is way below that agreed to in the contract. The worst thing about this scenario is that there is no reason or excuse why you should "suddenly" realize that you are three months behind schedule. You should know that you are behind schedule as soon as it starts happening. If you do not see a pattern emerging, and recognize a downward trend only when your schedule shows that you slipped from two weeks behind to three weeks behind, then you are not monitoring your project effectively. If your monitoring is ineffective, your project management is going to be ineffective also.

How to Recognize when Trouble Is Brewing

So how do you recognize the early warning signs that something is going awry with your best laid plans?

- Schedule Slippage—The schedule is starting to slip, and you are not seeing a recovery or much slow down in the rate of slippage. Your team is working longer hours consistently to try to catch up, or the tasks are being pushed out more and more each week, causing the project end date to keep moving further and further away.

- Project Is Running Over Budget—If you are running over budget, you are spending too much money. It could be due to the schedule slipping, it could be due to other project costs running too high, or it could be a combination of both.

- Scope or Feature Creep—If you start getting a lot of little extras added by the client, or you find that your team members are being a bit overzealous in the quality and functionality they are adding, you may be on the path to self destruction. Keep an eye on this, and manage it so that it does not get out of hand.

■ Lack of Quality—Your team are delivering regular builds to QA for testing, and there is an unusually high occurrence of bugs. This could be due to the developers not unit testing their code properly or rushing to get things finished, or you may be overstretching some team members with tasks that are too complex for them. Lack of quality will start to affect your schedule because your team will need to spend much more time than allocated on bug fixing, which in turn will affect their ability to get their other tasks completed on time.

■ Not Receiving Adequate Support from the Client—If your client is taking too long to approve specifications or is not getting back to you in a timely manner when questions are asked, this will start to affect your team's ability to implement tasks on schedule. You could have team members sitting around unable to continue while waiting for information or approval from the client.

■ Increase in Employee Turnover—Another sign that your project is in trouble is when your team members starting flying the coop. If you see a big increase in turnover, it usually indicates that your team is unhappy. This may be due to project issues or organizational issues. You need to do some damage control to try to minimize the issues. You also need to manage the issues created by losing developers midcycle. This can have a huge schedule impact, and even after you replace those employees, you have the ramp-up time and effort to deal with.

Once you see these kinds of problems occurring, start doing some root cause analysis immediately. If you stop these problems dead in their tracks—before you start to see the fallout from them affecting the schedule or the budget—you will spend less time putting out fires and more time proactively managing your project. The previous chapter gave you some great tools and techniques for monitoring and managing your project.

Where do you start with root cause analysis? Here are some questions that should help you to figure where the problem(s) are originating. If you answer, "don't know" to any of these questions, you need to focus some energy finding out the answer. An "I don't know" is a big red flag alerting you to an area of your project that needs more attention. If you answer "no" to any of these questions, you definitely need to focus some attention fixing these issues. Bear in mind that this is by no means a full list of everything that can cause your project to go off track. You should create your own list of questions to ask yourself every month or so, customizing them for your project and taking into account the identified areas of risk for your particular project.

■ Have the client expectations been set appropriately?

■ Do you and the client have a shared vision?

- Are you having regular, honest discussions with your client about the project's progress?

- Is your client delivering information required by team members in a timely manner?

- Are you soliciting feedback and status reports from team members on a weekly basis?

- Are you processing the status reports, updating the schedule, and distributing updated copies of the schedule to the development team in a timely manner?

- Are you running weekly reports on your schedule to check your use of resources and ensuring that your team members are not over allocated?

- Are the scheduled builds and releases to QA happening on time?

- Are you running defect reports and reviewing them with the QA manager regularly?

- Are the number and severity of defects in line with expectations?

- Is the scope of the project in line with that of the Project Definition?

- Is the scope of all the features in line with the original requirements?

- Is the change control process being used for every change?

- Are late-delivered tasks spread fairly evenly across the team (and not all originating from just one person)?

- Are you managing the triple constraints proactively?

- Are the code and security reviews being conducted before features are delivered to QA?

- Are you keeping a Risk Log and doing risk analysis regularly?

- Are you doing budget analysis on a regular basis?

- Are you meeting one-on-one with team members regularly and ensuring that they are happy with the way things are going?

- Are you holding weekly team status meetings?

- Are you holding regular project review meetings with the client?

- Do you have the full support of the sponsor and senior management for your project?

- Is your project buffer proving to be sufficient to cover tasks that run over schedule?

- Are you meeting your milestone deadlines?

If you take action now on any of the above questions where you answered "no" or "don't know", you may be able to avert a disaster. It would be surprising if you never had a "no" or "don't know" answer for any of the questions. There are always issues with projects; this is why project managers are needed to manage them. The proactive monitoring of your project, and your management of the project, will alert you to problems early on and enable you to resolve the issues and keep things moving along without too many hiccups.

Managing the Change Control Process

In the planning phase of your project, you created a Change Control Process document. The document may define the best change control process ever invented in the history of project management, but unless the process is used, it is not going to benefit your project one iota. It is your responsibility to enforce the rules regarding change control. Unless you have a highly disciplined team and an exceptionally responsible client, it is likely to take quite a bit of effort on your part to ensure that everything is going through the right channels and nothing is slipping through the net.

"Oh, by the way, this needs to be changed, but I don't want to pay any extra because I know it is just a small change so it cannot possible take long to do it. You can just add it to the schedule and give it to an engineer when they have nothing else to do and then you will still be able to finish the project in three months." As a project manager, you will grow to love *Change Requests*, especially if they are submitted via the formal change control process rather than in a phone call like the one above. Change Requests will be one of the things that you can be certain of on every project in which you are involved, so you need to be ready to deal with them. As soon as you start letting changes through the gate without them going through the change control process, you have lost control of the changes in your project. This will lead you down the slippery slope of uninhibited scope expansion. Believe us: You do not want to go there!

Change is not a bad thing. It is likely the reason that your project was required in the first place. You should embrace change enthusiastically, and while you are holding it tightly in your arms, you should run as fast as you can to the change control office and drop it into the inbox! Seriously, without change, there would be no need for project managers. You need to either grow to love it or grow to tolerate it. Either way, you need to learn how to manage it effectively.

As soon as the Project Definition is finalized, your client will start requesting changes. Often, they want changes implemented without affecting the timeline or the budget. They usually have no idea how big an effect one small change (as they see it) can have on the project schedule and costs. Before you start crying, working like crazy burning the midnight oil, or asking your team members to work overtime, remember that you have a change control process. If you don't have one, you need to create one as quickly as possible.

The *Change Request Form* is the standard written document used by any person who is requesting a change to the project. The form is designed to capture all the relevant information regarding the desired change request. The form should be simple enough to encourage its use and complete enough to provide the necessary information for an adequate preliminary review.

The Change Request Form should include, but not be limited to, the following fields. A sample Change Request Form is shown in Figure 10.1. A Change Request Form is included on the CD-ROM that accompanies this book.

- Change Request Title and Subject—The title and subject of the proposed change. The title is used for categorization and for tracking purposes.

- Change Request Number—The change request will be assigned a change request number after it is submitted to the change control board.

- Date Created—Date the change control form was created and submitted.

- Originator—The person who is requesting the change.

- Organization—The company the originator works for. Are they part of the client's company, the contractor's, a partner, or an internal group?

- Proposed Change Description—A full description of the proposed change.

- Justification—Why the originator feels the change is necessary and whether it is an addition, deletion, or change to the original plan.

- Benefits—Describe the anticipated benefits of the change. Who benefits from it?

- Impact Statement—What are the implications if the change is not implemented? What are the known impacts of the change on the existing product, code, or system?

- Action Taken—Describe the action taken by the change control board on the change request.

- Approvals—For both round one and two of change control, the decision on whether to approve, disapprove, or defer the change is recorded here. Both the change control board and a client representative sign the completed Change Request Form before it is closed.

Change Requests should be logged and managed using a *Change Log*. The project manager should own the Change Log, regardless of who the change control process owner is (it may not be the project manager). A sample Change Log is shown in Figure 10.2. A Change Log document is included on the CD-ROM that accompanies this book.

Fundamentals of Technology Project Management   Document Name Template
Project Name

Change Request Form

Project Name:	OFIS		CR Number:	
Project Manager:	Daryl Johnson		Process Owner:	Daryl Johnson
Change Request Title:	Add update functionality to customer order management screens			
Originator:	Robin English		Date Created:	June 23rd

Proposed Change Description

Add ability for retailers to update orders after they have been submitted. Will need notification process for warehouse shipping and can only accept changes if order not shipped yet

Justification

Will cut down customer support calls for customers who want to make changes soon after placing order.

Benefits

Increased ROI

Impact Statement

Impact on business is more customer support calls. Impact on other features unknown.

Action Taken

Approvals

Round One: Approved	YES	NO	DEFFERED
Round Two: Approved	YES	NO	DEFFERED

Approver Signature		Print Name	Date
Client Signature		Print Name	Date

Figure 10.1: Change Request Form.

Change Log

OFIS

No	Change Request Description	Originator	Date of Request	Status	Owner	Date Change Implemented	Description of Change	Implemented by
43	Add update functionality to customer order management screens	Robin English	13-May	Closed	Robin English	28-May	added update component A to order management component B	Manuel Gomez
44	add four new screens to product pages	UI designer	26-Jun	open	Robin English			

Figure 10.2: Change Log.

The purpose of a change control process is to enable you to continue developing your project while also managing changes that affect your project. The process is designed to manage and to communicate all changes to the Project Plan. The change process should help you protect your team from distractions that could affect their ability to successfully implement the project. Change Requests can easily upset the balance of the triple constraints of requirements, resources (time, people, equipment, and cost), and scope. As a result, you need to ensure that you are proactively managing the triple constraints and paying particular attention to them when approving change requests. Your client should never call an engineer directly to ask for additional features or functionality to be added to the project. They need a clearly defined process to follow, and they need to understand that changes will cost money and time. Some of the changes that you will be managing will be because of things that your team is doing and not because of the client asking you for something extra. For example, you may discover at some point during the project development cycle that to use the required technology to build the product, the client will need to upgrade their data center servers to a new version of the operating system (OS). You cannot just call their systems administrators and ask them to make this change. They could be using those systems for other projects or functions, and the changes could impact their other business processes. You need to determine with the client what the change procedures are for changes in their environment as well as for changes in yours.

Change is a natural process in everyday life and most especially in the life of a project manager. Understanding and managing change requires skill and knowledge. Change is good. You cannot have progress without change. Unmanaged change can be bad, however, and will not result in much progress. You need to be careful that you are not creating a monster. Well-managed changes in client's requirements can create additional revenue for both companies involved in the project. No matter how large or small, it is imperative to the success of your project that all changes be accurately tracked and documented. If changes are not documented, it can be a nightmare managing the consequences and could have a serious impact on the success of your project. If your team works on client-requested changes that have not been approved or documented, your team will be doing additional work, in the same timeframe, for the same amount of money. Worse still, you will be doing additional work that takes longer for the same amount of money. If you deliver the project late to the client, there could be contractual issues. This opens up a whole other can of worms. The moral here is to make sure you have every change approved, signed off, and documented. This will ensure that any contractual changes are made, and there will be no issues later on with the client questioning the changes. The contractual changes will include revisions to the project costs and timeline.

Some changes will be small and will not need contractual revisions or changes to the costs or timeline of the project. These changes still need to be documented because some impact always occurs from change, and specifications should always be kept up to date. If a design is changed because something did not work as initially thought, if an OS version is changed, or if the test plan needs to be revised, all these things need to be documented. The changes may not all have to go through a formal change request process with sign-off from the client, but they will need to follow a change process.

It is very important that all team members fully understand the change control process. Clients will sometimes try to get additional work from your project team without going through the process. Your team members may try to avoid updating the specifications to reflect changes because they dislike writing documents. You need to have a "no excuses" policy on change, or you will never be able to keep your project on track. It is very important that the team exercise discipline, and if a client calls a team member directly (this should be strongly discouraged), the team member should direct them to you, the project manager. If a team member makes a change for the client because they want to increase client satisfaction, they are allowing the client to work outside of the process, and the client will start to go directly to that person for everything he needs. The team member will have created his or her own monster! Even worse, the client will believe that all changes can be implemented in a quick and easy manner without documentation and without additional cost. It undermines your authority and creates a division on the team.

Ask your team members how they would feel if they made the small change that the client wanted, just to be nice, and then after the project was completed the client called and reported that the project had not been implemented correctly so they wanted some of their money back or they wanted it corrected. That small change could require a major effort to change it back to what was in the specification. The change was never documented so all the specs and the requirements do not show it as being requested. Perhaps the person who requested it did not have the authority to ask for that change, they do not work there anymore, or it caused problems so they conveniently "forgot" that they had asked for it. Both you and the engineer who made the change would be on the line for not following the specifications. At the end of the day, this issue cannot be traced back to the project manager because it was obviously done without their knowledge or consent. Therefore, the developer has to explain why they did not follow the specification. It could be a career-changing decision for the team member. Ensure that your team understands that documenting and approving changes is not about whether or not you are being nice to the client or making them jump through hoops for one small change, it is about being professional and responsible and maintaining the highest standards at all times. It is very important that team members comprehend the importance of the change control process and integrate it into their daily routines.

Any project can be difficult to manage, but technology and IT projects can have added complexities that may not be found in other industries. Change control in technology projects can be a highly challenging task for a project manager. It is not always clear what impact one small change can have on the project without getting input from others working on the project. There are so many interdependencies among tasks and features that no one person can manage this independently. Communicating change effectively is an art that requires a lot of time, attention, and practice to master. The good thing is that you will get lots of practice!

Emergency Change Requests (ECRs)

You will need a process for dealing with *Emergency Changes Requests (ECR)*. As you get closer to the end of the development phase, there will be situations where you cannot wait until a formal change control meeting to move forward with a critical change. If not making the change immediately has the potential to endanger the project, the project manager needs to be able to make the call on whether to implement it prior to it going through the change control process. Figure 10.3 shows a typical Emergency Change Request process workflow.

An ECR process typically will allow the project manager to authorize an emergency change with the approval of one senior-level manager, the senior-level manager being the most relevant person to give approval depending on what area of the product or system the change will impact. For example, a change that impacts the data center operations would need the second approval from a data center manager; a change that impacts the way the client will interact with the product should have second approval from the client project manager.

The project manager will need to complete an *ECR*

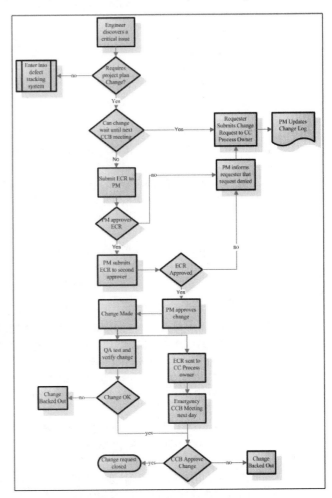

Figure 10.3: Emergency Change Request process workflow.

form that is submitted to the second approver before the change is made. (This can be done verbally if it is a dire emergency that needs attention within the hour.) Both the project manager and the second approver need to sign the ECR form as approved before the change is made.

The ECR form should be submitted to the change control board as soon as possible so that an emergency change control meeting can be scheduled to discuss the change that has already been made. This may be the next day, or it may be considered at the next regularly scheduled meeting. This will likely depend on where you are in the life cycle. If you are three weeks from deployment, the meeting should take place the next day, at the latest. If you are in the development phase, it may well wait for a week until the next regularly scheduled meeting.

An ECR form will need to contain the same information as the regular change request, in addition to:

- The reason the change could not wait until the next change control board meeting

- Signatures from the project manager and the second approver confirming that they feel the change is a valid emergency

It is important to make sure that the emergency change process is not abused. It is not a way to get around the process; it is a way to ensure that the process does not create critical problems that could adversely affect the outcome of the project.

An Emergency Changes Requests form is included on the CD-ROM that accompanies this book.

Managing Risk

During the planning phase of your project, you identified project risks. These risks need to be monitored and managed along with any new risks that arise during the course of the project. Managing the constraints of the project will go a long way toward minimizing the chances of creating unnecessary project risk by making bad decisions. However, it cannot prevent risk from occurring. Risk is inherent in every project.

The first step in managing risk is to use a process for identifying and evaluating risk as it occurs during the project life cycle. The second step is to document the risks using a *Risk Log*. It is important to ensure that the project team understands the risk criteria for your project. A risk is generally defined as something that could seriously affect your ability to complete the project successfully (on time, within budget, and with high quality).

The risk identification and evaluation process is as follows:

- Identify—This is the first step in the risk management process. Identify exactly what the risk is, how it will manifest itself, and where it will occur.

- Evaluate—Evaluate the potential risk to determine its level of criticality to the project and the likelihood of it happening. Potential risks with low criticality or low probability should be tracked as issues and not risks. They should be reevaluated as risks if more information becomes available or if the status of the problem changes.

- Analyze—Using the risk evaluation, rank the risk to determine how high up on the priority list it should be. Separate risks from issues, but continue to track both.

- Risk Action Plan—Specify what steps need to be taken to reduce or control the risk and the timeline in which the action needs to occur.

The risk management process will help you identify risks that are a serious threat to the project and need immediate action. Figure 10.4 shows the risk analysis process workflow.

Now that you have identified, evaluated, analyzed, and prepared an action plan for your risks, how are you going to manage them on an ongoing basis? This is where the Risk Log comes into play. A Risk Log enables you to track and manage all the risks and issues that are identified throughout the project life cycle. The Risk Log is an excellent way to communicate project risks with the project team, the client, and the various stakeholder groups.

A Risk Log is brief and concise but contains all the necessary information to ensure that the impact of each risk is clearly understood by everyone. The project manager owns the Risk

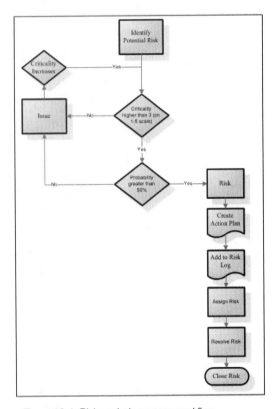

Figure 10.4: Risk analysis process workflow.

Log and, as such, is responsible for sharing it with the project team and relevant stakeholders. The project manager should review the Risk Log with the development team in the weekly project status meetings and should share relevant information with stakeholders at the formal project review meetings. The Risk Log can contain both the risks and the issues, or the project manager can create two logs, one for risks and one for issues.

A Risk Log should include the following:

- Risk Number—Each risk should be given its own unique number so that it can be tracked by number.

- Risk Description—Describe exactly what the risk is, how it will manifest itself, where it will occur, and what the impact will be on the end user.

- Originator—Document the name of the person who lets the team members or stakeholders know whom they should speak to if more information or clarification is needed.

- Date Found—Document the date that the risk was first identified.

- Assigned to—Identify to whom this risk has been assigned for evaluation, action, or resolution. This person becomes the "owner" of the risk.

- Criticality—Identify the criticality of the risk. Either you can assign a numbering system for this (for example, 1–5, with 1 being the highest and 5 being the lowest), or you can assign a High, Medium, or Low criticality.

- Probability—Identify the probability that the potential problem will occur. You can either assign a numbering system for this (for example, 1–5, with 1 being the highest and 5 being the lowest); you can assign a High, Medium, or Low probability; or you can use a percentage probability.

- Priority—Based on the criticality and probability, you should assign a priority. This can be High, Medium, or Low, or you could number the risks in order (updating the position on the list as more risks are added).

- Action Plan—Here you should document the action plan for the risk. Add as much detail as possible in this section to ensure that the owner is aware of what he is supposed to do.

- Status—Indicate the status of the risk. You should define a set of codes (for example, Resolved, In Progress, Under Investigation, Not Assigned, Need more Information) to group and track progress.

- Date Resolved—The date the risk was resolved or was no longer considered to be a risk.

Ensure that you keep your Risk Log up to date and that you are tracking all the highly critical issues on an ongoing basis. The Risk Log can be created and managed manually, or it can be created as a Web-based system, similar to a defect tracking system that all team members have access to. An example Risk Log is shown in Figure 10.5.

	Risk Log							OFIS		
No	Description	Originator	Date Found	Assigned To	Criticality	Probability	Priority	Action Plan	Status	Date Resolved
1	Unexpected technical problems	David Moss	04-Apr	David Moss	High	High	High	Evaluate the technical problem and make appropriate suggestions for workarounds.	Open	
2	Tim Timmons is out ill and expected to be out for 2 weeks	Daryl Johnson	10-Apr	Daryl Johnson	Medium	High	Medium	New team member to continue with the work.	Closed	20-May
3	Bug in code	Daryl Johnson	13-May	David Moss	Medium	Medium	Medium	Fix bug in code	Closed	21-May
4	Main graphic grainy	Paulette Green	18-May	Matsu Liu	Low	Low	Low	Graphic needs to be redesigned with more clarity	Open	

Figure 10.5: Risk Log.

Managing Obstacles and Delays

It is possible to minimize obstacles and delays on your project with some high-quality planning, good communication, and effective processes. Instructions to the client regarding their responsibilities should be clear, precise, and not open to interpretation. For instance, specify the required turnaround times for open issues and questions that your client needs to respond to. You should have specific deadlines for when documentation, feature requirements, or specifications need to be delivered. Similarly, you need documented and agreed-upon dates for the client sign-offs on all relevant documents.

When specifying deadlines, be sure to be specific about when on that date the task becomes due. Is it the beginning of the day? The end of the day? What time is the end of the day? 11:59 p.m.? Or is it the end of the working day at 5 p.m.? Is the beginning of the day 12 a.m. or 9 a.m.? In what time zone? Is it Pacific or Eastern Time? Do not assume that everyone has the same assumptions on what a delivery date means. To effectively schedule, you will need to know what time a deliverable is due. This is true of your developers as well as your client. For instance, if you have a specification due on Monday, can you schedule an engineer to start working on the implementation on Monday or not until Tuesday? If you assume a 9 a.m. delivery time and your client assumes a 6 p.m. delivery time, you will have a developer twiddling her thumbs all day waiting for the specification that she needs to implement the task she was scheduled to start on that day. The devil is in the details!

Here are some examples of how you can specify a precise time, in addition to the date, that a task is due:

- Beginning of Day (BOD)—No later than 8 a.m. (PST)

- Middle of Day (MOD)—No later than 12 p.m. (PST)

- End of Day (EOD)—No later than 5 p.m. (PST)

You can substitute any times for each of these. If you define a standard time for what "beginning of day," "middle of day," and "end of day" mean, and you use the same standard for every task on your project, you will have a shared understanding between client and team members. Your project schedule should specify what time a task is due if it is scheduled to be completed on that day. It is advisable to use the same time for every task. For instance, all tasks are due by EOD (5 p.m. PST) unless specified otherwise.

Poor instructions and lackluster communication will create confusion and uncertainty. This will result in unnecessary obstacles slowing down the progress of your project. It could result in the client having to come back to you for additional clarification, delivering the wrong thing, or delivering a task at the wrong time. Be sure to set realistic deadlines. If you send a document to the client at 4 p.m. on Monday, you cannot expect them to have reviewed it by 9 a.m. on Tuesday. Do not assume that they have nothing else to do but wait for a document from you. Depending on the size of the document and how thorough a review they need to do, you should give them at least a day and maybe even a week to complete a document review. Make sure that they know well in advance when they will receive the document and when you need the review completed by. Springing it on them at the last moment is not going to result in a smooth, seamless process.

Be sure to specify the consequences of late deliveries of documentation, information, or approvals. If it will result in the project schedule being pushed out, this needs to be clearly communicated. If the delay will mean that your team is dead in the water between the scheduled delivery time and the actual delivery time, your client must be aware of this. It could mean the necessity of additional resources and additional costs to complete the project on time if you are losing development hours waiting for client deliverables. The client needs to understand how much each hour of delay is costing. If the delay is holding up an entire team of 20 developers, they are losing 20 hours, or half a workweek, for each hour that the deliverable is late. If the average cost of an engineer is $45 per hour, this equates to $900 per hour in addition to the half a week of time. A simple example like this, presented up front, is worth a thousand words and a dozen phone calls after the fact!

Clients do not always understand what a detailed and precise art project scheduling is. They do not understand that they are creating project obstacles by not meeting their deliverables. Keeping costs and time under control takes careful management of every detail. If you can explain this process to them in simple and concise terms that they can relate to, your project has a much greater chance of running smoothly through to a successful conclusion.

Schedule Overrun

There are many reasons that a project can fall behind schedule. The most dangerous cause is when many tasks are all a little bit late. This is dangerous because such a situation can creep up on you very fast. One minute everything is fine, and the next you are in deep trouble! To illustrate this, imagine that you have a team of 20 developers working on a project. One of your developers is one day behind schedule. Is this a problem? Do you need to spring into action to resolve this as quickly as possible? Well, that depends on the status of all the other tasks on your project schedule and the progress that the other team members are making. If every team member is one day behind, then you are actually four weeks behind schedule. This is a significant schedule variance. If half your team is one day behind and the other half is one day ahead, then you may still be on track. If the late tasks have dependent tasks that will be delayed as a result of the lag, you will be behind schedule. If there are no dependencies on the late tasks, your schedule may be on track. As you can see, one day in the life of your project can make a huge difference to the outcome. If you did not see the trend when each developer was one day behind, and you waited until each one was two days behind, you will find yourself eight weeks—almost two months—behind schedule! So do not get completely distracted by the big issues and the obvious schedule impacts because while your back is turned, your schedule and your project could be headed for disaster!

What can you do if your project is falling behind and nothing seems to be getting it back on track again? The first thing you need to do is identify where the problems are. Is there just one developer who is delivering their tasks late? Is there one specific part of the project that is running over? If so, you may have a problem with underestimation or a developer whose skills are not in line with his assignments. You may need to replace your developer or move his tasks to someone else and assign him less complex tasks. If part of the project was underestimated, you will need to meet with your team and see whether it is possible to implement it in a way that will bring it back in line with the estimates.

People do not generally like to admit that they are having problems or falling behind schedule so don't expect everyone to come to you and tell you that they know they are going to be late. The usual behavior is to keep trying to catch up and hope for the best. It is like the gambler who is $5,000 down but keeps betting in the hope that she can regain the losses. She finally admits defeat when she is $10,000 in the red. It is up to you as the project manager to keep an eye on your team members and to be proactive in asking them when you suspect there may be a problem. You should strive to make your team feel comfortable informing you about problems as they arise, but if they are in denial, nothing you do will convince them to tell you there is a problem.

Another issue could be that one of your team members does not agree with you about what needs to be done to accomplish his tasks or refuses to work on his tasks in the order you have scheduled them. Instead, he chooses to work on what he feels is correct. He may avoid you and may be reticent about submitting status reports. This kind of behavior can cause major problems, especially if you have other team members scheduled to work on successor tasks. You need to have a serious talk with renegade team members as soon as you see any signs of this kind of behavior. Everyone on the team needs to understand the importance of teamwork. A one-man band cannot perform a symphony. Your project needs a symphony, not someone who can kick a bass drum and play the harmonica at the same time!

What do you do if a team member, client, or vendor is not communicating with you in a timely manner and it is causing schedule issues? Perhaps they are not returning phone calls or answering e-mails for days on end, and you have no idea what is happening or how much longer you will have to wait for their assignment to be delivered. This evasive behavior can be a serious problem because it can affect many dependent tasks and quickly cause your project to grind to a halt. It is something that needs drastic action and needs it quickly.

If the problem is with a team member who is located offsite, at another of your company's work sites, you should check in with someone else at that site to ensure that the person is turning up for work. Find a senior manager who works in the same building who can talk to the employee about the communication issues and the late delivery of work. If you are unable to resolve the issues quickly, you may have to remove the developer from your project and replace her with someone more team oriented, who can complete their tasks on time. Move any critical tasks to other team members as quickly as possible so as not to slow down anybody else while you are dealing with the problem. If the solution is to terminate employment, it can be a long process involving many other people within the organization, and you don't want your project on hold while you are waiting. If you do not take action quickly in this kind of situation, you will live to regret it.

What if the person telecommutes and is not answering your phone calls? How do you know if they are working at all? Are they checking in code regularly? Is anyone checking their code to make sure that it is OK? Ask your technical lead or a senior developer to look at what is being delivered. Does it conform to the quality standards? Is the work being done? Is the person making excuses about computer problems or saying that they are working locally on their own system because they are having problems transferring files? Any of these excuses is a big red flag. Have a frank discussion with the team member and tell him that if he cannot deliver high-quality work on time and cannot respond to your enquiries within a reasonable time (you should define what a "reasonable time" is), then you will need to replace him on the project. Again, move critical tasks to another developer as quickly as you can to avoid the delays trickling downstream.

You will need to follow your company's procedures for removing team members from projects whether they are full-time employees or contractors. Call an emergency meeting with your sponsor and senior management and let them know how critical the situation is and that it is risking the completion of your project. Ask for the person to be removed from your project. If a termination is necessary, involve human resources as early as possible. You must follow the law and your company policies.

We have an example of a team member who worked offsite and was not responsive to requests for updates. There were many red flags, but the project manager either did not see them or chose not to react to them. The developer was hired as a contractor and was telecommuting. She was not delivering code on schedule. She said that it was really slow uploading and downloading code during the check-out and check-in process so she was working locally on her machine and would deliver parts of the feature as she got them working. After a few weeks of delivering no code, receiving many phone calls, and giving numerous excuses, she reported a computer "crash" and said that she had no backups so she had to recreate all the code she had written so far.

By this time, it was a couple of months into the project and not one line of code had been delivered. The project manager continued to have faith that the code would be delivered albeit rather late. The excuses continued. She could not upload the code, it wasn't working correctly yet, and on and on. Eventually the developer stopped answering phone calls and e-mails altogether. The code was so late by this time that the product had to be delivered with that feature conspicuously absent. Luckily, it was a standalone feature with no interdependencies with other features so the rest of the code was completed and delivered on time with promises that the missing feature would be delivered very soon.

Still not being able to get any response to e-mails or phone calls, the project manager finally sent someone to the developer's house (she lived locally) to find out what was going on. The developer's mother was at home but there was no sign of the developer. Her mother told the employee that her daughter was depressed and had gone to stay with relatives. She said that her daughter had not written any code at all and, in fact, that she was not a qualified software engineer. She had lied on her resume. Her daughter had collected salary from the agency for her contract work for six months and had done no work at all. How could this happen? You would be amazed at what people will do if they want something badly. You may have heard stories of people posing as doctors who have no medical training at all. You also get people who pose as software engineers who have no programming training at all. Make sure that you *always* check references and always make sure that a new developer writes some test code that is reviewed by the technical lead for quality before assigning her project tasks.

If the client is not responding to your communications, you need to call an emergency meeting with client representatives and the project sponsor to communicate the issues and the impact that the delays are having on the project. The client organization must be informed if its employees are not doing their jobs. They can remedy the situation only if they know about it. If they are causing the project to run late, they need to know about it, in writing (not e-mail). Otherwise, they will assume that you are at fault for late (or non) delivery, no matter how many phone calls they have ignored!

It can be really tricky when vendors are not delivering on schedule, especially if it is paired with nonresponsiveness to enquiries. It is not always possible to replace a whole company, especially if what they do is very specialized. It is a good idea to ensure that contractual agreements with vendors clearly specify the consequences of late delivery. If it costs the vendor money every time they are late, they will make a concerted effort to be on time, or early, for every delivery. If you continue to have problems with vendors, you need to look for alternative solutions. The project team should be brought together to brainstorm on ideas and suggestions for alternative plans of action. You may want to include the client in these discussions, too, depending on their relationship with the vendor and their relationship with you.

It is extremely important that your team be clear about their assignments and what is expected of them. If they are not sure what they should be doing, how can you expect them to be doing it? Other causes of project schedule overruns are poor planning, procrastination, nondedicated resources, and task uncertainty. These are all manageable and controllable.

Have you allowed for your team members' company holidays, vacation time, and sick time in your project schedule? If not, you will quickly find yourself behind schedule if a couple of team members take two-week vacations or if you forgot that everyone gets the day off for Independence Day.

When your team members are working on multiple projects and are not dedicated to just yours, this can cause problems. If your team members are being pulled in different directions, and your company has not given either project top priority because they feel that both the projects are equally important, you are bound to end up with a problem. Lack of direction or conflicting direction can cause a team member to lose focus, feel confused about priorities, and get burned out very early in the project life cycle. In an ideal worl,d all your team members will be assigned to your project full time. If this is not the case, you must insist that there be clear direction about what the team member should do if either, or both, projects are making demands for more time.

Have you ever met anyone who continuously says, "No problem, it will get done," or "It is on my list of things to do," but they never seem to deliver anything? This is called "procrastination." Every one of us has procrastinated at one time or another in our lives, and as long we can separate the important things from the not-so-important things, it is usually OK not to jump on everything immediately. The habitual procrastinator, however, can be very destructive. Don't accept the "don't worry, it will get done" excuse. Insist on a specific deadline and make sure that the team member knows it is not negotiable. Do not allow your team members to wait until the very last minute before they start working on tasks. If you do, they will most likely deliver late. Your schedule buffer is not designed so that your team members can swan around working on unimportant tasks or taking long lunch breaks. If they can start working on a task earlier than scheduled, they should do so. The schedule buffer time is for emergencies, and there will be emergencies that you need that time for. The buffer can save your butt, so make sure it is not used for frivolous tasks!

Task uncertainties can also be damaging to your schedule. You team members should not be scheduled to work on tasks if the task is not defined yet (unless the task is to define the task, of course). They also need to be made aware of the status of other team members' tasks. If there are dependencies, they need to know whether they are able to start early on a task (because the predecessor was completed early) or whether they are going to be delayed starting work on something (because the predecessor is going to be delivered late). Removing uncertainties will decrease the chances of schedule overrun.

Don't try to sugar coat problems or protect your team from the truth if the project is in jeopardy. Your team needs to be aware of what is going on. They may have solutions that will get the project back on track. If you never communicate issues with your team, they will never be able to help resolve them.

Should You Hurry Up or Should You Wait?

We are going to describe two very negative behaviors that are rife in corporate America and that can lead to a lot of wasted time and a lot of frustration. We call them the "hurry up and wait syndrome," where you hurry up and then find that it was not an emergency after all; and the "wait and hurry up disorder," where something has been left to the very last minute, causing it to become an emergency even though it never really needed to be so in the first place.

Hurry Up and Wait Syndrome

"I need to get this new specification done immediately," says the client. "No problem," replies the project manager. "It will add a couple of extra days to the schedule. I will stop work on the 'B' feature and ask that engineer to work on the new specification instead. As soon as it is finished, I will e-mail it to you for approval and then we can submit it to the change control board before the end of the week."

This is a great example of a project manager taking decisive action to deal with a client emergency and responding to their request as fast as possible. The project manager delivers the specification two days later. The client is e-mailed the specification, and the project manager follows up with a phone call to ask them to review it as soon as possible so that it can be submitted for change control. The project manager wants to get any schedule changes finalized as early as possible in the project life cycle to minimize the impact on the team.

Days go by and there is still no word from the client. The project manager makes numerous phone calls and is getting the run-around from the client. Finally, the client says that though they had discussed the change, they had not really decided whether they needed it. Consequently, the project manager has wasted hours chasing this up, updating the schedule to take into account the two days needed to write the specification, and updating the engineer's schedule to reflect the two-day delay. The project is now two days behind schedule. The "emergency" turned out to be a false alarm. Few clients believe that they can be the cause of any wasted time on a project, but it is often the case. The hurry up and wait syndrome is extremely irritating for even the most effective project manager. How do you know whether an "urgent" request is really urgent? Unfortunately, you often don't know. You can start to figure out that some people always want things now. You can also start to see a pattern emerging where some people ask for everything they *may* need rather than for the things that they *do* need.

You will not only experience the hurry up and wait syndrome from your client, but you will also fall victim to this from your senior managers and your corporate officers. You may find yourself spending an entire weekend writing a report that your manager asked for at 4 p.m. on Friday because it must be delivered no later than 10 a.m. on Monday morning. Then you find that no one reads the report. How do you feel? Frustrated? Angry? How do you think your team members will feel if you start to do this to them? It is not very motivating to work with this kind of false pressure.

The perpetrators of hurry up and wait are using this technique to control others. They may not be consciously aware that they are trying to control you, but this is what it amounts to. They use this technique to force people to bend to their will. The request is often presented as something that someone else, someone much more senior and important, "must" have. The requester may tell you that the consequences will be dire if this is not done exactly on time. They are scaring you into doing what they want. You are afraid not to deliver on it because, if it really is an emergency, perhaps you will be fired or demoted for causing a disaster. It is often the case that if you ask the person who apparently needs this thing so desperately, they may know nothing about it. Sometimes a person is trying so hard to impress senior management that he tries to interpret everything he hears into some kind of action that can be taken that will impress his superiors. He then spends most of the time running around like a headless chicken trying to deliver something impressive. In fact, all this person is doing is wasting time and causing delays, which amounts to increased costs and lower productivity. Senior managers are not usually impressed by increased costs and lower productivity!

If you find yourself setting these artificial deadlines for your team or your client, then you need to evaluate what your true motivations are. If you do not need it until next Wednesday or possibly at all, then do not ask someone to deliver it to you tomorrow. Do you really need that much control over everything and everybody? If you are afraid that by not acting early you may have a last-minute scramble to get something completed, then plan for that possible last-minute request. Tell your team member, "The client is asking for a new specification for the 'X' feature. I have investigated what is behind the request and found that they have discussed the change but will not make a final decision until Monday. If they approve this on Monday, they will need the specification by Wednesday. It will be a stretch to get it completed in two days, so you may need to work some overtime to finish it, but I would rather do that than have you work on it now and then find out that it was a waste of time." Your team member will respect you far more for letting her know the real situation than if you ask for everything now "just in case." If you are setting artificial deadlines because you are trying to impress someone at the top of your organization, then you are not focusing on the most important priorities for your project. You need to reevaluate the driving force behind your actions.

Sometimes, the control issue behind the hurry up and wait syndrome is because the person making the request thinks that nothing else could possibly be more important than pandering to their every need. In other words, it is due to an inflated sense of self-importance on their part. It could also be due to a sense of insecurity on the part of the requester, who feels that to get anything done they have to present it as an emergency, thereby "threatening" you in some way to carry out the request. This could also be described as a deflated sense of self-importance. Though these two personality types are at opposite ends of the spectrum, their negative behaviors may be very similar. Don't mistake a quiet, personable nature as the sign that someone would never use a tactic like this to control you in some way. This type of personality often tends to use manipulative tactics for control. The use of hurry-up-and-wait behavior combined with the threat that someone more important is relying on this being done is a classic example of a manipulative tactic. Being able to understand and recognize the warning signs of negative behavior can help you avoid falling victim to the hurry-up-and-waiters quite so often. Avoiding it completely will be almost impossible, but reducing it will help you to manage your project more effectively.

So, what can you do? You can ask specific questions when asked for something "immediately." You can ask why it is urgent. You can ask who specifically has requested that this be done. You can clearly communicate what the impact will be on your project to drop everything and work on this. It would be wise to put the request, and the impact, in writing and copy the person who has been identified as the initiator. Better still, ask the requester to put it in writing. If they give you an "I am too busy to e-mail this to you, just get it done" excuse, then e-mail them a synopsis of the conversation, including what specifically they have asked you to do. You need to cover yourself with documentation because you will be surprised how often the hurry-up-and-waiters change their story after the fact. They will often deny that they asked you to work on the task or the report at all. They will state that they just told you that it might need doing and blame you for taking it upon yourself to make your entire team work the weekend on it. Cover yourself. People who continually cry wolf will hardly ever take responsibility for their actions.

Having said all this, real emergencies need to be dealt with quickly. You need to have a good, solid process in place that allows you to act quickly and effectively in an emergency situation. Flexibility and the ability to adapt to changing priorities are necessary to avoiding potential business and project disasters. If in doubt whether an emergency is really an emergency, go to the identified source or someone closer to the identified source and inform them what is at risk by this request taking priority over everything else. They can make an informed decision about whether they really want to drop everything to get this done. A half-hour spent researching a request will be time well spent. Don't overdo this, though. You cannot be calling the CEO every two days questioning them about every initiative that they launch. You do not want to be seen as inflexible or as a complainer or troublemaker. Use your judgment wisely and follow up in a professional and discreet manner. This is not about getting someone into trouble; it is about keeping your project on schedule and prioritizing requests appropriately.

Wait and Hurry Up Disorder

The hurry up and wait syndrome is frustrating, but equally frustrating is the hurry up and wait alter ego, the "wait and hurry up disorder." Wait and hurry up situations are the emergencies that arise due to procrastination on the part of someone else involved in, or who has an impact on, your project. They should have asked you for this "thing" four weeks ago when they identified the need for it, but they just remembered that it is due tomorrow, so can you please work all night to get it done or "Mr X" will be really angry and who knows what will happen?

Procrastinators are masters in the use of the name-dropping technique to get you to work late on something they forgot to communicate earlier. If you finish it on time, they get all the credit, but if it is late, they will likely try to find a way to make it someone else's fault, possibly yours. Be careful how you manage these situations. If you are too accommodating, you may end up spending most of your time dealing with other people's last-minute, procrastination-driven emergencies. It is far better to implement a process for requests that is immune to this kind of abuse. If you have clear, written proof of when requests are made, you can make sure that the procrastinator is on the spot for the delay and not you or your team!

Again, make sure that you are not doing this to your team members. It is easy to focus a lot of attention on what others are doing to make your job harder and thus forget to keep an eye on your own behavior. All leaders like to have control; this is why they have a desire to lead. Therefore, it takes a lot of self-discipline to ensure that you are utilizing your leadership skills in a positive manner to effectively manage and lead your team. Stay self-aware, and if you find yourself starting to exhibit negative behaviors, stop and think about what you are doing. Analyze the reasons and emotions behind your behavior, and identify a positive way to achieve the same result. Negative use of control tactics risks the well-being of your team and your project. Negative, controlling behaviors will start to rear their ugly heads more often when you are under pressure or feeling stressed, tired, demotivated, or disempowered. When you have any of these negative feelings or emotions, it is important for you to maintain an even tighter control and awareness of your own behavior.

Interestingly, the negative behaviors we have discussed result in feelings of high pressure, stress, demotivation, and disempowerment in the recipients of the negativity. This can then lead to negative behavior on their part, thereby creating a vicious circle. Remember that if you are a victim of negative control tactics, you could easily start to display the same negativity when dealing with your team members. Likewise, you could perpetuate the negativity by merely passing it straight on to your team. For example, if you have a hurry up and wait or a wait and hurry up situation, you could panic your team with the same threats and scenarios of disaster that were presented to you to force them to comply with your request to work the weekend without too much push-back. This tactic is designed to coerce your team members into fulfilling your request without argument. In other words, they will "go quietly." You are avoiding taking responsibility for the request by blaming the purported initiator for creating the need to work the weekend. Consequently, you are playing the "poor me" card. The result of all this is that your team feels frustrated, stressed, disempowered, and so on. Your team will feel disempowered if they think that the project manager does not have control of their destiny. It is important to be aware of this. They feel empowered because you are empowered. For them to feel like they have some control over the project, they need to know that you are making the decisions for the team .

Once again, it is important to note that teal emergencies arise that really do need to be dealt with quickly. Even if the emergency has been created by procrastination, it does not mean that it is not critical to the success of your project to act quickly. If this is the case, do the right thing to ensure the success of the project. You should follow up later, once the disaster has been averted, with a *lessons-learned* meeting to make certain that you will not have a repeat performance of this unnecessary "panic" again.

How to Recognize a Failing Project

Is your project out of control? Are you running around trying to get it back on track but finding that the project is both behind schedule and over budget? Is the client getting shaky on the whole thing? Is the technology just not working, no matter what the engineering team does? No matter how much effort you have put into making a project successful, the sad fact is that some projects fail. Projects fail for many different reasons. There are, however, clues that a project is on the road to, or needs to be on the road to, being canceled. They include:

- The client has gone AWOL (absent without official leave). No one is sure what has happened to the client or when they will reappear.

- You are hearing rumors that the client company is having financial problems.

- You are hearing rumors that your company is having financial problems and may need to cut back on some projects.

- The project is riddled with problems and is a technical disaster.

- More than half your team has quit.

- The project is running way over budget, and costs cannot be bought under control.

- The project is running way over schedule, and there is nothing you can do to get it back on track.

- The project was greatly underestimated.

- Team morale is at an all-time low.

- After the definition stage, it is clear that the project will not be cost effective.

- Senior management has withdrawn all practical support for the project.

- The budget for the project has been cut in half part way through development.

- The sponsor wants the project completed in half the estimated time.

- No requirements were documented at the beginning of the project, and verbal instructions from senior management are changing on a daily basis.

- The scope was not clearly defined in the planning phase, and the project keeps getting bigger and bigger—with no budget increase.

- Half your team has been moved to a different project, and you are being asked to finish the project without them.

- Market conditions have changed, and there is really no need for this product any longer.

The list could go on, but suffice to say that most projects fail due to lack of good planning, teamwork, and documentation.

When a project is spinning out of control, it won't do you any good to start pointing figures at the people you feel made the project fail. The lessons-learned meeting that you hold right before the project is closed will uncover all kinds of problems and causes. It is not up to you to be the judge and the jury. If you think you can salvage the project, then spring into action and start doing something about it. Make sure that you approach it in a positive way. If you are all doom and gloom about it, you will not be able to persuade anyone to come on board and help you in your quest. If your project is on the edge of failing, you will not be able to save it alone. Put together a plan for saving the project. Detail the additional resources and associated costs. If you plan to reduce the scope of the project, clearly document how you can do that and what the benefit will be from developing a scaled-down version of the project. Perhaps you need to increase the scope and increase costs significantly to make the project work. Perhaps it was not defined accurately in the first place. The project manager cannot usually cancel a project. The sponsor, the client, and the steering committee are typically responsible for these kinds of decisions. If the client is being "fired," your legal team will likely be heavily involved with the contractual issues surrounding the cancellation.

No matter what the cause, it is important to be aware of the symptoms and to know when to call time-out on your project. It is unusual for any project manager to have never worked on a project that was canceled or that failed miserably. Don't beat yourself up about it; move on, and start on the next project. You will have learned a lot, and hopefully you will be able to apply that knowledge to your next project.

CHAPTER 11

Managing Communication

Numerous methods of communication exist. Verbal and written communications are two distinct methods of communicating. Written communication also takes very different forms. A technical specification is very different from an e-mail. Meeting minutes are very different from a process document. Many times, it will be obvious what method is most appropriate. Other times it will not. When in doubt, communicate face to face, one on one. If the communication is personal or could be construed as something personal or something that should be kept confidential, then ensure that the communication takes place in private. Never use team settings to shame someone into doing what you want or to put them on the spot so that they cannot refuse your request. In this chapter, we will cover some of the forms that communications will take and some methods for using them effectively.

Verbal Communication

It is never too early, or too late, in your career to learn how to communicate effectively. The language we use affects how other people feel. It determines whether our words cause or prevent conflict. You can tell someone the same thing in two different ways, and one way will energize them while the other will deflate or de-energize them. Language is a powerful tool. Whether you communicate verbally or in written form, the way you express yourself, your words and your body language, affects whether your message is perceived in a positive or a negative way. Learning how to use language effectively takes a lot of practice, but you can start by following some simple rules. You should always try to use positive language and positive reinforcement, even if your message could be seen as negative.

Negative phrasing and language have the following characteristics:

- Focus on what cannot be done.
- Have a subtle (or unsubtle) tone of blame.
- Include words like "can't," "won't," or "unable."

- Do not stress appropriate positive actions or positive consequences.
- Use terms like "you failed to," "you claim that," "why didn't you," "you should have," "you must," "if you had."
- Use the word "but" in sentences, which usually takes away from something positive said in the first part of the sentence. (For instance, you did a great job on the Smith project, *but* you really messed up on that Brown project.)

Positive phrasing and language have the following qualities:

- Focus on what can be done.
- Suggest alternatives and identify the choices available.
- Sound helpful and encouraging.
- Stress positive actions and positive consequences.
- Use terms like "can I help you," "can I suggest," "a great way to handle a situation like that is."

Before you use the word "but," why not just finish the sentence? "You did a great job on the Smith project." If you need to discuss an issue with another task, do not use it to take away from a positive comment. You could then say, "Let's talk about the Brown project: How do you feel that went?"

Some additional examples would be:

- Don't Say: "You never finish work on time."
- Do Say: "It seems you are having some difficulty with the timelines. What can I do to help"

- Don't Say: "If you had bothered to read the report, you would know what I was talking about."
- Do Say: "It might be that the report wasn't clear on those points. Would you like me to explain?"

- Don't Say: "You did a terrible job on the Brown project. What were you thinking?"
- Do Say: "How do you think the Brown project went? Do you think there is anything we could improve on if we have a similar project again?"

E-mail

E-mail is great for things that are noncontroversial, nonthreatening, and nonpersonal. E-mail is *not* a good communication tool for letting someone know they are not doing a great job, telling them that they need to improve on something, disagreeing with something they said, discussing potentially controversial issues, or discussing issues that need a wide audience and would be better discussed in a meeting. Positive things are great in e-mails, but negative things are not. How you write something can be misconstrued and misunderstood. Take for instance, an honest slip of the caps button. It can be interpreted as yelling when, in actuality, it was a mistake, and you were just sending a polite reminder. It is a permanent record; it will be there forever, unless deleted. Most people do not delete e-mails that have upset them. They keep them for future reference, just in case. So be careful about what you say in e-mail.

Overuse of e-mail is one the biggest communication problems in corporate America today. Inboxes are full of nonsense that people send. It can take hours per week to sort through the messages to find those that are important. Complex and long-winded discussions involving numerous people take place. Some people are removed from certain threads of the e-mails (because the sender did not know how to use the "reply to all" button), so they only have partial information. Alternatively, everyone is copied on a reply meant for one person because the sender forgot they could use the "reply" button instead of the "reply to all" button. Some people are added to the thread two weeks into the discussion and have no idea what the discussion is about or how it is relevant to them. It is often not clear whether a decision has been made, who owns the decision, or who is asking for a decision. If you are copied on an e-mail, are you supposed to do something about it or just read it? If no one asks you to do anything, does that mean that you have no responsibility for the issue, or is there a need for you to take some action implied by the act of including you on the e-mail?

It would have saved hours of reading, writing, and agonizing over e-mails if the initiator had just scheduled an hour-long meeting to discuss the issue and resolve it. Due to the overload of e-mails, important messages can easily be missed. As a result, you have to take the extra time to call a person to tell them to read the e-mail you just sent, which defeats the purpose of using a nonverbal form of communication in the first place! E-mail does not need to be a waste of time; it has just been abused and overused. How many e-mails do you get in a week telling you that someone has left their headlights on in the parking lot, what is for lunch in the cafeteria today, a goodbye message from someone who is leaving (whom you have never even heard of), Jane Doe had a baby, John Smith retired, Susie is getting married, and on and on? That is not to mention the e-mails about project-related issues that are irrelevant or of no interest to you.

Think carefully about how much you communicate and to whom. More is not necessarily better. Covering all your bases is not going to make everything run more smoothly. Specific, directed communication is the key to successfully communicating. When you send an e-mail, you have no idea whether the recipients read it unless they reply to you. Some people only read the first two sentences and think they get it. If you hold a meeting, you know who is there, who is listening, and who is responding. There is a certainty about the communication that you do not get with e-mail.

Having said all this, e-mail is a great tool that can save you lots of time and can make communication easier, quicker, and more efficient as long as you use it appropriately. Writing and sending e-mail messages is very simple. E-mail is an effective means of communication when used correctly. You need to be aware of the dangers in the tone as well as the content of your e-mail messages. Humor and sarcasm are lost in e-mail and can easily offend. You need to make sure that your e-mails are straightforward and to the point and that they convey the right message. If the facts cannot be stated in a noncontentious way that is free of sarcasm, then communicate verbally instead. It is not difficult for e-mail arguments to get started, and often they are due to misinterpretation of what the author is trying to say.

Another danger is copying everyone on e-mails. This is especially bad if you are doing it to try to get someone to react or to make him or her look bad. What are you accomplishing by making someone feel bad or embarrassed? Make sure your message is clear, direct, and cannot be misinterpreted. You should *never* send an e-mail when you are in a bad mood. You can easily start something that you will wish you hadn't. You may think that e-mail cannot possibly convey what kind of mood you are in, but it can. The tone of your message will be clearer than you think. The worst danger of this is that you may not be angry with the person you are e-mailing, or about the issue you are e-mailing about, but it may come across that you are. The recipients of your message do not have the benefit of the clues they would have in a face-to-face conversation. They can't see or sense the body language or facial expressions that can alert them to how you are feeling, so they are not sure how to react. When you are face-to-face, you can usually tell whether someone is upset about something, and more often than not, you will know whether it is related to what you are talking about. You find yourself asking, "Are you OK? You don't seem like yourself this morning" or "Are you upset about anything. You seem quieter than usual?" Their body language tells you that they are upset, but it also tells you that they are not upset with you. In e-mail, the only thing that comes across is that someone is upset, abrupt, or angry about something. If you think that by putting a "smiley" face in the e-mail, it will represent your emotions and let people know that you are in a good mood, think again; emotion icons ("emoticons") may be appropriate for friends and family, but they are not appropriate in the workplace. Sometimes the use of emoticons can make your message appear sarcastic or suggest that you are not taking an issue seriously. Worse still, someone may think that you are making fun of him and not treating him with the appropriate respect.

The most important thing to remember about e-mail is to think twice before you send it. Always reread what you are about to send. E-mail makes it easy to fire off a message that you might regret later. Make sure that your e-mail conveys the right message and does not contain lots of typos or grammatical errors. If you have ever received an e-mail that is devoid of all capital letters, punctuation, grammar, and correct spelling, you will know how hard it is to read and understand them. Your e-mails need to be as professional and respectful as your verbal communication.

You should also avoid sending or forwarding joke e-mails in the workplace. It is unprofessional, and the messages may be considered disrespectful. It demonstrates that you are not focusing the appropriate attention on your project and perhaps do not have enough work to do.

Conducting Effective and Productive Meetings

Have you ever sat in a meeting that was soooooooooo long and boring that you started fantasizing about smashing your head into the wall just so you could go to the hospital and get out of the meeting? We are taught that time is money, so why do we waste so much time in meetings that half the time do not seem to be productive or useful? Wasted time organizational meetings has a significant impact on individual and business productivity.

Overcoming Resistance to Meetings

There are many reasons why people hate going to meetings. People feel that the meetings are nonproductive, repetitive, ineffective, and our personal favorite, confrontational. How can a room full of adults turn into a room full of preschoolers in a matter of minutes? In general, you will find that most of your team members think meetings are a waste of time, so they try not to show up. This is a very bad thing for the project manager. If a project manager cannot get her team together in a room to discuss a project, that project is going to be at risk. It is vitally important that all team members are on the same page throughout the project. Meetings are necessary to accomplish this.

Harnessing the Power of Meetings

Meetings can be very powerful ways to communicate and solve problems. It will be up to the project manager to conduct effective and productive meetings. If you can accomplish this, then your meetings will become a necessity and will be both positive and informative.

A project manager must create satisfying and energizing meetings. It is necessary in a meeting to get your team members involved and hold their attention. Remember, while meetings are in progress, the team members are not being productive with their assigned tasks. So, if you invite a team member to a meeting that is preventing him from working on the project, you must ensure that it is an important and necessary meeting that will be addressing project needs and issues. Make certain that your meetings are absolutely necessary. Having a status meeting every day when you know that receiving status on a daily basis is not critical to the project will be redundant and repetitive.

At times, though, it may be critical to have status meetings on a daily basis. For example, during the last week or two of the project when all the loose ends are being tied, you may need to track the remaining issues daily or even hourly to ensure that your product will be completed on time. If this criticality does not exist, let your team members focus on their primary responsibility—getting the product built! You can also help your team members with their focus by scheduling the various meetings that they need to attend on the same afternoon, or morning, of the week. They will be able to put this time aside for meetings and use the rest of the week for their project assignment work. The more frequent interruptions your team members get, the more it will affect their productivity.

Meeting Planning

Companies love employees who know how to conduct effective and productive meetings. Meeting planning and facilitation skills are highly valued in any organization. Nonproductive and long-winded meetings that never finish on time and do not accomplish much are a waste of the company's money and resources. Meetings should have a clear purpose and be relevant to the attendees. When you hold a successful meeting, it adds tremendous value to your project and to your organization. However, a poor meeting that lacks purpose, follow-up, and direction, combined with a lack of ownership or decision-making, will leverage failure throughout a company and could severely affect the success of your project.

Every meeting scheduled by a project manager should be carefully planned and have clear and achievable objectives. The Meeting Process Workflow is shown in Figure 11.1. If the meeting is a status meeting, to inform and gather status from team members, it may be relatively informal and have free-flowing, open discussion for all team members. If it is a meeting to inform stakeholders and clients of the project's progress (a "project review" meeting), then it should be a more formal meeting that includes a visual presentation, followed by a Q&A session. A team status meeting's focus is the project schedule and the team members' progress. A project review meeting with the stakeholders is focused on the project as whole and the project manager's ability to deliver on the agreed milestones and deliverables.

You should ensure that the roles within meetings are also clearly defined. For example, who owns the meeting? Who is facilitating or moderating? Is there an interpreter (techspeak to nontechspeak)? Your meeting attendees need to know who is responsible for what and to whom they should speak if they have any questions or concerns. The chances are that you will be filling all these roles.

When a person opens a meeting, she needs to ensure that all team members are aware of the goals of the meeting. What is the purpose? Don't assume that everyone is aware of what is going on and why they are there. Many team members work in their own little bubble, unaware of and unconcerned about what is going on outside of it. As long as they are on task and not impacted by other team members who may not be, they assume that the whole project is coming along nicely. You need to tell them why you need them in the meeting and clearly explain what the problems are that you are addressing. It is very important to set measurable objectives prior to each meeting. This will enable you to focus your meeting appropriately and will help you keep it on track. Never run meetings where you allow your team members to just walk in, sit down, and begin without a clear, common understanding of the goal of the meeting. If you do, then the chances of your meetings being successful will be minimal. You also risk alienating team members, who will then not turn up to future meetings because they feel that the meetings are a waste of time.

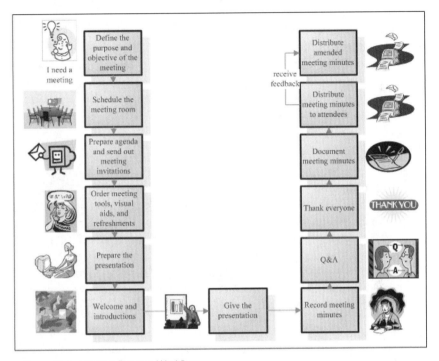

Figure 11.1: Meeting Process Workflow.

Let us assume that you have established the purpose and goals of your meeting. Did you prepare an agenda and send it out prior to the meeting? Having an agenda is not optional; it is a necessity. An agenda will clearly define what topics you will cover in the meeting. As with the Kick-Off Meeting Agenda, it is very important to distribute it to the team members in advance. This will enable your team members to prepare for the meeting and arrive ready to discuss the topics.

During the meeting, it is very important to stick to the agenda. As the meeting owner, it is your responsibility to keep the meeting on track both time-wise and topic-wise. You must set a start and a finish time for your meeting. Make sure that the time you allot for your meeting is appropriate. If you can accomplish your regular team status meeting in a half hour, schedule it for a half hour and manage the meeting so that it finishes on time. If your meetings consistently run under or over the scheduled time, you need to do some analysis of your meetings to understand why. If you run over consistently for a one-hour meeting, you are either adding too many items to your agenda or you are letting the meeting get off track and not controlling it effectively. You need to stop those side discussions that digress from the topic. You need to control idle chitchat and remind your attendees that you have an agenda and a time limit and that you need to move on. If the issue is important, ask them to take it offline and to speak to you about it after the meeting. Your meetings should be effective and efficient, which means scheduling them for the shortest time that you can without running out of time. You should never expect people to remain in your meeting if you run out of time. It is unprofessional, and it shows a total lack of regard for other people's time and schedules. If you need more time, apologize to the attendees for running out of time, and tell them you will reschedule an additional meeting to continue where you left off. Then allow them to leave the room on time.

Meeting Facilitation

There are times when you will need to enlist the help of independent meeting facilitators for your meetings. "Independent" does not mean that they do not work for your company. It means that they do not work on your project so they are able to maintain an unbiased and unemotional presence in the meeting. Their role is to facilitate and not to participate. This is a very different role from the one you play when you facilitate your own meetings. In those meetings, you are also a key contributor to the meetings and are likely taking minutes, tracking attendees, assigning tasks, and so on. You are in dual or multiple roles. The independent meeting facilitator, on the other hand, has one role only—to facilitate.

Independent meeting facilitators are more commonly used for very critical meetings, training or work sessions, meetings that are anticipated to become contentious, and lessons-learned meetings, to name but a few. An experienced facilitator will be able to effectively guide the meetings and can achieve the meeting's objectives in an unbiased and collaborative manner.

In critical or high-intensity meetings, it can be extremely difficult for a project manager to effectively contribute, participate, lead, guide, manage, take notes, summarize, and facilitate. As the project manager, your opinions may carry more weight than some other team members. This makes it is possible for you to lead the meeting and the team in the direction that you want to go. After all, that is what your job is most of the time.

This is not always the best way to run certain types of meetings. If you need everyone at the meeting to be equal and for their opinions to have equal weight, you need a facilitator. How can you, as the project manager, facilitate a meeting about your project without participating or contributing? It would be almost impossible. If it is necessary, call on one of your company's meeting facilitators. The facilitator's role is to keep the meeting focused, on task, and on schedule. He is responsible for making sure that everyone gets heard and that each participant has an equal voice. The facilitator will take the notes or will bring a note taker with him, and he will write up the minutes for the meeting. This maintains the objectivity through to completion.

There may be times when you are asked to act as a facilitator in a meeting. Perhaps another project manager needs a facilitator for a meeting about her project. Perhaps your company does not have its own designated facilitators, and you need to choose one of your peers and persuade them to facilitate your meeting. What skills does the facilitator need?

- Ability to remain neutral and objective
- Ability to hear what everyone has to say
- Ability to listen and understand
- Ability to get full cooperation and participation from the team members
- Ability to keep all team members engaged and involved
- Ability to accurately record minutes and action items
- A can-do attitude
- Ability to keep the meeting on track and stay focused on the key topics
- Ability to provide recommendations

Facilitation skills are broadened and improved with practice. Volunteer to assist in facilitating some smaller meetings until you feel confident that you can facilitate on your own. Then move onto larger meetings. Additional expertise can be gained by attending meeting facilitation classes. An effective facilitated meeting will require the same premeeting work as for your regular meetings.

The Bottom Line

When planning meetings, you should question whether the purpose of the meeting could be accomplished more effectively and efficiently via e-mail or the telephone. Alternatively, try to determine whether your meeting could be scheduled to include only two of your team members rather than the whole group? Remember, when you organize a meeting, you are asking people to stop what they are doing while they attend. You may also have consultants who do not work onsite who will need to travel to your site to attend your meetings. An interesting exercise when holding a meeting is to mentally add up how much the meeting is costing. Estimate the hourly rate for each person in the room (guessing is fine), multiplying the total by the number of hours the meeting is scheduled to run, and adding travel costs, refreshments, and supplies. You will be amazed at how costly an hour-long meeting can be. If the meeting is a waste of time for half the people in the room, you will have wasted a lot of money.

For example, suppose you are holding a meeting to discuss project status. The following people are in attendance. Remember, these are just sample figures. The numbers could be significantly more:

Resource	Title	Cost	Total
Daryl Johnson	Project Manager	35-55/hr × 1 hour	$35.00–$55.00
David Moss	Technical Lead	45-65/hr × 1 hour	$45.00–$65.00
Vin Patel	DBA	45-65/hr × 1 hour	$45.00 –$65.00
Jane Jones	Software Engineer	42-52/hr × 1 hour	$42.00–$52.00
Tim Timmons	Systems Engineer	46-56/hr × 1 hour	$46.00–$56.00
Matsu Liu	UI Designer	32-42/hr × 1 hour	$32.00–$42.00
Projector		10	$10.00
Computer		10	$10.00
Refreshments		45	$45.00
TOTAL			$310.00–$400.00

You can see that this meeting cost a whopping $310 to $400 for one hour! You can imagine how quickly meetings can eat up your project budget if your team members are expected to attend too many of them!

Every meeting that a project manager holds has associated costs. Don't think that meetings are free, especially if you have contractors involved in your project. You also need to take into account the time that you spend on the preparation and follow-up for the meetings you call. Your time is not free either! If you pull a salesperson into the meeting, it is costing your company money in lost working time as well as any potential sales that the salesperson could have been making during that time.

Do not underestimate travel costs for offsite personnel. You need to factor in the costs for any nonproductive time while offsite members are on the road traveling to and from the meeting as well as the actual travel costs. One last item to remember about meeting costs is the overhead and administration costs. Every time you use a room that is equipped with presentation equipment, telephones, and video conferencing, costs are associated with this. You may not directly see it, but your company has to pay for all this. The administrative costs include the paper used to print agendas and presentations, and the administrative assistant time to record and type up meeting minutes. A lot of time and money is invested in meetings so you need to ensure that the meetings you are scheduling are important and vital to the success of your project. If you need to get status from only one or two people on your team, then meet with them individually or send them an e-mail. Your whole team does not need to be involved in retrieving this information.

Leadership and Direction

Leadership is an essential ingredient for successful meetings. Leadership requires a unique combination of attitude, confidence, and motivation together with some highly developed skills. You need to use these skills to run effective meetings. You need to act in a professional manner at all times and treat your team members with dignity and respect. Never try to belittle anyone in front of the team. If you have issues with one team member, meet with that one team member to discuss them. Your team is looking to you for leadership and direction. Be sure that what you are demonstrating to them is what you want them to emulate.

Eliciting Full Participation

It is very important to have active participation in your meetings from all your team members. You may need to use a lot more encouragement for some team members than others. Some people are naturally more shy or don't like to talk in meetings because they just want it all to be over with as quickly as possible. Work with your team members and try to get as much participation as possible. It is vitally important, however, that you never try to force someone to participate by putting them on the spot in the middle of a meeting. It is embarrassing for them, and it is not going to win you any popularity contests either! Putting people on the spot is a sure way to lose the respect of your co-workers, lose control of your meeting, and create a negative environment. Some people are not comfortable speaking in front of people, but they could have great input. A good leader is able to draw out information from these more reticent personalities without making them feel embarrassed or belittled.

Here is an example of being put on the spot during a meeting. Imagine this scenario: You are the new project manager at a company, and it is your first week on the job. You are in a team meeting with about 25 people in attendance. They all know each other quite well. You are a bit nervous because you are still trying to figure out who is who and are struggling to remember the names and positions of all the people who report to you. You are hoping that you will not call someone by the wrong name or ask a question that indicates that you have no idea what his responsibilities are.

Your manager called the meeting and, after giving some team updates, he is now heading up a long and rather heated discussion about the pros and cons of adding a particular feature to the product. It is a controversial subject; some of the participants are very emotional and have very strong opinions about whether the feature should be added to the project. Some of the team members are looking down at the floor, looking as though they are uncomfortable with the raised voices and the emotional outbursts. Your manager, who is running the meeting (and not running it very well so far, based on the noise level), turns to you and says, "So, project manager (imagine that he actually calls you by your name), what do you think we should do?" Everyone goes deathly quiet, and all eyes are on you. You have no idea what they are talking about or why they are so upset about it. You feel totally embarrassed and stupid because you do not know what to say and everyone is waiting to see how you will handle this. You now understand why half the room was looking at the floor, no doubt avoiding eye contact so they were not the next person to be put on the spot.

This is a true story. The manager who did the putting on the spot would do this regularly to different people in the room, regardless of how long they had worked there. No one enjoyed those meetings, and they felt compelled to say something, anything, just to get off the hook. They were often arguing for something that they had no knowledge or interest in just so that they did not look stupid in front of the boss. This behavior was not very productive and certainly was not conducive to effective meeting facilitation or brainstorming. It also created a very negative environment both for the project manager and for the team. The team felt resentment because the project manager was new and had been unfairly put on the spot. The project manager had obviously not had the time yet to review all the necessary documents and get up to speed on the project before being thrown in at the deep end in this meeting.

Wondering what to do if this ever happens to you? Here is a tip on what to do when you have no idea what to say. This should help you dig yourself out of the hole and will not make you sound stupid. It should also demonstrate your integrity and intelligence.

> *Thank you. I appreciate that you value my opinion. I am not sure that I completely understand all the ins and outs of this particular issue. I have just heard some very compelling arguments from the team both for and against this (whatever the issue was about). However, I do not feel that I am currently familiar enough with all the details of this issue to be able to form a personal opinion. If it would benefit the group, I am happy to do some research into this issue and discuss my findings and recommendations at next week's meeting.*

That should get you off the hook, at least temporarily! It is far better than making something up. You never know what sort of hot water that could get you into. It demonstrates to your team that you make decisions based on facts and not on who is shouting the loudest. They will respect you for refusing to be bullied into commenting on something that you do not feel you are qualified to comment on.

Stating that you value everyone's opinion is a great way to start eliciting feedback from your team. If you find that only a small percentage of your attendees are participating, listen to their suggestions, thank them, and ask if anyone else has any ideas. You will often find that the same few people are actively participating in every meeting, and the rest of the room is quiet. If you consistently have problems with specific team members' lack of participation, talk to them individually and explain to them why it is important that you get their input. If they are really embarrassed about speaking up, tell them that they can talk to you before the meeting with their input and that you will share it with the group. You can present it to the group in such a way that they do not feel embarrassed that they did not speak up themselves. For instance, "John and I were discussing this same issue just this morning, and he had a great point that perhaps we should implement this as an optional feature." Once the discussion gets going on that point, you will probably find that John cannot help but join in to defend his idea or to add more compelling arguments for why it is a good idea. You may not see an overnight change, but as time goes by, you should start to see broader participation. It is a good idea in these situations to talk one-on-one with the person. Sending an e-mail or leaving them a voice mail about it will probably make them feel embarrassed and perhaps more nervous about it and could well make matters worse. They may feel too shy about approaching you to talk about how they feel.

Setting the Tone

One very important thing to remember is to ensure that you are creating a positive environment for your meetings. As stated previously, participation is a key factor in productive and effective meetings. There should be no criticizing or negative behavior from anyone involved in the meetings. It is your responsibility to ensure that your team behaves in a professional and respectful manner at your meetings as well as those owned or run by other people. If your meeting starts on a negative note, it will be hard to get it back on a positive track unless you change the tone before you move on. One negative person can set the tone for your whole meeting unless you know how to recognize and deal with negativity as soon as it rears its ugly head.

For instance, a developer might walk into your meeting and loudly declare to the room, "Ok, I'm here; let's hurry it up and get this over with; I have more important things to do." People in the room may laugh, and she may think that she is stating the truth in an amusing way. She may even think that she is helping you to get the meeting finished more quickly and efficiently. In fact, all she is doing is setting a negative tone for the meeting and implying that it is unimportant and a waste of time. You need to manage this situation before you get your meeting started. A meeting attendee with a negative attitude can make it very difficult to run an effective and successful meeting.

It is not always clear at the beginning of the meeting that you have a negative attitude in the room, so you need to be vigilant and aware of what is going on in the room at all times. Sometimes the negativity will manifest itself as whispering and under-the-breath remarks that are made during the meeting. Do not ignore this. Ask participants to speak up, and if they do so with a negative remark, respond to it in a respectful but assertive way. You do not need your meeting disrupted by negative or childish behavior. If the disruptive person refuses to participate in the meeting, you can ask them to leave, or you can adjourn the meeting and reschedule for a later time. If you adjourn the meeting early, be sure to speak with the offending person before the next meeting to ensure that you have resolved his issues first.

Usually, if someone is being negative and disruptive, there is a good reason for him to feel unhappy. You need to find out what that reason is. It is not always as easy as you asking and him telling you, though. You may need to dig a bit deeper. The conflict management section later in this chapter will help you with ideas and strategies on how to handle these situations and how to diffuse anger and conflict. A meeting with positive energy will be a successful meeting. You may not resolve all the issues, but that does not mean that your meeting was not successful. Project management is a continual process, and your meetings will be part of that continual process.

Meeting Minutes

Realtors will tell you that there are three key points to remember when investing in real estate: location, location, location! Here are the three key points to remember when managing a project: documentation, documentation, documentation! There are many selfless reasons for documenting everything, but first let's talk about the most selfish reason: It is to protect yourself! Whether the meeting is formal or informal, it is necessary to write down what was discussed and agreed to, and to distribute the notes to the meeting attendees and appropriate stakeholders. The recording of meeting minutes is a very important task. It may be one of the least-favorite responsibilities of many project managers, but that does not diminish its importance. The ability to record and transcribe meeting minutes in an accurate, concise, and coherent manner is a very valuable skill.

Creating meeting minutes for status or other meetings is the same as documenting the meeting minutes for the kick-off meeting. When conducting a formal meeting, it is important not to make the mistake of trying to document every single comment that was made, verbatim, but to concentrate on the big picture and summarize what is being communicated. If you know shorthand, your life will be much easier! But how many people know shorthand these days? If you do not feel that you are a good note-taker, you can take a class that will help you to develop note-taking and speed writing skills. For now, you could take a tape recorder into the meeting so that you don't miss anything, but be sure to let everyone know that you are recording the meeting before you start. You could also delegate the note-taking to someone else. However, learning to recognize important points and being able to summarize them is a skill that you will need for more than creating meeting minutes and status reports. This is great skill to learn for verbal communication as well as written communication.

When creating meeting minutes, make sure you document all the important elements of the meeting. This includes the type of meeting, client name, attendees, date and time, facilitator's name, main topics, action items, and adjournment time. Use the agenda as the template for taking notes and for how to organize your minutes in a meaningful way. You can either handwrite your meeting notes or use a computer. If you decide to handwrite, leave plenty of space on your copy of the agenda to take the notes and ensure that you have plenty of spare paper available if the discussion gets lengthy and you have to take a lot of notes. Have your list of invitees in front of you so you can check off their names as they come into the room. This way you will not have to try and think back when creating the meeting minutes to remember who was in attendance. Another idea is to have a sign-in sheet that can be passed around the room while the meeting is in progress. However, this method is usually used for more formal meetings or meetings where people do not know each other well. It is not as common to see this method used in regularly scheduled meetings.

As discussed in previous chapters, meeting minutes should be typed up and distributed to the attendees within three days of the meeting. You should give a deadline for the recipients to get back to you with comments, additions, or corrections so that you can send out an amendment to the minutes within a few days, if necessary.

Communicating with Formal Presentations

To be effective and successful, formal presentations require preparation. Formal presentations will most likely be given in front of clients, stakeholders, and sometimes, upper-level (senior) management. Presentation meetings are designed to inform about project status or to sell new ideas. You should never go into a presentation meeting unprepared.

When preparing for a formal presentation, first define the desired output, which is what you would like to see as a result of your presentation. This will help you decide how much detail you need in the presentation. What are you trying to accomplish in the meeting? Are you trying to get approval to continue the project, or are you trying to sell the client new ideas? Either way, you need to be clear on what you want the outcome of the meeting to be. Unless you have a clearly defined objective, you are not in a position to create a cohesive presentation.

Don't wait until the very last minute to work on your presentation. You need to get an early start on your presentation so that you have time to incorporate any last-minute changes or late-breaking news. Being able to give a polished presentation will require some rehearsal time. If you finish working on your presentation ten minutes before the meeting starts, you are not going to be prepared to give a confident and streamlined presentation. Remember that the people who are attending the meeting are there for knowledge purposes, not to "ooh" and "ah" over the dazzling affects or fancy graphics that you put into your presentation. Don't use smoke and mirrors to try to impress your audience. Keep the presentation simple, informative, accurate, and to the point. Figure 11.2 shows an example PowerPoint presentation. A blank PowerPoint Presentation template is included on the CD-ROM that accompanies this book.

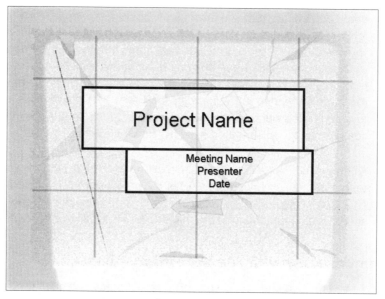

Figure 11.2: PowerPoint presentation screen.

When creating formal presentations you also need to decide which presentation tools are the most appropriate. Many different tools available.

Presentation tools include:

- PowerPoint Presentations
- LCD Projectors
- Laptops
- Video
- Laser Pointers
- Remote Mouse
- LCD Panels
- Multimedia and Sound
- Overhead Projectors
- Printers
- Interactive White Boards
- Video Conferencing
- Phone Conferencing

Determine your communication needs, the environment, and the message you want to get across. Then, you can choose the right tools. Base your decisions on the functionality the tools will give you as well as your comfort level with using them. If you are unfamiliar with the use of the video conferencing equipment, for instance, you do not want to spend the first 20 minutes of your meeting trying to get it working with your white board software. You would have been better off using phone conferencing for your remote attendees and e-mailing the presentation to them beforehand so they could follow along during the meeting. There are many different options, and often the simplest are best. The more technology you are using, the more things can go wrong.

Just as you did for your kick-off meeting, you need to create support materials for the meeting. Make sure you have a copy of the agenda and any other handouts to give to your attendees. These handouts will allow the attendees to review the material again later and to go back to their supervisors or team members and give them an overview of your presentation.

We want to stress once again that prior to the meeting, you should try to rehearse your presentation. This ensures that you have everything you need included in the presentation and the tools to present it. Most important, you need to know what you are going to say. Merely reading from the presentation screen is not going to be very compelling or interesting for your audience. They could sit and read it themselves! You should use exactly the same equipment for your rehearsal that you will be using in the meeting. If you have access to the same meeting room, it would be a good idea to rehearse there, so you will know your way around. You should also test your equipment to make sure that it works and that you know how to use it. Go through your whole presentation to make sure that all the screens are there, in the right order, with no typos and no deleted text still showing up on the screen.

A smart presenter always has a backup plan. What if the computer crashes or the projector dies? What will you do? What if there is a plumbing leak and your meeting is moved to a different conference room? Many things can happen toaffect your presentation. Always have hard copies of everything. You can just as easily give your presentation with your audience following along using the printouts. If you have example documents printed, you can share those, too. What would you do if your lead engineer were not available? Do you have a backup person who can stand in? Think simple when devising your backup plan. Imagine that there is a fire drill, and you have to give your presentation out in the parking lot. Do you have what you need to do it? If you know how you could accomplish this, then you know you have a foolproof backup plan!

One of the biggest fears for many project managers is public speaking. Remember that the more presentations you give, the more comfortable you will feel about speaking in front of an audience. Giving presentations is a big part of a project manager's job, so there is no way to avoid it. Giving formal presentations is very different from giving informal presentations to your team members. In meetings with your team members, it is a much more relaxed and friendly environment. You will probably have more humor in your meetings and perhaps a bit of chitchat here and there about not-so-critical issues.

When giving formal presentations to clients and stakeholders, your whole demeanor needs to be professional. When presenting, you should:

- Be dressed professionally and appropriately and remember that you are representing your company and your team members.

- Face your audience. Do not sit behind the computer hiding your face. It will be beneficial to have a remote mouse so you can stand in front of the room and click through the slides. Your audience should have sight of you at all times.

- Be sure to not read your presentation word for word, and don't try to memorize it. Use your notes sparingly and talk about what is up on the screen knowledgably and confidently. You should know your project inside and out. Too much time spent reading your notes or reading from the screen demonstrates to your audience that you are unprepared.

- Establish eye contact with all attendees in the room. (Not all at the same time, of course, or you will look cross-eyed and crazed!) You should move your gaze around the room so that you establish eye contact regularly with each and every person in the room. Try not to stare at the same person for too long, or you will make them feel uncomfortable.

- Try not to talk too fast or rush through the presentation. This will make you look nervous and uncomfortable. If you look as though you can't wait to get it over with and get out of the room, your audience will start to feel the same way. Remember, you are the project manager and the speaker, and the room will feed off your enthusiasm, confidence, and energy. It is your responsibility to know your material and your project.

- Try not to fall apart if someone asks a question that you cannot answer. Don't panic! Tell them that you do not feel that you can give an accurate answer right now and that you will follow up with them as soon as possible after the meeting. Let the attendees know that you will also include the information in the meeting minutes. It is OK if you do not have every single piece of information at hand. You will look more professional if you admit you do not know than if you guess and then have to retract the answer later if you guessed wrong.

Remember, just as in the kick-off meeting, you should keep your meeting upbeat and interesting because you don't want your attendees to fall asleep from boredom. However, be careful if you use humor. Too many jokes can hurt your presentation and your reputation. You have to be careful not to offend anyone with jokes so when in doubt, leave it out!

Display enthusiasm and confidence about your project. If you truly believe in the project, it will be obvious to your attendees. You should ensure that you keep the meeting in control and that you finish on time. Show respect for other people's schedules, and make sure that your meeting does not run over the time limit. If you are running out of time, skip over some of the less important parts of your presentation so that you cover the critical points. You can also consider scheduling a follow up meeting.

Do not wait until 1 minute before the end before you realize you need 20 more minutes to finish. Do regular time checks. You can let the team know that you are doing time checks every 15 or 30 minutes. Let them know if unnecessary discussion is slowing you down. Tell them that the presentation is going slower than you had expected so you are going to skip over some of the presentation to finish on time. Offer to schedule another meeting to discuss other issues that are being raised so that you can put them aside for now. This is often referred to as the "parking lot." If you put a topic in the parking lot, it is off limits for this meeting but will not be forgotten because someone will take an action item to follow up on it or schedule a meeting to discuss it further. Your audience will appreciate you keeping track of time and being respectful of their schedules.

Keep the meeting interactive and answer any questions that arise. Allow time at the end of each section, or at the end of the presentation, for questions. When you time your presentation, remember that when you give the real presentation, you will need some additional time to allow for questions from your audience. Remember to factor this in when figuring out how much time you need to schedule for your presentation. You need to answer questions and be sure that everyone understands what you are presenting. If it is more pertinent to answer a particular question later in the meeting, defer the question. Reply with, "I will be covering milestones later in the meeting, so I would like to address your question then." You should let your audience know at the start of your presentation whether you would like to take questions as you speak or whether you would like them to make a note of their questions and ask you at the specified Q&A times. Letting your audience know what process you would like to follow for your meeting will help you run your meeting more smoothly.

Once the meeting is over, thank the attendees for taking the time out of their busy schedules to be there. Ask for feedback on your presentation and on the material. Feedback will help you make the next presentation even better. Make all materials available, but most important, make yourself available to answer any questions that attendees may have after they leave the meeting. Make sure that they all know how to contact you and what your availability is. For instance, let them know whether you will be on vacation next week or out of the office for a couple of days so they know the best time to contact you.

The Importance of Documentation

Every stage of the project life cycle has associated documentation. It is vitally important to your project, and to the success of future projects, that this documentation is written, reviewed, and finalized during each phase of the life cycle.

No one on your team should be operating in a vacuum: They need to document and review designs and specifications documents with the team. Without a good, solid documentation process, your project may still be completed on time and within budget, but it will be debatable whether it was really completed with high quality. It will certainly not be completed in a way that makes it robust, reusable, or extensible.

In addition to the formal technical documentation, your team should be documenting their code, keeping release notes up to date, and making sure that defect resolution reports are completed when bugs are resolved. Not only will this serve you well if you need to do more work on this project later on—a subsequent release for instance—but it can also be used for new projects that require similar technology or features.

Ensure that your team members know that documentation is not optional; it is mandatory and must be completed on schedule just as the rest of their assigned tasks. Ensure that you include the documentation tasks on their schedules and that they are assigned time to complete those tasks. It takes time to write a specification or a design document. Your team members should not be expected to fit this into their spare time. You may have heard the expression "suck it up." It is used in technology companies to describe tasks that some people do not think should be assigned schedule time. Getting into the habit of assigning tasks that your team members have to "suck up" is a very bad thing. You will overstretch your resources, work your team into the ground, and alienate your team members. Documentation is not a spare-time task; it is an important part of the project life cycle.

It is important that roles, responsibilities, and processes be documented for your project. Your team members need to be aware of the existence of these documents and know where to find them. It is the responsibility of the project manager to ensure that process documents are kept up to date, so make sure that each of the documents has an assigned owner and that those owners have scheduled time to update the documents.

Open Communication

Team morale has been recognized increasingly as an important element in team productivity. The higher the team morale and motivation, the higher the productivity of the team. As projects are approved and kicked off, members of your project team may be working together for the first time. Resources may be moved from one project to another, and these changes can cause some level of anxiety on your team. If your team has not worked together before, the unfamiliar environment and the new faces may be a little overwhelming for them. If your team has not worked with you before, then it is only natural that they will be concerned about your leadership style and how it will affect their everyday work lives.

Whatever the size of a project, it will require a specific set of activities, tools, and processes, which will require a lot of communication. Being an efficient task manager does not necessarily mean that a project manager will be a good people manager. People management is a whole different ball game, with lots of subtle and not-so-subtle complexities. If you have never managed people before, you may find that you are not very well prepared for this aspect of project management. Remember that tasks do not have personalities, but people do! You cannot just put together a schedule and expect your team to get the job done without any input or coordination from you.

In addition to excitement and anticipation, anxiety and stress will likely be two very strong factors when dealing with a new project team. You will likely be suffering from some of these feelings yourself. It is your responsibility as the project manager to relieve some of the anxiety and stress your new team members are feeling. If a member of your team feels out of place, unsure about her responsibilities, or unsure about the project, you will need to work with her to resolve her uncertainties. The sooner you deal with uncertainties on your team the better. Everyone on your team needs a clear understanding of why his is there and what the goals of the project are. The team members need to communicate with you and with the rest of the team. They need to feel comfortable talking to each other as well as going through their manager to get things done. A highly skilled and talented engineer is not much use to you in a team setting if her communication skills are appalling.

An example of this is taken from the experience of a technology project manager. The team comprised a group of very talented engineers. They ranged in experience level from 12 years on the job to graduates just out of college. The project manager was new to the team, though the team had been working together for a year. The team had a senior engineer who was very talented. The project manager and other senior team members enjoyed working with her. She was helpful and accommodating. She was very knowledgeable and had great communication skills. You could not ask for anything more. Or could you? All the team members had to work with this engineer in some capacity during the development stage of the project, so some level of technical discussion was necessary. Everything seemed to be going pretty well.

Then after a couple of months one of the junior engineers resigned. The project manager was surprised because the team was very strong and the project was very exciting, and she knew that the engineer loved what he was working on. She met with him to see whether she could persuade him to stay, but he was adamant that he needed to leave. He did, however, tell her why he was leaving. The senior engineer was bullying and threatening the junior engineers, and it had been going on for a year. The previous manager would not hear a word against the senior engineer and raved about how great she was at every team meeting. Other team members were made to feel inadequate if they complained about her and were told that they should listen to her because maybe they would learn something. The junior team members were too scared to say anything because they thought they would get fired.

The new manager had walked into a situation where open communication was talked about all the time but was not really present. The team seemed happy on the surface, but it was rife with conflict and inequality underneath the friendly facade. Working with the engineer on behavioral problems that she had been allowed to get away with for a year was challenging for the project manager. More importantly, building the trust and open communication that had been missing for so long took a lot of effort and a long time.

So just because it all looks good on the surface does not mean that it is. It's like a Monet picture—beautiful when standing far away, but completely horrible close up. You need to pay attention to what you see, hear, and feel and follow your instincts. Bullies do not put signs on their office doors that read, "beware of the bully." They only bully those whom they believe are weaker than them. They do not behave badly in front of their manager or anyone else they think they need to impress. You need to be vigilant and open minded. Bullies are also very often the people whom you would least suspect would behave in such a way.

So, what are some of the key contributors to poor communication and low team morale on a project team? These are some things to look out for:

- Inappropriate Communication
- Over Communicating
- Under Communicating
- Lack of Empowerment
- Lack of Direction from the Project Manager
- Lack of Accountability
- Overcommitting Resources
- Making Important Team Decisions without Team Input
- Unrealistic Expectations and Timelines
- The "What's in it for me" Syndrome
- Dissention among Team Members
- Undefined Process or a Lack of Understanding of the Process
- No Clear Goals or Objectives
- Lack of Clarity about Who the Decision-Makers Are
- Language Barriers
- Fear or Resistance to Asking Questions
- High Staff Turnover

Political Correctness in the Workplace

What can you say and what can't you say? Some people are touchy feely, and some are not. What is appropriate, and what is inappropriate? When it comes to political correctness and workplace humor, it can be very confusing knowing what is OK and what is not OK. There is a lot of diversity in companies these days, and it is not always obvious what might be offensive. You may not find out what comments are offensive to someone until it's too late. You may have said something in a joking manner to one person that was quoted out of context to another. Worse yet, you may have said something to one person that another person overheard. Though the person you were talking to may have been OK with what you said, you may have offended the person who overheard you. It is a terrible day when you receive the dreaded phone call from human resources to let you know that they received a complaint against you and you now have to prepare to defend yourself. This is not a phone call that you want, or need, to receive. It is completely avoidable. Just because you do not think that something is offensive does not mean that someone else will not be offended by it.

We have all been in a situation, at one time or another, when what we say has been taken out of context or when we unintentionally offended someone by something that we thought was quite innocent. Some people feel that having to watch every single word that comes out of their mouth is ridiculous. However, others feel safer and more comfortable knowing that their personal beliefs, religion, nationality, race, marital status, sexual preferences, or disabilities will not hinder them in their career or make them an object of ridicule or abuse. Whether you believe that political correctness in the workplace has gone too far or not, you have a responsibility to follow the rules and enforce them on your team. Political correctness is a way of life in the corporate world, and it is important that you take it seriously. Not only do you have a responsibility to ensure that you treat everyone with dignity and respect, but you also are a role model for your team, and you need to lead by example. Everyone is different, and they find different things offensive. It should not be difficult to anticipate that something you are about to say could be taken the wrong way. If you are in any doubt, then do not say it. When team members are respectful of others, it makes for a healthier and happier workplace. Remember, a joke that may be funny to you may not be funny to someone else.

Everyone wants to be in a healthy work environment. What is a healthy work environment? A healthy work environment is an environment where everyone feels safe, secure, appreciated, and respected. Employees can go about their jobs secure in the knowledge that they will be measured on their performance and not their sex, color, race, sexual orientation, or religion. A healthy environment means no one having to worry about being harassed or made fun of.

The reality of the workplace today is different from the way it was years ago. As the workforce has changed, so have the rules related to communication in the workplace. What used to be considered OK in terms of humor is not necessarily considered OK any longer. Some negative behaviors were tolerated in the past, and anyone who was offended was encouraged to grin and bear it. Complaining may have resulted in their being fired especially if they were complaining about their manager. Today, employees have much more protection under the law and do not have to grin and bear unacceptable and disrespectful behavior.

Here are some examples of political incorrectness that you need to be careful to avoid:

- Don't discriminate against *anyone*. This means people of different sex, race, color, religion, sexuality, marital or child status, health, or disability, to mention just a few.

- Don't discuss anything that might be considered sexual in the workplace, even if you consider it joking. People may find your discussion offensive even if you were speaking to someone else. People overhear conversations and can be offended by what is said. Sending e-mail to a friend that contains sexual remarks or connotations can be dangerous. If your e-mail is personal mail, then send it from home and do not use work computers or work time to send it. Not only is it unprofessional to be sending these kinds of e-mails, but also anything that is sent to or from your work e-mail address has a copy left on the server, so it is not private or personal.

- Ask your friends not to send jokes or rude e-mails to your work e-mail address. Even if you are just the recipient, you are responsible for what is in your inbox.

- Don't make jokes about people's appearance. Most people are very sensitive about their appearance, so you should never go there!

- Be careful about discussing personal things that someone else may find embarrassing or rude. For instance, a nursing mother may think that it is OK to discuss breast-feeding in front of the whole team or to leave her breast pump apparatus in the team kitchen. She may be very comfortable with her body and the idea of breast-feeding, but others may find it embarrassing or distasteful.

- Do not make fun of people's accents. People from other countries speak and pronounce words differently. People from some countries have difficulty with certain sounds in the English language. Those people should not be laughed at or made fun of. A professional person does not need to be informed, while they are in the middle of a serious technical discussion, that they are pronouncing a word incorrectly or that you "love their accent." They want you to listen to what they are saying and take them seriously.

- Be aware of team members who do not like physical contact. It can make some people feel uneasy if you touch their arm to get their attention, and they may take it as a sexual advance. You will learn quickly who is uncomfortable about physical contact. You will be able to read their body language. When you go to touch their shoulder, they may shrug or if you touch their hand when passing them a document, they may pull away quickly.

- Do *not* put pictures of scantily clad people in your office.

You never know what can offend, so be sensitive and overly cautious. Unfortunately, some people are easily offended and appear to be oversensitive. If you are practicing political correctness in the workplace, however, even the most sensitive people will have nothing to be offended about. As a manager, you must always behave appropriately. You cannot make up your own rules for your team because you think the company rules are too strict. You must show your team that you value diversity by doing everything you can to ensure that everyone is treated with dignity and respect.

Ask your team members to let you know whether something offends them or makes them uncomfortable. This way you can deal with issues on your team before human resources gets involved. If a team member tells you that another team member talking about breast-feeding embarrasses them, you can step in and resolve the situation before it goes any further. You do not need to tell the breast-feeding–discusser who complained about her. You can just say that some team members find it embarrassing and ask her not to discuss this topic at work. Both of the team members should appreciate your involvement, because it is likely that neither of them wanted to offend the other. If you cannot resolve the issue, then it will inevitably end up as an official complaint to human resources. Talk to your team about the process for complaining when they feel someone has acted in a discriminatory way. Let the team know that they can file a formal complaint with human resources, but that they can also come to you first so that you can try to resolve the issue before it goes that far. If the discrimination or harassment is indicative of gross misconduct, though, then you should not try to resolve it yourself but should report it to your human resources department as soon as possible.

Sometimes complications and misunderstandings happen when one person is "more open" than someone else. One person thinks that the other should lighten up and the other feels that the "offender" should control him- or herself and not discuss such disgusting or embarrassing things in the workplace. You may be thinking, "Man, what is left to joke about? Humor is a big part of relieving tension. Can I never joke?" You can still use humor to make a fun environment for your team members. You just have to be careful about what you are joking about. You can joke about yourself and your own flaws. Everyone loves to laugh at someone else, and if you are poking fun at yourself, then it is OK to laugh and you know you won't write yourself up! You still need to be careful that someone else in the room does not think you are poking fun at them in a roundabout way, so be sensitive about how personal you get.

Sometimes joking about situations that have happened prior to the team getting together is fun. An example would be a programmer talking about a difficult client he had to work with, or the project manager talking about how she tripped on the stairs and managed to save herself injury by landing on her laptop and then spent the next three weeks having to recreate the schedule. The moral of the story being, of course, to make regular backups and always take the elevator!

Just because no one complains to you about inappropriate behavior does not mean that you should not deal with it before it gets out of hand. The following story is an example of a situation where the manager decided to take no action, and it resulted in all kinds of problems.

A young female programmer enjoyed hanging out with the male programmers. She got along well with all of them and eventually became "one of the boys." She was not a timid or shy person. She was just the opposite. She was very loud and, at times, vulgar. She told sexual jokes and dressed inappropriately for her job. She wore tight skirts and low-cut blouses. Because none of the male programmers seemed to mind, and no one complained about it, the manager took no action.

One day, the female programmer jokingly made a comment about one of the male programmer's clothing being boring and "geeky," and he jokingly reciprocated, making a comment about her plunging necklines and short skirts. She went directly to human resources and filed an official harassment complaint. The male programmer was called in and was completely embarrassed and amazed that he had to defend himself in a situation that was, to him, completely innocent. He was written up for sexual harassment, and she, of course, was not because no one had complained about her behavior.

His work performance suffered because of the incident, and the two could not work together because he was afraid to say anything at all to her. His happy-go-lucky attitude changed overnight because of a comment that he felt was justified and appropriate in the circumstances but was against the rules of the company. Everyone knew what had happened and was nervous about saying anything to the female programmer. He stayed in his cubicle and hardly spoke to anyone on the team any longer. She, however, continued to act in the same inappropriate way, making sexual comments and wearing tight clothing. No one said anything because they were afraid she would go to human resources and report them for sexual harassment.

This is not such an unusual situation. The rules are there to protect *everyone*, but some people use them to gain control and advantages for themselves. The moral of this story is that you should deal with these kinds of situations immediately. It would have been very easy for the manager, in this instance, to speak to the young woman as soon as she joined the team and ask her to dress more professionally at work and to tone down her sexual remarks and behavior. If this had occurred, and the manager had documented the conversation, either the situation would never have happened or it would have had a very different outcome.

CHAPTER 12

Integration and Testing

Once your project has reached the "feature complete" milestone, you are in the integration phase. During the integration phase the code, or the system components, are integrated together to form the final product. This phase often seems short and lacking in diversity compared to the rest of the phases in the project life cycle. Do not be fooled by this narrowly focused approach; it can be an extremely stressful and intense time. Do you remember the old adage, "The proof is in the pudding"? Well, this is the pudding! When working with very complex products or projects designed to interface with many existing systems, there is the potential for some really scary problems to arise during the integration phase. After you have the components working together, the systems talking to each other, and everything seamlessly integrated, you need to ensure that you have acceptable performance statistics for each area of the system. There is no point in having a great product that integrates seamlessly with all the business and technical systems if you find that it can support only 10 concurrent users, rather than the 2,000 that it was supposed to support!

On some projects, some administrative product functionality may be implemented during the integration phase rather than during the development phase. These tasks will be limited to tasks not on the critical path that are not required to complete the project. For example, these tasks may include:

- Errors and Alerts Monitoring and Reporting Engine
- Decision Support
- Automation of Back-End Administrative Functions
    - Automated install and setup
    - Automated system backups

Any functionality that is not required for the end-to-end testing to be completed or for the product or service to be deployed may be implemented during the integration or deployment phase. This functionality may be highly desirable and may be a requirement for project completion; however, scheduling the implementation of the tasks to occur post-development is an effective way to fast-track the project and schedule the completion date as early as possible. It also helps to balance the workload more evenly across the life cycle phases because there may not ordinarily be as much work for the development team in the integration phase as in the development phase of the project. The Integration Process Flowchart is shown in Figure 12.1.

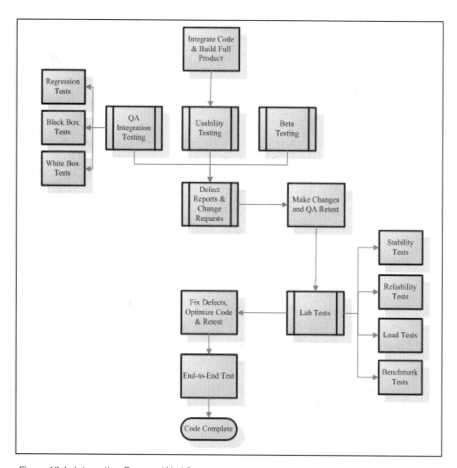

Figure 12.1: Integration Process Workflow.

Understanding Quality Assurance (QA) and Quality Control (QC)

"Quality control" is the term used to describe the verification testing of a *manufactured* product. Examples of a manufactured product would be a hardware product such as a server or a software product such as a CD-ROM. This testing occurs during the Deployment (or Post-Deployment) phase of the life cycle and is completely separate (and totally different) from the quality assurance testing performed during the Development and Integration phases of a project. The manufacturer of the product is responsible for quality control testing, whereas the developer of the product is responsible for the quality assurance testing. Quality assurance tests the functionality of the product; quality control measures the quality of individual units of the product. For example, you may have noticed that when you purchase a new network router or a CD player, there is often a small "QC" sticker on the product. This sticker indicates that the unit passed a quality control test before it was released from the manufacturer. Each unit (or a sampling of units) goes through a predefined set of tests to ensure that it meets the specification before it is released for sale. Quality control testing for hardware products is much more complex and costly than it is for software products. Hardware products are composed of many different electronic and mechanical parts, so there are many more defect opportunities than in software manufacturing. The costs of fixing hardware defects are much higher than for fixing software defects in manufactured products. Consequently, the quality control process for hardware is much more complex and time consuming, and the costs associated with it are significantly higher.

Quality assurance refers to the testing of the product that takes place during the Development and Integration phases of the project. It also incorporates the testing of the final integration of the project components and the performance tests that take place before the final product is released (delivered) to the client. All this testing needs to be planned in the early stages of the project. Project documentation is a critical requirement for quality assurance. The project requirements, specification, and design documents serve as the basis for the quality assurance process planning.

Chances are that your company will have a quality assurance manager who oversees the quality assurance team. Even though you may not be managing the quality assurance team, you will need a basic understanding of quality assurance to be able to communicate effectively with the quality assurance team members. You also need to understand the dependencies between the teams and the importance of the timely delivery of the project documentation and the project releases to the quality assurance team. The QA team needs the documents early in the process so that they can create test plans for the project releases. You need to ensure that the quality assurance team has adequate time for testing the releases and that you incorporate those timelines into your project schedule so that you are delivering on time. Your project cannot be delivered to the client until it has been tested and passed by quality assurance.

The more coordination and cooperation existing between the development team and the quality assurance team, the more you lower the risk factor of your project.

In many companies, a kind of rivalry exists between development and quality assurance teams. The developers consider themselves superior in some way to the quality assurance team members. Quality assurance team members feel that the developers do not respect their knowledge or their contribution to the project. It is critical to the success of your project that you break down any of these barriers and create an environment of mutual respect and cooperation between the teams. Engineers from both teams perform very specific and specialized functions, and each and every person is needed to create a successful project. The more involvement you have from quality assurance early in the process, the more successful your project will be.

Being able to adequately test a product is as important as meeting the user-defined requirements. How do you know that the project meets requirements if you cannot test it? How can you find what is broken if there is no test mechanism to help track down problems? It is the responsibility of every developer to ensure that her code is testable. If she cannot write code that is testable, then she should not be writing the code. Quality assurance engineers can review requirements and designs and identify where there will be testing problems. The developers should use this specialized knowledge of QA to improve their designs and their code. Developers may need to write test programs that quality assurance can use to test the code that they have written. The more efficiently that quality assurance can test the product, the more cost effective your project will be; the greater the test coverage, the higher quality the product. Project management does not just mean managing your team; it means taking responsibility for working with other groups to ensure that the entire project process is as efficient and effective as possible. The more teamwork and cooperation that exists between groups, the higher the morale and motivation will be for members of all teams.

The Role of Quality Assurance

The goals of the quality assurance team are to reduce risk and ensure quality by verifying and validating the project. For quality assurance to achieve these goals, they need to be involved at the beginning of the project. The earlier in the process that quality assurance is involved, the greater the time and budget savings will be for your project. Quality cannot be added to a product after the fact; it must be built into the development process. A quality assurance team can measure quality and identify areas where the code fails to meet the requirements and specification, but it cannot add quality into the product.

Quality Assurance Organization

Depending on the organizational structure of the company, the quality assurance team may be part of the development team or may be a separate group entirely. The team may be assigned to one project only or may be a centralized group that is responsible for QA on all projects. The quality assurance manager may report to a group manager, a project manager, or a group quality assurance manager (Figure 12.2), or the project manager may also be the quality assurance manager. There is no right or wrong way to organize a QA team, but in our experience, we have found that combining the role of project manager and quality assurance manager does not work very well. It removes some checks and balances from the development equation and spreads the project manager too thin. These situations can only lead to compromised quality.

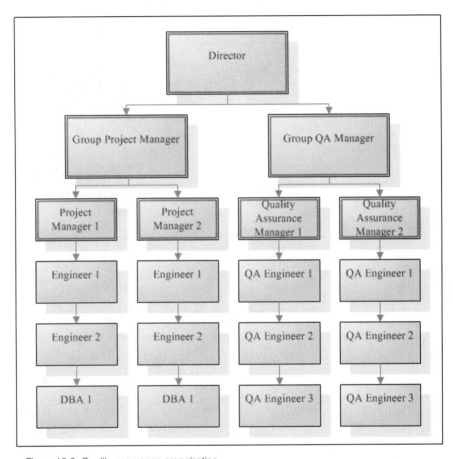

Figure 12.2: Quality assurance organization.

Quality Assurance Process

There are seven main QA steps that are covered during the quality assurance process, as shown in Figure 12.3.

- Test Matrix
- Test Plan
- Traceability Matrix
- Test Case
- Test Script
- Defect Reports
- Quality Risk Assessment

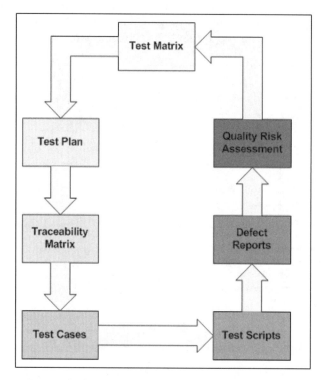

Figure 12.3: Quality assurance process.

Test Matrix

The test matrix is used to analyze the project requirements and identify any holes that exist in the requirements. This benefits both the development and the QA team and ensures that requirements are watertight and appropriately detailed from day one. This will minimize problems later on and will avoid requirement inconsistencies or gaps being discovered later in the process. The test matrix identifies the QA methodologies that will be utilized for that particular project.

Test Plan

The test plan is, in effect, a quality assurance project plan. It identifies the activities and the resources required for each project. The plan is tailored to the unique needs of the project and is based on all the information available at that point. It takes a lot of work to get the test plan right, and it must be finalized before the project begins. The test plan is the foundation that the quality assurance activities and scheduling will be based on for the duration of the project, and as such, it cannot evolve or change as the project progresses.

Traceability Matrix

The traceability matrix is a QA plan and schedule that documents and tracks progress on all tasks. It is a living document that is updated and revised as the project progresses. The traceability matrix tracks which resource, or group of resources, is responsible for testing each of the requirements. It tracks which test plans and scripts are completed as well as what features and functionality have been completed by the development team and are ready for testing. This is the tool for ensuring that every single requirement is validated and verified before product release.

Test Cases

A test case is used for manual testing. It lists the requirements and functionality for each area and the methods that will be used to exercise that specific piece of code. Test cases are usually written so that testing can be started at any place in the test suite rather than having to run from beginning to end. Test cases are broken down into separate modules so that tests can be grouped according to requirements and functionality rather than features. Features may share functionality, which could lead to a lot of redundant testing if QA were to focus all their testing efforts on features rather than functionality. Test cases are mapped to requirements to ensure complete code coverage. A test case will include fields for input, expected output, and actual output. The development team needs to work closely with the quality assurance team to be sure of a common understanding of expected output for a given input. Anomalies between expected and actual output are tracked as defects.

Test Scripts

A test script is scenario based and, as such, requires that the process be stepped through from start to finish. The scripts can be automated or can be run manually, but they must run through the entire process flow. A test script contains fields for input actions, input steps, expected output, and actual output. Test scripts are more detailed than test cases, and they run through a predefined path of the application. This type of testing works well for repetitive and time-consuming testing, such as regression testing. It is not a great tool for measuring the effects of users entering invalid data or using the product in a way that is inconsistent with its intended use.

Defect Reports

Defect tracking or bug tracking is an essential part of both quality assurance and project management. A defect needs to be clearly defined and provide the necessary information for both quality assurance and development team members. Bug reports are used by QA to document problems found in the code that they test. The project manager or project lead will distribute the bug reports to the relevant developer for analysis and resolution. If the required information is not available in the defect report, the developer is not going to be able to reproduce the problem to diagnose the root cause. Once a defect is marked as resolved, QA needs to understand what was changed in the code so that they are able to effectively test the fix and any other code that may have been affected by the change. Defect tracking metrics are used to determine the "readiness for release" level of a product at any given time, so it is critical that the tools and process used for defect tracking be kept up-to-date.

The development team will spend a larger percentage of their time working on defect resolution, also known as "bug fixing," during the integration phase than any other phase of the life cycle. This is the time when those really critical but elusive bugs often rear their ugly heads. It can sometimes take days or weeks for the engineering team to track down the root cause(s) of critical problems. It is important to ensure that any other tasks your team members are assigned to during the integration phase do not take priority over critical bug fixes.

During the development phase, it is likely that most defect reports were approved and assigned to a developer to resolve. During the integration phase, the criteria for approving a defect for resolution will be much stricter. If a bug is not considered critical or a high risk to the success of the project, it will likely be deferred or denied. It is good practice to start using the change control process for bugs as you get close to the end of the integration phase of the project. Once the product is stable, it is important not to make too many changes that may destabilize it again. The change control process is an excellent way of evaluating and tracking changes very closely so that no miscommunication or misunderstanding occurs about what needs to be fixed and what does not.

Quality Risk Assessment

The Quality Risk Assessment is the final document produced by quality assurance upon completion of testing. It identifies what areas of code were tested and what the results of the tests were. It also clearly identifies areas of the code that were specifically not tested, together with the reasons why that testing was not completed. There can be numerous reasons for not testing areas of the code. For instance, lack of time, lack of tools required for testing, budget restrictions, low risk factor, and so on. The quality risk assessment details any areas in the code that are considered at risk, and the level of risk, if the product is released in its current state. This document is reviewed by the various stakeholders and decision-makers and is used as input into their final decision on whether the project is ready for release. A Quality Risk Assessment document is included on the CD-ROM that accompanies this book.

The quality assurance process is used in conjunction with the standard six-step project life cycle.

White-Box versus Black-Box Testing

White-box testing is also referred to as "clear box," "glass box," "open box," and "structural testing." White-box is a testing method that requires explicit knowledge of the internal workings of the code by the tester (see Figure 12.4). The tester must know what the program is supposed to do and must be able to read and understand the code so that he is able to analyze and verify the test outputs.

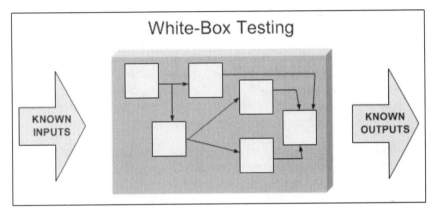

Figure 12.4: White-box testing.

Black-box testing is also referred to as "functional testing." Black-box testing is a testing method that requires no knowledge of the internal workings of the code by the tester (see Figure 12.5). For example, in a black-box test the tester will know the inputs and the expected outputs but will not know how the program arrives at those outputs. The tester does not need to examine the code and needs only to understand the specification.

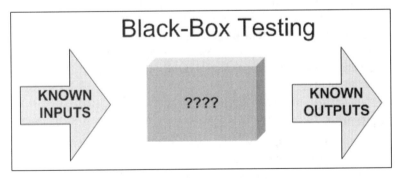

Figure 12.5: Black-box testing.

The majority of testing performed by quality assurance is black-box testing.

Understanding the Different Types of Testing

Numerous quality assurance methods of testing exist. Here is an overview of some of the most common methods. Most of these tests will be black-box tests.

Integration Tests

Integration tests are designed to test the interoperability of components in a system. Integration tests are used to test graphical user interface (GUI), portability, performance, and security of the product. Early in the development phase of the project, the separate components of the system will be tested as they are completed. As development progresses and more areas of the system are completed, it is critical that these interoperability tests be performed to ensure that the separate components will function as one complete application. During integration testing, the development team needs to work to fix problems as quickly as possible so that the QA team can continue testing the product without unnecessary delays.

Integration testing includes testing the installation and setup of the product, as well as testing any administrative functions. If the project is designed to integrate with systems at the client site, that testing will generally start during the integration phase and continue through the deployment phase. The client may be responsible for some of that testing, but it is common for development or quality assurance team members to assist with the testing and to ensure that any issues are identified and documented thoroughly. For Internet or enterprise systems, networking integration testing is also performed during this phase. It is essential to iron out any creases at this stage so that integration problems are not being identified as late as the deployment phase. If problems are not found early, they may not be able to be resolved in time for an on-time release.

During the Integration phase of the life cycle, it is common for complete end-to-end integration testing to be performed on the product and systems. For complex systems this can require a large coordinated effort involving people from every company or department whose system is connected in some way with the project's system. It is important that the system as a whole has been verified. One should never assume that adding a new component to an existing system will not affect any of the existing components.

Acceptance Testing

Acceptance testing is typically the final phase in the quality assurance process, where the finished software is used in the same way that it will be used in the field. The testers will run through various scenarios to verify that the product behaves as expected. The tests will include common mistakes made by users, such as entering text into a numeric field, leaving a field blank, or jumping around within the application rather than proceeding from start to finish. This is to ensure that the application has been programmed to handle use in the real world. This testing is performed by quality assurance engineers and can be extended to include beta testers.

Beta Testing

In *beta testing* the product is given to members of the user community to be tested for functionality. Beta tests can be private tests for selected users, either internally or externally, or they can be public tests, where the product is available to the general public. The goal of beta testing is to get feedback from users to identify bugs in the product or usability issues that need to be resolved before releasing the final product to the end user.

If the project is going to be beta tested, t typically occurs during the Integration phase. Beta tests are purposefully not performed by the project team or quality assurance team members because they have too much knowledge of the product and its functionality. The beta users will invariably find ways of using the product, or navigating through the product, that the project team never envisioned, which will result in the uncovering of all kinds of issues. Beta testers are required to submit defect reports. Those defect reports should be verified by quality assurance (to ensure that they are not the result of user error), and once verified, they should go through the same defect tracking and approval process as the defects found by the quality assurance team.

Usability Testing

Usability testing is generally carried out in a controlled and monitored environment. The goals of usability testing are to verify that the product meets the needs of the user, that the user interface (UI) is intuitive and easy to understand, and that the product will be used in the way the designer had anticipated. Companies often utilize *usability labs* that are set up similar to the interrogation rooms that you see on TV detective shows. The users are put in a room with the system (product) and asked to perform specific functions. The usability specialists, together with members of the development team, stand behind a two-way mirror where they can observe the user at the same time as being able to monitor their actions with the product via a computer interface. The results of these tests are used to improve the product functionality and flow as well as to provide information to the quality assurance and performance testing teams to enable them to develop accurate test plans and scripts based on real user data. Usability testing may begin during the Development phase, as specific areas of the product are completed, or it may occur during the Integration phase, when most of the functionality has been tested and verified.

Regression Testing

Regression testing is the method of rerunning exactly the same test on an application or system that has been changed. The goals of the test are to verify that any defects have been fixed and that no other previously working functions have failed as a result of the changes. Regression tests are generally run with each new build of a product to test bug fixes and new features. These tests can be very time consuming because they generally need to cover a large percentage of the code base. To evaluate the results, the tests must be run exactly the same way every single time. For these reasons regression tests are usually scripted and automated tests.

Benchmarking

Benchmarking is used to compare the performance of hardware or software to a standard. The standard may be an industry standard benchmark, or it may be an internal benchmark used within your company for testing and evaluating products. It is critical when comparing test results that it is very clear what the benchmarks are designed to test and that the tests are run identically so it is an apples-to-apples comparison. Companies often use benchmarks to determine minimum standards for performance of their products. For instance, they can be used to determine minimum (user) system requirements for software products.

Performance Testing

Performance tests measure the performance of each component and the performance of the system as a whole. Performance testing includes load, stress, and stability and reliability testing. Performance tests are generally run in a lab using automated tests. The lab needs to mimic the production or end-user environment as closely as possible, though this will often be on a much smaller scale. Tests are run to simulate users and to measure the performance of the system with increasing load until the breaking point is reached.

Load tests on individual components are often run during the development phase to find bottlenecks in the system. Those bottlenecks can often be removed by making code adjustments. The majority of load tests are run on the full product during the integration phase of the life cycle. Load tests are typically run for a few hours until the required load is reached. These tests are run to ensure that the product will meet the load and performance criteria as specified in the project definition. If the product is required to support 8,000 users but only supports 4,000 users, the team has a lot of work to do before project completion!

Stress tests are similar to load tests and often include running test scenarios where user behavior puts additional stress on the system. This could include denial of service (DoS) attacks.

Stability and reliability tests are run on the fully integrated product (during the Integration phase) to measure the stability and reliability of a system over a longer time period. Stability and reliability tests are run for days or weeks, and the system performance is measured over that period to ensure that there are no time-related issues. For instance, memory leaks over time will crash a system but may not be apparent in a shorter test. There is no point in having a great-looking product with excellent functionality only to find that it crashes every 20 minutes! An apparent intermittent problem may occur regularly but over a broad timescale. For instance, if a problem occurs every 27 hours, it may appear to be a problem that is intermittent and cannot be duplicated. By running a test that lasts for 100 hours, you will see the problem occur 3 times, at 27 hours, 54 hours, and 81 hours. It will be fairly obvious that this problem is time related and is not intermittent.

Security Testing

Security tests are run to test the security robustness of software, hardware, and networking systems. Outside companies are often employed to perform security reviews and tests on systems that contain sensitive information. The tests include reviewing code for security holes and running tests to try to hack into the system. These tests are called "attack and penetration" (A&P) tests. The security tests are designed to ensure that the system handles attempted security breaches gracefully and without crashing the system. Most important, it ensures that the system is secure so that a break-in cannot occur either accidentally or maliciously and, in the event that the system is compromised, that the system contains the necessary monitoring components to alert the security team as quickly as possible.

Product Optimization

Optimization is the tweaking of the product to improve its performance. This means improving the speed, the number of functions that can be performed at one time, or the number of concurrent users that can be supported. It is not always easy to know when you have optimized enough. Make sure that you know when to stop, so that you can move on and get the project ready to deploy and close. As long as your product meets the required performance specification, you can stop optimizing. If you have identified areas that could be optimized even more, document them for consideration for a subsequent release. Remember that every single change you make to the code risks the stability of the product. Be conservative and be safe.

Product Help

The help content for your Web site needs to be written, tested, and verified. The help may have already been written and just needs updating. Help content is typically written by a technical writer and not by an engineer. You have probably seen products or Web sites where an engineer obviously wrote some, or all, of the help content. It generally lacks the polish that you would expect from a professional product. If the development team is required to write the help content, try to assign it to someone whom you know has good writing skills. It could save you a lot of complaints from end users later on!

Code Complete

Code complete is a major project milestone that signifies that all post-feature-complete coding is complete. This includes coding of noncritical areas of the product and bug fixing. The only changes to the code that are allowed to occur after code complete are fixes for critical problems that must be resolved for the project to be completed. Any changes that occur after code complete must go through a change control process. Absolutely no code changes should occur unless approved by the change control board.

Developing the Deployment Plan

The deployment plan will need to be updated to ensure that it is complete and accurate. Many of the post-deployment documents also need to be created during this phase because they will be required prior to deployment, for testing and verification of processes and procedures, as well as for training purposes.

Developing an Operational Support Plan

Who is going handle any issues that come up after the project has been handed-off to the client? It is very easy to forget that the product will continue to have a life of its own after you hand it off to the client. In addition to regular maintenance and monitoring, it is likely that the product will also go through some changes and upgrades farther down the road. When you hand-off the project, make sure that your client understands what they have been given. Believe it or not, there are clients that will be clueless about what to do once they have taken ownership of the project. The client can choose to do the operational and maintenance support for the product themselves, they can hire a third party to manage it on their behalf, or they can purchase a service and maintenance contract with the company that developed the product (if that option is available). Regardless of who will be managing the operational support for the product, an *Operations Plan* is going to be required. It is important to note that the Operations Plan will be different for each project. Depending on the specifics of the project, the product, the client, and the end users, the information and documentation required for post-deployment support will differ greatly.

An Operations Plan will have been started during the Planning phase. The document will need to be updated to ensure that it is complete and accurate. It is not typical for these documents to be created by the project manager. However, the project manager should ensure that these documents are tracked on the schedule. Without the necessary documentation and training, the deployment and hand-off to the client will be delayed. If these documents are delivered late, it could cause your project to become unsuccessful. It doesn't matter whether it was your fault, the end result will be the same. If the people responsible for these documents are behind schedule, you need to track these tasks in your risk log. Likewise, if there are any problems with the training sessions being scheduled or the required students being unable to attend, you need to raise this as a risk and escalate the problem to the appropriate party as soon as possible.

The Operations Plan consists of the following documents:

- Operations Document
- System Administrator Guide
- User Guide
- Technical Support Guide
- Customer Support Guide
- Release Notes

An Operations Plan document is included on the CD-ROM that accompanies this book. The sample plan includes all six documents. These six documents can easily be split and created as separate documents.

Operations Document

A typical Operations Document will contain, at a minimum, the following information:

- Network and System Diagrams
- Technical Specifications for All Hardware and Software Components
- Interoperability Specification
- Network Specification
- Security
- Decision Support
- Required Regular Maintenance
- Bug Fix Releases
- Product Update Mechanism and Process
- System Monitoring
  - Error logging
  - Error severity
  - Escalation and notification
- Change Control Process
- List of Related Documents
- Service or Maintenance Contracts
  - Contract Details
  - Contact Information
  - Renewal Date
- Scheduled System Downtime
- Escalation Process
- Roles and Responsibilities

The Operations Plan also needs to include a System Administrator Guide. This can either be part of the main document, or it can be created as a separate document. Often, operations groups prefer to have two separate documents. This enables them to give their system administrators a document that is limited to just the functions that they need to carry out.

It is unlikely that the project manager will be responsible for the creation of this document though he may be a key contributor to the content and a reviewer for the document.

System Administrator Guide

A typical system administrator guide may include the following information:

- Network and System Diagrams
- Technical and Functional Specifications for All Hardware and Software Components
- Server Hardware and Software Installation and Setup Guide
- Required Regular Maintenance Procedures
- Monitoring and Reporting System
  - Process
  - Error detection method
  - Error codes
  - Escalation procedures
- Troubleshooting
  - Criteria
  - Procedures
- Restart and Recovery Procedures
  - For each part of the system
  - Processes launched on startup
- Backup and Restore Procedures
- Scheduled Processes and Scripts
  - Manual reports or processes
  - Activity log

It is unlikely that the project manager will be responsible for the creation of this document though he may be required to supply input and review with the assistance of his team.

The User Guide

The product user guide gives clear, precise instructions on all aspects of using the product. If the project will have different groups of end users, who will interact with the product in different ways, there will be multiple user guides. Using our case study example, five variations would be likely on the user guides for the following end users.

- Call Center
- Warehouse
- Shipping
- Accounting
- Retailers

A typical user guide will contain the following information:

- Description of the Functionality and Features
- Client Hardware and Software Installation and Setup Instructions
  - Step-by-step instructions
  - Screenshots
- Step-by-step Instructions on How to Use Each Feature and Component
- Customizing Views
- How to Print Reports
- How to Submit Defect Reports
- How to Contact Technical and Customer Support
- How to Use Knowledgebase
- How to Use Help
- Accessibility
- Troubleshooting
- Whom to Contact
- How to Manually Process Orders, Shipments, and Deliveries

It is unlikely that the project manager will be responsible for the creation of this document though she may be required to supply input or review.

Technical Support Guide

This is pretty much a technical user guide. It contains all the information in the user guide with the addition of some technical tips and tricks on how to get end users out of trouble if they are experiencing problems. The quality assurance team will provide a lot of input for the technical support guide. They will provide information on known bugs and work arounds for those bugs. They will know what to do in the event that a user has crashed their system and is possibly unable to get the product or service working again. For Internet products, the technical support guide may include instructions on how to view, update, or delete a user's file from the server. It is unlikely that the project manager will be responsible for the creation of this document.

Customer Support Guide

The customer support guide will contain information for dealing with customer enqui-ries. Most of the information for a customer support guide will come from the company that owns the end product. The guide may contain some of the information from the user guides, and it will likely also contain a lot of company policies and processes—for instance, how to create Return Material Authorization (RMAs) or how to process a re-fund for an overcharged customer. It would be highly unusual for the project manager to be responsible for the creation of this document. The project manager should, how-ever, ensure that this document is completed on schedule. Without the documentation and training, the deployment and hand-off of the project will be delayed.

Release Notes

Release notes will be prepared during the Deployment phase. They contain all late changes and additions that did not make it into the finalized Operations Plan documents.

The Training Plan

The training plan created during the planning phase will need to be reviewed and up-dated to ensure that it is still accurate. To implement the training plan, the following training materials will need to be created for each specific type of training:

- Training Agendas
- End User Training Manuals and Lessons
- Teacher Training Manuals and Lessons
- Exercise Manuals
- Examination and Certification

The training manuals and lessons should contain the following information:

- An introduction to the Lesson
- Objectives
- Scope
- Process Flows
- Written Instruction
- Visual Instruction (Screenshots)
- Examples
- Lesson Review

Writing training materials is not usually the responsibility of the project manager, but you should ensure that they are written and that they are accurate (to the best of your knowledge). A sample training manual is included on the CD-ROM that accompanies this book.

Service Level Agreement (SLA)

During the Integration or Deployment phase, a Service Level Agreement (SLA) will be created, if applicable. Data center groups commonly use this document to specify the level of service they are committed to for the systems they manage. For example, the SLA will contain the percentage uptime for Internet systems (it is rarely 100%), the scheduled system downtime required for maintenance, and the times at which that maintenance would be performed. If the client has purchased a Service Agreement from your company, the SLA will outline the level of service that has been agreed to. The MRD contains a Service Level Agreement Requirements section, and the SLA should be in line with those requirements. A typical Service Level Agreement will contain the following sections:

- Introduction
- Services Delivered
- System Uptime
- Scheduled Maintenance and System Downtime
- Performance, Monitoring, and Reporting
- Problem Management
- Client Duties and Responsibilities
- Warranties and Remedies
- Security
- Disaster Recovery
- Intellectual Property Rights and Confidential Information
- Legal Compliance and Resolution of Disputes
- Compensation
- Termination
- Approval and Signatures

A Service Level Agreement template is included on the CD-ROM that accompanies this book.

CHAPTER 13

Deployment

All right! You are almost there. The Deployment phase of the life cycle is where you prepare for project hand-off. For most people, this is the most rewarding phase of the project. It is not unusual to get to this point and be amazed that the team has actually managed to pull it off! Don't get too full of yourselves quite yet, though; there is still a lot to be accomplished before you can get the client's signature on the "project completed and approved" signature line! It is very exciting for everyone who has been involved in the project to finally get to see the end product working as designed and meeting all the client's requirements. It is a great feeling to know that all the hard work and agonizing moments were worth the effort and that they have ultimately paid off. Having said all that, after the initial excitement about having created a great product, there can be a bit of an anticlimax as you work your way through all the deployment tasks. It can be very tedious tying up all those loose ends to get your project finalized. It can also be challenging trying to keep your team motivated when they are either anxious to start on a new project or nervous because they aren't sure what is going to happen next. After all, the client hasn't accepted the project yet. It can be a bit disconcerting, especially if some project compromises had to be made along the way and, in retrospect, the client or the project team is not sure they made the right decision.

It is possible that the project you are completing has not been completely successful. You may be delivering the project late, it may be way over budget, or it may not meet the quality standards. If any of these scenarios are indicative of what is happening on your project, the team will be under a lot of pressure to wrap things up with as little additional cost as possible. If the problem is with quality, and the decision has been made to deploy with limited functionality, the team may still be trying to figure out how some issues can be solved post-deployment. If this is the case, the team may be required to continue to work on releases and updates after the project has been delivered. The client may have decided to take the project "as is" and to find another company to fix the problems, or they may have decided to take the project and to pay a reduced fee for it.

If any of these situations are occurring on your project, you will have your work cut out for you trying to keep the team motivated and productive. It is not unusual for a project to have some problems. How much the problems affect the morale on your team will depend on how bad the problems are. For example, if you are delivering one week late, it may not be a major issue. If you are a very small amount over budget, it may not be the end of the world. Projects can be unsuccessful by a small margin or hugely unsuccessful.

No matter where you find yourself as far as project success goes at this point, the best thing to do is to focus on that light at the end of the tunnel (you should be able to see it by now) while keeping your team as focused and energized as you can about the project closure. No matter what happens, you cannot afford for your team to lose interest or momentum at this point in the life cycle.

In some organizations, the project manager hands over the final product to a "deployment team," which performs the deployment and post-deployment tasks. In this situation, the project manager will move on to a new project, and the team members will either be disbanded or will continue to work for the deployment team as necessary.

Six key elements are involved in deploying the project and achieving project hand-off (as shown in Figure 13.1):

- Finalize the Deployment Plan
- Training
- Prepare Final Release Notes
- Deployment
- Client Acceptance and Approval
- Project Hand-off

Finalizing the Deployment Plan

In the planning phase, you created a Deployment Plan. The plan will not have been complete when you created it. Before you do anything else in this phase of the project, you need to update and finalize the Deployment Plan. It is important that each team member and the client understand their roles and responsibilities. The plan will be customized for your project and will look very different depending on whether it is a software, Internet, or hardware product. No matter how small the details, you need to ensure that they are captured in the plan. You need to include step-by-step instructions, with exact times associated with each step. For some deployments, this will include steps that are less than an hour apart. For example, an Internet deployment takes a lot of coordination because each step has to be completed exactly in order and on time to meet the launch deadline. You will need a list of steps and a strict process for ensuring that no task is started unless the previous step has been completed and verified first.

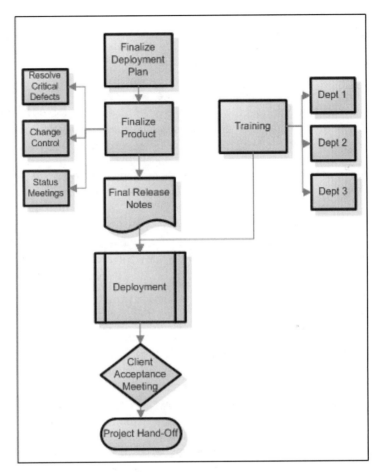

Figure 13.1: Project hand-off workflow.

Deployment Steps

It is common at this stage of the project for there to be more regular status meetings. As the deployment date gets closer, it may be necessary to meet daily. If there are a lot of critical issues leading up to deployment, you may need to meet more than once per day. The attendees for these meetings will consist of various stakeholders. You will need key decision-makers involved, especially if you are still working on resolving critical issues and may need to make some last minute tradeoffs. You will need representatives of the groups and teams working on the deployment tasks. Most of the tasks in the Deployment Plan are interdependent. Therefore, everyone involved in the deployment needs to be aware of any issues or delays. We like to refer to this deployment stakeholder group as the "deployment task force."

Deployment Status Meetings

The project manager needs to lead the deployment task force to a successful conclusion, whether that is to deploy as scheduled, to delay deployment, or to deploy with trade offs or compromises. A successful conclusion does not necessarily mean that the project meets the project success criteria. It means that the task force reached deployment and closure based on the decisions made during the days or weeks leading up to the deployment date. An unsuccessful conclusion occurs when the project is not deployed at all due to the project being canceled or postponed.

While you are focusing a lot of attention during the project life cycle on minimizing meetings and keeping productivity as high as possible, it is critical to the success of your project that you schedule meetings when necessary and that you insist on the right people attending. They may be busy, and so are you, but deploying the project is the most critical task that you have to complete, and you will not be able to accomplish it without high quality commitment, teamwork, and coordination.

Training

Do you remember when you first learned how to drive? For most of us, we had to take a drivers education class prior to being allowed behind the wheel. A drivers education class teaches the basics of how the car works, and many of them include the use of simulated cars, like those you see in video games. Once you have passed the drivers education class, you are placed behind the wheel of a big, scary piece of machinery that appears, at times, to have a mind of its own. The teacher proceeds to teach you how to handle the car properly and how to maintain control at all times. Can you image being put into a car and being told just to drive and do the best you can? Well, that is exactly what technology projects can be like if you don't have a good training plan. If the key people do not have appropriate training on the final product, they will not be able to use or keep control of it. It will be only a matter of time before they crash and burn.

The training classes will take place during the deployment phase. If the relevant people have not received adequate training on the product or service, it is possible that the deployment and hand-off will need to be delayed. Make sure that you are tracking the training progress and that you know exactly who has had training and who has not. You should track the training progress in your deployment status meetings.

One of the major causes of project issues (or failures) from the client's perspective is lack of skill and comfort level with the new product, service, or process on the part of their employees. If they are not ready to start using or supporting the new product, it could have a serious effect on the client's ability to do business. If the team supporting the product is not properly trained, they may cause the product to not work correctly by doing something harmful to the system, or they may be unable to resolve minor issues that lead to a major problem. Make sure that the trainers get feedback from the students at the end of the training sessions regarding the usefulness of the training and their comfort level with starting to use or support the new product. If they see a lack of confidence in the students, the client needs to be made aware of that before they make the decision to go ahead and deploy the product.

Final Release Notes

The operations, user, system administrator, and support guides were completed and distributed during the integration phase. It is typical for issues to be discovered after these documents have been finalized and printed, so release notes are used to communicate late-breaking updates for any of the user or support documentation. Copies of the release notes should be sent to the trainers as soon as possible, because they may need to make updates to the course material to reflect the changes. For desktop software projects, the final release notes will need to be sent to the printer so that they are included when the product is assembled and shrink wrapped.

Release notes include changes to features or functionality, known issues, work arounds for known issues, and corrections to information contained in the printed guides.

Deployment

This is where you actually deploy your project. Here, the client sees or receives the final product for approval before they sign-off that it is being acceptable.

For a software (shrink wrap) product the following steps need to be followed (see Figure 13.2):

- Producing the CD Master
- Testing and Verification of the Master
- Client Approval and Sign-off for Deployment to Proceed
- Delivery to the CD Manufacturer
- Finalizing Artwork and Packaging
- Delivery of Artwork to Packaging Manufacturer
- Delivery of User Manuals to Printers
- Delivery of Release Notes to Printers
- CD's (or Disks), Packaging, Release Notes and Manuals Sent to Assembler
- Assembly and Shrink Wrap of Final Product
- Approval of Final Packaged Product
- Client Approval and Acceptance

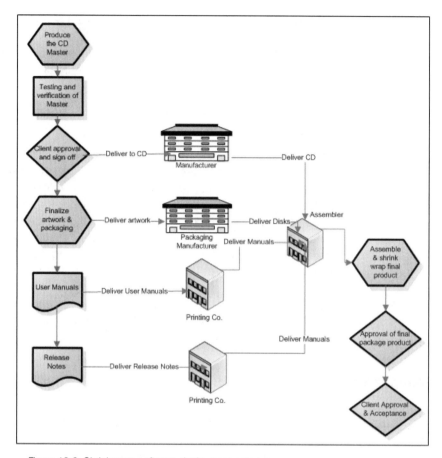

Figure 13.2: Shrink wrap software deployment process.

For Internet products the following steps need to be followed (see Figure 13.3):

- All Hardware, Networking, and Systems Are in Place
- Connectivity Is Tested and Verified
- Software or Product Is Installed on Hardware
- Final System Test and Verification Is Performed
- Client Approval and Sign-off for Deployment to Proceed
- The Site Goes "Live"
- Site Is Retested and Verified
- Client Acceptance Testing

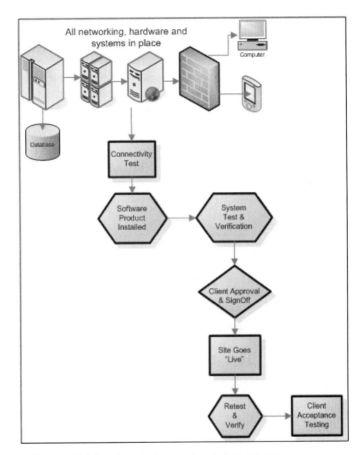

Figure 13.3: Internet product or service deployment process.

Project Acceptance and Hand-off

To complete project closure, the project manager must ensure that all terms and conditions specified in the contract have been fulfilled. It is important that all deliverables and documentation be delivered, approved, and accepted by the designated decision-makers, and the client acceptance testing should be completed before the client acceptance meeting. Copies of documentation should be available and ready for review at the acceptance meeting. Documentation will include technical documentation, user documentation, plans, specifications, training documentation, and any other documentation required to meet the conditions of the project contract.

Client Acceptance Agreement

The acceptance meeting should be a formal meeting, run by the project manager, and it should occur immediately following deployment—on the same day if possible. The project manager should have a visual or multimedia presentation prepared (a PowerPoint presentation for example) that covers the project, the final deliverables, the client acceptance criteria, next steps, and recommendations. The meeting should be attended by the steering committee and possibly some additional senior executives from each company. A sample PowerPoint presentation is shown in Figure 13.4, and a copy of the full presentation is included on the CD-ROM that accompanies this book.

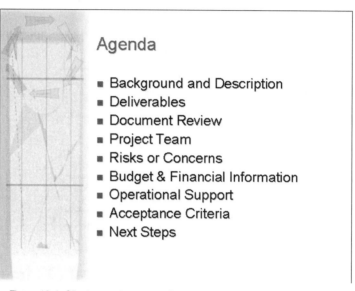

Agenda

- Background and Description
- Deliverables
- Document Review
- Project Team
- Risks or Concerns
- Budget & Financial Information
- Operational Support
- Acceptance Criteria
- Next Steps

Figure 13.4: Client acceptance meeting presentation.

Client approval and signoff for specific parts of the project will have occurred at various stages throughout the project life cycle. The acceptance agreement is the final approval for the whole project. A client acceptance agreement should be prepared beforehand and should be distributed for review prior to the acceptance meeting. The document should be prepared by your legal department because it will be a legally binding agreement between your company and the client. By signing the document, the client agrees that all project deliverables have been received and that they meet the acceptance criteria as specified in the contractual agreement.

The client acceptance agreement can be a very simple document, or it can be extremely detailed. This will depend on the size and complexity of the project, as well as the legal processes and procedures at your company. Much of the information contained in the acceptance agreement will be taken word for word from the Contractual Agreement, the Project Definition, and the Project Plan documents.

Typically, a client acceptance agreement will include the following information:

- Client—Client's name.

- Name of Document Preparer—The name of the person who prepared the document so if there are any questions, the client knows who to contact.

- Date—Date the document was issued.

- Project Description—Full and detailed description of the project, including the goals and objectives, the solution, the scope, and the prerequisites.

- Costs—The agreed-upon costs for the project and the payment terms and conditions.

- Acceptance Criteria—The acceptance criteria as defined in the project plan.

- Post Deployment Deliverables—Any deliverables scheduled for post-deployment, either because they were originally scheduled to be delivered later or because they were not ready in time for deployment, along with costs and payment terms, if applicable.

- Client Approval Section—Final approval statement for client signoff. Example: I have done a complete and thorough review of the project deliverables and results and agree that the project meets the documented client acceptance criteria.

- Signatures—The client and development company authorized representative(s) must sign the acceptance agreement.

Once the client has signed off on the final acceptance of the project, final payment will be due in accordance with the terms of the contract.

A sample Client Acceptance Agreement document is shown in Figure 13.5.

Figure 13.5: Client Acceptance Agreement.

A Client Acceptance Agreement is included on the CD-ROM that accompanies this book.

Success! Congratulations! You have deployed your project, you have client acceptance, and you are ready to celebrate! What feels like an eternity of hard work has finally come to an end. Or has it? Well, not quite. Before you can celebrate, you have to hand project responsibility off to the client and figure out how to disband your team.

Project Hand-off

It is time for the project manager to turn his baby over to someone else to take care of on a day-to-day basis. It can be quite painful preparing yourself to hand off your project to someone else. It is amazing how attached to it you can get! Although it is complete, there is life for your project after deployment, and you can't just walk away. It is common for the client to settle their account before the final project hand-off can occur. The hand-off can include several things:

- Handing over source code to the client (if the source code is part of the contractual agreement; often it is not)

- Handing over designs and specifications

- Giving the client passwords to all systems

- Handing over knowledgebase or other information depositories

- Handing over 100% of the management of the software and systems to the client

- Manufacturing rights

- Distribution rights

The specific hand-off tasks for your project should be detailed in the Deployment Plan. Once you have handed-off the project to the client, you are ready to prepare for project closure.

CHAPTER 14

Project Closure

As you sit back in your chair with your feet up on the desk breathing a huge sigh of relief that the implementation of your project is finally completed, come back to reality for just a minute. It's not quite over yet! It is true that you are almost ready to close the project and disband your team, but before you let your team members move full time onto new projects, a few additional tasks need to be completed. At this time some, or all, of your team members are very likely assigned to new projects and may be shared between the projects for some period of time. If they are starting on new projects that are still in the planning phase, the chances are that they may not be required on those projects on a full time basis yet, so there should be adequate time available to complete the closure of your project.

It is common for some project support to continue for at least a couple of weeks after the project has been handed-off to the client. In some cases, it will continue for a much longer period of time. During the first few weeks after project hand-off, it is common for a few "teething problems" to occur with the new product or the processes being used to support it. The client's various support teams may not be totally comfortable with the new product yet, and there could be a few panic phone calls from them when they need some technical assistance. Until the client organization feels totally comfortable with the new product, they may contract with your company to continue offering support for a specified amount of time.

It is important to remember that implementation is only the beginning of what could be a long-term relationship with your client. If you wash your hands of the whole project the minute you hand it off to the client, rather than the start of a long term relationship, you may find that this becomes the end of a very short-lived acquaintanceship! How you handle any post-deployment issues—and (unless a miracle occurs) believe us when we tell you that there will be post-deployment issues—will leave a lasting impression on the client on the professionalism of both you personally and your organization. As eager as you may be to move onto your next assignment, remember that without the ability to nurture long-term client relationships, you may one day find yourself without a next assignment. A Project Closure Process workflow is shown in Figure 14.1.

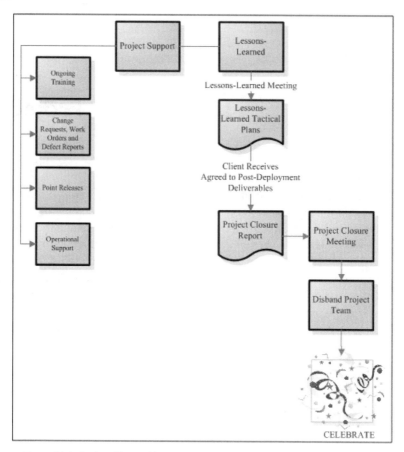

Figure 14.1: Project Closure Process workflow.

Ongoing Training

It is not uncommon for some of the client training to continue after the project hand-off has occurred. This training may occur in-house, for example, if the support staff and users that have been trained are training the rest of their teams; or your company may still be involved in training the client's employees. Often, training is not completed before hand-off because there are just too many people that need training in a short time, and the client is anxious to launch the new product as quickly as possible. If the initial training took place over a short time period, some of the students may have missed the training due to being out of the office on vacation, sick, or on business travel.

Change Requests, Work Orders, and Defect Reports

At this time the project manager needs to ensure that there are well-documented processes and contractual agreements (if necessary) for managing change requests, defect reports, and work orders from the client. Your organization may or may not have an agreement to continue offering support for change requests, but your company may be liable for defects if they are critical or serious enough to cause the product to be unusable in some way. If a Service Level Agreement exists between the two companies, this information will be contained in that agreement.

Point Releases

If your company is responsible for *point releases* of the product, you will need a clearly defined schedule for those. Point releases are so called because they refer to the 1.1, 1.2, and so on releases that are created as updates to a full version releases. Point releases may contain new features or functionality that were purposely scheduled for a later release. They could include support for different platforms, operating systems, or browsers. The point release may be a result of the project not being completed on time so some features were pushed out for later release. Additionally, point releases may be scheduled bug fix releases.

Lessons Learned

Post-implementation reviews are important to identify and discuss the lessons that have been learned during the course of the project life cycle. All areas of the project are under analysis, including technical, managerial, organization, business processes, communication, and so on. Lessons-learned meetings are not always easy, so be prepared to attend with an open mind and a willingness to be completely honest in sharing your opinions and observations. The desired outcome of a lessons-learned meeting is an improved process for enhancing both client and team satisfaction for future projects.

The Lessons-Learned Meeting

Lessons-learned meetings can sometimes be contentious. For this reason, we suggest that you utilize the services of an independent facilitator for your meeting. This can be a manager from another department if you do not have a specific department at your company that can supply facilitators for these kinds of meetings. It is not a good idea to facilitate the meeting yourself. You need to be prepared to hear some things about your management style and some of the decisions you made during the course of the project that someone else is not happy about. No matter how successful your project outcome, there are always things that can be improved, and that goes for everyone on the entire team. If you try to facilitate your own lessons-learned meeting, it is very likely that your team members will not be honest. It may make you feel good to hear only positive things about yourself and your project, but it is not going to help improve the process and will be a waste of all the time that you and your team spend on it.

A sample Lessons-Learned Agenda is shown in Figure 14.2. A copy of the Lessons-Learned Agenda is also included on the CD-ROM that accompanies this book.

Fundamentals of Technology Project Management | Lessons-Learned Template
Project Name

Lessons-Learned Agenda

Project Name: OFIS
Date: Friday, January 1, 2XXX
Time: 8:00 AM PST – 5:00 PM PST
Location: XYZ Corporation Board Room #5

8:00 Welcome and Agenda – Marie Brown (facilitator)
- Purpose of the meeting
- Rules:
  - You can say anything about anything
  - You cannot name people or blame people
  - You cannot defend yourself or others
  - Everyone's opinions are valid
  - All comments are welcomed on any part of the process, the organization, the product.
  - Nothing discussed in this room should leave this room.
- Agenda

8:30 Categories
Team members collectively create a list of broad categories that can be used to sort issues. This does not have to be a full list - categories can be added later in necessary. For example, scheduling, communication, escalation procedures, feature sets, change control, meetings, etc. Categories are transferred onto large white sheets and pasted up around the room.

9:00 Things that could have been improved on
Team members write one issue on one sticky note (all stickies must be the same color) and continue until all the issues have been captured. These stickies are confidential. Be honest.

9:20 Things that went well, that we are proud of, that we must do again
Using a different color of sticky note, team members write one accomplishment or success on one sticky note and continue until all have been captured. These stickies are confidential. Be honest.

9:40 Categorize the stickies
The whole team participates in putting their own stickies onto the category sheets on the wall. Add categories if any are missing.

10:00 15 minute break

10:15 Re-categorize stickies
The whole team should go around the room and read the stickies. If you feel a sticky is in the wrong category then move it to the appropriate one. If you feel it should be in more than one category then copy it (mark it as a copy) and add it to the other category as well.

10:45 Summarize Categories
Each team member volunteers to summarize one or more category (in writing). Team members should try not to choose a category that they will find it hard to be unbiased about (for instance the project manager should not choose scheduling). The summary should include both the positive and the negative comments. There may be conflicting comments -- be sure to mention these in the summary as they may be significant (perhaps something worked very well for one group but was a hindrance to another).

Page 1 of 2
Created by "Author"

Figure 14.2: Lessons-Learned Agenda.

The Process

The purpose of the lessons-learned meeting is to discuss the things that went well and the things that could be improved for the project that just completed. The desired outcome of the meeting is to have a clearly defined action plan that will define specific steps to be taken to fix existing problems and to improve processes for future projects. The purpose of the meeting is *not* to apportion blame or to take out frustrations on other team members.

Rules

- You can say anything about anything.
- You cannot name people or blame people.
- You cannot defend yourself or others.
- Everyone's opinions are valid.
- All comments are welcomed on any part of the process, the organization, or the product.
- Nothing discussed in this room should leave this room.

Define Categories

Team members collectively create a list of broad categories that can be used to sort issues. This does not have to be a full list; categories can be added later if and when necessary. For example, a category list would likely include scheduling, communication, escalation procedures, feature sets, change control, meetings, and so on. Categories are transferred onto large white sheets and pasted up around the room.

Capture the Things That Could Have Been Done Better

Team members write one issue on one sticky note (all stickies must be the same color) and continue until all the issues have been captured. These stickies are confidential. Everyone must be 100% honest. No names should be mentioned.

Capture the Things That Went Well, That the Team Should Be Proud of, and That the Team Should Try to Do Again

Use a different color sticky note for the positive items, but ensure that each team member is using the same color. Team members write one accomplishment or success on one sticky note and continue until all have been captured. These stickies are confidential. Team members should be 100% honest.

Categorize the Stickies

The whole team participates in putting their stickies onto the category sheets on the wall. The team members will add category sheets for categories not captured earlier.

Recategorize Stickies

The whole team should go around the room and read the stickies silently. If anyone feels a sticky is in the wrong category, they should move it to the appropriate one. If they feel it should be in more than one category then they should copy it (mark it as a copy) and add it to the other category as well.

Summarize Categories

Each team member volunteers to summarize one or more category (in writing). These can be worked on individually or in small groups. Team members should not choose categories that they may find difficult to summarize in an unbiased and unemotional way (for instance, the project manager should not choose the scheduling category). The summary should include both the positive and the negative comments. There may be conflicting comments; be sure that the team members mention these in the summaries because they may be significant (for example, perhaps something worked very well for one group but was a hindrance to another).

Present Summaries

Going around the room, each summary is presented to the group by the team member who summarized the stickies. The summary must not contain any opinions, comments, or defensive or supportive statements by the presenter. They must present only the facts as stated in the stickies. Both positive and negative comments should be presented.

Select Highest-Priority Issues

Each team member is given six sticky-colored dots. Each sticky dot is equal to one vote. They use their dots to vote for the categories that they feel have the most pressing issues that need to be addressed. Team members can spread their dots among categories or put them all on one category. When all dots are posted, the facilitator counts up the dots, writes the totals on the sheets, and uses these numbers to identify the top 10 categories.

Discuss the Top 10 Categories

The whole team should participate in reviewing each of the identified top 10 categories one at a time. The team should discuss the issues, the reasons for the issues, and whether a lessons-learned tactical plan is necessary to resolve the issue. Allow approximately 15 minutes for each issue. Make sure that someone is taking notes for this part of the meeting. This discussion must be documented. Between 5 and 10 categories should be selected for lessons learned-tactical plans. Plan owners will be identified. Those owners will select team members to assist them. Deadlines for lessons learned tactical plans are set.

Next Steps

- Summarize action items and tactical plans.
- Confirm date that all meeting notes will be sent out to team.
- Schedule a follow-up meeting, If necessary.

The lessons-learned process is shown in Figure 14.3.

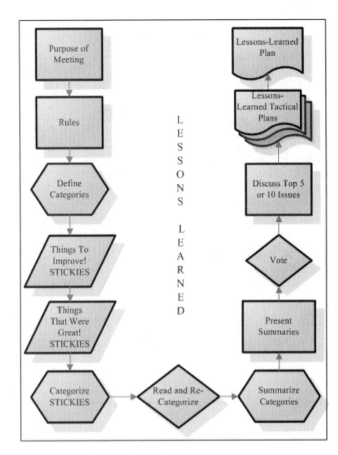

Figure 14.3: Lessons-learned process.

Lesson-Learned Tactical Plans

Each Tactical Plan owner will be required to submit a formal Tactical Plan document on the due date. The Tactical Plan (shown in Figure 14.4) will contain the following information:

- Plan owner
- Committee members
- Due date
- Problem
- Solution

- Identify any processes or procedures that will need updating as a result of this tactical plan
- Describe how results will be measured
- Next steps
- Risks

Fundamentals of Technology Project Management Document Name Template
Project Name

Lessons-Learned Tactical Plan

1. Tactical Plan Owner

Plan owner

2. Tactical Plan Committee Members

List all committee members

3. Tactical Plan Due Date

Date due

4. The Problem

Describe the problem. You may want to quote some of the "sticky" comments here

5. Describe the Solution

How the problem will be solved. Who will implement solution. How soon the results will be measurable

6. Describe any processes or procedures that will need updating as a result of this tactical plan

List all existing processes, procedures, documents that will have to be updated

7. How Results Will be Measured

Describe how results will be measured

8. Next Steps

Describe any next steps

9. Risks

Identify any outstanding risks or any new potential risks as result of the tactical plan

Page 1 of 2
Created by "Author"

Figure 14.4: Lessons-Learned Tactical Plan.

The project manager will create a Lessons-Learned Plan that will be used to track progress on the individual tactical plans. The Lessons-Learned Plan will include the following information about each Tactical Plan (See Figure 14.5):

- ID—A name or number used to identify the tactical plan
- Description—A detailed description of the problem that the tactical plan needs to address
- Date Assigned—Date the tactical plan was assigned
- Owner—Identify the person who has been assigned ownership of the tactical plan
- Tactical Plan Committee—The group assigned to work with the owner to create the tactical plan
- Due Date—The date the tactical plan is due
- Status—The current status of the tactical plan (For example, in progress, late, completed, approved)
- Date Finalized and Closed—The closure date, so there is no confusion about whether the lessons learned tactical plan has been reviewed, updated, approved, and finalized
- Tactical Plan Location and Filename—Document the location and unique filename of the final version of the tactical plan

The Tactical Plan owners will deliver the tactical plans to the whole team on or before the agreed-upon deadline. The team members should be given a deadline for feedback on each plan, and the Tactical Plan owners will incorporate or respond to feedback in a timely manner so the overall project Lessons-Learned Plan can be finalized, approved, closed, and put into action as soon as possible.

Lessons-Learned Plan								
Project Manager:				**OFIS**				
ID	Description	Date Assigned	Owner	Tactical Plan Committee	Due Date	Status	Date Closed	Tactical Plan Filename and Location
1	Technical risk not evaluated effectively during planning phase	14-Mar	David Moss	Tim Timmons, Vin Patel	21-Mar	in progress		
2	Builds breaking consistently during development season. Causing delays.	14-Mar	Roger Brady	Jane Jones, Manual Gomez	21-Mar	in progress		

Figure 14.5: Lessons-Learned Plan.

A sample *Tactical Plan* and *Lessons Learned Plan* are included on the CD-ROM that accompanies this book.

Project Closure

The project closure signifies the official end of the project. The project closure should not take place until the client has received all agreed to deliverables. The closure meeting may take place before all operational support has been completed. This is to enable the project manager to disband the team so that team members may be assigned to new projects while retaining only the team members necessary to offer client support. The team members needed for post-deployment support will continue working on the project either full or part time, either under direction of the project manager or under whichever manager is assigned to supervising operational support. Some companies have operational teams whose sole responsibility is to handle post-deployment support. In this case, the project manager will be assigned to a new project.

The *Project Closure Report* is written for a broad audience including the project team, steering committee, stakeholders, and senior management.

It is good practice to present the Project Closure Report to your team members at a formal project closure meeting. It is a great way to signify the end of a project and to include the whole team in a summary of the project, the successes, and the final outcome. The project manager should acknowledge that it has been a team effort and that the team has come a long way since the kick-off meeting, however long ago that was. Make sure that you give this milestone, and your team, the recognition that it deserves.

As with other meetings, you should pass out an agenda at least 24 hours in advance so the team is aware of what will be discussed and will be able to come to the meeting prepared. Be sure to have someone take meeting notes and distribute the minutes to the project team within three business days.

The meeting will verify that all project activities have been completed and will ensure that any outstanding work is assigned and not forgotten. You will review the Project Closure Report with the team to get their feedback. You should also discuss the release of team members and how the project team will be wound down. You may need some resources available for client issues if the closure meeting is taking place prior to the teething period being complete.

If the project is closed without a major deliverable to the client having taken place, there may or not may be the need for a formal project closure meeting that includes all the team members. That will really depend on the reason the project was closed and at which point in the life cycle it was closed. The format for the meeting will be at your (or your manager's) discretion.

The Project Closure Report should be a summary report of the project from start to finish. A sample Project Closure Report is shown in Figure 14.6. It is usual for the Project Closure Report to be presented to the team in a visual or multimedia format.

A PowerPoint presentation is recommended. A sample Project Closure Report and a Project Closure Meeting Presentation are included on the CD-ROM that accompanies this book.

The Project Closure Report should contain the following information:

- Background and Description—Briefly describe the background, the business case, and the objectives of the project.

- Reason for Closing the Project—State the reason why the project is being closed. This may be because the project was completed, or it may have been canceled or postponed for some reason.

- Deliverables—List the planned and actual project deliverables. Include information on relevant change requests.

- Project Schedule—List the planned and actual project completion dates.

- Project Team—List the names of everyone who worked on the project, including their titles, project roles, and steps taken to move the team members from the project to other projects, including the time frame of their move.

- Outstanding Risks—Identify any outstanding risks as defined in the Quality Risk Assessment Document and any planned actions or steps related to those risks.

- Budget and Financial Information—Compare the budget to actual costs. Explain any discrepancies. Include ROI information if available. Identify any non–project budget related financial issues or concerns.

- Lessons-Learned Plan—Cut and paste the project Lessons-Learned Tactical Plans.

- Ongoing Support—Describe the plan for ongoing support for the project. Include operational support, defect reports, change requests, and technical and customer support.

- Next Steps—Identify the next steps. For example, any tasks moved to post-deployment (late features, for instance) or any plans for point releases. Detail the process and the timing for disbanding the team.

- Project Closure Approval—Both the project manager and the project sponsor will sign off on the project closure document. Be sure to include a copy of the acceptance agreement from the client.

The steering committee will officially close the project. The steering committee will then be disbanded.

Figure 14.6: Project Closure Report.

Closing a Canceled Project

Even if the project wasn't a success and was closed before completion, you still need to go through the closure process. As much as you may wish that the ground would open and that you could disappear into it, you must close the project first. Closing a project can be done at any point during the project life cycle. During the course of your career, it is likely that you will work on at least one unsuccessful or canceled project.

If a project must be closed before completion, it is the responsibility of the steering committee to close it, just as it is with a project that has run to completion. It may be that you were the person that suggested the project should be canceled due to obvious signs that it had little chance of coming to a successful conclusion. However, you will unlikely have the authority to close the project yourself.

There are many reasons that a project may be deemed unsuccessful and warrant cancellation. Some examples are:

- The project team is unable to meet major project milestones on a consistent basis.
- Key team members leave the project, and you are unable to fill those spaces with compatible resources who have the same experience and skill set.
- Project risks have been identified as major risks and cannot be managed.
- The client is unable to accept or meet project deliverables.
- The client is unable to pay for the project.
- The client continuously makes unrealistic demands to the point that the two companies are unable to continue working together.
- The client cancels the project.
- The initial scope has completely changed, so the project needs to be closed and a new project started in its place.

Once a project has been deemed a failure, it will be up to the steering committee to take the necessary steps to close the uncompleted project. Whatever the reason to close a project, the decision can be demoralizing for the project manager and the project team, especially if the project had been going well and was canceled for financial or business reasons. Remember, the reasons for project failures can be very complex and are seldom completely the fault of the project team. The project manager should reiterate to the team that the responsibility of failure doesn't rest entirely with one or two individuals. There will be numerous reasons that the project was incomplete. The team should not feel that they failed, but should take the lessons that they have learned on this project to try and make the next one even better. Be sure to have a debriefing session, hold a lessons-learned meeting (if appropriate), and have the team redeployed to other projects as quickly as possible.

Let's Party!!

Now it is time to disband the project team, do some dancing in the hallways, slap a few high fives here and there, have a big party, and move on to bigger and better things!

Disbanding the Project Team

The project closure meeting was the official end to the project. You now need to put the plan for disbanding the team into motion. Some of the team members may be retained for some length of time working on operational tasks.

While coming to the end of a project should be an ecstatic time, it can also be very traumatic for your team members. Some team members may resist the project end because they are uncertain about what lies ahead for them in their careers. You should be compassionate when disbanding the team. Remember that the team members have put a lot of heart and soul into the success of this project, and they may be feeling quite emotional about it coming to an end. Do not make insensitive remarks or make fun of team members who are upset. You do not want to create any bad feelings at this stage of the project. If the project team has been together for a long period of time, the team members have likely developed close bonds with each other. The thought of starting over with a new team and a new manager can be quite unsettling. Team members may feel nervous about having to prove themselves all over again in a new position or project role. This can be especially troubling for someone who has achieved exceptional personal performance on a project. They may be feeling a lot of pressure to live up to that reputation on the next project and may be concerned about whether they can do so and achieve those same results again. Help your team members with the transition to their new positions by ensuring that the new project managers have all the necessary information about the team members they will inherit, including any copies of any formal written reviews, growth and development plans, and written project objectives.

When dealing with subcontractors and consultants, make sure they have returned all project documentation and property to you. Ensure that you have received any security related items, such as ID badges or network IDs. Hold an exit meeting with each contractor and consultant and give them copies of any signed confidentiality or nondisclosure agreements you have with them. They will have been given a copy when they signed the agreements, but this acts as a reminder that they are still legally obligated under those agreements even though the project has ended. It also ensures that they have not lost the agreements or forgotten what they agreed to. Make sure that you receive any final bills for work performed and outstanding expenses before, or at, the exit meeting. Prepare a *Project Completion Agreement* document for you both to sign (see Figure 14.7). The document should include the following information:

- That the work has been completed to the best of our knowledge
- That all deliverables have been met as laid out in the contract
- That all project related property and documentation has been returned
- That the contractor or consultant has not retained any copies of any documents and any documents not returned have been destroyed
- That the project manager has received the final invoice

- That the contractor or consultant has received copies of signed confidentiality and nondisclosure agreements
- That any ID badges and network IDs have been returned
- Date that the project is complete (last day for contractor or consultant)

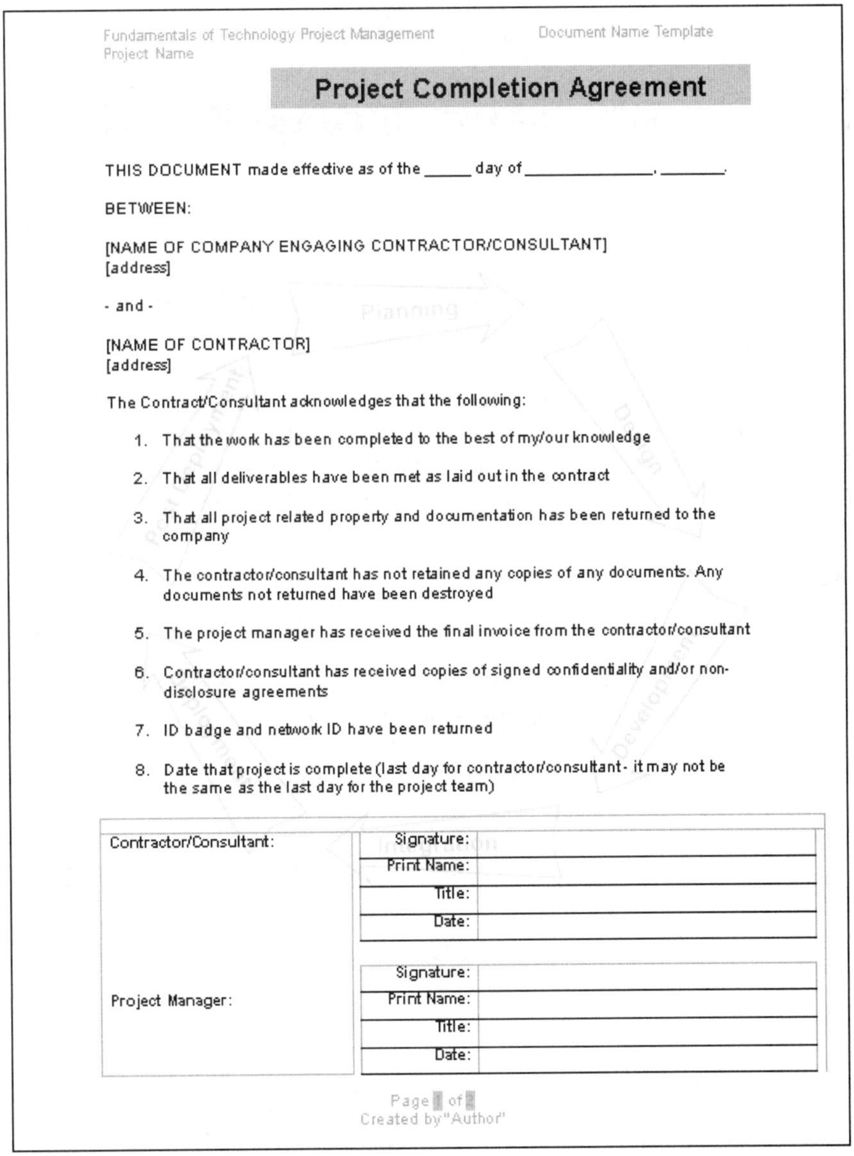

Fundamentals of Technology Project Management
Project Name

Document Name Template

Project Completion Agreement

THIS DOCUMENT made effective as of the _____ day of _____, _____.

BETWEEN:

[NAME OF COMPANY ENGAGING CONTRACTOR/CONSULTANT]
[address]

- and -

[NAME OF CONTRACTOR]
[address]

The Contract/Consultant acknowledges that the following:

1. That the work has been completed to the best of my/our knowledge

2. That all deliverables have been met as laid out in the contract

3. That all project related property and documentation has been returned to the company

4. The contractor/consultant has not retained any copies of any documents. Any documents not returned have been destroyed

5. The project manager has received the final invoice from the contractor/consultant

6. Contractor/consultant has received copies of signed confidentiality and/or non-disclosure agreements

7. ID badge and network ID have been returned

8. Date that project is complete (last day for contractor/consultant - it may not be the same as the last day for the project team)

Contractor/Consultant:	Signature:	
	Print Name:	
	Title:	
	Date:	
Project Manager:	Signature:	
	Print Name:	
	Title:	
	Date:	

Page ▮ of ▮
Created by "Author"

Figure 14.7: Project Completion Agreement.

A Project Completion Agreement document is included on the CD-ROM that accompanies this book.

Celebration

You and your team have worked hard, and sadly it is time to say goodbye to the project even if not to each other! The end of a project should be celebrated, and it should be done in style. That does not mean that you have to spend lots and lots of money. You may not have been given enough budget for a really big party with gifts for everyone, so use your discretion when deciding the best way to spend whatever money you have allocated. You can have a big formal party or an informal lunch at a local restaurant. If you are celebrating on a tight budget or on no budget, you can still do it in style and have a lot of fun. Here are some ideas for different budgets:

No Budget

- Ask the team members to go to lunch and all chip in to pay the bill.

- Rather than giving gifts, write a poem or a song about the team that you can share at your "goodbye" lunch.

- Ask the team to come to the lunch with one funny story from the project that can either be about themselves or about someone else on the team.

- Have a gift exchange. Everyone buys one gift, and you each pick a number to select a gift.

- Have a potluck lunch or dinner at a team member's house or at the office.

Low Budget

- A number of the no-budget ideas would be good.

- Have lunch at an informal restaurant.

- Hand out t-shirts or mugs with the project or team name or slogan on them.

High Budget

- You can still implement some of the above ideas in addition to spending lots of money.

- Go to a fancy restaurant.

- Arrange a fun team outing to a local event.

- Have a catered event at a local beach or park (if the weather is conducive to such an event).

- Plan a weekend trip to Las Vegas or a ski resort.

- Provide stock options or project bonuses.

- Give out some nice gifts: jackets, sports bags, or golf clubs (just kidding on the golf clubs).

Whether you were able to have a formal or informal gathering for those involved in your project, a party is a good way to acknowledge individual and team contributions and is a great way to mark the end of a great project.

Make sure that you organize an event that is appropriate for your team members. For example, if 80% of your team members are nondrinkers, do not organize an event to go wine tasting. Likewise, if you have disabled team members, make sure that, whatever you are doing or wherever you are going is accessible and that they will be able to join in with the activities. If you decide to go on a boat trip, make sure that you don't have a lot of team members who get seasick.

It is better if the project closure party is limited to team members. It is not a good idea to invite their family members. It is also not a good idea to invite the client or the steering committee. The celebration is for your development team. It is your team's opportunity to celebrate success and say goodbye.

However you decide to mark this momentous occasion, your team will be pleased that they are recognized as contributors and that you are doing something special for the team. Ending the project on a positive note is a great way to set the stage for future successful work.

How to Be an Effective Leader

Many characteristics define good leaders. Regardless of their leadership styles, effective leaders need to develop skills in many areas. Effective leaders need to:

- Be good decision-makers
- Take ownership and responsibility for decisions
- Have good problem-solving skills
- Be assertive and willing to stand up for their beliefs
- Have a positive attitude and an eagerness to learn
- Have good listening skills
- Behave respectfully towards all team members
- Value diversity
- Have the ability to recognize and resolve conflict
- Be able to empower others
- Have effective meeting-management skills
- Have a sense of dedication and loyalty to the project, the team, and the company
- Be able to formulate a clear vision of the final product and share it with others
- Have effective delegation skills
- Have the ability to keep people enthused and motivated
- Have good writing and presentation skills
- Have excellent verbal communication skills
- Be good negotiators
- Have an abundance of energy
- Be patient
- Be able to keep calm in a crisis

These are just a few examples of the characteristics, talents, and skills required to be a good leader. It will take time to develop the skills you need to be a great project manager. The most important characteristics that will help you grow as a leader are a great attitude and a willingness to learn. Great leaders never stop learning and growing. They learn from every situation, both successes and failures. They learn from others. They do not assume that they can only learn from people who are higher up the corporate ladder than they are. They are willing to learn from interns as well as CEOs. If you go through life assuming that you can learn something from every single person that you meet, you will learn quickly and you will develop a high level of leadership skill. As soon as you think you know it all, you will stop learning, and as soon as you stop learning you will start to stagnate. Stagnation and technology do not make very good partners!

A leader seeks to bring out the best in everyone on her team. You would not have chosen team members if you were not confident that they could give you a high level of performance. Once you have recruited them onto your team, you must figure out where their talents lie and work with them to achieve the highest performance possible. A leader strives to keep all the team members enthused and engaged at all times. Active participation from everyone on the project team is vital to the success of your project. If your team is excited and inspired by what they are doing, they will not need to be pushed to actively participate in team meetings or events.

Developing and Leading a Successful Team

Make sure you know what is important to your team members as individuals as well as what is important to them as a team. Support them and guide them. It is your responsibility to make sure that your team members are getting what they need from you and the company and that you and the company are getting what you need from them. Your team needs you to protect them from things going on in the company that do not concern them. You are the umbrella preventing all that unnecessary information from falling on them. You need to be a filter so that they get the information they need without having to plow through it all themselves. You need to ensure that your team members know what is going on with regards to their tasks, their projects, and their careers. Appropriate and timely communication is the tool you should use to achieve this.

You will need to coach your team members and, from time to time, will need to work with them to change negative behaviors. However, do not make this your only focus of coaching and development. Encouraging positive behaviors and recognizing successful outcomes is necessary to building a strong, positive, forward-thinking team. In today's fast-paced work environments, there is a great need to continually focus on what could have been done better and what can be improved on in the future. While it is important to strive to better oneself, one's team, and one's company, do not forget to celebrate successes. No matter how small or insignificant they may seem to outsiders, if they are important achievements for your team, then celebrate them. Give your team the credit it deserves for a job well done, particularly when the client or executive management expresses satisfaction. You should never take all the credit for yourself. Your job is to build a successful team, and if you give the impression that you are the one doing all the work, you are not demonstrating that you have good team leadership skills. A project is a team effort. However, as the leader of the project, you are responsible for failures.

This may seem unfair, but do you remember the analogy we used in Chapter 1 about the conductor being the glue that holds the symphony together? The orchestra is comprised of highly talented musicians, but they need the conductor to blend their talents to produce the end product. Well, the same applies here. Your team may be comprised of highly talented and productive individuals, but without effective leadership they will not be working towards a successful outcome. You are responsible for the failures of your team. If you are unable to manage the problems or replace ineffective team members, then you are not doing your job as a project manager. Never try to blame your team for failures. Never try to single out individuals to blame for failures and most definitely never try to blame the client. It will only demonstrate even more clearly to your senior managers that you are an ineffective leader. If you can come up with valid reasons for the failures, admit that you made misjudgments, tell them that with hindsight you would have handled situations differently, but take full responsibility for whatever went wrong, you will demonstrate that you have good leadership potential. You will confirm that you have learned from your mistakes, that you are able and willing to take responsibility and ownership for your projects, and that you have loyalty and trust in your team. These qualities should earn you the trust and support of your superiors. At the same time, you will be demonstrating to your team that you have trust and confidence in them, and they will be willing to work even harder to resolve the issues and get the project back on track again.

You learned earlier that a great strategy for getting your team members emotionally invested in the project is to involve them in the planning and scheduling of the activities that they will be involved in. This creates team camaraderie and gives each team member a sense of ownership in the project. No one wants to work on a project where they feel they are unappreciated or their opinions and suggestions are unimportant or ignored. An important tool for effective leadership is open and direct communication. When team members feel that their ideas are important to the team and that any idea is valid for discussion, they will start sharing more and more ideas with the team. If you cut them down at every point, then you will have a bunch of clones who just sit in meetings not saying a word.

You may find that your team is quiet and unwilling to participate very much in your meetings in the early days of your project. No matter how hard you try to get some participation, you find that you are doing most of the talking. This is because the team is not yet comfortable sharing their ideas, because they are unsure whether the environment is hostile or friendly. Don't panic if it takes a little while to establish trust and openness in your meetings. You do not know what past experiences team members have had in meetings. Perhaps they worked for a manager who used anything they said in a meeting against them. Perhaps they have been misquoted or made to feel stupid. There can be any number of reasons that your team members are reluctant to speak up. They are waiting to see proof that it is safe to offer an opinion, so it might take a few weeks until your meetings are going the way you want them to. Remember too that it is far better to encourage participation than to try and force it. People will participate when they feel comfortable, and this will happen at different times for different team members.

Corporate America is a very different beast than it used to be thirty years ago. Back then, it was acceptable in many companies to work in an environment where intimidation, yelling, and fear for your job was used to get you to do or say whatever your superiors wanted. If you would not do something that your boss told you to, you would suffer the consequences. The military is a good example of this style of management. If you have ever been in the military, or if you have seen one of those TV documentaries where they follow a group of rookies through boot camp, you will know what we mean. They are yelled and screamed at, threatened, deprived of sleep, and emotionally battered into submission. In the military, it is important to develop the mentality to do whatever your superior officers tell you to do and not to question their orders. This responsiveness is critical for their personal survival and that of their unit. They are being trained for war, where mistakes can be deadly. They need to be able to act quickly and without hesitation. For these reasons, you are unlikely to find a friendlier military anytime soon, but you will definitely see a friendlier corporate America. Doing whatever your boss told you to was not conducive to the survival of many companies, most especially technology companies. That way of managing assumes that only one person can have good ideas, and they do not need any involvement from others to validate or to improve them. Corporate America understands today that, rather than shouting, it is better to nurture and that, rather than telling, it is better to ask.

Project managers are expected to coach their team members, to motivate and encourage them, and to help develop their critical and creative thinking. Without these skill developments, there would be no out-of-the-box thinking. It is that kind of creative and technical innovation that today's companies thrive on. Companies know that team members who have a positive attitude towards their work and the company they work for will consistently deliver great performance and high-quality products.

It is not always possible for team members to increase their knowledge and skills and gain sufficient on-the-job training to successfully implement their tasks to complete the project. Therefore, there will be times when you need to send team members for specialized training to gain the necessary skills and knowledge. This company-paid training is seen as an additional perk for a lot of team members. Technical people need to continually keep their skills up to date, and if employees know that a project manager encourages developing skills while working on their projects, they will be keen to be assigned to your team. If the training involved is in an area that is currently in high demand, then they will be even more excited about joining your team.

Leadership requires a diverse skill set. You need to grow and develop your team members and keep them motivated and excited about what the team is working on. You will have high expectations and high demands of your team. As a project manager, your attitude about the team and about the project will have a huge impact on the effectiveness of the group. You have the authority to expand or restrict activities that will impact many aspects of a team member's working day. This position of authority or power that you hold carries with it a lot of responsibility.

If you are excited and enthusiastic about the project and have a positive attitude towards the other companies and teams that you will be working with, then this positive energy will rub off on your team. If you continually complain about other teams, about the client, or about your manager, your team will start to think badly about those people too and will eventually get fed up with hearing the complaints from you. Just as you should never try to blame your team members for things, you should not blame other groups for things. If a team member is complaining about the client continually changing their mind, you should not agree with him and say, "Yes, they are a pain in the butt and you will never guess what else they did, blah, blah, blah." This is not building rapport with your team member; it is encouraging a negative attitude. Instead, you should say something like, "Well, I understand that you feel frustrated about the situation but in today's fast-changing business world, requirements often change mid-project. The client needs to analyze and respond to changes that affect their business and because we are not involved in the reasons behind the changes, we cannot really judge whether they are making the right decision asking for this change. If it were easy to implement these projects, then everybody would be doing it for themselves, and they would not need a top-notch team like ours to produce it for them. It is our job to ensure that they get the best product possible even if that means making changes mid-cycle. After all, the customer is paying for those changes and pushing out the schedule so that we can accommodate them."

By having this type of conversation you are changing the focus from the problem to the solution. You are coaching your team member by helping him understand that projects have business as well as technical requirements and that requirements can change. Allowing him to express anger at things changing, or even worse, encouraging it, is unhealthy and unproductive. Though your team member may wish that you would join in bitching session, he will have more trust and confidence in your leadership abilities if he sees you demonstrating maturity and understanding of the business needs of the customer.

Leading a team requires that you know how to deal with difficult employees. Punishing them for poor performance or a bad attitude is not usually the answer. For example, let's say you have an engineer who has been up all night because his baby was ill during the night. The engineer is tired and grumpy and is obviously not going to be alert and focused enough to get much work done. Even if he can work, he will be unhappy and will likely not produce very high-quality work. This situation has the potential to affect the entire project team. This is a problem that can be easily and quickly resolved. Sending the engineer home to catch up on his sleep is the best thing to do. Even if you know the engineer is behind schedule and has a tight deadline, you should make sure that he goes home and gets some sleep so that he can return to work later in the day or tomorrow refreshed and ready to work. This will allow your other team members to continue working in a more relaxed atmosphere, and your team members will know that you appreciate them and are understanding about family issues.

It is highly unlikely that your team members will try to take unfair advantage of your generosity and all start to have family "issues" to get time off. They are more likely to work even harder to ensure that the work is finished. You may even find that other team members volunteer to help with that person's work if they need to take additional time off to attend to a sick child. This is what great teamwork is all about. When the team members are pulling together to get things done and are taking care of each other at the same time, you know you have built a great team! Not all problems can be fixed that quickly or easily, but you must ensure that you are doing whatever you can to maintain a positive and comfortable environment for all your team members. If you cannot resolve an issue quickly, then do what you can to contain it and prevent it from affecting anyone else on the team.

So, you have figured out how to fix other peoples problems, but what about your own? As we mentioned earlier, you need to remember that you have the power to personally impact the effectiveness of the whole group. You are responsible for containing problems that occur on your team, and this includes ensuring that your own behavior is appropriate at all times and that your own frustration and anger is managed. Project management can sometimes be a very stressful job. You may be dealing with highly stressful or volatile situations. You may work long hours and feel worn out. Regardless of the reasons for how you are feeling, it is very important that you do not display negative behavior in the presence of your team or stakeholders. Someone else displaying negative behavior is not an excuse for you doing so, whether they are your superior, your peer, or your subordinate.

For example, perhaps your manager has just yelled at you because the schedule has slipped. You should not go to the team and tell them that your manager was yelling at you or, worse still, start yelling at them for schedule slippage. Instead, you should try to resolve the problem in a positive manner. The best piece of advice we can offer here is to never respond to a problem, or talk to someone about a problem, if you are feeling upset, emotional, angry, frustrated, or overwhelmed. If you are upset that your manager yelled at you, then go out to lunch for an hour, calm down, put things into perspective, and either talk to your team when you get back or wait until the next morning. Presumably you knew you were behind schedule, you knew why you were behind schedule, and your team is working on trying to catch up, so talking to them about it again is not going to make things happen any faster.

It is hard to do nothing when you are feeling very pressured, but if you can learn to do this, it will help you in many, many situations both in your professional and your personal life. There will be times when you want to yell and scream or where you want to play the "poor me" role because someone chewed you out. However, you must contain your emotions, act maturely, and demonstrate the qualities of great leadership. Investing in a punching bag may help relieve some of the pressure, but be sure to leave it at home. It is not a good idea for your team to see you practicing to punch as hard as you can!

No matter what happens, it is imperative that you continue to support and motivate your team. Your team members may be aware that you were yelled at by your boss. They may have heard it. They may even ask you about it. Do not get drawn into a discussion about it. Tell them that, rather than talking about what you have discussed with your manager, you need to talk about the issues with the schedule, and you need the team to work with you on that. They will respect you all the more for not going into the details about it. It reinforces their trust that you keep conversations confidential—no matter how loud they get. Self-control is critical for effective leadership.

A team is not the same thing as a group of individuals working together. A team is an entity in its own right. It is greater than the sum of the parts. A team works together for the overall success of the project; in a group of individuals, people work independently from each other for the success of their own tasks.

Coaching and Development

Your team members will have a different working styles, different motivations, and different personalities. Some will be humorous, some scary, some quiet, and some loud, and you will need to work effectively with them all. As a project manager, you will quickly learn which team members need more attention and which team members need to be left alone. You will need to do more coaching with some team members than others. All your team members will need some coaching and development from you to accomplish their goals. If they do not, then they have not been set appropriate goals. All team members, no matter how senior, need stretch goals. Everyone on your team needs to continue to learn and grow, including you. In technology, it is imperative that all team members continue to acquire and develop new skills. Technology changes very fast, and no one can afford to get left behind.

Coaching and development is not restricted to acquiring new technical skills. A project manager will spend a lot of time coaching her team members to improve communication skills and time management skills and to develop new skills in areas that are not needed for their current position but are a requirement for the position they are hoping to advance to. Your team members will more than likely gain their technical skills from books, classes, and each other. They need you to help with the other aspects of growth and development that will "round out" the technical skills that they have. Your team members may not know what skills they need to improve on. As their manager, you will know pretty quickly where there are gaps that need filling. Coaching can take many different forms. You may meet one-on-one and teach them. You may help them to figure out how to find the resources they need to learn or develop a skill. You may work with them to guide them in the right direction so that they are not trying to learn everything just in case they need to know it for later. You need to help your team members focus on specific areas and not be all over the place trying to grow and develop in 20 different areas at the same time. Coaching may mean that you assign team members certain tasks that help prepare them for positions they hope to advance to.

Feedback is vitally important. You need to be sure to give both positive and negative feedback. When you give positive feedback, be sure to explain what the person did and why it was good. Was it the result he achieved or how he achieved it that was good? If you are giving negative feedback, ensure that the person understands why there was a problem and what behavior or outcome you would have expected. If he does not understand how to fix the problem or the behavior, then help him with suggestions. If he is not aware when he is displaying the behavior, then come up with a plan to alert him immediately when you see it. When giving feedback, do not compare your team members to each other. For instance, do not say, "What you did was wrong, and in future I would like you to be more like John" or "Observe how John handles those situations and try to copy him." This is not going to promote good teamwork. Each team member needs to find their own style of doing things, so help them to develop their own right way of doing things rather than just trying to copy someone else's.

Here is an example of correcting a behavior that a team member was aware was a problem but did not realize when he was doing it. It was such a habit that by the time he realized he had done it again, it was too late, and the chance to correct it was gone. This team member was committed to self-improvement and was not at all defensive about the issue. He was a senior developer who was knowledgeable and highly skilled. The problem was that he went into too much detail about everything. The level of detail was excruciatingly painful at times. He would get very technical when talking to nontechnical people, which totally confused them, and he would talk for 10 minutes when all that was needed was a "yes" or a "no". He thought that he was a good communicator, because he told people everything that they needed to know plus a bit extra as a bonus.

After his manager spoke to him about this being an area for improvement, he started to become aware that people were hesitant to ask him questions because they did not want to listen to a long-winded answer. He wanted to advance in his career into a supervisory role but knew that this behavior was holding him back, so he was very motivated to try and change it. For a while, he would invite his manager to attend meetings where he knew he would be answering questions or offering opinions so that she could give him feedback afterwards. Unfortunately, although this was helpful to him in recognizing after-the-fact that he had gone into too much detail, it was not helpful in stopping him while he was doing it.

His manager decided to try a different approach. It sounds rather simplistic and silly, but it worked. When he was speaking in a meeting she told him to be sure to glance at her every few seconds. If he was going into too much detail she would touch her ear, and he would know to bring himself back down to earth and to speak at a more understandable level. No one else in the room had any idea that this was going on. He would see the ear touch and say, "I am going into way too much detail here so let me bring it up to a higher level," and he would finish his statement clearly and concisely.

It took about two to three weeks until he no longer needed the signal. He would catch himself midsentence and correct himself right away. The manager knew that he was "cured" when she sat in a meeting where he was a key participant and she heard him politely cut in when another developer was speaking to say "I think we are getting into too much technical detail. Most of the attendees are nontechnical, so we really should be talking about this at a much higher level so that they can understand the issues and follow the discussion." He scored huge points with the nontechnical managers that day. His teammates were not in the least offended. In fact, they thought that he was demonstrating some great leadership skill. A few months later, he got the promotion he wanted.

So coaching is not always about being very clever and important and coming up with sophisticated ways of achieving results. It is about trying different approaches and working with your team members to really help them to help themselves. Just telling them what they need to improve on is not necessarily going to help them. They may already know what they need to improve on; they may just be struggling with how to do it!

Delegation

One of the biggest challenges for a project manager is deciding how and to whom to delegate tasks. Your team members will already have their development work assignments, and now you need to delegate some tasks from senior to more junior team members and very likely delegate some of your own tasks to other team members too. There are a few things to consider before you do this. Does the person you wish to delegate the task to have the schedule time available to be able to complete the task, as well as their other assigned tasks, on time? How much "rope" should you give to the team member along with each delegated task? Can they manage it independently? Can you bear to let go and let someone else work on the task without your direction?

Delegation is a very important skill for any manager, and it can be very challenging figuring how and when to delegate.

Delegation is the process by which a project manager examines the various responsibilities and tasks for both themselves and their senior team members and evaluates whether to assign some of those tasks to others. Delegation is used to balance the workload across the team, to offer advancement and growth opportunities for team members, and to take the pressure off the more senior team members so that they can spend more time leading the team and managing the project.

Some of the tasks that you delegate from senior to more junior team members will end up taking more time to complete. You cannot expect a junior developer to be able to complete tasks as quickly as a senior developer. If it is new area for them, they will need some ramp-up time. They may need to work on the task with supervision from a senior team member. Do not make the mistake of assigning every task to the person who can complete it the fastest. That will not grow and develop your team. You will not have a highly productive and cross-trained team unless you spend time developing and cross-training them. You will also end up with a top-heavy schedule, meaning that your senior people will be over scheduled, and your junior people will be under scheduled.

Keeping tight parameters on the more inexperienced team members is often a necessity. If you are giving them stretch tasks and goals, they will need clear and direct instructions and easy access to their project manager or senior team members for support. However, be careful with giving too much instruction to the more experienced team members. This approach is likely to have the opposite effect from what you get with your junior team members. If they are used to working independently, they will not enjoy being told "how" to accomplish their tasks or working under a microscope. If you do not manage delegation of tasks to senior team members well, they may end up resenting you and feel that you do not have confidence in their abilities.

One of the hardest things about delegating is letting the person you delegate to approach the task in her own way. It will likely be different from your way. You may not feel that it is as good as your way or as effective or efficient as your way, but you delegated the task to her so she now owns the task. You cannot dictate how it gets done or pick holes in her implementation of it. It is not a competition to see who does it the best. It is working as a team and sharing the load. You must trust your team members and let them learn, grow, and develop as individuals. If you see them heading for disaster, by all means head them off at the pass and prevent the train wreck, but don't be a mother hen pecking and picking at every step of the way. You could end up with a team that will refuse to be delegated to, and then you really will have a plate that is too full to manage!

When you delegate, it can be a little scary at first. As the project manager, you maintain accountability for all tasks no matter who works on them. If the project succeeds, it is a team success, but if the project fails, it will be your reputation on the line. That is not to say that every project you work on will succeed. Some will fail, but hopefully it will not be due to poor performance or bad judgment on your part. It is only natural to be nervous when you are delegating your own tasks. Many project managers are perfectionists, and it is often that quality that makes them good at the job. The old saying, "If you want it done right, then do it yourself," is not going to be a very helpful mentality when trying to manage a project. If one person could do it all, then teams and project managers would not be needed to implement projects. It is very important that you learn to be comfortable with delegating tasks to other members of your team. It is even more important that your team members believe that you have confidence in them to be able to successfully complete those tasks. Whether you chose your team or you had it chosen for you, they are now your team, and you must believe in them both individually and as a whole.

A project manager is at liberty to assign or delegate any tasks or deliverables that are included in the project plan. However, you should be wary of delegating tasks associated with project strategy or the creation of the project schedule. As a project manager, you are responsible for making sure that you have a well-balanced project schedule. The tasks should be appropriately distributed among team members, each team member should have some stretch tasks, and each team member should be assigned some tasks that they are really excited about working on.

Building your schedule is like a multidimensional puzzle. There are many facets to the schedule, and they all need to be accounted for and appropriately balanced. When you get the final piece in place, you will have a wonderful sense of achievement. It is not an easy task. To do it well takes practice, experience, and a desire to do a great job. The project manager "owns" the schedule, so the project manager should create it.

After you have assigned or delegated tasks and assignments to your team members, it is very important to communicate. Your schedule will need monitoring, updating, and managing. You will need to reprioritize tasks from time to time and intervene when necessary. Your ultimate goal is to deliver a successful project. Have faith that you have a strong project team and that they will be able to successfully implement the project. If you have faith in them, they will have faith in themselves. If you delegate successfully, you will have more time to concentrate on the critical, strategic, and managerial aspects of the project. You are empowering your team by working with them to take on more important responsibilities. Your team is acquiring new skills and gaining more confidence in their abilities. The more you trust and empower your team, the more they will respect you for your project management and leadership skills.

Motivation

What exactly is involved in motivating team members? To effectively manage and motivate people, you need some knowledge and understanding of the human psyche. You will be working with multiple personalities, sometimes in the same person! Everyone is different; they have different work ethics and styles, and they are motivated by different things. Trying to motivate 20 different people with 20 different needs is a challenge. However, once you have mastered motivation, your life as a project manager will get easier and your team will be happier and stronger.

Motivating people starts with finding out *what* motivates them. You need to understand what motivates the individuals on your team as well as what motivates the team as a whole. Remember that your team is a personality and has needs in its own right. Just as no two people are the same, no two teams are the same either. How do you discover what motivates? Ask! It is that simple. A highly motivated team is an enthusiastic and energized team. Your team will be willing to do whatever it takes to make the project successful if they truly believe in it. So, the first task on your agenda as a project manager should be to sit down one-on-one with each team member and find out a bit about them. Let them know how happy you are to have them on your team and how happy you are to be on the team. Tell them how excited you are about the project and the project team that will be working on it.

Find out what the personal goals are for your team members for this project and beyond. What skills do each of them want to develop in the next six months and the next one to two years? Ask them where they see themselves in two years or five years and listen to what they tell you about what they want. Ask questions to make sure that you understand exactly what is being said. Your team members may talk to you about both professional and personal goals, and this is fine. It indicates that you are establishing some rapport with the person and that she feels comfortable talking to you.

However, don't specifically ask your team members to talk about their personal lives. About 80% to 90% of people will do so naturally, because they will want to share with you. If they do not offer this information, then do not ask for it. Some people prefer to keep their personal lives very private, and you must respect that.

You should ask your team members what they are interested in, such as their hobbies and activities. Ask what motivates them at work. Is it money, recognition, being given more responsibility, a day off, or a team outing? The list is endless. You will be surprised how many different answers you can get to this question. Ask your team members to give some thought to the questions you have asked, so that they are aware of what it is that motivates them. Sometimes people don't think about it too much, so they are surprised when someone asks them. They may be used to getting whatever reward their manager thinks is appropriate rather than being asked what they think would be a great reward.

Most of your team members will probably need to go away and think about what is important to them before they can discuss it with you. Ask each of them to write a *Personal Development Plan* (see Figure 15.1). This should fit onto one page (two pages maximum). They should write down their short- and long-term goals, what they think they are best at, what they would like to improve on, and what motivates them. This information is the most valuable information you will have about each team member. It will help you to be a better manager because you will know how to keep each person motivated.

Fundamentals of Technology Project Management Personal Development Plan

Personal Development Plan

Name:
Daryl Johnson
Date:
June 28th
Where I am Today:
I am a project manager working for XYZ Corporation. I have worked for XYZ for 14 months. I have a degree in computer science and have been working in project management for 3 years. I am currently working on an order management project for a fashion distributor. I am 32 years old, single (engaged) and have no children.
Short Term Goals (1-2 years):
- Get promoted to senior project management position with XYZ
- Get assigned larger and more complex projects
- Get married

Medium Term Goals (2-5 years):
- Move up into group project management and director positions
- Be managing other managers
- Be more involved in strategic direction for the company
- Complete my masters in business management
- Start a family

Long Term Goals (5 - 10 years):
- Move into the business side of the company (instead of technology)
- Vice President position in company in new business or emerging markets/technologies
- Be financially secure and well on the way towards a healthy retirement plan

What I am best at:
- Organizational skills
- Scheduling
- Data analysis

Things I would like to improve on:
- People management /team motivation
- Working with business groups
- Project management skills - get to senior level
- People management skills
- Time management
- Communication

New Skills I would like to learn /training I would like to take:
- Quality management methodologies
- Skiing
- Conflict management
- Business classes (for my MA)

What Motivates me:
- Recognition and praise (from manager especially)
- Money
- Promotion
- Stock options

Time off

Page of
Created by Daryl Johnson

Figure 15.1: Personal Development Plan.

You should try writing a Personal Development Plan for yourself too. You might be surprised at how difficult it is to put into words and also at what you find out about yourself! It is an enlightening exercise. In a few months' time ask your team members to review and update their plans. Many of them will want to make changes. Our goals and motivations are not constant throughout our lives; they change often. Major life events change our outlook and our goals. Reaching short-term goals sometimes changes our perspective on the longer-term goals. Our likes and dislikes change as we mature, as we develop new skills, and as we gain more confidence. Never assume that because someone once had a goal once that they still have the same goal. Do you remember what you wanted to do when you grew up when you were six or eight years old? If you had written down your goals, dreams, and motivations at that time, do you think if you read them now that they would be same? It is possible that some of them would still be the same, but many, if not all, of your goals and motivations will have changed over time. If you write your own Personal Development Plan, consider sharing it with your manager. You may find that you also start to get rewarded with the things that motivate you the most. A Personal Development Plan document is included on the CD-ROM that accompanies this book.

When you meet with your team members to find out more about them, make sure that you let each one know that your door is always open and that they can come to talk to you at any time about anything. Depending on the size of your team, you will likely meet with each person for at least half an hour every week or two. You will need to meet with your team leads more often because you will have a lot more to discuss. Ask them how often they would like to meet with you one on one. For example, you could let each person decide whether they would like to meet with you for half an hour each week or one hour every two weeks. You could ask whether they prefer to meet in the mornings or the afternoons. You may not be able to accommodate all requests, but it is good to know what each person is the most comfortable with. Let each person know that anything you discuss is confidential and that you will ask for their permission before sharing anything you discuss with others.

You should also plan to meet with your whole team to talk about team motivations. To start, you will probably have to make suggestions and perhaps get the team to vote on what they would like. This can be as simple as whether they want donuts or bagels for the team meeting or whether they want something different each week. As time goes by and the team develops its own personality, it will become easier for you to suggest things that you know they will like. You should start to see suggestions from the team members as they get more comfortable with the team and start to feel and act like a team. We have discovered that, as a project manager, you can have donut teams and bagel teams, lunch outing teams and happy hour teams, sporting event teams and movie event teams, zoo teams and BBQ teams. They are all different, but the team naturally settles into liking some common things that become "team" things to do.

Team likes and dislikes work as they do in relationships. When a couple gets together, they like some of the same things and some different things. As the relationship develops, couples have "their" places and things that become special to that particular relationship. The special restaurant, the favorite food, their song, volleyball or tennis on the weekends, movie nights or games nights with friends, hiking or snorkeling vacations, and so on. It is never an exact duplicate of either person's past relationship(s), but rather it develops as a result of their combined personalities and likes and dislikes. Your team things will develop in the same way. You cannot do exactly the same things with a team because your last team liked those things and assume that the new team will too. You need to find the right combination that makes this team unique. You should certainly use your experience working with other teams to try some of those things to see whether the new team responds to them. You never know what will happen! You will learn to treasure the things that are special to each team because they will last only as long as the project (or as long as the team is together). After that, you will get to start all over again with a new team for your next project.

Manage the team and the team activities by meeting, communicating, supporting, and helping with decisions, both individually and as a team. It is important to thank team members for a job well done. Do this often, but do not overdo it. Do not keep praising someone for good work if the other 50% of his work is substandard. He will think he is doing a great job, and you are not helping him by reinforcing this belief. Be careful of how you use praise in a team environment. Depending on the nature and personality of your team, you might find that praising someone for doing a great job makes others feel that they are not being noticed. Perhaps someone else did something even more spectacular but did not make a big deal out of it so it went relatively unnoticed. You do not want your team meetings to become blowing-your-own-trumpet sessions or the place where the least modest team members get their egos fed!.

On most teams, it works better to celebrate team successes publicly and individual successes privately. The main thing to watch out for is that you are not publicly praising the same person over and over again. It will look as though you have favorites. If you have someone on your team who is a real star, then presumably you are rewarding them appropriately in salary and bonuses, so you do not need to go on and on about their accomplishments to the whole team. The more senior members of your team may be working on the higher-profile features, but that does not mean that they are contributing more to the team than the more junior members are. This is assuming that they are being paid more handsomely for their contributions. You need to maintain a delicate balance on your team of reinforcing good behavior without making the environment too competitive. If everyone on a soccer team wanted to be the one scoring all the goals, you would not have an effective or successful team. It takes a whole team effort for that one person to score the goal, just as it takes your whole team's effort for each person to successfully implement her features and tasks, resulting in the completion of the project.

One other danger to be careful to avoid is giving too much praise to people for working long hours or weekends. You are looking for high-quality results from your team, not longer hours. Longer hours may indicate that a person is underperforming. If someone worked long and hard to solve a problem, then focus your celebration of this success on the fact that she solved the problem, not the time that went into it. Someone else could argue that they solved a similar problem in two hours and didn't even have to work late. Does that mean that she is a lesser performer? It is more likely that she is a higher performer and much more productive. If you have a situation where some team members worked all night to solve an eleventh-hour problem just before the project was due for release so as to meet the deadline, then you should applaud them for this. This is demonstrating great loyalty and commitment to the team and the project. You should celebrate and reward this kind of positive behavior. However, you need to be on the lookout for team members who are consistently working long hours to complete their work. This is not displaying loyalty and dedication; it is demonstrating that the team member is consistently unable to complete the assigned tasks in the scheduled time.

If you are experiencing problems with a team member who is underperforming, do not confront him about this in front of other team members. Meet with him privately in your office to discuss the problem and work together to find a solution. The one thing that you should never do is to just ignore it and hope that it will get better. This could end up destroying your team, your project, the individual, and you! It is your responsibility to let your team members know if they need to change their behavior in some way. How can they ever learn and grow if you refuse to talk to them about issues? Even if they are upset about what you discuss, it is the appropriate and right thing to do. If you cannot respond to these issues quickly before other team members notice that there are problems, then you are heading for big trouble. If your team members start to feel that they have dead wood on the team and that you are covering it up or putting your head in the sand, you will have conflict between your team members as well as a lack of confidence in your leadership. These two problems individually are hard to resolve; together they could seriously impact your ability to continue to manage the project team. Never let things escalate out of control due to lack of prompt action.

An important thing to be aware of is that most people do not purposely underperform. Sometimes a person may need help understanding why her work is not considered good enough. People can sometimes confuse effort with achievement. Working 12 hours per day is not an achievement. Why is she working twelve hours? Does she have to redo everything she works on because it does not work the first time? Does she have too many bugs? Does she not understand the task sufficiently? Does she need help and is not asking for it? Is she adding too much functionality to her features so that she needs more time than estimated to complete them? Working more hours than everyone else does not make someone a more dedicated or better engineer compared with someone who is working a standard eight-hour day. Working smarter and getting better quality results in a shorter time period is what makes someone a better engineer. Make sure that your team members understand that you are evaluating them on results and not on how hard or long they work.

Sometimes you will find that someone is just assigned to the wrong types of tasks. He may be a real star but is being asked to perform the wrong act. If someone is an excellent operatic singer, he will likely not be an outstanding pianist. You would not ask him to play piano in the symphony based on his vocal ability. This sometimes happens with engineers. If you have a low performer, explore the options before you write him off. He may the biggest star you have ever had on your team, but his talents have not yet been utilized appropriately.

Your team members will not always know where their best talents lie, so you need to help them figure it out. They may be getting more and more frustrated and losing their confidence as they continue to be told that they are underperforming. It is important that you continue to encourage these team members, and if you know that there is untapped talent there, be prepared to take a chance on them and assign them to some different and possibly more complex tasks. It will show them that you believe in them, will restore some self-esteem, and will give them the motivation to succeed. They will want to show you that you were right to trust them. They will want to reward you for taking a chance on them and will try as hard as they can to succeed. Sometimes you will find that you have a team member who is just not cut out for the job, and no matter how hard you try and how much time you invest in working with her to assign different tasks, she just doesn't get it. You need to be smart and know when to cut someone loose. It is hard to do but in the end will be the best thing for you, the individual, and the team. Keeping an underperformer on your team will affect the performance and the morale of your whole team. The longer you wait to act, the worse the problem will get.

Team members can also be motivated by recognition and advancement. By recognizing outstanding work and working with your team members to reward them appropriately, you will inspire and motivate them. Working on promotions or salary increases for team members who have earned them is also very important. Your team members need to feel appreciated. Everyone loves to be recognized by their manager and the company they work for. They strive for that. If you do not show recognition, your team members may think that you have not noticed or that you do not care. As mentioned previously, the recognition does not have to be public. Recognizing individuals in your one-on-one meetings with them is usually sufficient. As long as their manager has noticed, they know that they are getting closer to achieving their goals. The feedback that you give your project team members about their work is fundamentally important. Team members need to know how well they are doing, what they need to improve on, and what is expected from them in the future. Everyone needs goals to work towards so that they can measure their own progress and feel satisfaction in the job they are doing.

Change Management

During these times of financial turmoil, corporations are bracing themselves for a rough ride. Planning for continued business growth and survival requires some tough decisions and often involves drastic organizational changes. As senior management struggles with newly imposed financial constraints that can include reduced running costs and hiring and pay freezes, they sometimes forget about the impact that these changes are having on their team members. While the focus is on departmental costs and wondering which group will be targeted for senior management scrutiny next, who is taking care of your team's concerns? You may not be aware of it, but rumors are rife in the hallways about reductions in workforce and projects being canceled. These rumors are likely not substantiated by any hard facts, but when there is instability in the workplace, everyone starts to get paranoid and read between the lines.

One of the worse crimes that companies commit against their employees is to allow them to learn about expected layoffs through press and media announcements. Ideally, this kind of news should come from employees' direct managers. If the first time the manager hears about a major organizational change is in a company meeting with all the employees, she is hardly prepared to answer questions or concerns that her team may have right after the meeting. As many companies have not yet figured out how to communicate organizational change in a way that reduces employee panic, you will need to learn effective damage control techniques for those situations when you learn about change in a public forum. In addition, you will need to learn how to handle the change communication that your company makes you responsible for.

Within any organization, fear and anxiety will be at extremely high levels among employees after an announcement has been made about expected layoffs, regardless of how the news was communicated. This anxiety will continue to increase in the days leading up to the internal announcement about which departments and individuals will be affected. The less information the employees have, the more anxious they will be. It will be difficult at a time like this for your team to continue working on the project with the same level of focus, enthusiasm, and energy. Do not try to make them feel better by telling them that they will not be affected by the changes, even if you have heard rumors or official statements that your team will not lose any employees. You must always be honest with your team members and let them know that no one's job is ever completely safe no matter what the financial climate.

If you have been told that their jobs are safe, then you should share this information cautiously with them. Explain that in any organization no one has a 100% guarantee that their job is safe. Tell them that you have been informed no layoffs are anticipated in your department. Follow this up with a statement about the unpredictability that exists when a company is in the midst of major organizational change and that things can often change quickly. You are not telling them this to panic them or to make them feel more scared. You are telling them this because it is true, and you want them to make decisions based on this information.

For example, imagine that you had totally convinced your team that there would be no layoffs on your team because you had been told this by your manager. One of your team members was thinking of buying a new house, but after the initial layoff announcement had decided to wait to make sure that her job was still safe. If that person now believes she is safe, she may go ahead and buy the new house, increasing her monthly outgoings by 20%. Three weeks down the line, the company may have a board meeting and find that the shareholders do not agree that the planned layoffs are sufficient and are insisting on an additional 10% reduction in the workforce. The company needs to keep the shareholders happy. Without their support, they risk losing the whole business. The company makes a decision to cut an additional 5% of the workforce and to offer some percentage of other employees the opportunity to keep their jobs if they take a 20% decrease in salary. What does this new decision mean to your team? Perhaps some will lose their jobs and perhaps some will need to take a pay cut. Where does this leave the employee who just bought a new house? Not in a very good position if she is about to become unemployed or reduce her income by 20%. It may be that the team is not affected at all, but how long will this be the case? If your team members believed you last time you told them everything was OK and you were wrong, how long will it be until they have confidence in your predictions again?

Until the company has become stable again, it is not possible to predict what may happen in the next few months. It is very common for change to escalate. Companies start with the minimum cuts and increase them as necessary. They are trying to retain as much consumer and shareholder confidence as possible, so they need to find the delicate balance between cuts and business as usual. This balance can sometimes take some time to get right. They want to be seen as doing something to reduce costs but they do not want to be seen as reducing them so much that they are unable to continue running a profitable business. For these reasons, do not try to lull your team into a false sense of security. Tell them the facts but do not try to gloss over how serious the situation is. During times of financial upheaval, team morale and productivity will be affected. You need to work with your team to keep them as focused on the project as you can. You also need to remember that during this time you will be as worried about your job as your team members will be worried about theirs. Try not to let your own fears fuel theirs. It is important to be professional at all times, and having concern for your team members and encouraging them to be careful about making any long-term financial commitments while things are unstable is definitely the right thing to do.

When people are laid off from a company or if changes have triggered a high number of resignations, employees start to feel very insecure. If the layoffs or resignations were on your own team, then you really have your work cut out to manage the fallout from those events. Pep talks about teamwork from the CEO and COO will not eliminate peoples' feelings of insecurity nor allay the fear that things will never be the same again. If the environment before the change was very people-focused and nurturing, it will be a big adjustment for people to get used to the company becoming more task and cost oriented. Employees will perceive that the company is no longer the nurturing or fun environment that it used to be. If you have lost some team members, you will need to do some "damage control" to ensure that the rest of your team do not give up on the company and start looking for other jobs. Your team and your project can recover from some amount of disruption, but there is a limit to how much change you can absorb in a given time period and still complete your project successfully. "Successfully" meaning that the schedule, timelines, costs, and so on have been revised to take the organizational changes into account.

Not all organizational changes involve people losing their jobs. Some change is driven by changes in the business environment or the type of business that your company is in or has evolved to. To ensure that they stay competitive and profitable, some companies reevaluate their organizational structure from time to time to ensure that it is optimal for the current business and technology environments. Some companies have an organizational shake-up every year or two because they feel that it maintains flexibility and adaptability in their employees.

Although the vision for change may come from the top, your team members will look to their project manager and immediate supervisors for guidance and reassurance. As a role model, you need to ensure that you are communicating change positively. If it is a standard organizational "shake-up," you should have no problems communicating the change and the benefits of the change to your team members. Feeling passionate about positive change is a good thing. If your team is aware that you feel passionate and enthusiastic about it, they will feel more comfortable and will adapt to the changes more easily. Communication is an essential ingredient in managing change. No amount of communication is too much, as long as it is positive and appropriate. Never communicate change to your team as a complaint about the change or the person who made the decision for the change. You can tell them that you understand that change can be difficult and disruptive, but be sure to focus on the fact that the benefits are worth the upheaval.

Change can also be necessary due to growth. Often, when companies experience rapid growth, their executives and employees are not positioned well to manage the changes that go along with that growth. Growth is good for the company, but too much growth too quickly can be disastrous. There are many reasons why rapid growth can cause organizational chaos. When you add a lot of new people to a company at the same time, you risk losing the cozy feel that you had before, when perhaps everyone knew everyone else.

To manage a rapidly growing organization, you need to ensure that your team members have current and appropriate skills. You may need to start using new technologies or upgrade to new development systems. If you worked on projects in the $20,000 to $100,000 range for the past three years and are suddenly winning contracts for multi-million-dollar projects, do your managers and team members know how to handle this? As a project manager, how hard is it if over 50% of your team members are new recruits? How much time do they need to get up to speed, and how much time do your other team members need to spend with the "newbies" helping them to get up to speed? How productive will your team be during this time? How cohesive a plan will you be able to develop for the project? Will plans be constantly changing? Most likely, yes. How will the increase in team size affect your processes and procedures? How will the addition of a large number of new employees impact the dynamics on the team and within the company? How will the team's personality change? Will you still have a bagel team, or will it now be a donut team? How will your original team members feel when so many things start to change?

Growth can be incredibly exciting, but it needs to be managed well if you are to keep your team members engaged and motivated. Do not assume that your team will be excited just because they are getting to work on larger projects. They may have been perfectly happy working on the smaller projects and working on a smaller team! Growth can mean a location change for your company's offices too. You may outgrow the building(s) you are in and have to move. You may then outgrow the new building in a year and have to move again. You may be thinking that surely companies would know how rapid their growth will be and would not move and then realize that they need to move again after a short time. Well, believe it or not, it happens all the time.

Moving to a new office, driving to a different part of town, possibly adding half an hour to commute time—there are many reasons that location change can be stressful for employees. As companies grow and recruit new team members, the original team members may feel that they are less important than they were before. Jobs become more "specialized," so they do not get to interact as much with other groups or contribute to decisions about product planning. Whereas they used to know everything that was going on, now they find out about decisions and events at quarterly company meetings along with everyone else. They no longer get invited to barbeques at the CEO's house on the weekends. In fact, they no longer even see the CEO in the building! They may feel that they have lost some status. These feelings of being less important to the direction of the company may exist even if the team member has received a substantial salary increase or bonus. Do not assume that more money makes everything OK. Not all of your team members will be primarily motivated by money. It is unlikely that any of your team members will be motivated by money alone.

It is critical that, no matter who makes the decision to initiate change, it is clearly understood by everyone on the team. The team needs to be aware of who specifically is going to be affected by the change. The various groups, individuals, and companies that will be affected must be identified and informed. Forgetting to inform people about change is a sure way to make it more painful for everyone and to make managing the results very difficult.

The emotional state of employees in the workplace can motivate them to build, stagnate, or destroy the value of a business. In a well-organized emotional environment, emotions motivate people to be productively engaged in their jobs, and to adapt well to growth and organizational change. When people are motivated to perform productively and with flexibility (especially the core contributors on your team), the company's value tends to grow. In a poorly organized emotional environment, whether it has too much emotional interaction or too little, and whether it suffers from chaotically under-structured emotional interactions or brutally over scripted ones, emotions motivate people primarily to protect themselves in, and from, the workplace. Most especially they are protecting themselves from changes in the workplace. This causes the organization to drift towards low productivity, stagnation, brittleness, and slow-growing, or even sinking, value. It is very important, as a project manager, that you nurture your team members and communicate change in a positive and honest manner. You need to ensure they understand that in today's fast-paced business environments, change is inevitable. Let your team members know that you are there to assist them with working through any insecurities or fears they have and to help them positively and successfully adapt to change.

Managing Performance and Performance Reviews

Feedback can be given informally or in a more structured format. For example, you may verbally discuss performance with your team members in one-on-one meetings, or you may create formal written reviews. Most companies use a combination of both these methods in managing performance.

Based on performance reviews provided by the employees' managers, companies give bonuses, raises, and other rewards to their employees. Therefore, feedback is critical to team members. You must be honest and straightforward when giving feedback. Feedback should never be ambiguous. Make sure that, if there is a problem, it is clear what the problem is. Give an example of the issue and give an example of what you would have expected.

For instance, if you tell someone that they were rude in a meeting, give an example of the meeting and what was said: "Julie, in the project meeting last week, John Smith stated that he thought the 'X' feature should be implemented to support multiple OS platforms. You replied that he must be crazy to suggest something so stupid and asked him if he realized how much time and effort that would take. By using the words 'crazy' and 'stupid' your comments became personal attacks. Your tone of voice and body language was aggressive and the way you shot down his idea without being prepared to discuss it further was disrespectful and rude. A better way to state your opinion would have been to tell him that although the suggested approach would allow the customer to support multi-platform clients, that was not a requirement from the customer as far as you were aware. You could also have stated that it would require a substantial amount of additional work and a large cost increase to the customer to make this change. Additionally, you could have asked him if anyone had spoken to the customer about this request. Being respectful is not only what you say but also how you say it and how you look (your body language) when you say it." This method of describing the issue, ensuring that it is clear why it is an issue, and following it with an example of the expected behavior or outcome, is a great method to use when giving feedback on an area that needs improvement.

You should not blame someone else for negative feedback. For example "John Smith thinks that you are rude in meetings" or "John Smith thinks you are rude in meetings. I have never observed this myself, but you should be aware of it and work on it." You do not need to tell your team members who complained about them, just that you received feedback. You should be sure to verify that the issue raised is really an issue. Just because one person complained does not necessarily mean that your team member has a problem or that they were in the wrong in that particular incidence. If you have received a complaint about how someone behaved in a meeting that you were not present at and if it seems out of character for that person to behave or communicate in that way, then ask other people who were at the meeting what they thought. A second opinion can be very insightful.

You must make sure that you inform team members right away if you feel they need to improve on something. Do not wait until the next formal review to tell them about it. The quickest way to lose the respect and trust of your team members is to write something in their performance reviews that they did not know about beforehand. A great rule for review feedback is, if you have not talked to the team member about it previously and given him sufficient time to correct it, then it should not go into his review. Talk to him about it and save it for the next review. It is totally inappropriate to tell someone about a problem a week before you present his review (especially if you have already written it), giving him no opportunity to fix the problem or change the behavior. Do not blindside your team members. They deserve the same respect that you expect from your manager. Your team members will not be motivated or energized if they are getting mixed messages from you about their performance.

Here is an example of a poorly managed performance review: An employee has been performing well for the entire year. At each meeting with her manager during the past year, the employee has been told that she is doing a fantastic job both on her results and on how she has been achieving the results. The project was completed successfully, and it was delivered on time and with high quality. The project team was motivated and productive, and everyone asked to continue working with the employee, their project manager, again on the next project. The client could not say enough good things about her. From all accounts, the employee looks like a rising star in the company. She knows that things went well, and when her manager asks for her self input into her review, the employee mentions that she is interested in a promotion to a higher level and feels that she has proved herself over the last few years. Her manager makes note of her feedback and tells her she will have her review ready in four weeks.

Two weeks later her manager meets with her and tells her that she was unhappy with the employee's communication style. She says that she feels the employee gave her too many details when she was asked for status updates and that this kind of communication issue is not indicative of a good leader. The employee asks for examples (because she does not understand exactly what it is that her manager is referring to). Her manager states that she does not have any examples "off the top of her head" and that she will need a couple of weeks to get back to her. She also tells the employee that this issue is in her review, so be prepared. The employee asks why she has not been told about this before because all the previous feedback has been so positive. Her manager tells her that she is telling her about it before her review so it is OK. She also tells her that she learned in some recent classes that managers should avoid giving too much detailed information when giving status updates.

The employee feels very upset about the conversation with her manager. She knows that if her manager gives her a bad review, she will not be considered for any promotions that come up in the following year. She feels angry because all year she has been given excellent feedback. She has not been given any opportunity to work on this problem (if indeed it was a problem) and has been blind sided by this sudden "issue." She feels that her manager is looking for ways to use something that she learned in class and that she is being used as the guinea pig.

Of course it was not OK for her manager to tell her two weeks before her review. The review was already written. The manager could give no examples of the "giving too much detail" problem when asked by the employee. If a manager cannot cite examples of situations where the employee demonstrated an issue, then she has no business asking an employee to improve on it. The manager also never got back to the employee with any examples. The results were excellent for her project, the feedback was excellent from clients, stakeholders, and team members, and this was all reflected in the review, but the manager made a huge deal about the "too much information" issue and downgraded her review rating as a result of it.

When presenting the review to the employee, the manager stated that when receiving a review it was important to be open to feedback. She also stated that the employee should feel energized and motivated by the feedback about things to improve on because it was giving clarity to what was needed to improve and advance.

Do you think the employee felt energized or motivated? No, she did not. Do you think that hearing a statement like that before receiving the review made her feel more angry and resentful than she already was? Yes, of course it did. The end result of this was that the employee was not considered for promotion that year. A highly motivated employee who had loved her job now woke up each morning and did not want to go to work. She had no desire to work her butt off again because she felt that nothing she did really made a difference. This is neither an effective nor an appropriate way to manage team members or performance reviews.

If you want to have motivated team members, be honest and direct with your feedback and do not try to protect them from bad news. They need to know what the issues are so they can be aware of them and work on them. More than one mistake was made by this employee's manager:

- Not telling the employee about the communication problem immediately and giving her ongoing feedback about how she was doing with correcting the problem.

- Not having any examples of the issues when she told the employee about it.

- Not following up with examples as promised. This made the employee feel that there were no examples and perhaps her manager was wrong about it.

- Not telling the employee about the issue until the review was already written, giving the employee no opportunity to work on the issue pre-review.

- Stating that because she was telling the employee about the issue before the review was presented that it was appropriate to put it in the review.

- Telling the employee that she should feel "energized" and "motivated" by the things to improve on (ridiculous in the circumstances).

- Assuming that, because the employee was on a good salary and received a bonus for the project, this would be sufficient to keep the employee motivated.

- Allowing a poorly organized review process to lead to a highly productive and successful employee being disempowered.

Companies often assume that if someone leaves after receiving an annual review, it is because the review was bad, and deservedly so, and the people who left were dead wood. This is often far from the truth. The underperformers usually stay exactly where they are because they know it will be hard to find and keep another job if they are not achieving good results. A company can lose very valuable team members when a manager focuses too much attention on relatively unimportant details and springs surprise issues on team members during performance reviews.

Focus on the hundred positive things that your team members do well and not one easily correctable behavior or one incident that was not executed perfectly, especially if it was not critical to the project. No one is perfect 100% of the time. Managing employees is not about constantly focusing on what they can improve on. It is about helping them to develop and grow in the areas where they excel as well as improving in areas that need some work. If the things they are not good at are not necessary or important for them to be able to do their work, then why waste lots of time and energy trying to teach them how to be good at it? Your time would be better spent leveraging their strengths.

Management Effectiveness

Most of us, at least once in our professional lives, have had the displeasure of working for, or with, a bad manager. So what sets a good manager apart from the bad ones? What are the different management styles and how effective are they?

Being nice does not make you a good manager. In fact, this can be the most destructive kind of manager. At least if you are being yelled at on a daily basis, you have some idea of where you stand. A manager who says, "yes" to everyone is not going to build strong, productive, and effective teams. Here is an example of a situation in a company where there was a manager whom everyone liked—or appeared to like: The manager was personable and pleasant to everyone and always agreed with whatever a team member said and made the person feel like he really knew what they were talking about. Once someone had worked for this manager for a few months, they wished desperately that they reported to one of the managers whom nobody liked much. Why? Because when you agree with everyone, your opinion is always the same as the one held by the last person who left your office. You agree to something and then you change the decision based on what the next person in your office says. The person or people with whom you agreed earlier have no idea that you just changed your opinion and the decision. The result? Chaos, uncertainty, anger, frustration, and a lack of empowerment.

If you cannot make a decision and then follow through on it, you will never be an effective manager. If your only goal is to make everyone like you, then you will never oppose anyone else's opinion and you will never fight for anything that you believe in. Perhaps you won't even know what you believe in. What will happen if you never openly support any of your team members or you tell four people four different things? They go into meetings to argue their cases, believing that you are going to back them up and then you don't. You may even openly disagree with them based on what someone else in the meeting says. Does this inspire trust or confidence in you? Do they feel that you trust and respect them? No, of course they don't. They feel powerless. Management and leadership are not about being nice; they are about doing the right thing, standing up for what you believe in, and having personal and professional integrity.

What about the kind of manager who uses intimidation instead of encouragement? There are two different kinds of intimidator: the "bully" and the "blackmailer." The bully shouts and screams and makes a lot of noise. The blackmailer threatens in a more quiet and subtle way. They are both threatening to you, they will both scare you, and both styles are just as destructive as each other. How do you feel when your manager starts yelling at you or threatening that you might lose your job if you don't meet the deadline next week? How do you feel if your manager quietly tells you that she understands how you feel, but if you cannot resolve the issues then perhaps you are in the wrong job; or you are told that it is up to you how you proceed, but he cannot protect your job if you are unable to deliver? How would you feel if you went to your manager to tell her about a problem and to ask for some advice on what to do about it and this was the reaction? It is unlikely that you will feel motivated and inspired to do your best. It is more likely that you will start looking for another job and counting the days until you can hand in your resignation. In this situation some people may even start trying to make the project fail so that the manager is fired. This kind of management will result in a project team that is resentful, angry, frustrated, and ready to become job hoppers.

There are also the "poor me" managers. They present everything to their team as a problem that must be resolved or the manager will lose his job, will have to cancel his vacation, or will be the victim of some other dreadful outcome. These managers also make others feel badly about needing time off or scheduling vacations and will say things like "Hmmmm, well, I suppose you could take a vacation then but we will be very busy. I haven't taken a vacation in two years because the project really needs me, and if the team is not committed enough to the project then it is definitely going to fail." This kind of manager makes his team feel guilty about everything and tries to make the team think that their actions are making life harder for someone else, usually the manager. This type of manager is constantly letting his team know how many hours he is working, how many weekends he is giving up to work on things for the team, how he never sees his family, and so on. No one wants to work for a martyr, so don't do this to your team. People do not work hard for you because they feel sorry for you; they do it because they respect you and they believe in the project and the team.

Another nonproductive and ineffective management style is the "it is not my fault" style. Similar to the poor me style, this type of manager also behaves like a victim but in a slightly different way. Rather than making people feel sorry for them, the "it's not my fault" manager will just blame everyone else for whatever goes wrong. They do not take responsibility for decisions. Often, they never really make decisions—that way they can always blame someone else if it doesn't work out. Like the manager who agrees with everyone, if they have no opinion of their own, how can they be responsible when things go wrong? These managers blame their managers, peers, team members, and clients—anyone they can, as long as it is not their fault. They say things like, "Well, we only made that decision because my boss told us to," or "It was really the client's fault; they kept changing their minds and we got confused." Another classic is, "If I had a more experienced team working with me these kinds of things would not happen."

How about the "interrogator" manager? You know the ones: They question you about every single thing that you do and keep going until they find something that they can say you are doing wrong or could have done better. They always make you feel inadequate. They compare you unfavorably to others, and no matter how many things you do well, they always manage to burst your bubble with something that you did wrong.

Then there is the "micromanager." The micromanager is the one who watches every single little thing that you do down to the minutest detail. She will tell you exactly how she wants every task done, exactly what time you can go to lunch, and exactly what time you are allowed to go home. The micromanager handles the financials down to the very last cent. You are not allowed to buy a book without her permission or remove an extra chair from your office. Like the interrogator, she too makes you feel inadequate and are not empowering you in any way to do a great job. She doesn't trust that the job can get done right so she checks in with you every half hour to see what kind of progress you are making. She checks everything that you do because everything must get her seal of approval before it is considered final.

These are a lot of management mistakes that you may think you would never find yourself making, but be careful: Many managers slip into one or more of these styles from time to time, especially when the pressure is on, so beware. Think about your own personality and how you interact with your family and friends. Think about what your gut reaction is when you feel threatened. Do you get defensive, offensive, cry, shout, or withdraw? We all have negative behaviors, and they are increased when we feel under pressure or frustrated. Whatever your reaction is in a personal situation, you risk slipping into it in a professional situation. Being aware of this will help you to control your reactions. Remember earlier we talked about not reacting or dealing with things while you felt emotional, upset, or frustrated? Well this is the main reason for it. You will likely behave in a way that is out of character for you professionally, and once you have said it or done it, there is no taking it back. You can ruin months or years of teamwork and mutual respect with one sentence. It is just not worth it.

A good manager or leader is an effective leader. It is about getting the job done, and it is about getting it done the right way. It does not mean that everyone will always like you. You will not always agree with your team members, and they will not always agree with you. They will be upset when you talk to them about substandard work. They will sometimes be upset because you made a decision that they did not agree with. Leadership is not about consensus. It is about making a decision, implementing it, and taking responsibility for it. It is your job to do this. If you never do anything unless everyone on your team agrees with you, then you will never get anything done. You will not be leading the team at all; you will be facilitating ineffective teamwork. Leadership is not a popularity contest. A leader is a coach, a mentor, a manager, a peacemaker, a problem-solver, a meeting facilitator, and a psychologist.

No one likes to be nagged or picked at all the time. To achieve high-quality results, it is important that you lead your team through a well-defined process that allows them to effectively plan, control, and monitor their own contributions to the project. You can create a motivated and empowered team in many different ways. Some suggestions are listed here:

- Plan the project around deliverables, not individual tasks. This way your team members are focused on the destination rather than the journey.

- If a crisis hits, try to step back and let the project team members handle it. This can be a very difficult process because your initial reaction will be to fix it or tell them how to fix it. That's what a project manager does; he solves problems to help the team and allow them to move forward. If you step in and fix everything every time there is a problem, your team will start using you as a crutch. They will start relying on you for every little decision or want you to fix every little problem. You need to sit back and let the team members work it out. They own the project; let them own the crisis. If they are unable to resolve it in a reasonable amount of time, you may need to step in and help. Try not to tell them what to do, but use discussion to lead them down the path of discovery so that they find the solution themselves. It will take longer to resolve the issue, but it will help them develop better analytical and problem solving skills. The next time something like that happens they will have a much better idea of what to do.

- Make sure the team has the necessary resources to complete the project on time. Give the project team as much support and guidance as they need for a successful outcome, but let them make the decision on how things get done. Remember, they are the professionals that you recruited onto your team, and you hired them for a good reason. Let them do what you are paying them to do. Let them do their job.

Management effectiveness is leading your team using a structured process that allows team members the flexibility to make decisions within that process. They have the flexibility to decide how to implement the best possible solution to the problem that the project is trying to solve. It gives each team member the feeling that they are part of the process and not just an engineer hired to implement a predefined solution. They are all part of a team, and it should be a team that they can be proud of.

Empowerment

While you are leading your team, making decisions, and taking responsibility, you also need to be *empowering* your team members. What is empowerment? Empowerment is making people feel that they have some control over their work, their day, and their job. A lot of studies have been done on stress in the workplace. Most people believe that the highest stress jobs are the ones with the most responsibility. For instance, people often assume that managers, CEOs, or pilots are more prone to stress than manual workers. It is interesting to note that very high stress levels are found in blue-collar workers, such as people who work in factories or in manufacturing industries. These are people who go to work and do exactly what they are told all day, every day. They make no decisions and take no responsibility. So why are their stress levels so high? Their stress levels are high because they have no control over their own lives while in the workplace. It is frustrating to be in a position where you have no voice, no opinion, and no power. A lot of those people have little control over their personal lives, either, especially if they are living in low-income households where life is about surviving and they do not have the opportunity to make decisions about things that some of us take for granted. For instance, they may have no choice about what to buy their children for their birthdays or where to go on vacation. Having some level of control over your environment gives you security, confidence, and a sense of well-being and accomplishment.

Empowering your team members means that you have to work on your ability to let go of the control for some things. This can be a very hard thing to do, especially if you are a bit of a control freak. Great leaders like to be in control. That is why they want to lead and not follow. You need to use good judgment when deciding what you empower your team members to do. It does not have to mean that they get to make final decisions, but they do need to feel that they have a voice and that they contribute to some of the decisions. You may think that you are able to effectively and efficiently control every little aspect of everyone's life on your team, but it is very important that you resist this urge. You must trust your team members, and you must respect them. You need to give them some control so that they feel the security, confidence, and sense of accomplishment that comes with empowerment. As the project manager, you are accountable for what happens to the project so letting go of some control means that you are giving away some of yours. If you use good judgment and you monitor progress you may be surprised at how well this works. Empowerment goes hand in hand with the delegation that we covered earlier. Remember that your team members are the ones who are doing the work, so you cannot control everything that they do. You can coach, lead, persuade, and entice, but you cannot control. Your team members will be the best judges of how to accomplish their tasks. If there is mutual trust, they will ask for help when they need it because they will value your opinion.

Empowerment is not about giving responsibility for the project to someone else and then blaming that person if something goes wrong. You still have the ultimate responsibility for the outcome, so be careful about what decisions or responsibilities you are empowering your team members to make. Empowerment is a delicate balance between the control that the project manager has and the individual and shared responsibilities of your team members. Often empowerment can mean as little as your team members knowing that you have an open door policy and that they can make suggestions about any aspect of the project. They do not have to always get what they want, but they need to know that they were involved in the process that culminated in the final decision. Empowerment is also about choices. We all like choices.

- The choice that you may attend the planning meetings if you want to, even though your presence is not needed.

- The choice that you may work flexi-hours two days a week.

- The choice that you do not have to wear a suit and tie to the office.

- The choice that you may implement one of your features before the other one as long as the work all gets completed in time to meet the milestone deadline.

- The choice that you can have doughnuts at this week's team meeting rather than bagels.

It is not only the big important decisions that people care about. It is the small, every-day decisions that don't have much impact on the project that can make the biggest difference to how people feel about their jobs and about their manager. Control freaks want to control everything, even if it really doesn't matter whether it is done differently. Keep control of the things that are critical to your project, and encourage your team members to take control of some other things. You might be surprised at how much easier it will make your life when you have your whole team involved in those things and not just you. It will allow you to focus on the important things and not waste so much time and energy on the less important ones. Empowering your team members will make you a more effective leader and will result in a stronger and more productive team.

Managing Conflict

Regardless of how well-planned a project may be, constant unforeseen changes and demands can take their toll on you and your team members. Conflicts will arise from time to time, and resolution of those conflicts is part of the project manager's core re-sponsibilities. The root causes of conflict in a project setting can often be tracked down to flaws in the project plan, process, communication, or organization and personality clashes. Conflict also arises from decisions that team members do not agree with. These may be bad decisions, or they may be good decisions that are essential to the success of the project. Regardless of whether the decision turns out to be a good or a bad one, any conflict that results will need to be managed effectively.

Workplace conflict can be defined as any disagreement between two or more co-workers over policies, procedures, or attitudes related to the work environment. Since no two peo-ple view the world in exactly the same way, disagreements are quite normal. In fact, if you have team members who agree all the time, you should be concerned. They are likely afraid to tell the truth about their opinions. Your team needs to be encouraged to tell you what you need to know and not what they think you want to hear.

With this said, if your project falls behind, the fingers can start pointing to identify who is to blame. This blaming mentality needs to be managed by the project manager. Work with your team to get them to focus on the solution rather than on dissecting the problem to apportion blame. Everyone makes mistakes. A team needs to work together to resolve problems. Blaming each other will only create more problems.

Technical disagreements are common within a group of engineers. They may disagree with one another, or they may disagree with their manager. Differing opinions are not necessarily a bad thing. Challenging and improving on ideas is part of the technical development process. When a difference of opinion turns into a conflict, the project manager needs to act to ensure that the conflict is resolved quickly and before other people get involved. Sometimes a conflict arises because the project manager rejects a solution proposed by a team member on technical, financial, or scheduling grounds.

Conflicts arise when interests or ideas that are personally meaningful to either one or both of the parties involved are challenged or rejected. You should work with your team on open communication and sharing ideas so that if a solution is rejected it is not taken personally. The team's responsibility is to do what is best for the project regardless of whose idea it was. However, regardless of all the training, coaching, and encouragement you give to your team, sometimes these things will be taken personally.

At times, conflict arises not due to one specific decision but because of personality clashes. These can be harder to manage because the conflict can be an ongoing situation that needs to be constantly monitored and managed. These conflicts can escalate to the point where neither party is willing to agree with anything that the other party says or does. The two people involved both feel that the other does not respect them or their ideas. The other person makes them feel defensive and sometimes intimidated. The longer the situation is allowed to continue, the harder it will be to resolve it.

Unmanaged conflict can lead to arguments and insubordination. The conflict can start out between two people but, left unmanaged, can escalate to the point that it encompasses the entire project team. The key to managing conflict effectively is to deal with it as soon as it rears its ugly head. Waiting to see whether it will "blow over" on its own is a sure way to create a conflict that escalates out of control. The longer you wait to do something about it, the harder you will have to work to resolve it. If you are one of the people involved in the conflict, it is critical that you deal with it as soon as possible. You cannot effectively manage a project team if you are unable to manage your own personal conflicts.

When conflict arises between team members, you might not always be aware of the problems immediately. People can be good at hiding their emotions, and sometimes they are hoping that the problem will go away on its own. Your team members will not always come to you to tell you about a problem with someone else or a problem that they have with you. You need to be observant and aware of the subtle undertones that exist on your team. If someone who is normally funny, outgoing, and energetic seems to change overnight and is distant and moody, there is usually a reason.

It is very important to determine whether the team member has a problem with you, the project manager, or with another team member. You should always set up a face-to-face meeting to discuss any problems. Discussing these kinds of issues over the phone or by e-mail is going to make things worse. If you start trying to resolve an issue in an impersonal way, then you are never going to be able to change that. Open communication means face-to-face communication. Hiding behind communication tools is not going to help uncover or resolve any conflicts, and you risk the team member getting the impression that you feel the problem is not worthy of taking time out of your schedule to discuss it. You need to be able to see the reactions of your team member and to read the body language to ascertain whether there is a problem. You are at a disadvantage on the phone because you cannot see either of these things.

The meeting should *always* be held in a nonconfrontational manner. Do not attack the person or make accusations. You would be surprised by how much you can find out by simply asking whether there is a problem. You can just ask, "Is everything OK? You seem very quiet this week." If they say that everything is OK and they are sitting wringing their hands or looking very upset, then don't give up too easily. You can ask them if they are sure they are OK and perhaps ask them if you have done something that has upset them.

You need to be prepared to take some flack. You might hear something about yourself that you do not like. You cannot be defensive. It is very important that the team members feel that they can talk to you and that you are there to listen and try to work out a solution. If they tell you that you never listen to their input, you should not tell them that you do or try to justify your behavior. Ask them for an example. Discuss the example. It doesn't matter whether or not you were listening to them in the example they give, what is important is the perception that you were not listening. You can discuss the situation and you can assure them that you had no intention of making them feel that way.

Discuss with the team members some options around how you could communicate with them differently that would make them feel more comfortable. Use active listening skills. *Active listening* is repeating back to the person you are listening to what they are telling you. You do not have to agree with them; just let them know that you heard them. Listen to the example they give you and then repeat back to them what they said. For example, "I understand that you are upset because you do not think I was listening to your input on the X project at last week's team meeting. You feel that I dismissed your remarks and that I had already made my decision before I talked to the team. You also feel that I listen to Paul's input all the time and that he is only one I really listen to." You are not agreeing, you are just stating back what you heard (calmly). This will let your team member know that you are listening and that you have heard what he said.

Ask him if there is anything else that you missed. The problem could have been caused by something as simple as you stating "OK, thanks" in a meeting after hearing his input, and he took this as you dismissing his remarks. The solution may be just as simple. If you had instead said, "Thank you for your input, I have made a note of the points that you made and will consider those when making my decision." That might have been enough to make him feel heard.

Perhaps you did not explain enough about why you made the decision you made. Ask your team member if more data on the decision, the reasons, and the process for the decision would have been helpful to him. You could probably have explained this in a couple of sentences in an e-mail. "I met with the project team and other groups involved in the project, including the client, and discussed the issue with project X. Based on that input together with the budgetary and time constraints, the decision has been made to do 'blah'. I want to thank everyone for their input and their great ideas, all of which contributed to an efficient and informed decision with minimal impact on the project schedule." Once your team members understand that you are open to feedback and that you listen without becoming defensive or accusatory, they will trust you enough to come to you with problems in the future without having to be prompted by you. They may even start to come to you to discuss problems other team members are having, too, because they will trust that you will handle it tactfully and appropriately.

Becoming an effective conflict manager requires practice. The more that you do, the better you get at it. In the early days you might find yourself hesitating and procrastinating before dealing with a problem. You are just delaying the inevitable. The longer the conflict has existed, the bigger it will have grown. If you just take a deep breath and go for it, you will find yourself dealing with more molehills than mountains, and you will be able to resolve issues before they become full-blown conflicts. The main goal of conflict management is avoiding conflict. It is recognizing when something is brewing and dealing with it before it matures into conflict. Once you have a conflict on your hands, remember that the goal is to reach a compromise that all parties involved can live with. Ideally all parties will be happy with the resolution, but agreeing to it and moving on is the ultimate goal. If it is possible to find a way that everyone can walk away feeling like a winner, then kudos to your conflict management skills!

How do you recognize conflict? A number of organizational and management issues will lead to conflict, including poor communication, lack of openness, general lack of respect, not showing appreciation, disempowerment, unclear goals, lack of discussion regarding progress, and a weakness in leadership. You will also learn to recognize signs in your team members that are clues that conflict is brewing—for example, avoidance (of the issue or each other), negative body language, strong public statements, constant disagreements, increasing demonstrations of disrespect, insensitivity to others, personality changes, or taking an unusual number of sick days. Conflict can become very destructive when no action is taken to resolve it. Conflict needs to be met head on, and communication needs to be open and honest. Remember, you can agree to disagree. As long as a decision is made and all parties agree to move on and accept the final decision, you have avoided or resolved the conflict. It is important not to let conflict fester, because it can take the attention away from other important activities. If your team members are using up 25% of their energy on conflicts, then that is 25% of their time that is not focused on their scheduled tasks. Conflict can lead to harmful and disrespectful behavior, such as name calling and fighting. Do not think that these kinds of conflicts only happen in elementary school. Adults are just as susceptible to this kind of destructive behavior.

There are many approaches to conflict resolution, and one of the most successful is the *collaboration technique*. The collaboration technique requires both assertiveness and cooperativeness from the parties involved. This balance ensures that all parties feel heard and feel that they have equality in designing a resolution. The interests of all parties are represented by a successful collaborative solution. The project manager acts as a facilitator in the collaborative conflict resolution process. The conflicting parties must be willing to actively participate in the process if it is going to be successful. The concept, basically, is that the conflicting parties find a compromise that they can both (or all) agree to, and the project manager acts as the facilitator and peace-keeper. The facilitator should document the conflict and the agreed-upon solution and ensure that all involved parties receive copies. These should, of course, be kept confidential by all parties involved. Creating a workplace setting in which conflicts are resolved locally, informally, and quickly by those closest to the situation will build a strong and nurturing environment for your team. Conflict is best handled early and locally.

In addition to the collaborative technique, informal, constructive dialogue and problem-solving techniques can help team members deal with the root causes of conflict, rather than just the symptoms. Relationship dynamics need to be considered in conjunction with the conflict issues. As you learned earlier, personality clashes can be a key contributor to workplace conflict. As a project manager, you need to be empowered by your manager to make decisions so that you can effectively manage conflict on your team. If necessary, you should take additional specialized conflict management training to strengthen your skills in dispute resolution. If you are going to be managing a project or a team with a history of conflict, or there are current conflicts that you are aware of, you should seriously think about signing up for specialized conflict management training as soon as possible. Even if you are not aware of any conflict currently, you can never get enough training in this area. What you will learn is how to prevent conflicts from starting in the first place, which means that you will not have to spend too much time managing conflict situations. Depending on the level of autonomy that you have in your role as a project manager, your conflict management decisions may be subject to review by more senior management. Whether or not your senior managers get involved in these kinds of decisions, as the manager, you will be held accountable for the results. If the problem has escalated out of control, ask for help. Your manager should be able to offer you some good advice on how to proceed. You should ensure that you always handle issues and conflicts equitably and effectively.

In addition to handling issues and conflicts equitably and effectively, it is just as important to document everything. This means how you found out about the problem, who is involved, the actions you have taken, the actions the people involved have taken, any agreements made, and the end result. If the conflict has been serious, or has been between you and a team member, it would be wise to have the parties involved sign off on your document and the agreement that has been made. At the very least, you should follow up with an e-mail to the people involved that specifies the issues, the resolution, and the agreements made. Make sure you print a copy of your e-mail and any responses that you receive to it, and keep it on file for future reference. It is possible that a conflict will arise again or one party to the agreement will decide not to follow through with their side of the bargain. This can make the original conflict much worse and can sometimes result in human resources needing to get involved.

Conflict can sometimes lead to people either leaving the company or being asked to leave. Your human resources department will want as much information as possible on the conflict and what was done to resolve it. This is helpful to them in evaluating the situation and helpful to you in covering your own butt. You do not want to be implicated in any human resources issues. If a conflict has arisen due to an alleged gross misconduct including harassment (of any kind), bullying, physical harm, stealing, and so on, then you must report the situation to your human resources department immediately. This is not a conflict that should be dealt with locally or independently. Your human resources department will guide you in how to proceed.

A number of methods can be used to help diffuse situations before they become conflicts. Two that will be of particular interest to project managers are:

1. Self-directed initiative

2. Open door policy

Self-directed initiative or "direct action" is used in conjunction with constructive dialog and problem-solving. The project manager encourages team members to speak directly to the person with whom they have a problem to seek a satisfactory solution. Use your judgment wisely when suggesting this approach to team members. If the conflict has escalated out of control, and there is a high level of animosity, this approach will likely serve only to make things much worse. Your goal is to encourage open communication, not to force people into uncomfortable or intimidating situations. For smaller, less critical conflicts, this is a great approach to try before getting management involved.

The open door policy encourages open communication among team members and management to enhance team member morale and resolve work-related issues at a local level. A team member may consult informally with any project manager without fear of retaliation and in complete confidence. As a project manager, you may be approached by team members who report to other managers, and your team members may also approach other managers.

Here are some guidelines for setting up an effective open door policy:

- When a team member requests your assistance, make yourself immediately available or find time to meet as soon as possible.

- Talk in a private place so that no one overhears the conversation.

- Assure the team member of absolute confidentiality.

- Listen actively to the team member. Remember that "active listening" is repeating back what you hear to ensure that you have completely understood and that the person who is talking to you knows that you are listening.

- Ask questions to help the team member clarify the facts and separate them from assumptions or emotions.

- Ask the team member what assistance they are looking for. For instance:
  - Do they want you to just listen?
  - Do they want you to provide a referral for additional assistance for things that may be outside your area of authority or control?
  - Do they want you to contact human resources?
  - Do they want you to act as a facilitator or an advocate in a face-to-face meeting?
  - Are they requesting that you make a decision or take action?

- Close the meeting by summarizing what you have discussed and the team member's decision on how to proceed.

It is very difficult to trust someone you don't know. Consequently, if project managers want to earn and build trust, they must share their feelings and beliefs so that team members gain a clear picture of the project manager's values and priorities. In other words, let them get to know you as well as you are trying to get to know them. Project managers truly must lead the way in creating a culture that reinforces and models open, honest, and direct communication.

The most important skill to learn in conflict management is *conflict avoidance*. This does not mean pretending that it is not happening or not dealing with it; it means recognizing when conflict could result and managing the communication so that it does not. The more skilled you become at conflict avoidance, the less conflict resolution you will need to do!

In summary, this list of managerial tips that help you to avoid potential conflict:

- "If you lead through fear you will have little to respect; but if you lead through respect, you will have little to fear." - Anonymous

- Conflict is best handled early and locally.

- Informal, constructive dialogue and problem-solving approaches help team members deal with the root causes of conflict, rather than just the symptoms. Consider relationship dynamics in conjunction with the issues.

- Managers should always handle issues and conflicts equitably and effectively.

- Don't say, "You never finish the work on time." Do say, "It seems like you are having some difficulty with the timelines. What can I do to help?"

- Don't say, "If you had bothered to read the report, you would know what I was talking about." Do say, "It might be that the report wasn't clear on those points. Would you like me to explain?"

- If a team member is acting out of character, ask them if everything is OK.

Few of us enjoy dealing with conflicts, whether those conflicts are with bosses, peers, subordinates, or family members. This is particularly true when the conflict becomes hostile and when strong feelings are expressed. Resolving conflict can be mentally exhausting and emotionally draining. However, it is important to understand that conflict is neither good nor bad. There can be positive and negative outcomes. It can be destructive, but it can also play a productive role for you personally and for your relationships, both personal and professional. The key to resolving conflict with a positive outcome includes looking for a win-win situation, cutting losses when necessary, formulating proactive conflict management strategies, using effective negotiation and communication, and appreciating cultural differences. The important point is to manage the conflict, not to suppress conflict, and not to let conflict escalate out of control.

Most important, a great tip for avoiding conflict is to build a strong, motivated, and productive team that is committed to the project and that has respect and admiration for both their manager and one another.

Leadership and Communication Styles

Each of us has a distinctive way of interacting with others. The type of behavior we use most often defines what we call our leadership style, communication style, or management style. Leadership style influences the way we communicate, react, and respond to others. It also influences the way we approach and resolve conflicts. Understanding leadership styles will help you understand your own approach to management and identify that of others as well. You can use this knowledge to analyze, and perhaps modify, your own management approach. You can also use it to learn how to interact more effectively with others who have a different style from yours. Everyone has a leadership or communication style, not just leaders and managers. We all manage our own lives and relationships based on our style. Understanding the different styles and knowing how to identify what style a person is will help you greatly in conflict management.

A *communication style* is the pattern of behavior that a person displays for the majority of the time. It is the way other people perceive him or her and his or her actions. When we talk about leadership and communication styles, we are referring to people's *observable behavior*.

The characteristics of the different styles are shown in Figure 15.2. Many organizations use the Style Characteristics in team building activities. Psychologist, David Merril helped develop the Wilson Learning Social Styles Profile. A leadership style is derived from the level of assertiveness versus responsiveness. Assertiveness defines whether a person is more likely to "ask" or to "tell." Responsiveness defines whether a person is more task oriented or more people focused. Exactly where you are positioned on this chart is dependant upon exactly where you fall on each of these scales.

Each of your team members, including you, has a distinctive way of interacting with others. Your different ways of communicating and behaving can help or hinder you in both avoiding and resolving conflict.

The differences in the way people communicate can lead to misunderstandings. It's important to understand the different communication styles, and to know how to adapt your own style to

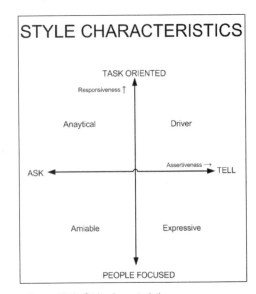

Figure 15.2: Style characteristics.

different situations. This will enable you to communicate more clearly and avoid misunderstandings.

The characteristics define four main leadership styles.

- Analytical
- Driver
- Amiable
- Expressive

Most people do not fit exactly into just one style. They will have characteristics of more than one style, which will be evident from where you fall on the chart in Figure 15.2. It is usually clear that one style dominates, with sprinklings of other styles here and there. It is interesting to note that what you think your style is may not be what your peers, employees, or family members think your style is. When analyzing the styles to figure out where you fall on the chart, ask other people where they see you too. Do not tell them what you think your style is beforehand because you may influence them to tell you what you want to hear. This is the only way that you will truly know your style. Remember that it is based on observable behaviors and not on how you think others perceive you or where you wish you were on the chart.

Each style has its own characteristics, strengths, and challenges. Figure 15.3 shows the strengths associated with each style.

Being aware of the driving forces behind each of the communication or leadership styles will help you to adapt your style to whomever you are communicating with. For example, if you are a driver and you are working with an amiable, it is possible that you will intimidate them so they will go along with you to avoid conflict. They may feel that you are too direct and are trying to force your opinions on them. You may feel that they are too wishy-washy and that they should be more forceful. On the other hand, you may be an expressive working with an analytical. They may view you as loud and unstable and think that you spend way too much time

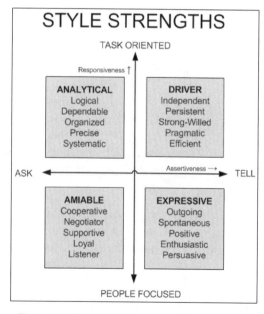

Figure 15.3: Style strengths.

socializing and chitchatting. You may view them as too serious and unsociable and think that a couple of margaritas might lighten them up a bit. None of the styles is right or wrong. They are just different from each other. We all communicate in our own way, and we all need to understand and respect that others are doing the same thing. The most successful teams comprise diverse team members with very different styles. If you learn how to leverage the power of these different styles and to utilize the potential that exists to create a really strong and versatile team, you will be a highly successful project manager.

The positive aspects of style characteristics are style strengths. The negative aspects are style weaknesses or "style challenges" as we prefer to call them. These are the behaviors that emerge when each style is under pressure or dealing with conflict. The style challenges are detailed in Figure 15.4.

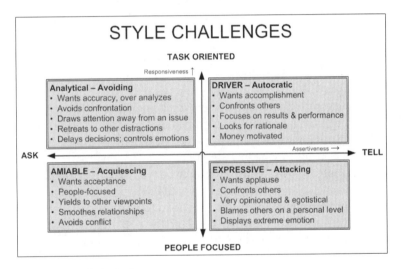

Figure 15.4: Style challenges.

It is important to be aware of these style challenges. No matter what your style or your combination of styles, you will have a tendency to slip into one of these negative behaviors if you are feeling stressed, tired, conflicted, disempowered, or frustrated. Being aware of these tendencies should help you control them. To become skilled at control, you must first be very honest with yourself about your style and your style challenges.

The chart in Figure 15.5 shows some alternative behaviors that you can use to help add more balance to your leadership style.

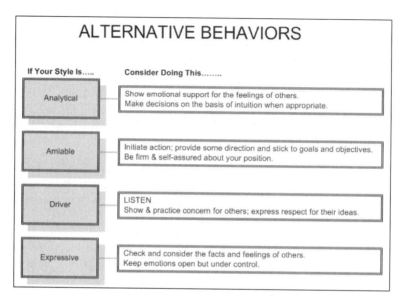

Figure 15.5: Alternative behaviors.

Making some adjustments to how you communicate with others can make a huge difference to the success of your outcomes. Think about a person's style before you talk to them and practice adapting to their style. Amiables will love it if you start the conversation by asking them how their family is and then answering questions about your own. Then, rather than telling them what you want them to do, explain what you are trying to achieve and ask for their help and support in achieving it. This approach will have the opposite affect on Drivers. You need to be direct and get to the point with drivers, or they will lose interest before you get to the punch line. Tell them what you need, when you need it, skip the pleasantries, and let them get back to work as quickly as possible. Expressives will respond well if you invite them out for a happy hour drink or lunch. They will be much more open to being enlisted to help you out if you are prepared to socialize and have fun with them. If you need something from an Analytical, go armed with lots of documentation. They will want to know all the symptoms, so they can be sure that you have the right diagnosis and have chosen the right cure. Analyticals like data and lots of it!

Figuring out people's styles and learning how to interact most effectively with each of them is fun! Don't get too stressed out about it. You can start off by practicing on your friends and family. You will be amazed at the results.

CHAPTER 16

Personal Growth and Development

You have learned in this book how to manage a project and how to coach, develop, and motivate your team members. You have learned techniques for keeping your team energized and enthusiastic and for helping them to avoid burnout. All the things that you have learned about managing other people also apply to you. As a manager, you must take a more active role in your own career development than perhaps you would if you were an individual contributor. You may be fortunate enough to have a manager who is as focused on developing his direct reports as you are on developing yours, but chances are that this will not be the case. Often when a person is managing other managers, he forgets that personal growth and development are just as important to a manager as they are to an individual contributor.

It is not your manager's responsibility to manage your career for you. Only you can do that. You will need to win the support of your manager if you are to grow and develop in the areas that are important to you. Your manager may be so focused on achieving results that she doesn't have the time or the inclination to talk to you about your career goals. You need to work with your manager to make time for those discussions. You do not want to end up in a situation where the only way to advance your career is to move to a different company. Changing employers to advance may prove difficult if you have not developed the new skills that you need for a higher management position.

In this chapter we will give you some tools and methods for managing your personal growth and development.

Avoiding Burnout

So what happens when you find yourself focusing so much time and attention on ensuring that your team members are motivated and not getting burnt out that you are consistently working long hours to get your own tasks accomplished? In addition, perhaps your manager is pushing you to get more and more accomplished, and the only way you can deliver is to work 12 or 14 hours every day. If working long hours and weekends is becoming a pattern, you are heading for disaster. This solution to achieving your goals is self destructive and, in the long term, will also prove to be detrimental to the projects you work on. Though you may be seeing short-term results, and your tasks may be getting completed on time, this success will be short lived. You will end up hating your job and exhausted, and your personal and social life will be affected. When you do get time off you will be too worn out to do anything apart from sleeping or lying around watching TV. You will be burnt out and will have no fun!

You can avoid falling into this trap, but it is going to require some assertiveness and focused time management on your part. The most important thing to remember is that you are the one who puts the schedule together. Make sure that you are scheduling your own tasks in the same way that you are scheduling your team members' tasks. You do not need to list every single thing that you do, but you can estimate how much of your time per week is spent in regular meetings, updating the schedule, and other weekly tasks. You should then schedule your other tasks during the remaining time you have available each week. If your manager asks you to work on something extra, re-schedule one of your other tasks to a later date to accommodate it. Alternatively, if it does not seem to be a critical task to you, ask your manager how urgent it is. Ensure that you communicate the impact of taking on the additional work. Schedule your time so that you are working 40 hours per week (or whatever your standard work hours are per week). There will be times when you have to work late or on the weekend, but those should be for unanticipated issues or problems. If you find that you are unable to schedule all your tasks into your standard workweek, you need to work on prioritizing your tasks and either delegating them or dropping some all together. The "Personal Time Management" section later in this chapter goes into more detail and includes some valuable tools and techniques for managing your time more effectively.

Burnout can also occur from stress. Stress is not usually caused by having too much responsibility; it is caused by having too much to do or having too little control over your own time. For example, if you work for a micromanager, if your manager is constantly changing his mind about what his priorities are, or if your manager is pressuring and threatening you to continually deliver more than you are able, you are likely to be under a lot of stress. The constant changing of direction or being told how to do things will wear you down until you just don't care anymore. The feeling that, no matter how many hours you work, you will never be able to meet your manager's expectations will demotivate and exhaust you. You will feel lethargic, you will stop making decisions, you will not be leading your team effectively, you will dread going to work each day, and you will be watching the clock waiting for the time when you can get out of there. That is not a career; that is torture.

If you find yourself in this situation, you must talk to your manager about it. It is important to be frank without being accusatory. Tell your manager that the constant direction changes are taking up so much of your time, due to the rework that is involved, that you are unable to spend the time you need managing your team and your project effectively. Be forthright about the level of risk that this is introducing to your project. If she tells you to work more hours, be firm and let her know that it is not going to solve the root cause of the problem. It is treating the symptoms and not curing the disease.

If your manager is micromanaging, you need to be direct about that too. Tell him that you are finding it impossible to do your job effectively because he insists on you doing everything his way. Explain that you have good project management and leadership skills, which is why you were hired to manage the project. Make it clear that you need to manage things your way, in your own style, and that trying to do your job someone else's way is causing problems and not allowing you to perform at the level you are capable of.

If you are being pushed to take on more and more work, tell your manager that it is impossible for you to complete your tasks with quality if you do not have adequate time to work on them. Communicate to her that you are going to prioritize your work daily, and the noncritical tasks will go to the end of the to-do list. Let her know that your to-do list is available to her for review and that you are open to feedback about where specific tasks are on the prioritization list. Be clear that you see your first priority as making sure that the project is completed successfully (on time, on budget, and with high quality) and that you need to manage your tasks very closely to be able to achieve that. You should be respectful at all times, but remember that you have a responsibility to yourself and to your team to make sure that you have the support you need to manage the project in the most effective way. It is worth bearing in mind that your manager may be feeling the same pressure that he is piling on to you. A manager has a responsibility to protect his direct reports from unnecessary stress. Your manager may be protecting himself by passing the tasks on to you instead. Try to have some empathy and see the world through your manager's eyes because he could also be suffering from burnout. Being aware of this may help you in your approach to talking with your manager about the problem.

The signs that you are burnt-out may not be as obvious to you at work as they will be at home. If you find yourself too tired or unenthusiastic to do anything apart from work and sleep, you are burnt-out. If you have lost the desire to go out with your friends or to spend time with your family, you are burnt-out. If you are getting sick a lot and not able to fully recover from a cold before you get the next one, you are definitely run down and heading for trouble. If you are suffering from a lot of respiratory problems, your burnout could be compromising your immune system. If you are feeling short-tempered and defensive when dealing with everyday problems at work, this could be a sign that you are burnt-out. If you are constantly having dreams or nightmares about your job, you are displaying a classic sign of burnout that causes you to be unable to "switch off" even when you are outside the office.

Burnout can affect you both mentally and physically. It is important to balance a good, quality work life with a good, quality personal life. If your personal and social life is suffering, it will start to affect your work and vice versa. If you have given up working out at the gym because you "don't have the time," you are increasing your chances of getting burnt-out as well as increasing your chances of getting run down and becoming more susceptible to illness. You need to be happy and healthy and have good balance in your life to be an effective leader. You need to believe in your project and your team, and you need to enjoy the challenges that you face at work each day.

So what do you do if the preventative measures have not worked and you suddenly (or not so suddenly) find yourself in burnout mode? First, try to be aware of your body and your actions and recognize the early signs of burnout. The most important thing that you need to do is rest and spend time on things that are not related to work! If you are getting sick a lot, and you are taking time off but working while in your sick bed, you are not going to get better. You may appear to get better, but you will get sick again soon afterwards. The best cure for burnout is to go on vacation and not check your e-mail or voice mail. If you cannot take a week off from work then take a long weekend. Even if you can't get out of town, you can pretend you are a tourist for a day or two and do things locally in your own town that you would not usually do. Forget about work and forget about things that need to be done around the house. Get out and enjoy yourself and do not feel guilty about it. You will be amazed at how therapeutic it is to just get away from the stress for a while.

Another positive thing you can do is make sure that you have a regular exercise or work out routine. Exercise strengthens the immune system and is beneficial both physically and mentally. It is a great stress reliever. Once you are feeling more relaxed, you will need to take a good look at how you are managing your time both at work and at home and will need to be prepared to make some adjustments. Have you been spending a lot of your personal time complaining about your job or how much work you have to do? If you have, you really need to make some changes, and you need to make them fast! If you have not been out on the weekend for months, make it a point to go out for a day each weekend and do something fun. Make it a high priority task, so that when you have too many things to do and need to drop something, this is not the thing that you drop first. Drop going to the grocery store and eat out for a couple days until you have time to shop instead!

If you manage your mental health, your physical health will be improved too. If you manage your physical health, your mental health will improve. It's all about balance. If you avoid burnout, you will continue to love your job just as much after five years as you did after four months. If you really hate your job, and nothing you do is making it any better, it is probably time to look for another job. A word of warning: Beware of falling into the same trap again at a new company. If you work yourself into the ground again, let your manager push you into doing too much work, let your social life dwindle away, and stop going to the gym, it will be just a matter of time until you find yourself just as disillusioned in the new job as you were in the old one.

Personal Time Management

Time management is an important skill that is critical for you to learn and to put into practice. We are not talking about managing other people's time; we are talking about managing your time. This chapter is all about you and what you need to do for yourself. Without proper time management, you won't be concentrating on the most important tasks and could very likely end up running around in a frenzy without accomplishing very much. We can help you to avoid the "headless chicken" syndrome simply by introducing some effective time management techniques into your daily (and weekly) routine.

So many distracting things are going on around you, from people walking into your office to ask questions, to e-mails constantly arriving in your inbox, to phone calls from your manager. Even the hardest-working employee with the best of intentions can get sidetracked. How many times have you been in the middle of working on something and were called into a last-minute meeting? You get out of the meeting, get back to your desk, and try to continue working on your previous task, and then the phone rings. Your boss wants some numbers from you as soon as possible. You start working on the numbers, and your original task is pushed out once again. As your day progresses, more and more last-minute tasks come your way, and more and more distractions occur that make it difficult to accomplish any of them. After a few more days, you have started about 50 different tasks and completed none of them. How do you break out of this vicious cycle? How do you decide which tasks to work on first and which can wait? How do you figure out how to actually finish something that you have started?

To be a successful project manager, you need good time management skills. To appropriately prioritize and complete your tasks on time, you must learn how to use your time management skills effectively. Time is a precious resource and is always going to be in short supply. Because the time that you have available to you is so limited, you must learn how to make the most out of it and use every possible minute in the most appropriate way.

Working effectively is about getting things done and planning for the future. By effectively learning how to time manage, you learn how to focus on the right tasks and not sweat over the small, less-important tasks. Decision-making is a key aspect of time management. You need to make informed decisions about which tasks are important and which tasks can wait.

To be really organized and stay on top of your tasks, you should plan the next day at the end of the day before. If you maintain a high-level weekly and monthly schedule of tasks, this should not take too much time. By planning your day in advance, you avoid any distractions at the start of the day that may prevent you from accomplishing this task—for instance, your boss calling and telling you that you are needed in a last-minute meeting or your co-workers popping in to ask if you want to go get some coffee in the cafeteria. You will get a lot more accomplished if you know what you need to do each day as soon as you walk into work. You will be able to start working on it immediately and will not get sidetracked into doing 10 other things first.

Many tools and processes are available to project managers to assist with managing the project and the developers' time. Can these tools and processes be applied to the manager's own time? Yes, some of them can. As we mentioned before, the important thing to remember is that you are the one who puts the schedule together. You can schedule your own tasks in the same way that you are scheduling your team members' tasks. Before you can do this effectively, you need to ask yourself some really important questions. If you can answer these questions, you are already part way to being able to manage your time.

1. What are the most important things that you need to do to accomplish the project objectives?

2. Do you know how to prioritize your workload?

3. How much time do you spend each week working on recurring weekly and monthly tasks?

4. How much time do you spend on coaching and developing your team members?

5. How much time do you spend on average per week dealing with emergencies and putting out fires?

Whether you are able to answer these questions, there are some things that you can do right away to prepare for managing and scheduling your time.

First, keep a log of what you spend your time on each day. Log your time as you work on tasks. Do not wait until the end of the day or the week, because you will forget a lot of the things you worked on, and you will be guessing how much time you spent on those you can remember. It is not easy to log your time when you are constantly changing tasks and getting distracted, we know, but the data you are gathering is critical to your personal time management so you must make time to do it. You should continue with the time tracking for at least four weeks to build a really accurate picture of where you are spending your time.

After one week, you will be able start some analysis of your time-tracking data. You will have an idea of where you are spending most of your time, and you will very likely find some time that has been wasted working on relatively unimportant tasks. Each week that you analyze the data, you will find more and more eye-opening surprises about the way you use your time. After four weeks, you will be able to average how much time you spend on each task per week. You are accomplishing two goals with this data: The first is that you are identifying how much time you spend on specific tasks. The second is that you are identifying areas where you are spending too much time on low priority tasks. Figure 16.1 shows an example Personal Time Log. A Personal Time Log document is included on the CD-ROM that accompanies this book.

Date	Task/Activity	Scheduling	Meetings	Conflict resolution	Putting out fires	Documentation	Client meetings	Change Control	Personnel Issues	Recruitment	Training				TOTAL HRS
5/23	Client Meeting						2								2
	Scheduling	4													4
	Dealing with broken build issue				2										2
	Coordination meeting		1												1
															0
															0
															0
	TOTAL HOURS	4	1	0	2	0	2	0	0	0	0	0	0	0	9

Personal Time Log — *Project Name*

Figure 16.1: Personal Time Log.

At the same time that you track your actual time you also need to work on a plan to schedule your time. To accomplish this task, you will need to follow the four steps below:

1. Identify—List all of the tasks that need to be completed by you. Just make a list; don't worry about which ones are of higher importance just yet. This list should include attending meetings, coaching and developing your team members, responding to emergencies, taking the client out to lunch—basically anything and everything that is expected of you during the course of the project.

2. Separate Meetings from Tasks—Separate the meetings from the tasks on your list. The meetings should be entered into your calendar or time tracking software. The tasks should go onto your prioritized list.

3. Prioritize—Prioritize the tasks in order of importance. Is writing the project plan more important than getting quotes for the new development server? Make sure you identify only real priorities and tasks. Don't put on your list that you need to have lunch with your friend from the accounting depart-

ment. Unless it is required for the successful completion of the project, it doesn't belong on this list. Ask yourself whether you need to have one-on-one meetings with everyone on your team weekly or bi-weekly?

4. Set Deadlines—When does each task need to completed? Identify tasks that have specific and inflexible completion dates attached to them and make sure that they are prioritized accordingly. Give yourself deadlines to complete the tasks that do not have hard completion dates. If a task is highly critical but is not due for another eight weeks, then it should not necessarily be at the top of your priority list, yet. Make sure that you are accomplishing tasks in a methodical way. Do not make the mistake of prioritizing the easy tasks first just because you can complete them quickly. It is tempting, but it is not good time management.

5. Delegate—Can you, or should you, delegate any of your tasks to someone else? There may be sections of documents that can be delegated to members of your technical team. There could be some PowerPoint presentations that your administrative assistant could create for you. Do you really need to attend all the meetings on your calendar? If your technical lead is also invited to the same meeting, could one or the other of you go rather than both of you?

We included meetings in the original list so that you could add them to your calendar or delegate them to someone else, if appropriate. Some of your tasks will be driven by your meetings—for example, writing minutes, reading minutes and documents, and meeting preparation. If you deleted some meetings from your schedule, you may also be able to delete some of the tasks associated with them.

Now what? You have your prioritized list; what do you do with it?

- Once you have your list of priorities completed, start on the most important one first (not the ones that you can complete the fastest). If you feel that a task is too big, reduce the scope by breaking it down into smaller subtasks.

- As you complete each task, mark it off your list and start working on the next one. At the end of each day, you will be able to see what you have accomplished and feel like you are making progress. By checking the tasks off the list as you complete them, you will easily be able to pick up where you left off if you are pulled into meetings or have to take phone calls while you are in the middle of a task.

- Update and reprioritize your list on a daily basis. At the beginning of each day your list should be complete and accurate. If your boss asks you to do something, prioritize it and add it to the list. It may not need to be done immediately.

- Concentrate on completing one task at a time. Don't try to do multiple items at once because you will start to get frustrated when, instead of having one task 100% complete, you have three tasks at 33% complete each. You will not feel like you have accomplished very much at the end of the day or the week. At times you will have tasks that are started but not completed because you may start one and then de-prioritize it due to project changes, or you may be waiting for information from someone else to complete the task. If this is the case, you should move onto the next task until you are able (or it is appropriate) to complete the partially completed ones.

Lastly, don't procrastinate. Everyone has done it at some time. If there is a less-than-exciting task that needs to be done, it is tempting to move it down the list, regardless of the importance level. This is not going to help you in the long run. There will always be something that you have to do that you just don't want to do. Don't drag it out. If it belongs at the top of the priority list, make sure that is where it is. Get started and get it completed as soon as you can. If you are one of those people who always wait until the very last minute (you know who you are), you need to change that behavior. Otherwise the work is going to be completed with low quality and very likely behind schedule. The longer you leave it, the higher your anxiety level will be when you are rushing to complete it on time. Figure 16.2 shows the Task List Process workflow.

If you are a procrastinator, you need to overcome it. It is no excuse for not getting things done in a timely manner and with the appropriate level of quality. Imagine that you really dislike (despise even) the financial part of project management, so you wait until the very last minute to get the numbers done. You rush the job, and it turns out that the figures you deliver are not accurate. This, in turn, causes the project to have cost overruns and results in the project not being completed within budget. Consequently, your project has an unsuccessful outcome because you waited until the last minute and then rushed putting the numbers together. How easily that could have been avoided!

Here is a great technique for minimizing stress: If you have two tasks that are of the same importance, work on the one that you consider "the worst" or "the hardest" one first. Commit to getting that task completed no matter what distractions you experience. This will lower your anxiety level because once the task is complete you can move on with your other tasks without the thought of the big gnarly task haunting you.

At the end of each day, ask yourself, "What did I accomplish today?" and, "What took up too much of my time?" If you are spending way too much time attending unnecessary or relatively unimportant meetings, or engaged in inappropriately lengthy or irrelevant conversations, you need to be aware of the problem so that you can resolve it. In the technology industry, we tend to spend quite a bit of time in meetings that turn out to have little value to us or to our projects. Make sure that you know where you are spending your time. Be cognizant of the time-waster tasks and distractions that affect your ability to complete your tasks efficiently. Time wasters are the unimportant things that interrupt you from getting your work done, like phone calls, e-mails, and co-workers dropping by just to say "hi" or discuss their weekend. Some of these distractions will be important, and it will be appropriate for you to put aside what you are doing to deal with them. Others will most definitely not be worthy of your precious time. They key to good time management is to be aware of where you are spending your time. Don't spend too much time documenting your day, but make time to do it. In the final analysis, don't be surprised if you find that you can reclaim about 20% of your time that was being lost on unimportant and inappropriate tasks.

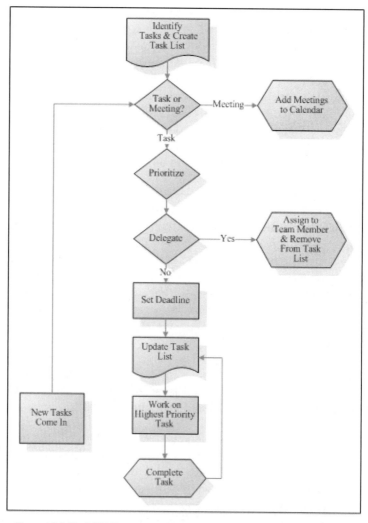

Figure 16.2: Task List Process workflow.

Ongoing Growth and Development

Earlier in the book, you learned some great techniques for growing and developing your team members. Who is working on your growth and development? If your manager is working with you on your growth and development and takes an active role in your career development, then you are very fortunate and are probably in the minority. Even with a very supportive manager, it is you that has to put in the effort to continually work on your growth and development. Just because you are busy, don't put this on the back burner thinking that you will get to it one day when you have more time. You will never have more time. You need to prioritize this with your other tasks and responsibilities and make time to work on it. Prioritizing it does not necessarily mean that it will be more critical than all your other responsibilities and tasks, but it does mean that you need to schedule time to work on it.

First thing give some thought to what is important to you. Create your own Personal Development Plan and use it as your template for deciding in what areas you want to improve or learn new skills. If you are new in a job, don't think that you need to wait a couple of years before focusing on this. If you do not focus some time and energy on your personal growth and development–planning now, you will be in exactly the same place in two years as you are today. Then, in two years time it may take you two more years to get to where you want to be. It is really important to have a plan, even if you do not need to do very much immediately to implement your plan. Without a plan, you will be working each day with no direction and no end result in mind. You would not manage your project from day to day without having a plan or a schedule with milestones and a clearly defined objective. If you did, your project would not be successful. You would have no way of knowing whether it was completed on time or whether you met the objectives if you had no specified timeline or objectives before you started! Your life and your career are more important in the whole scheme of things than one technology project, so give your life plan the attention that it deserves.

In your Personal Development Plan, you will be able to define some obvious areas where you need to develop more skill or have formal training, and your manager may have already pointed those areas out to you. Some of your learning will be done on the job and will develop through experience, and some will need some focused learning. You may have some other development areas that are not as obvious to you or your manager. For example, there will be some areas where you want to learn and gain more knowledge and understanding even though it is not critical to your current role. There will be some new skills that you want to develop so that you can take on more responsibility or be assigned to more complex projects. All these things need to be planned so that you do not get too busy or forget to work on them.

Your Personal Development Plan can be a bulleted list or can be written essay style. Sharing your plan with your manager is a great idea, but there is no guarantee that she will see the value of it. Imagine seeing these kinds of plans from everyone on your team. How much insight are you gaining into how they think and what motivates them? You will likely gain just as much insight into what makes you tick by writing your own plan. It is often surprising to put down your own goals and dreams in writing and realize that you had never really thought about your life in such a complete way before. Make sure that you date your plan. You will need to update it every few months (or more often if you have a significant life event). It is a great way to keep track of your career progress and to see how your goals and dreams change over the years.

A blank Personal Development Plan template is included on the CD-ROM that accompanies this book.

Just because the Personal Development Plan separates short-, medium-, and long-term goals, it does not mean that you should only focus on the short-term ones. To achieve the medium- and long-term goals, you will need to start working on some of them in the short to medium term to complete them on time. The Personal Development Plan can be used as a basis to create a Career Plan that contains the hows as well as the whats that you need to achieve your goals. We cover Career Plans in the next section. You will likely need help from your manager, a human resources person, or a mentor at your company on some of things in your plan—how to get promoted is one area, for instance. Find out what qualities and skills the company seeks in senior project managers, directors, and vice presidents. Make sure that you are developing those qualities and skills. You need to be prepared!!

Not all of your personal development can be accomplished on company time. Some of it is not appropriate to be worked on during company time. Many Personal Development Plans include personal items that are important to the individual. These are obviously not things that will be accomplished during the time the individual is in the workplace. Having personal goals on a development plan can be really helpful, especially where it indicates significant life events (getting married, having children, buying a house, or going back to school part-time, for instance) because these things indicate where the individual's primary focus may switch from work to personal at certain times. These times happen for everyone. If you are able to schedule some of them, you are able to work them into the plan. You will never be able to anticipate every event in your life, so expect some surprises during your career. Some people are not comfortable putting personal goals into a work document and that is fine. Whatever works for the individual is appropriate for the plan. Do whatever you feel most comfortable with.

To grow and develop, you will need feedback from your manager. Ensure that you get some time to meet with her to discuss your personal goals. You may find that many of the meetings you have with your boss are very task oriented. It is your responsibility to ask your manager for what you need. You definitely need more than status and task assignment meetings!

A great way to identify areas for growth and development is to check the career Web sites or the career section of the classified ads in the newspaper. What specific skills, education, and experience are companies seeking for their project manager positions? Are most companies requiring that candidates hold a specific degree or be certified or licensed by a professional organization? By staying aware of industry trends, you can be sure that you are keeping current with the trends (or perhaps even a little ahead of them). You will be well positioned for any major changes that occur in regards to project manager qualifications and training. For example, if the industry standard is becoming that all project managers need a master's degree, how long will it be before your organization is asking the same from you?

You should always be striving to improve. If not, you will be underperforming. Your company will expect more from you as you gain more experience and they pay you more money each year. Status quo does not go hand in hand with good project management skills. There are always more classes, books, online training, and in-house learning that you can do to keep your skills up to date and your knowledge current. Technology changes so quickly that you need to be constantly vigilant to keep up with it. Do not let yourself slip behind with your skills or knowledge. It will suddenly creep up on you, and you will realize that you are no longer very employable. You may see more inexperienced project managers assigned the prime projects because they have knowledge and understanding of the new technology. The worst crime you can commit against yourself is deciding that you do not need to learn about these new-fangled technologies because there will always be a demand for the things you know. You are an experienced project manager after all, right?

Don't delude yourself. You may still find projects that need you, but you will end up working on the maintenance projects rather than new development projects. You could find yourself managing a team that works on bug fixes for systems that went out of production 6, 10, or 12 years ago. If this was your career choice—perhaps you were ready for a less demanding project—then all is well and good. However, if you had plans to be vice president of technology or CIO, you will have definitely gone in the wrong direction! We have seen this happen to project managers so many times, and it is very difficult to catch up on lost time once you are a year or two behind your peers. Don't be fooled into thinking that no one else is working on their long-term career plans, either. Believe us, if they are ambitious and career oriented, they are.

Great ways of identifying areas for improvement are by taking part in a 360 feedback program. A 360 is where your superiors, your peers, and your subordinates are asked for anonymous feedback on how you perform in a large number of specific areas. You are also asked to rate yourself in the same areas. You will be given an analysis of your performance based on the feedback, together with where the gaps are between how well you think you are doing and how well the respondents think you are doing.

It is interesting to note where you might be doing a great job in the eyes of your team but not in the eyes of your superiors. This indicates that you need to do some campaigning and advertising of your methods and results to the more senior management team. On the other hand, you may see that your superiors think you are doing great, but your subordinates are very disappointed in your performance in a specific area. This indicates that you are spending a lot of time talking yourself up to your superiors and not enough time managing your team effectively. You need to find out what your team need from you, what is lacking, and how you can fix the problem.

Whatever the results, you will see that there is a lot of room for improvement. The 360s are tough, and it is always hard to get so much honest feedback. It is a great opportunity to focus on improvements, but you must first get over your sulking about people saying bad things about you (it will happen). Believe us when we tell you that you need to prepare yourself for it and be open to whatever feedback you get. You don't get to defend yourself. Get to work on the issues, improve in the areas that need improvement, and hopefully you will get better results next time.

Career Planning

Career planning is vitally important to any professional, yet it is amazing how many people leave their careers to chance. Some have a vague idea of where they see themselves in a few years, and others have a really clear idea of where they want to be in the future. Interestingly, there are not many people from either group who have planned how they are going to get there. They just assume that if they work hard, it will happen. It is possible to achieve your goals without a Career Plan, but it is far more likely that you will get what you want, and within your desired time frame, if you are consistently working in a focused manner towards your goals.

Career planning goes hand in hand with personal development. To successfully manage your career and deliver on your personal objectives, you will need a clearly defined Career Plan in addition to your Personal Development Plan. Both of these plans will need to be updated from time to time. It is good practice to review your plans every three to six months and update them as necessary. Even if there have been no changes, it is good for you to get a regular change of perspective from short-term (your project) to long-term (your career goals) lest you forget, in the mayhem of your day-to-day life, that you have a master plan.

Your Career Plan should take your career goals from your Personal Development Plan. If the goals in these two documents are not in synch with one another, then you have a problem. You should review both documents to find out where the anomalies lie and fix them. The Career Plan will take only the career-related goals and will put a timeline on achieving them. It will also list the steps that you need to take and the things that you need to achieve to reach those goals. Be realistic with your timelines. It is highly unlikely that you will rise from junior project manager to CIO in three years! Defining the steps that lead to the attainment of each goal will help you with putting a realistic timeline on your Career Plan. For example, if you need to complete your master's degree before one of your goals can be reached and you know that it will take four years to get the master's (assuming that you spend X number of hours per week working on it), then you know that you are not going to be able to achieve that goal in less than four years.

A sample Career Plan can be found in Figure 16.3, and a blank Career Plan Document is included on the CD-ROM that accompanies this book.

Fundamentals of Technology Project Management
Project Name

Document Name Template

Career Plan

Name: Daryl Johnson
Date: May 26th

Date	Milestone	Steps to achieve milestone
20XX	Promotion to senior project management position	• Get assigned larger and more complex projects • Increase Project management skills • Certification in PM discipline • Certification or training in people management and conflict management
20XX	Promotion to group project management position	• Work on multiple projects at a time • Project manager for different technology groups and departments • More interaction with clients • Certification in management • Continued learning in new technologies • Certification in quality management
20XX	Promotion to director position	• Proven track record managing other managers • Experience managing different departments across the organization • Certification or training in public speaking / communication • Gain understanding of business groups and their role • Work more closely with senior management on strategic projects • Continued learning on business management, managing managers and new technologies
20XX	Move into the business side of the company (instead of technology) at Director level	• Complete masters in business management • Get involved in strategic direction/planning for the company • Take business writing & visual presentation classes • Continued learning in areas of business/finance
20XX	Vice President position in company in new business or emerging markets/technologies	• Get assigned projects that help shape strategic direction for company • Lead and implement some key business initiatives • Gain specialized knowledge and experience in new business areas • Contributing at executive level on high visibility initiatives

Page █ of █
Created by "Author"

Figure 16.3: Career plan.

To move to the next level in an organization, you will need to demonstrate specific skills that are required to be effective in the desired role. It is not always possible to gain experience with the necessary skills while you are in your current position. So, what happens if you cannot get the promotion unless you can demonstrate competency in specific areas and you do not have the required level of competency because you have not had the opportunity to work on those things in your current role? The most likely consequence is that you will be passed over for promotion. It is unlikely that your employers will overlook a lack of competency just because you don't need that skill in your current job.

In addition, you should not assume that your manager, or the company you work for, is grooming you for promotion and that because you have been there for x years that you are in line for a more senior position. If you have not been told explicitly that you are being groomed for a new position, you should ask whether you are. You can ask your manager for help while you are building and enhancing the skills that you need for your next career move, but you cannot expect him to do the work for you. You may need to take classes or self-study during your own time to be ready to ask for the promotion you want.

If you have a Career Plan that has you moving into a more senior role in two years, do you know whether that is possible with your current company? How do you get promoted? Is the company growing and creating more openings at that level regularly enough for you to stand a chance? Does someone have to leave the company (or be promoted up) for an opportunity to become available? If so, what is the current and historical attrition rate? Are there any employees in those positions who look ready to be promoted, retire, or leave the company in your desired time frame? How many other employees at your level have their eyes on the same prize that you do? Is the company you work for a small, family-owned business where no positions are available above the one that you have?

If you can see that the opportunities are not going to be available with your current employer, then you need to think about how you are going to achieve your goals. You may need to consider changing employers. It may not be possible for you to make a move to a new company and a step up at the same time. You may need to consider a sideways move to a new company that can offer you the promotion opportunities that you desire.

Career planning can be a complex process. Timing is as important as preparation. Recognizing opportunities when they present themselves is vital to successful career management. It is no good if you find out about a great promotion opportunity by reading the e-mail announcing that one of your peers has just been promoted to the position that you are interested in! Most companies have an online career Web site where they list all the current open positions. Check the Web site weekly and keep up to date about what is going on within the company, which departments are hiring, and why new positions are opening (growth, attrition, or promotion). Talk to someone in the human resources department about your goals and ask them to let you know whether a position is about to become available that would be a great opportunity for you. Network with other managers and other executives and let them know your career goals. Find a mentor to help you prepare for that next step. All these suggested actions are geared towards you actively managing your own career and creating your own opportunities.

A well-managed career, just like a well-managed project, will result in a successful outcome!

Developing New Skills

You may be thinking that it is really hard to find the time to work on developing new skills when you are so overwhelmed and overworked managing the everyday tasks of being a project manager. However, if you do not learn new skills, you will stagnate, and after a time, you will start to get bored with your job. You will also become less effective in your current role because you will be falling behind your team members and peers in experience and knowledge.

You not only need to develop new skills to move to the next rung on your career ladder; you also need to learn new skills to maintain and increase your effectiveness in your current role.

Much of the new skill development will occur as part of doing your job everyday. For example, after you have created and managed four or five project schedules, you will have a higher level of skill with scheduling than when you started. If you have not done much scheduling yet, you may find it hard to believe that scheduling requires skill that goes beyond understanding how the tools work. You will learn that there is an art to creative and effective scheduling. The more skilled you become, the more smoothly your projects will run, and the less schedule risk you have to assume for your project.

Communication is an area where we never stop learning. You can always improve. The better your communication skills, the more effective a leader you will be. It is relatively easy to tell how junior someone is—whether they are on the technical team or the management team—by their level of skill in communicating. The polish, the nonconfrontational manner, the lack of defensiveness, and the ability to make others feel that their contributions are valuable are all traits of an experienced communicator.

As you develop your communication skills, you will learn how to leave personal feelings and emotions outside the boardroom or meeting room. Good communication skills allow you to manage up, manage down, and manage your peers. Being able to influence others and reach consensus in a calm and dignified manner are highly valuable skills. Remember though that one outburst in a meeting, or one negative comment that is overheard in the hallway, could set you back years. Your credibility could go down the toilet overnight. At all times, be respectful and honest, manage negativity in others, nurture positivism in yourself, and most important of all, leave a good impression.

People management is another area where you can never stop learning. You can learn both on the job and by reading books or attending classes. The more skilled you become, the more productive your team will be and the more smoothly your project(s) will run.

Staying on top of new technologies; new project management tools, techniques, and processes; and new development tools and processes are all essential for effective project management. Make time to develop your skills and knowledge in the areas that are important to you, your team, and your company. Track your progress so that you can identify in which areas you have developed a higher level of skill or knowledge. Make a point of asking for feedback from your manager on the areas that you should be developing or improving.

Continued skill development is necessary to ensure that you maintain a high level of employability. No matter how great you are doing in your job, it is always possible that something could happen that would cause the company to downsize or go out of business. It can happen to even the most (seemingly) successful businesses. Don't assume that you are indispensable or irreplaceable. Never get overconfident about your position or importance to the company. If you maintain employability, you are planning for the worst and hoping for the best—the project manager's mantra!

Employability is relevant to your current role too. Not everyone can be assigned the best or the highest-profile projects. Your project management skills will determine where you are in relation to your peers when it comes to who gets assigned what. Keep yourself at the top of the list. Working on the high-visibility projects will get you noticed and, if your Career Plan includes promotions, will make sure that senior management knows who you are and what you can do when they see your resume submitted for that directorship.

Climbing the Corporate Ladder

Before you embark on your journey to get to each consecutive rung on the corporate ladder as fast as possible, ask yourself why you want to get there. What is it about the next rung on the ladder that appeals to you? More responsibility can bring with it more headaches, more risk, and longer working hours. Are you ready for that? What are you going to do at that next rung that will be significant? What will you be remembered for? It is fine and dandy to have a goal to be promoted, but do you fully understand what you might be getting yourself into? Do you want the promotion, or are you trying to get it because your partner wants you to and is already planning the new things you will be able to afford with your higher salary? Is it because your parents expect it? Are you following in a father's, mother's, or sibling's footsteps? Are you sure that it is what you want? Are you climbing the right ladder? If the answer is "yes", how do you know?

These are tough questions, and you should give them a lot of thought. If you are happy in your current job, be sure that you really want to change it before you get glassy eyed over that window office on the third floor! Once you move up, it is not possible to move down gracefully. It is not common for someone who is underperforming in a new (promotion) position to be demoted back to their previous role with all their benefits and self-respect intact. It is more common that they will be fired and lose all their benefits along with quite a lot of confidence. Make sure that you are up to the job. Do not lie about your knowledge, skills, or enthusiasm to get a promotion. It is bound to backfire on you at some point. The higher up the corporate ladder you go, the less room there is for mistakes. You will have more eyes on you, and the stakes are much higher. A small mistake at a higher level could have monumental repercussions.

If you get an interview for a promotion, the chances are that you will be asked some thought-provoking questions. It is common to be asked what it is about the new role that appeals to you and why you believe you are a good fit for the position. Make sure that you are well prepared with honest and insightful answers.

Advancing up the corporate ladder can be done in a variety of ways. We would recommend that you do it by building relationships, earning respect, and proving your effectiveness and value to the company. We would not recommend that you get there by backstabbing, taking no prisoners, and leaving a trail of dead bodies in your wake. Both of these methods may result in a promotion, but only one of them will result in you feeling good about your achievements. Remember that success is also measured by how you achieve something and not just what you achieve. Getting a promotion and having no friends to celebrate with because you stomped all over them to get what you wanted is a pretty sad state of affairs. Though it is possible for people with little integrity to get promoted, and most of us have worked with someone who appears to be in this category, it is not the best way to advance in your career. Making other people look bad to get positive attention for yourself is only going to get you so far. The higher up the ladder you go, the fewer peers you have, so the harder it becomes to cheat and lie your way to the next level.

It is a sad fact of life in corporate America that people who suck up to the boss but are otherwise incompetent can often do well in an organization. Everyone knows that the person is incompetent, it seems, apart from the boss! How can this happen? It happens when there is a lack of open communication within the company and particularly on the senior management team. It also happens when people allow their judgment to be influenced by flattery or hearsay. Evaluate people on their personal merit and do not allow gossip and backstabbing to affect your judgment or decision-making. Most important of all, do not allow your ego to get in the way of making good, common sense decisions.

Playing fair is important in the business world. In recent times, we have been shocked to hear about some high-profile companies where personal ambition and greed on the part of senior executives overruled common sense. These behaviors resulted in the collapse of the companies, losses of millions of dollars for many investors, and prison terms for some of the employees. There is no excuse for not conducting yourself with integrity, honesty, and good ethics. This is true no matter where you are in the organization today or where you want to be tomorrow and into the future. Do not allow greed to lead you down the path of making bad or illegal decisions. Aside from your personal integrity, you could be arrested and you could go to prison. It really isn't worth it.

If you strive for advancement without cutting corners, you will achieve personal success as well as the respect of your co-workers. You will be proud of yourself for climbing the ladder in a way that sets an example to others, and you will be able to truly enjoy your success. It will be a success that is honestly earned and well deserved.

The most important thing you should remember about climbing the corporate ladder is to never burn your bridges. Be courteous and polite to everyone you encounter on your journey to the top. If they do not treat you with the same respect, that is no excuse for lowering yourself to their level. If you refuse to rise to the bait, others will stop trying to bait you! Never think that because someone or something is not important to you now that the person or thing will never be important to you. You should treat people well whether they are important to your career or not. Everyone deserves to be treated with dignity and respect. If this is not enough to convince you, consider this old proverb: "Be careful how you treat those you meet on the way up as you may meet them again on the way down." There is a lot of truth to this statement. You never know whom you will encounter during your career. The intern who delivers the mail to your desk today may be the CEO of a company that you want to work for in 20 years. One of your developers may be your boss one day. Make sure that what they learn from you about management is how you would like to be managed.

Most important, remember that this journey is supposed to be fun, and it is supposed to enrich your life, not prevent you from having one! Happiness is success.

Case Study

Project Name: OFIS
(Order Fulfillment and Inventory System)

XYZ Corporation is the company that implemented the OFIS project. XYZ is a software and Internet development company located in Tucson, Arizona and Boston, Massachusetts, USA. XYZ has a development team of 500 employees and a total workforce of 750 employees. XYZ Corporation has a successful business model demonstrated by consistent growth and increased revenues over the past eight years.

ABC Inc. is a Florida-based fashion wholesale distributor specializing in mass-produced designer label clothing. After a successful merger, in 1997, between AB Designs and Chloe Fashions, ABC Inc. became the leading distributor of designer fashion products in the Western United States. As of today, ABC Inc. has grown its staff to over 5,000 employees and its distribution network to all 50 States.

Project Team

XYZ Corporation

- Sponsor—Paulette Green
- Project Manager—Daryl Johnson
- Subject Matter Expert (SME) Consultant—Kevin Roth
- Technical Lead—David Moss
- Software Engineer—Roger Brady
- Software Engineer—Sharon Helstrom
- Software Engineer—Manuel Gomez
- Software Engineer—Jane Jones
- UI Designer and Programmer—Matsu Liu
- Graphic Designer—Maria Brown

- Systems Engineer—Tim Timmons
- Database Administrator (DBA)—Vin Patel
- Marketing and Product Manager—Stuart Perry
- Usability Coordinator—Ginger Freeman
- Quality Assurance (QA) Manager—Jeff Sterling
- QA Engineer—Mark Terry
- QA Engineer—Melanie Charles
- Administrative Assistant—Terri Compton
- Business Analyst—Susan Chen

ABC Inc. (Client)

- Project Manager—Cal Smith
- Program Manager—Robin English

External Partners (Vendors)

- TLC Hardware Ltd
- ACME Consulting

Project Description

The goal of the OFIS (Order Fulfillment and Inventory System) project was to port ABC'S existing internal enterprise order management software system to the Internet.

Business Case

Over the past seven years, ABC has grown from having a relatively small retailer customer base in a few states to a distribution network of over 2,000 retailers in 50 states. ABC is in the process of securing wholesale distribution contracts with a number of international businesses.

ABC's call center has grown significantly over the last few years. Due to the multiple time zones they are servicing, the call center needs to be operational for approximately 12 hours per day. By integrating the current order management system with the inventory system and moving it to the Internet, the company could offer access to retailers to place orders, get status on current orders, get quotes, view the current catalogue, and check available inventory 24/7 while reducing costs as follows:

- Call center 60%
- Sales 20%
- Marketing 60%

The Problem

The current ordering and inventory management system requires that ABC's retailers phone or fax their orders to the ABC sales office in Florida. The retailers are sent printed catalogues that are updated every two months. The operators take over-the-phone orders from retailers and enter the orders manually into the existing Order Management System (OMS). Orders are also received by fax and by mail on ABC order forms. The OMS is a proprietary system that was written in 1995, for Chloe Fashions and that ABC continued to use after the merger in 1997.

The order management and the inventory system are not seamlessly integrated. Both the order management and inventory systems use the same back-end Oracle database, but the operators have to open the inventory screen to check availability before switching to the order screen to enter the order. The order management component of the system does not know whether there is sufficient inventory to fulfill the order. Two of the biggest problems with this process are that the shipping department has to manually update the inventory database every time an order is sent out, and the current process is that they update the inventory in the database after the order has been packaged for shipping. The inventory is also manually updated by the warehouse when supplies are received from manufacturers, but there is often a one or two day delay between the order being received and the inventory system being updated by the warehouse manager.

The end result of these issues is that the inventory screen is never 100% accurate. This leads to all kinds of problems with retailers being told that the goods are in stock when they are not. The operators often tell retailers that the goods are on back order when the database shows that the stock is available but where the stock levels are looking a bit low. They do this to allow for the inaccuracy.

Another problem that arises from the inaccurate inventory is that the operators are unable to give retailers an accurate date for when their back ordered stock is due to come in. The operator checks the manufacturer order screen to find out when the stock is due to arrive. What they do not see is how many other back orders there are for those items. As a result, managing back orders is a hit-and-miss process.

Key Business Requirements

- System needs the ability to significantly increase distribution network without increasing headcount.
- System must be implemented to support 4,000 retailers and have the scalability to support 8,000 retailers.
- Order management, back orders, inventory, and account information must be seamlessly integrated.
- Call center screen must have ability to show all account and order information on one screen.
- Existing Oracle database must be used for back-end.
- Retailer account numbers must not change.
- Product numbers must not change.
- System must integrate with the billing and accounting system.
- Warehouse system must support bar codes.
- Processes need to be created and documented for sales, warehouse, and shipping.
- Functional training for sales, warehouse, shipping, and accounting.
- Technical training for onsite webmaster, systems administrator, and database administrator.

Challenges

- Switching from the old system to the new system when they are both using the same database (the existing database)
- Testing the new system using a production database
- Training staff on new systems and processes
- Convincing retailers to switch from the phone to the Internet without giving the retailers any training on the new system

Solution

Frontend

- The OFIS system is a Business to Business (B2B) online order fulfillment system. The Web site utilizes a shopping cart technology. The online catalogue is available for viewing to anyone on the Internet, but the shopping cart functionality is available only to authenticated users. All users must have a user name and password to log on to the Web site.

- The call center continues to use the existing desktop PC computer systems. The retailer Web site and the operator interface utilize the existing Oracle database on the back-end, allowing the operators access to the operator screens via the Web interface similar to that used on the Web site by the retailers. The operators have the ability to assist users with entering their order on the Web site real time. They also have the ability to change or cancel orders for retailers. The operators have the ability to enter orders for retailers who continue to phone, fax, or mail their orders.

- The shopping cart calculates shipping costs, discounts (both volume and customer).

- The site is designed for ease of use. The screens are logical and intuitive. A comprehensive demo and help system is built into the Web site. The Web site includes full search functionality. Retailers can view and copy past orders to save time reentering similar orders multiple times. All retailer account numbers and product ID numbers are the same as the ones used in the old computer system.

Backend

- ABC's current business systems are on the Unix platform and their data center team has a high level of skill working in a Unix environment. Therefore, XYZ implemented the OFIS system on the Unix platform.

- The site supports automated e-mails that notify retailers that an order has been received, processed, or shipped. They also notify retailers when back ordered items are received in stock or if the back order delivery date changes.

- The warehouse and shipping departments utilize bar code scanners for checking inventory in and out. The bar code readers interface directly with the inventory database, removing the manual steps required for updating the system.

- The administrative functions (for system administrators) are accessible via a full GUI interface.

- The shopping cart is integrated with the existing accounting system so that invoices can be printed and mailed by the accounts department without reentering any data.

- Retailers' order histories are stored in the database and linked to their accounts.

- The database has an update function for editing, adding, or removing products. These functions are accessible via a user-friendly GUI interface.

- OFIS manages back orders on a first-come-first-served basis, and the back ordered inventory is calculated to give an accurate due by date for product. This date is automatically updated if the supplier changes the ship date.

Process

- Training programs were offered for both functional and technical users of the OFIS system who are employees of ABC.

- Business analysts created workflow process for warehouse, shipping, and accounting departments.

Benefits

- Decrease call center, marketing, and sales costs

- 100% Return on Investment (ROI) within one year

- Improve coordination and productivity

- Improve retailer experience

- Competitive advantage by giving customers real-time access to product information and simplifying the procurement process, making it easier for retailers to do business with ABC

What Went Right

- Offered discounts to retailers who used the online services, which exceeded the anticipated early adoption rate.

- The project team's Subject Matter Expert (SME) had extensive international e-commerce business experience, which resulted in a very high-quality, bug-free Web site that supported multiple currencies.

- To have a competitive advantage in the global market, XYZ's project team implemented multiple language GUI frontends and built-in the ability to add additional language GUIs with ease.

- The formal and informal communication between XYZ Corporation, ABC Inc., ACME Consulting, and TLC Hardware Ltd. project managers led to minimal integration issues and superior cross-organization teamwork.

- The deployment was completed on schedule within the planned 12-hour time frame.

What Went Wrong

- Language barriers with the warehouse and shipping departments were a problem. There were a large number of employees that were limited in their English language skills. Training of the staff took more time because most of the training had to be done verbally because the staff was not able to comprehend the English training manual.

- Staff members were resistant to changes because they foresaw a potential downsize in the company. ABC Inc. held a meeting with senior management to inform them that there were no potential layoffs in the immediate future and that the new system was merely allowing the company to minimize hiring any new employees. Workforce would be reduced only through attrition and not through layoffs.

- The system was not handled to check for duplicate orders. After launch, it was found that if retailers were on a slow connection, it took some time to get the confirmation page. Some retailers clicked the submit button more than once and received multiple orders. The quick fix for this was to put in a warning to inform the retailers to only press the submit button once. The DBA at ABC Inc. set up an automatic duplicate order report to run at the end of each day. This report was reviewed by the call center each morning to check for multiple orders and contact retailers for verification and manually delete duplicate orders.

Project Success

Over the course of your career as a project manager, you will learn a lot of tips and tricks that will help you to complete your projects successfully. You will find that project success factors are generally process or people related. Whether you are a new project manager with no list of success tips or a more experienced project manager with a few projects under your belt, we would advise that you take note of the Five Keys to Project Success and keep them handy. They may be obvious, but they are often overlooked.

The factors that can make a project unsuccessful go hand in hand with the factors that make a project successful. Though some projects will fail due to forces outside your control, most failures are avoidable. If you are aware of the most common pitfalls, you can focus on taking preventative action. The Top 10 Reasons Projects Fail are key hazards to avoid for project success.

Five Keys to Project Success

1. The project has an a clearly defined sponsor as well as the necessary organizational (senior management) and client support, which includes project input and feedback on an ongoing basis.

2. The project goals, objectives, and scope are clearly defined. Everyone on the project team has a common understanding of, and fully supports, the goals and objectives.

3. The project plan is clearly defined and documented. The tasks, responsibilities, budget, and schedule included in the project plan are agreed upon, and each project team member understands and accepts their personal responsibilities.

4. The project team embraces open and honest communication and work together towards building a strong, productive, and mutually respectful team.

5. The project has clearly defined and understandable processes and procedures.

Top 10 Reasons Projects Fail

1. Lack of buy-in or support from the project sponsor, senior management, or the client.

2. Lack of clearly defined and documented project management and technical processes.

3. Inaccurate estimates.

4. Unrealistic expectations.

5. Team members are inexperienced or lack the appropriate training or skill sets.

6. Ineffective or nonexistent of change control.

7. Poor team motivation.

8. Adding new team members mid-project.

9. Lack of client input or involvement in the project.

10. Lack of adequate quality assurance testing.

The Project Manager's Toolkit

Various project management, planning, and organizational tools are available. Most companies have standard software and tracking tools that employees are required to use. There are so many options available when choosing what software to use for tracking and managing your projects that it can make your head spin. In this appendix, we have listed a few of the more popular packages.

Project Planning and Control Software

- Microsoft Project (largest market share)
- Kidasa
- Kidasa Milestones
- AMS Realtime
- Primavera SureTrak Project Manager
- eProject Enterprises

E-Mail and Calendaring

- Microsoft Outlook
- Eudora

Presentations

- Microsoft PowerPoint
- Webex

Diagrams and Flowcharts

- Microsoft Visio
- Smartdraw

List of Recommended Reading

There are thousands of books available about project management, quality management, people management, and project management tools and methodologies. Here we have listed a few personal recommendations:

The Management and Control of Quality by James Evans and William Lindsay

Project Management: A Systems Approach to Planning, Scheduling, and Controlling by Harold Kerzner

Quality Software Project Management by Robert Futrell and Donald Shafer.

Project Management in the Fast Lane: Applying the Theory of Constraints" by Robert Newbold

Microsoft Office Project 2003 Step by Step by Carl Chatfield and Timothy Johnson

First, Break all the Rules by Marcus Buckingham and Curt Coffman

You should make it a point to speak to other project managers in your organization to ask for book recommendations. Be sure to ask them why they recommend each book, what they learned from it, and how it helped them to be more successful. Getting involved in a local or online project management group is an excellent way of sharing ideas, successes, and concerns with other project managers. You can learn a lot from your peers.

If you need help with overcoming your fear of public speaking, or you would like to improve your ability to "think on your feet" during meetings and presentations, organizations like Toastmasters are excellent for increasing one's skill, confidence, and comfort level with public speaking. More information on Toastmasters is available at http://www.toastmasters.org/.

APPENDIX D

Document Templates

Numerous documents are required for managing the project life cycle and completing a successful project. The diagrams D1 to D60 show the templates included on the CD-ROM. Using these templates will save you hours of time creating the documents and presentations from scratch. The following chart provides you with the information you need to find the templates on the CD-ROM. The templates are listed in the order that they are mentioned in the book. This is also the order in which you will need to create them for managing a real project. The Document Process Workflow diagram (shown in Figure D.1) shows each document in the phase in which it should be created.

Document Name	Document Number	Life cycle Phase	File Type	Filename on CD-ROM
Project Life cycle Presentation	D1	Planning	PowerPoint	001 Project Lifecycle.ppt
Request for Quote (RFQ)	D2	Planning	Word	002 RFQ.doc
Request for Information (RFI)	D3	Planning	Word	003 RFI.doc
Request for Proposal (RFP)	D4	Planning	Word	004 RFP.doc
Project Proposal Document	D5	Planning	Word	005 Proposal.doc
Estimate Document	D6	Planning, Design	Excel	006 Estimate.xls
Project Definition	D7	Planning	Word	007 Project Definition.doc
Marketing Requirements Document (MRD)	D8	Planning	Word	008 MRD.doc

Document Name	Document Number	Life cycle Phase	File Type	Filename on CD-ROM
Statement of Work (SOW)	D9	Planning	Word	009 SOW.doc
Project Plan	D10	Planning	Word	010 Project Plan.doc
Staffing Plan	D11	Planning	Word	011 Staffing Plan.doc
Development Environment	D12	Planning	Word	012 Development Environment.doc
Functional Requirements	D13	Planning	Word	013 Functional Requirements.doc
Technical Requirements	D14	Planning	Word	014 Technical Requirements.doc
Decision Support System Plan	D15	Planning, Deployment	Word	015 Decision Support Plan.doc
Quality Assurance Plan	D16	Planning, Integration	Word	016 Quality Assurance Plan.doc
Communication Plan	D17	Planning	Word	017 Communication Plan.doc
Deployment Plan	D18	Planning, Integration, Deployment	Word	018 Deployment Plan.doc
Operations Plan	D19	Planning, Integration, Deployment, Post-Deployment	Word	019 Operations Plan.doc
Training Plan	D20	Planning, Integration. Deployment	Word	020 Training Plan.doc
Risk Management Plan	D21	Planning, Development	Word	021 Risk Management Plan.doc
Measurement Plan	D22	Planning	Word	022 Measurement Plan.doc
Project Approach	D23	Planning	Word	023 Project Approach.doc
Change Control Process	D24	Planning, Development	Word	024 Change Control Process.doc
Technical Processes	D25	Planning	Word	025 Technical Processes.doc
Organizational Processes	D26	Planning	Word	026 Organizational Processes.doc
Defect Tracking Process	D27	Planning, Integration	Word	027 Defect Tracking Process.doc

Document Name	Document Number	Life cycle Phase	File Type	Filename on CD-ROM
Monitoring and Reporting Process	D28	Planning, Deployment, Post-Deployment	Word	028 Monitoring and Reporting Process.doc
Escalation Procedures	D29	Planning, Deployment	Word	029 Escalation Procedures.doc
Kick-Off Meeting Agenda	D30	Planning	Word	030 Kick-Off Meeting Agenda.doc
Kick-Off Meeting Presentation	D31	Planning	PowerPoint	031 Kick-Off Meeting Presentation.ppt
Kick-Off Meeting Minutes	D32	Planning	Word	032 Kick-Off Meeting Minutes.doc
Network and System Architecture and Design	D33	Design	Word	033 Network and System Architecture & Design.doc
Software System Architecture and Design	D34	Design	Word	034 Software System Architecture & Design.doc
Technical Design and Specification	D35	Design	Word	035 Technical Design & Specification.doc
Database Design and Specification	D36	Design	Word	036 Database Design & Specification.doc
UI Design and Specification	D37	Design	Word	037 UI Design & Specification.doc
Detailed Task List	D38	Design	Excel	038 Detailed Task List.xls
Status Report Form	D39	Development, Integration, Deployment	Word	039 Status Report Form.doc
Status Communication	D40	Development, Integration, Deployment	Word	040 Status Communication.doc
Project Review Meeting Presentation	D41	Development, Integration, Deployment	PowerPoint	041 Project Review Meeting Presentation.ppt
Change Request Form	D42	Development, Integration,	Word	042 Change Request Form.doc
Change Log	D43	Development, Integration,	Excel	043 Change Log.xls

Document Name	Document Number	Life cycle Phase	File Type	Filename on CD-ROM
Emergency Change Request Form	D44	Development, Integration, Deployment	Word	044 Emergency Change Request Form.doc
Risk Log	D45	Development, Integration, Deployment	Excel	045 Risk Log.xls
Blank PowerPoint Presentation	D46	Development	PowerPoint	046 Blank Power Point Presentation.ppt
Quality Risk Assessment	D47	Integration, Deployment	Word	047 Quality Risk Assessment.doc
Training Manual	D48	Integration, Deployment	Word	048 Training Manual.doc
Service Level Agreement (SLA)	D49	Integration, Deployment	Word	049 Service Level Agreement.doc
Client Acceptance Meeting Presentation	D50	Deployment	PowerPoint	050 Client Acceptance Meeting Presentation.ppt
Client Acceptance Agreement	D51	Deployment	Word	051 Client Acceptance Agreement.doc
Lessons-Learned Agenda	D52	Post-Deployment	Word	052 Lessons Learned Agenda.doc
Lessons-Learned Plan	D53	Post Deployment	Excel	053 Lessons Learned Plan.xls
Lessons-Learned Tactical Plan	D54	Post-Deployment	Word	054 Tactical Plan.doc
Project Closure Report	D55	Post-Deployment	Word	055 Project Closure Report.doc
Project Closure Meeting Presentation	D56	Post-Deployment	PowerPoint	056 Project Closure Meeting Presentation.ppt
Project Completion Agreement	D57	Post-Deployment	Word	057 Project Completion Agreement.doc
Personal Development Plan	D58	All Phases	Word	058 Personal Development Plan.doc
Personal Time Log	D59	All Phases	Excel	059 Personal Time Log.xls
Career Plan	D60	All Phases	Word	060 Career Plan.doc

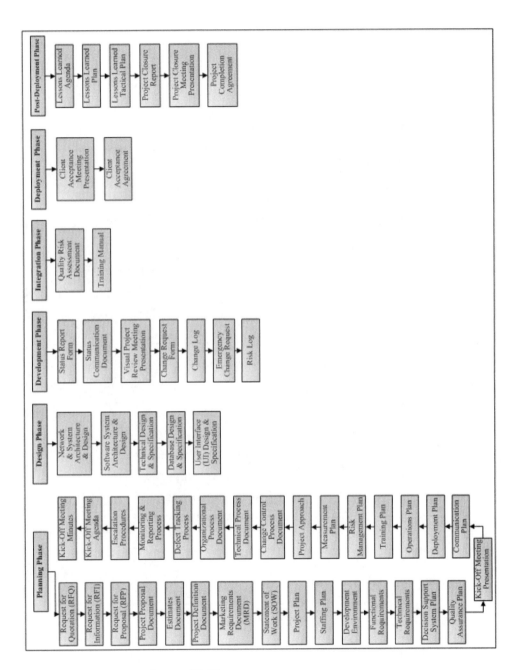

Figure D.1: The Document Process Workflow.

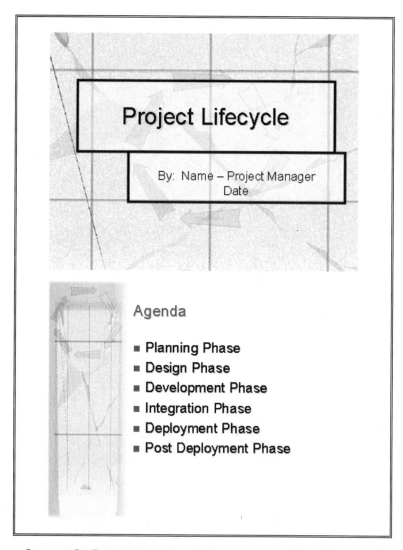

Document D1: Project Lifecycle Presentation

Request for Quotation (RFQ)

1. *Introduction*

2. *Date Request for Quotation Sent:*

   [   ]

3. **Request from:**

Name:	
Address:	
Fax:	
Phone:	

4. *Please supply a quotation for the following items:*

   -
   -
   -

5. *Please respond to this request:*

   ☐ Immediately
   ☐ By the end of the week
   ☐ By [date]

Document D2: Request for Quote (RFQ)

Request for Information (RFI)

1. Introduction

2. Company

> Name of organization requesting the RFI. Brief overview of business if necessary.

3. Information Requested

Please supply the following information:

4. Additional Information

> Any necessary background or supporting information that might be needed to respond to the request.

5. Response Submission and Questions

Please submit RFI response no later than [**date**] to [**full address**]. Questions should be addressed to [**Contact Name, title, phone, e-mail**].

6. Terms and Conditions

> Insert any confidentiality or legal terms or conditions here.

Document D3: Request for Information (RFI)

Request for Proposal (RFP)

1. Introduction

2. Executive Summary

This section should include a summary of the requester's company and market space.

3. Purpose

This section will be a description of the project, the problem, and the proposed solution that the requester needs to achieve.

4. Key Business and Technical Requirements

This section will include the key business and technical requirements.

5. Proposed Project Phases and Milestones

This section will include a high-level description of project phases (if applicable) and milestones.

6. Quality Assurance Requirements

This section will include any and all quality assurance requirements, including processes, procedures, and methodologies.

7. Budget

This section will detail the budget that has been established to complete the project.

8. Schedule of Events

This section will include a schedule of events with timelines for the proposal through awarding of contract to vendor.

9. Proposal Template

This section will indicate whether a proposal document template is included and any instructions for completing it.

Document D4: Request for Proposal (RFP)

Proposal Document

1. Introduction

2. Executive Summary

3. Corporate and Cultural Information

4. Previous Projects and Clients

5. Client References

6. Development Methodologies and Process

7. Quality Assurance and Testing Processes and Procedures

8. Development Environment

9. Assumptions

10. The Problem

11. Proposed Solution(s)

12. Constraints, Limitations, and Risks

13. Proposed Project Phases

14. Milestones and Deliverables

15. The Proposed Project Team

16. Costs and Payment Details

17. Terms and Conditions

18. Proposal Submission and Questions

19. Proposal Acceptance and Approval

Document D5: Project Proposal Document

Estimate				Project Name											
Feature No.	Feature / Task	PM	S/W Engineer	UI Designer	Technical Lead / Architect	DBA	Systems Engineer	Business Analyst	QA Manager	QA Engineer	Product Manager	Usability	Graphic Design	Consultant	Contractor	Vendor	TOTAL HRS
1																	0
2																	0
3																	0
4																	0
5																	0
6																	0
7																	0
8																	0
9																	0
10																	0
11																	0
12																	0
13																	0
14																	0
15																	0
16																	0
17																	0
18																	0
TOTAL HOURS		0	0	0	0	0	0	0	0	0	0	0	0	0	0	0	0
Charge Per Hour																	
Total $		0	0	0	0	0	0	0	0	0	0	0	0	0	0	0	0

Document D6: Estimate Document

Project Definition

1. **Introduction**
    1.1. General Information
2. **Project Name**
3. **Client Name**
4. **Decision-Makers**
5. **Project Description and Goals**
6. **Business Case**
7. **Key Business Requirements**
8. **Project Objectives**
9. **Benefits**
10. **Target Audience**
11. **The Problem**
12. **The Solution**
13. **Project Scope**
    13.1.   In Scope
    13.2.   Out of Scope
14. **Prerequisites**
15. **Assumptions**
16. **Project Constraints**
17. **Project Risks**
18. **Time and Costs**
19. **Project Organization**
    19.1.   Organization Chart
20. **Project Definition Approval**

Document D7: Project Definition

Marketing Requirements Document (MRD)

1. *Introduction*
2. *Strategy and Overview*
   - 2.1. Description of Project
   - 2.2. Goals and Objectives
   - 2.3. Project Scope
   - 2.4. Target Audience
   - 2.5. Competitive Strengths and Weaknesses
   - 2.6. Cost Analysis And Strategy
   - 2.7. Budget
3. *Business Model*
   - 3.1. Value Proposition/Benefits
   - 3.2. Market Space
   - 3.3. Cost Structure
   - 3.4. Competitive Strategy
4. *Affected Groups*
   - 4.1. Internal
   - 4.2. External
5. *External Partners/Vendors*
6. *Hardware, Equipment, and Tools Requirements*
   - 6.1. Development
   - 6.2. Support
   - 6.3. Operations
   - 6.4. Sales
7. *Product Requirements*
   - 7.1. Performance and Stability Requirements
   - 7.2. Backward Compatibility
   - 7.3. Physical and Logical Architecture
   - 7.4. Platforms and Protocols
   - 7.5. Uptime and Quality of Service
   - 7.6. Security
   - 7.7. Benchmarking
   - 7.8. Special Requirements
8. *Functional Requirements*
   - 8.1. Must Have
   - 8.2. Highly Desirable
   - 8.3. Nice to Have
9. *Usability Requirements*
   - 9.1. GUI
   - 9.2. Usability Testing
   - 9.3. Beta Program
10. *Service Level Agreements (SLA's)*
11. *Deliverables*
12. *Future Requirements*
    - 12.1. Extendibility
    - 12.2. Scalability
    - 12.3. Upgrades and Enhancements
    - 12.4. Desired Future Features
13. *Out of Scope/Specifically Not Being Implemented*
    - 13.1. Out of Scope

Document D8: Marketing Requirements Document (MRD)

Statement of Work (SOW)

1. *Introduction*
2. *Purpose*
3. *Milestones*
4. *Scope*
    4.1.   Stakeholders
    4.2.   Data
    4.3.   Processes
    4.4.   Locations
5. *Deliverables*
6. *Constraints*
    6.1.   Start date
    6.2.   Deadlines
    6.3.   Budget
    6.4.   Technology
7. *Assumptions*
8. *Acceptance Criteria*

Document D9: Statement of Work (SOW)

Project Plan

1. *Introduction*
2. *Project Definition Overview*
3. *Changes Since Project Definition Was Approved*
4. *Staffing Plan*
5. *Development Environment*
6. *High-Level Schedule*
7. *Deliverables and Milestones*
8. *Functional Requirements*
9. *Technical Requirements*
10. *Decision Support System (DSS) Plan*
11. *Quality Assurance (QA) Plan*
12. *Communications Plan*
13. *Deployment Plan*
14. *Post-Deployment Plan*
15. *Training Plan*
16. *Risk Management*
17. *Measurement Plan*
18. *Client Acceptance Criteria*
19. *Project Plan Approval*

Document D10: Project Plan

Staffing Plan

1. **Introduction**

2. **General Information**

   Project Name: _____

   Project Manager: _____

   Project Begin Date: _XX/XX/XXXX_   Project End Date: _XX/XX/XXXX_

3. **Skills Assessment**

Milestone/Objective	Title	Source	#	Skill Level/Special Requirements
Milestone # 1	Project Manager	Internal		
	Technical Lead	Internal	1	

4. **Staffing Profile**

Calendar (month or quarter)	Title (personnel category)	Resource Name	Level of Commitment (utilization rate)
Period #1	Project Manager		1 – Full time
	Technical Lead		1 – Quarter time

5. **Organization Chart**

6. **Outside Resource Profile**

Calendar (month or quarter)	Title (personnel category)	Resource Name	Company	Level of Commitment (utilization rate)
May-July	Project Manager			1 – Full time

7. **Project Roles and Responsibilities**

Resource Name	Title	Project Role	Responsibilities
	Project Manager	Manager and owner for development and delivery of product	

Document D11: Staffing Plan

Development Environment

2. *Development Environment for In-House Project Development Team*

   2.1.   Platform

   2.2.   Operating System (and Version)

   2.3.   Development Tools (editors, compilers, debuggers)

   2.4.   Design Tools

   2.5.   Unit Test Tools

   2.6.   Other Equipment or Tools

3. *Development Environment for Client Developers or Quality Assurance*

   3.1.   Platform

   3.2.   Operating System (and Version)

   3.3.   Development Tools (editors, compilers, debuggers)

   3.4.   Design Tools

   3.5.   Unit Test Tools

   3.6.   Other Equipment or Tools

4. *Development Environment for Consultants and Contractors*

   4.1.   Platform

   4.2.   Operating System (and Version)

   4.3.   Development Tools (editors, compilers, debuggers)

   4.4.   Design Tools

   4.5.   Unit Test Tools

   4.6.   Other Equipment or Tools

5. *Development Environment for Vendors*

   5.1.   Platform

   5.2.   Operating System (and Version)

   5.3.   Development Tools (editors, compilers, debuggers)

   5.4.   Design Tools

   5.5.   Unit Test Tools

   5.6.   Other Equipment or Tools

6. *Special Instructions*

Document D12: Development Environment

Functional Requirements

1. *Introduction*
2. *Features*
3. *Performance*
4. *Speed*
5. *Ease of Use*
6. *Use Cases*
   - 6.1. Define Different Types of Users
   - 6.2. Interaction with Product
   - 6.3. Workflow Diagrams
   - 6.4. Alternative Workflows
7. *Usability*
   - 7.1. User Interface
   - 7.2. Look and Feel
8. *Legal Requirements*
   - 8.1. Regulatory Requirements
   - 8.2. Security
   - 8.3. Privacy
9. *Decision Support Requirements*
   - 9.1. Data Requirements
   - 9.2. User Requirements
   - 9.3. User Interface
10. *Access Requirements*
    - 10.1. Remote (VPN, Internet, etc.)
    - 10.2. Local
11. *Backup Requirements*

Document D13: Functional Requirements

Technical Requirements

1. *Introduction*
2. *Network Requirements*
   - 2.1. Hardware
   - 2.2. Software
3. *Server Requirements*
   - 3.1. Hardware
   - 3.2. Software
4. *Workstation Requirements*
   - 4.1. Hardware
   - 4.2. Software
5. *Database Requirements*
   - 5.1. Hardware
   - 5.2. Software
6. *Error Handling*
7. *Error Logging, Reporting, Monitoring*
8. *Redundancy*
9. *Capacity*
10. *Reliability*
11. *Interoperability*
12. *Scalability*
13. *Stability*
14. *Extensibility*
15. *Flexibility*
16. *Portability*
17. *Security*
    - 17.1. Authentication
    - 17.2. Monitoring
18. *Decision Support*
    - 18.1. Logging
    - 18.2. Data Collection
    - 18.3. Data Storage (Database)
    - 18.4. Reporting Mechanism
19. *Systems Monitoring*
    - 19.1. Monitoring Mechanism
    - 19.2. Reporting and Alert System
20. *Backup Technical Requirements*

Document D14: Technical Requirements

Decision Support System Plan

1. Introduction
2. Demographic Information Required
3. Accuracy of Data
4. Data Collection Strategy
5. Data Storage Requirements
6. Data Mining Tools
7. Reports and Analysis
8. Network and Hardware Requirements
9. Backup Requirements
10. Roles and Responsibilities
11. Privacy Policy

Document D15: Decision Support System Plan

Quality Assurance Plan

1. Introduction
- 1.1. Project Overview
- 1.2. Project Scope
- 1.3. Testing
- 1.4. Completion Criteria
- 1.5. Schedule

2. Test Matrix
- 2.1. QA Methodologies
- 2.2. Test Summary Report

3. Test Plan
- 3.1. Activities
- 3.2. Resources

4. Traceability Matrix

5. Test Cases

6. Test Scripts

7. Defect Reports

8. Quality Risk Assessment

9. Performance Test Plan

Document D16: Quality Assurance Plan

Communication Plan

1. Introduction

2. List of Steering Committee and Stakeholder Groups and Members

List steering committee and all stakeholder groups with a description of the purpose of the group and a list of all members for each group.

Stakeholder Group Name	Description	Members

3. Formal Communication Schedule/Plan

Communication	Content	Objective	Owner	Audience	Method	Frequency / Date

4. Informal Communication Plan

Issue	Description	Action	Owner (escalate to)	Audience	Method	Timeline

5. Communication Rules

Here you should list any rules, either company or regulatory, that exist at your company, the client company, or the vendor's company on what and how things can be communicated.

Document D17: Communication Plan

Deployment Plan

1. Introduction
   1.1.   General Information

2. Network Deployment
   2.1.   Network Setup
   2.2.   Network Test

3. Server Deployment
   3.1.   Directory Structure
   3.2.   Deployment Steps

4. Workstation Deployment
   4.1.   Directory Structure
   4.2.   Deployment Steps

5. Database Deployment
   5.1.   Directory Structure
   5.2.   Deployment Steps

6. Database Access

7. Data Conversion

8. Security

9. For Software Project
   9.1.   CD Mastering and Duplication
   9.2.   Artwork and Packaging
   9.3.   Printing
   9.4.   Assembly
   9.5.   Distribution
   9.6.   Shipping

10. Deployment Schedule of Events and Timelines

11. Roles and Responsibilities

12. Verification and Test

13. Acceptance Criteria

14. Project Hand-Off

Document D18: Deployment Plan

Operations Plan

1. *Introduction*
2. *Operations Document*
    2.1.   Network and System Diagrams
    2.2.   Technical Specifications for All Hardware and Software Components
    2.3.   Interoperability Specification
    2.4.   Network Specification
    2.5.   Security
    2.6.   Decision Support
    2.7.   Required Regular Maintenance
    2.8.   Bug Fix Releases
    2.9.   Product Update Mechanism and Process
    2.10. System Monitoring
    2.11. Change Control Process
    2.12. List of Related Documents
    2.13. Service or Maintenance Contracts
    2.14. Scheduled System Downtime
    2.15. Escalation Process
    2.16. Roles and Responsibilities
3. *System Administrator Guide*
    3.1.   Network and System Diagrams
    3.2.   Technical and Functional Specifications for All Hardware and Software Components
    3.3.   Server Hardware and Software Installation and Setup Guide
    3.4.   Required Regular Maintenance Procedures
    3.5.   Monitoring and Reporting System
    3.6.   Troubleshooting
    3.7.   Restart and Recovery Procedures
    3.8.   Backup and Restore Procedures
    3.9.   Scheduled Processes and Scripts
4. *User Guide*
    4.1.   Description of the Functionality and Features
    4.2.   Client Hardware and Software Installation and Setup Instructions
    4.3.   Step-by-Step Instructions on How to Use Each Feature and Component\
    4.4.   Customizing Views
    4.5.   How to Print Reports
    4.6.   How to Submit Defect Reports
    4.7.   How to Contact Technical and Customer Support
    4.8.   How to Use Knowledgebase
    4.9.   How to Use Help
    4.10. Accessibility
    4.11. Troubleshooting
    4.12. Who to Contact
    4.13. How to Manually Process Order, Shipment, and Delivery
5. *Technical Support Guide*
6. *Customer Support Guide*
7. *Release Notes*

Document D19: Operations Plan

Training Plan

1. **Introduction**
   1.1. General Information

2. **Purpose / Goal**

3. **Objectives**

4. **Scope**

5. **Assumptions**

6. **Training Requirements**

7. **Training Strategy**
   7.1. Training Resources
   7.2. Hardware Environment to Be Used
   7.3. Software Environment to Be Used

8. **Dependencies, Constraints, and Limitations**

9. **Types of Training Manuals Required and Number of Each**

10. **Course Description (For Each Course Define):**
    10.1. Course Outline
    10.2. Target Audience
    10.3. Goals and Objectives
    10.4. Content
    10.5. Learning Methods and Activities
    10.6. Attendee Prerequisites
    10.7. Training Resources
    10.8. Training Environment
    10.9. Training Materials
    10.10. Training Evaluation
    10.11. Certification

11. **Constraints and Risks**

12. **Roles and Responsibilities**

13. **Training Schedule**

14. **Training Log**

Document D20: Training Plan

Risk Management Plan

1. *Introduction*
2. *Risks Identified During Planning Phase*
3. *The Risk Identification and Evaluation Process*
    3.1. Identify
    3.2. Evaluate
    3.3. Analyze
    3.4. Risk Action Plan
4. *Prioritization Process*
5. *Management of Risks*
    5.1. Risk Log
    5.2. Risk Status Reporting
6. *Roles and Responsibilities*

Document D21: Risk Management Plan

Measurement Plan

1. *Introduction*
2. *Overview of Measurement Plan*
   2.1. Requirements
   2.2. Scope
3. *Measurement Criteria*
4. *Description of How Each Objective Will Be Measured*
   4.1. Objective 1

Measurement	Reason	Method	Frequency	Expected Results	Person Responsible

   4.2. Objective 2

Measurement	Reason	Method	Frequency	Expected Results	Person Responsible

5. *Roles and Responsibilities*

Document D22: Measurement Plan

Project Approach

1. Introduction

2. Executive Summary

3. Corporate and Cultural Information

4. Previous Projects and Clients

5. Client References

6. Development Methodologies and Process

7. Quality Assurance and Testing Processes and Procedures

8. Development Environment

9. Assumptions

10. The Problem

11. Proposed Solution(s)

12. Constraints, Limitations, and Risks

13. Proposed Project Phases

14. Milestones and Deliverables

15. The Proposed Project Team

16. Costs and Payment Details

17. Terms and Conditions

18. Proposal Submission and Questions

19. Proposal Acceptance and Approval

Document D23: Project Approach

Change Control Process

1. *Introduction*
2. *Change Control Process*
    - 2.1. Description Overview and Process Flowchart
    - 2.2. Planning Phase
    - 2.3. Design Phase
    - 2.4. Development Phase
    - 2.5. Integration Phase
    - 2.6. Deployment Phase
    - 2.7. Post-Deployment Phase
3. *Bug Change Control Process*
4. *Appeal Process for Change Request Denials*
5. *Roles and Responsibilities*
    - 5.1. Process Owner
    - 5.2. Change Control Board

Document D24: Change Control Process

Technical Processes

1. Introduction

   1.1.   General Information

2. The Build Process

   2.1.   Build Schedule

   2.2.   Time Builds Are Kicked Off

   2.3.   Approximate Completion Time

   2.4.   Who Kicks Off the Build (If It Is Not Automated)

   2.5.   Who Is Responsible for Ensuring the Build Is Done

   2.6.   Who Is Responsible for Fixing Problems That Break The Build

   2.7.   Which Builds Are Given to QA for Testing

3. Source Control Process

The process should define the source code used, the process for checking in and checking out code, who is responsible for the source code system, and procedures for dealing with problems that require the source code to be restored or rebuilt.

4. Versioning

The process should define the versioning method and who is responsible for tracking the current version.

5. Configuration Management

The configuration management process should be defined—who owns it, who uses it, and the process for using the CM system for building the final products.

6. Roles and Responsibilities

   6.1.   Process Owner

Document D25: Technical Processes Document

Organizational Processes

1. Introduction
   1.1.   General Information

2. Interdepartmental Builds and Releases Process

3. Time Tracking
   3.1.   Project
   3.2.   Personal

4. Time-Off Request
   4.1.   Vacation
   4.2.   Sick
   4.3.   Family Leave

5. Information Requests
   5.1.   Team
   5.2.   Other Departments
   5.3.   Client
   5.4.   Vendors

6. Organizational Information
   6.1.   Links to Company Employee and Team Web Sites

7. New Hire Information

8. HR Information

9. Roles and Responsibilities
   9.1.   Process Owner(s)

Document D26: Organizational Processes Document

Defect Tracking Process

1. *Introduction*
   1.1.   General Information
2. *Definition of Defect*
   2.1.   Defect Bug
   2.2.   Enhancement
   2.3.   New Feature
3. *Who Can Submit Defects*
4. *How to Complete a Defect Report*
5. *Defect Process*
6. *How to Reopen a Defect Report If the Defect Is Not Fixed*
7. *How to Appeal a Decision to Defer or Close a Defect Report*
8. *Roles and Responsibilities*
   8.1.   Process Owner

Document D27: Defect Tracking Process Document

Monitoring and Reporting Process

1. *Introduction*
   1.1.   General Information

2. *Error Categorization and Definition*
   2.1.   Level 1
   2.2.   Level 2
   2.3.   Level 3
   2.4.   Level 4

3. *Process for Each Type of Error*
   3.1.   Level 1
   3.2.   Level 2
   3.3.   Level 3
   3.4.   Level 4

4. *Alerts*
   4.1.   E-mail
   4.2.   Pager

5. *Storage and Backup*

6. *Reporting*

7. *Analysis*

8. *Roles and Responsibilities*
   8.1.   Process Owner

Document D28: Monitoring and Reporting Process Document

Escalation Procedures

1. Introduction

1.1. General Information

2. Escalation Path

Level	Definition	Expected Response	Call Intervals
Priority 1	Critical Security Issue	Security team takes ownership of problem and implements security emergency plan. No alerts or discussion of issues allowed via e-mail. No details to be discussed outside of security team.	Immediate
Priority 2	Major Impact—Impact to the Client's Business	Problem is worked on continuously until it is resolved.	Immediate
Priority 3	Large impact—significant inconvenience to customers where a workaround might be implemented	Work is expected to continue on a workday basis until a more permanent solution is in place.	2 hour maximum
Priority 4	Small to Minor Impact—Minor to small inconvenience	Resolution is worked into a planned project list and schedule or it can be deferred until there is time allowed in the project schedule.	24 hours maximum

3. Notification

Sequence	Contact/Name	Work Phone#	Home Phone#	Mobile/Pager #	Title/Description
Priority 1					
Priority 2					
Priority 3					
Priority 4					

4. Roles and Responsibilities

4.1. Process Owner

Document D29: Escalation Procedures

Kick-Off Meeting Agenda

Date:
Time:
Location:

8:00   Welcome and Agenda (Sponsor and Project Manager)
(The sponsor welcomes everyone to the meeting, and the project manager briefly reads the day's agenda.)

8:15   Introductions (All Attendees)
(Introductions—team members introduce themselves and briefly describe their professional and technical backgrounds.)

8:30   Purpose of Meeting (Sponsor)
(The sponsor will present to the team the purpose of the meeting and the goals and objectives of the meeting.)

8:45   Project Background (Sponsor)
(The project's sponsor will give a description of the project's background and the needs and expectations of the customer.)

9:00   Presentation of Project Plan (Project Manager)

12:00 Lunch

1:00   Presentation of Project Approach (Project Manager)

3:30 Open Discussion (Team)
- Any other business
- General Q & A

4:30 Action Items (Project Manager or whomever is documenting action items)
- Recap action items, owners, and timelines

4:45 Next Steps (Project Manager)
- Summary of key issues discussed
- Next Steps
- Schedule follow up meeting(s)

5:00 Adjourn *(The project manager will adjourn the meeting.)*

Invited Attendees:
List all the invited attendees.

Document D30: Kick-Off Meeting Agenda

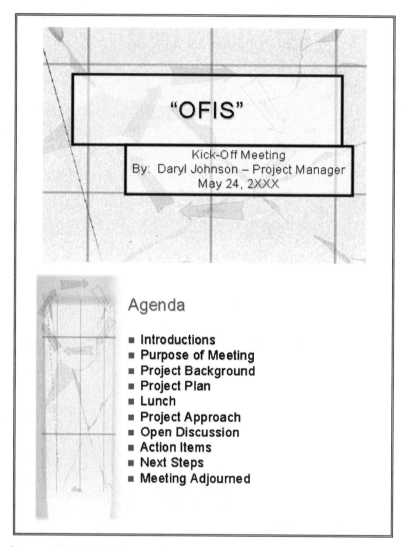

Document D31: Kick-Off Meeting Presentation

Kick-Off Meeting Minutes

Date:
Time:
Location:

Welcome and Agenda (Sponsor and Project Manager)

Introductions (Each member introduced themselves and their backgrounds.)

Purpose of the meeting (Sponsor)
Recap the purpose of the meeting.

Project Background (Sponsor)
Recap the project background.

Presentation of Project Plan (Project Manager)
Recap discussion regarding:

Presentation of Project Approach (Project Manager)
Recap discussion regarding:

Open Discussion (Open Forum)
Recap the discussion that took place in the meeting.

Action Items (Project Manager)
Document action items.

Next Steps (Project Manager)
- Summary of key issues discussed.
- Next steps.
- Follow up meetings scheduled.

Adjourn (Project Manager)
The meeting was adjourned at 5pm.

Attendees

Name	Agency/Organization
Jane Doe	XYZ Corporation
Bob Smith	XYZ Corporation
Jon Rocket	Contractor
Lisa Miller	Contractor

Document D32: Kick-Off Meeting Minutes

Network and System Architecture and Design

1. **Introduction**
   - 1.1   General Information
   - 1.2   Related Documents
2. **Overview of the System**
3. **Requirements Overview**
   - 3.1   Servers
   - 3.2   Capacity
   - 3.3   Connectivity
   - 3.4   Storage
   - 3.5   Availability
   - 3.6   Backup
4. **Network and System Management**
   - 4.1   System Monitoring
   - 4.2   Logging
   - 4.3   Notification Engine
5. **Security**
6. **Current Architecture**
   - 6.1   Overview
   - 6.2   Network Diagram
   - 6.3   Hardware Diagram
7. **Proposed Architecture**
   - 7.1   Overview
   - 7.2   Network Diagram
   - 7.3   Hardware Diagram
8. **Required Changes**
   - 8.1   Identify Gaps
   - 8.2   Define Change Plan
9. **Quality of Service**
10. **Nonimplemented Tasks**
11. **Summary**

Document D33: Network and System Architecture and Design

Software System Architecture and Design

1. *Introduction*
2. *Overview of the System*
   - 2.1   Purpose of the System
   - 2.2   Related Documents
3. *Design Goals*
   - 3.1   Features and Components
   - 3.2   Connectivity
   - 3.3   Performance, Capacity, and Optimization
   - 3.4   Backup and Restore
   - 3.5   Disaster Recovery
   - 3.6   Deployment
   - 3.7   Installer
   - 3.8   Launch Application
   - 3.9   Monitoring and Notification System
   - 3.10   Code Reuse
4. *Security*
   - 4.1   Authentication
   - 4.2   Remote Access
5. *Current Software Architecture*
6. *Proposed Software Architecture*
   - 6.1   File Hierarchy
   - 6.2   Component Map
   - 6.3   Data Management
   - 6.4   Links to Other Systems
7. *Platforms and Protocols*
8. *Nonimplemented Tasks*
9. *Summary*

Document D34: Software System Architecture and Design

Technical Design and Specification

1. *Introduction*
2. *Design Overview*
3. *Detailed Design*
4. *Components and Processes*
5. *Interfaces*
6. *Security*
7. *Reuse*
8. *Test Plan*
9. *Extensibility*
10. *Nonimplemented tasks*
11. *Summary*

Document D35: Technical Design and Specification

Database Design and Specification

1. *Introduction*
2. *Design Overview*
3. *Detailed Design*
   3.1   Logical Design
   3.2   Physical Design
4. *Data Diagrams*
5. *Database Structure*
6. *Process Flow Diagrams*
7. *Test Plan*
8. *Extensibility*
9. *Nonimplemented Tasks*
10. *Summary*

Document D36: Database Design and Specification

UI Design and Specification

1. *Introduction*
2. *Design Overview*
3. *Detailed Design*
4. *Site Structure and Navigation*
   4.1   Describe Different Types of Users
   4.2   Workflow Diagrams
   4.3   Alternative Workflows
   4.4   Site Map
5. *User Interface*
   5.1   Graphic Design
   5.2   Look and Feel
   5.3   Screen Mockups
   5.4   Form Mockups
   5.5   Report Mockups
   5.6   Tabbing Order
6. *Online Demo Prototype*
7. *Help Screens*
8. *Test Plan*
9. *Nonimplemented Tasks*
10. *Summary*

Document D37: UI Design and Specification

Detailed Task List			Feature				Project Name						
	Prepared by:			Estimate:									
Task No.	Task	Planning	Design	Coding	Unit Test	Bug Fix	Update Docs	Integration	QA Support	Other		TOTAL HRS	Dependencies
1												0	
2												0	
3												0	
4												0	
5												0	
6												0	
7												0	
8												0	
	TOTAL HOURS	0	0	0	0	0	0	0	0	0	0	0	

Document D38: Detailed Task List

Status Report Form

Project Name:	
Project Manager:	
Date:	
Contact Name:	
Phone / E-mail:	
Reporting Period:	

Are All Tasks:				
On or Ahead of Schedule?	Yes		No	
Meeting Requirements?	Yes		No	

1. Current status

  1.1. Scheduled Work

  1.2. Unscheduled Work

  1.3. Issues

2. Status of tasks completed during this reporting period

3. Planned work for next period

1. Recommendations

  Status reports needs to be turned into the Project Manager by (insert day(s))

Document D39: Status Report Form

Status Communication

Project Name:	
Project Manager:	
Phone / E-mail:	
Today's Date:	
Reporting Period:	

Is the Project					
Meeting milestones and deliverables?	Yes		No		
On track for an on-time completion	Yes		No		

1. *Overall status*

2. *Progress since last update*

3. *Issues, concerns, and changes*

4. *Risk update*

5. *Budget and costs*

6. *Milestones and deliverables for next period*

7. *Action items*

Document D40: Status Communication

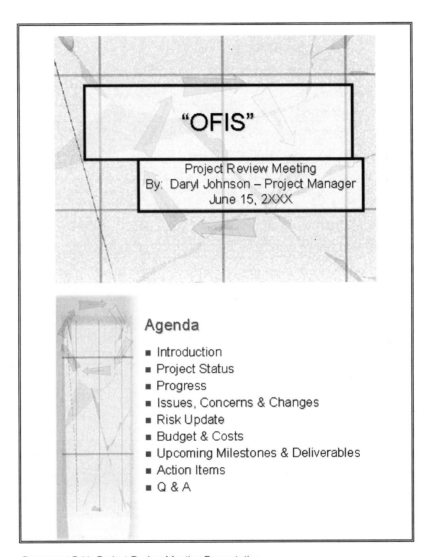

Document D41: Project Review Meeting Presentation

Change Request Form

Project Name:		CR Number:	
Project Manager:		Process Owner :	
Change Request Title:			
Originator:		Date Created:	

Proposed Change Description

The originator describes the proposed change.

Justification

The originator describes why is the change is necessary and whether it is an addition, deletion or, change to the original plan.

Benefits

What are the benefits of making this change? Who benefits from it?

Impact Statement

What are the implications if the change is not implemented? What are the known impacts of the change on the existing product, code, or system?

Action Taken

What action is being taken regarding this change request? Is more information needed? Is the change being made? Is the change being made different from the one requested?

Approvals

Round One: Approved	YES	NO	DEFFERED
Round Two: Approved	YES	NO	DEFFERED

Approver Signature	Print Name Date
Client Signature	Print Name Date

Document D42: Change Request Form

No	Change Request Description	Originator	Date of Request	Status	Owner	Date Change Implemented	Description of Change	Implemented by
	Change Log							
						Project Name		

Document D43: Change Log

Emergency Change Request

Project Name:		ECR Number:	
Project Manager:		Process Owner :	
Change Request Title:			
Originator:		Date Created:	

Proposed Change Description

The originator describes the proposed change.

Justification

The originator describes why the change is necessary and whether it is an addition, deletion, or change to the original plan.

Benefits

What are the benefits of making this change? Who benefits from it?

Impact Statement

What are the implications if the change is not implemented? What are the known impacts of the change on the existing product, code, or system?

Action Taken

What action is being taken regarding this change request? Is more information needed? Is the change being made? Is the change being made different from the one requested?

Reason for ECR

Why is change an emergency? Why could it not wait until the next Change Control Board meeting?

ECR Approvals

Project Manager Signature		Print Name	Date
Second Approver Manager Signature		Print Name	Date

Change Control Board Approvals

Emergency Change Approved:	YES	NO	
Approval Signature		Print Name	Date

Document D44: Emergency Change Request Form

No.	Description	Originator	Date Found	Assigned To	Criticality	Probability	Priority	Action Plan	Status	Date Resolved
Risk Log						**Project Name**				

Document D45: Risk Log

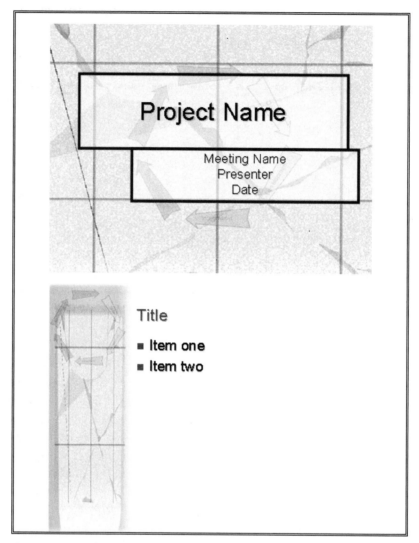

Document D46: Blank PowerPoint Presentation

Quality Risk Assessment

1. *Introduction*
2. *Areas of Code Tested*
3. *Code Not Tested*
4. *Result Summaries*
5. *Defects*
   5.1   Open
   5.2   Deferred
   5.3   Pending
   5.4   Closed
6. *Risks*
   6.1   Critical
   6.2   High
   6.3   Medium
7. *Quality Assurance Recommendation*

Document D47: Quality Risk Assessment

Training Manual

1. *An Introduction to the Lesson*
2. *Objectives*
3. *Scope*
4. *Process Flows*
5. *Written Instruction*
6. *Visual Instruction (Screenshots)*
7. *Examples*
8. *Lesson Review*

Document D48: Training Manual

Service Level Agreement (SLA)

1.   Introduction

2.   Services Delivered

3.   System Uptime

4.   Scheduled Maintenance and System Downtime

5.   Performance, Monitoring, and Reporting

6.   Problem Management

7.   Client Duties and Responsibilities

8.   Warranties and Remedies

9.   Security

10. Disaster Recovery

11. Intellectual Property Rights and Confidential Information

12. Legal Compliance and Resolution of Disputes

13. Compensation

14. Termination

15. Approval and Signatures

Document D49: Service Level Agreement (SLA)

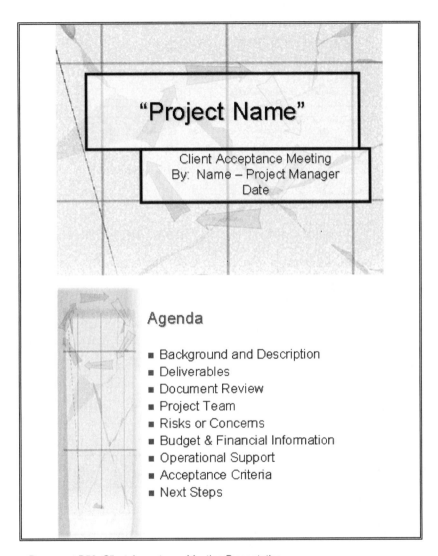

Document D50: Client Acceptance Meeting Presentation

Client Acceptance Agreement

Client:

This agreement has been prepared by: **Date Issued:**

Project Description
Full and detailed description of the project, including the goals and objectives, the solution, the scope and the prerequisites.

Costs, Terms and Conditions
The agreed to costs for the project and the payment terms and conditions.

Acceptance Criteria
The acceptance criteria as defined in the project plan.

Post-Deployment Deliverables
Make a note of any deliverables delayed until post-deployment together with costs and payment terms for those deliverables.

Client Approval Section
Final approval statement for client signoff. Example: I have done a complete and thorough review of the project deliverables and results and I agree that the project meets the documented client acceptance criteria.

Client	**Signature:**	
	Print Name:	
	Title:	
	Date:	
Sponsor	**Signature:**	
	Print Name:	
	Title:	
	Date:	
Project Manager	**Signature:**	
	Print Name:	
	Title:	
	Date:	

Document D51: Client Acceptance Agreement

Lessons-Learned Agenda

Company Name
Project Name

Date: **Friday, January 1, 2XXX**
Time: **8:00 AM PST – 5:00 PM PST**
Location: **XYZ Corporation Board Room #5**

8:00   **Welcome and Agenda** – Marie Brown (facilitator)
- Purpose of the meeting
- Rules
- Agenda

8:30   **Categories**

9:00   **Things that could have been improved on**

9:20   **Things that went well, that we are proud of, and that we must do again**

9:40   **Categorize the stickies**

10:00   **15-minute break**

10:15   **Recategorize stickies**

10:45   **Summarize categories**

11:15   **Present summaries**

12:15   **Lunch**

1:15   **Select highest-priority issues**

1:45   **Discuss the top 10 categories**

4:30   **Next steps**

Invited attendees:

Name	Position	Company
Person one	engineer	XYZ

Preparation for this meeting:

Document D52: Lessons-Learned Agenda

Lessons-Learned Plan								
	Project Manager:			Project Name				
ID	Description	Date Assigned	Owner	Tactical Plan Committee	Due Date	Status	Date Closed	Tactical Plan Filename and Location

Document D53: Lessons-Learned Plan

Lessons-Learned Tactical Plan

1. Tactical Plan Owner

Plan owner

2. Tactical Plan Committee Members

List all committee members

3. Tactical Plan Due Date

Date due

4. The Problem

Describe the problem. You may want to quote some of the "sticky" comments here.

5. Describe the Solution

How will the problem be solved, who will implement solution, and how soon will results be measurable

6. Describe Any Processes or Procedures That Will Need Updating as a Result of this Tactical Plan

List all existing processes, procedures, and documents that will have to be updated.

7. How Will Results be Measured

Describe how results will be measured.

8. Next Steps

Describe any next steps.

9. Risks

Identify any outstanding risks or any new potential risks as result of the tactical plan.

Document D54: Lessons-Learned Tactical Plan

Project Closure Report

1. Client Name

This project was undertaken at the request of

2. Background and Description

Briefly describe the background, the business case, and the objectives of the project.

3. Reason for Closing the Project

State the reason why the project is being closed. This may be because the project was completed, or it may have been cancelled or postponed for some reason.

4. Deliverables

List the planned and actual project deliverables. Include information on relevant change requests.

5. Project Schedule

List the planned and actual project completion dates.

6. Project Team

List the names of everyone who worked on the project, including their titles, project roles, and steps taken to move the team members from the project to other projects, including the timeframe of their move.

7. Outstanding Risks

Identify any outstanding risks as defined in the Quality Risk Assessment document and any planned actions or steps related to those risks.

8. Budget and Financial Information

Compare the budget to actual costs. Explain any discrepancies. Include ROI information if available. Identify any non-project, budget-related financial issues or concerns.

9. Action Plan

Insert the project action plan.

10. Ongoing Support

Describe the plan for ongoing support for the project. Include operational support, defect reports, change requests, and technical and customer support.

11. Next Steps

Identify next steps. For example, any tasks moved to post-deployment (late features, for instance) or any plans for point releases. Detail the process and the timing for disbanding the team.

12. Project Closure Approval

Document D55: Project Closure Report

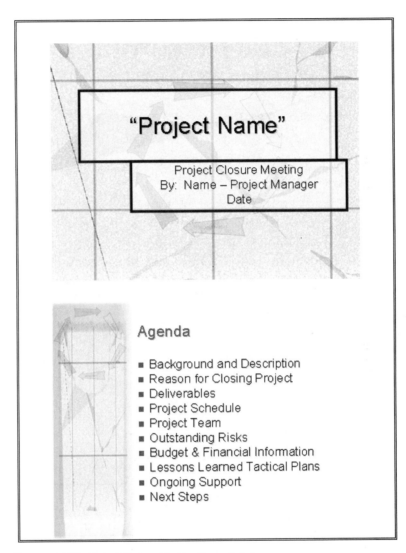

Document D56: Project Closure Meeting Presentation

Project Completion Agreement

THIS DOCUMENT made effective as of the _____ day of _____, _____.

BETWEEN:

[NAME OF COMPANY ENGAGING CONTRACTOR/CONSULTANT]
[address]

- and -

[NAME OF CONTRACTOR]
[address]

The Contract/Consultant acknowledges that the following:

1. That the work has been completed to the best of my knowledge

2. That all deliverables have been met as laid out in the contract

3. That all project related property and documentation has been returned to the company

4. The contractor/consultant has not retained any copies of any documents. Any documents not returned have been destroyed.

5. The project manager has received the final invoice from the contractor/consultant.

6. Contractor/consultant has received copies of signed confidentiality and/or non-disclosure agreements.

7. ID badge and network ID have been returned.

8. Date that project is complete (last day for contractor/consultant; it may not be the same as the last day for the project team)

Contractor/Consultant:	Signature:	
	Print Name:	
	Title:	
	Date:	
Project Manager:	Signature:	
	Print Name:	
	Title:	
	Date:	

Document D57: Project Completion Agreement

Personal Development Plan

Name:

Date:

Where I Am Today:

-
-
-

Short-Term Goals (1-2 years):

-
-
-

Medium-Term Goals (2-5 years):

-
-
-

Long-Term Goals (5 - 10 years):

-
-
-

What I Am Best at:

-
-
-

Things I Would Like to Improve on:

-
-
-

New Skills I Would Like to Learn and Training I Would Like to Take:

-
-
-

What Motivates Me:

-
-
-

Document D58: Personal Development Plan

Date	Task/Activity	Scheduling	Meetings	Conflict resolution	Putting out fires	Team 1x1 Meetings	Client meetings	Change Control	Personnel Issues	Recruitment	Training	Documentation					TOTAL HRS
																	0
																	0
																	0
																	0
																	0
																	0
																	0
																	0
																	0
																	0
																	0
																	0
																	0
																	0
																	0
																	0
																	0
TOTAL HOURS		0	0	0	0	0	0	0	0	0	0	0	0	0	0	0	0

Personal Time Log — Name: — Project Name

Document D59: Personal Time Log

Career Plan

Name:
Date:

Due Date	Milestone	Steps to achieve milestone
20XX		• • • • •
20XX		• • • • •
20XX		• • • • •
20XX		• • • • •
20XX		• • • • •

Document D60: Career Plan

Index

NOTE: Boldface numbers indicate illustrations or code listing; t indicates a table.

C

NOTE: Boldface numbers indicate illustrations or code listing; t indicates a table.

NOTE: Boldface numbers indicate illustrations or code listing; t indicates a table.